Pennsylvania Land Records

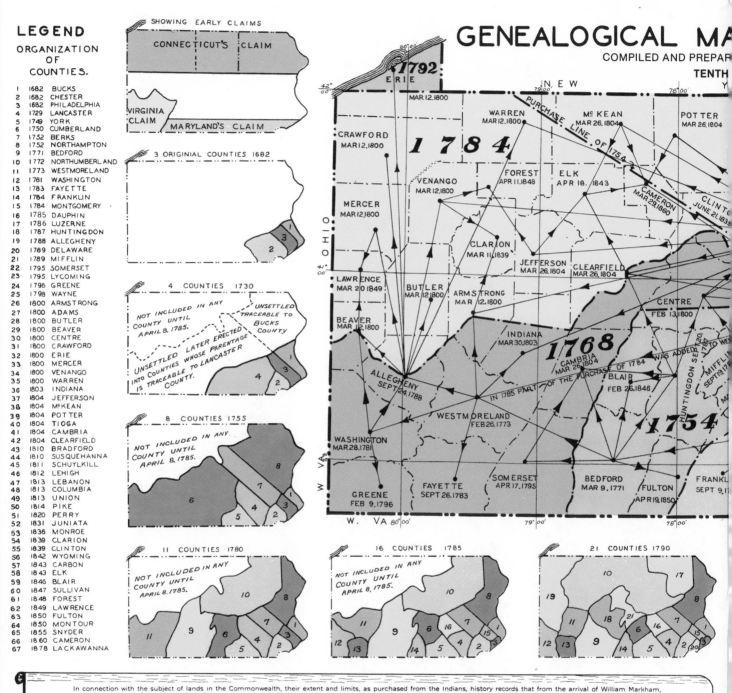

LEGEND
ORGANIZATION OF COUNTIES.

1	1682	BUCKS
2	1682	CHESTER
3	1682	PHILADELPHIA
4	1729	LANCASTER
5	1749	YORK
6	1750	CUMBERLAND
7	1752	BERKS
8	1752	NORTHAMPTON
9	1771	BEDFORD
10	1772	NORTHUMBERLAND
11	1773	WESTMORELAND
12	1781	WASHINGTON
13	1783	FAYETTE
14	1784	FRANKLIN
15	1784	MONTGOMERY
16	1785	DAUPHIN
17	1786	LUZERNE
18	1787	HUNTINGDON
19	1788	ALLEGHENY
20	1789	DELAWARE
21	1789	MIFFLIN
22	1795	SOMERSET
23	1795	LYCOMING
24	1796	GREENE
25	1798	WAYNE
26	1800	ARMSTRONG
27	1800	ADAMS
28	1800	BUTLER
29	1800	BEAVER
30	1800	CENTRE
31	1800	CRAWFORD
32	1800	ERIE
33	1800	MERCER
34	1800	VENANGO
35	1800	WARREN
36	1803	INDIANA
37	1804	JEFFERSON
38	1804	McKEAN
39	1804	POTTER
40	1804	TIOGA
41	1804	CAMBRIA
42	1804	CLEARFIELD
43	1810	BRADFORD
44	1810	SUSQUEHANNA
45	1811	SCHUYLKILL
46	1812	LEHIGH
47	1813	LEBANON
48	1813	COLUMBIA
49	1813	UNION
50	1814	PIKE
51	1820	PERRY
52	1831	JUNIATA
53	1836	MONROE
54	1839	CLARION
55	1839	CLINTON
56	1842	WYOMING
57	1843	CARBON
58	1843	ELK
59	1846	BLAIR
60	1847	SULLIVAN
61	1848	FOREST
62	1849	LAWRENCE
63	1850	FULTON
64	1850	MONTOUR
65	1855	SNYDER
66	1860	CAMERON
67	1878	LACKAWANNA

SHOWING EARLY CLAIMS

CONNECTICUT'S CLAIM

VIRGINIA CLAIM

MARYLAND'S CLAIM

3 ORIGIINAL COUNTIES 1682

4 COUNTIES 1730

NOT INCLUDED IN ANY COUNTY UNTIL APRIL 8, 1785.

UNSETTLED TRACEABLE TO BUCKS County

UNSETTLED LATER ERECTED INTO COUNTIES WHOSE PARENTAGE IS TRACEABLE TO LANCASTER COUNTY.

8 COUNTIES 1755

NOT INCLUDED IN ANY COUNTY UNTIL APRIL 8, 1785.

11 COUNTIES 1780

NOT INCLUDED IN ANY COUNTY UNTIL APRIL 8, 1785.

16 COUNTIES 1785

NOT INCLUDED IN ANY COUNTY UNTIL APRIL 8, 1785.

21 COUNTIES 1790

In connection with the subject of lands in the Commonwealth, their extent and limits, as purchased from the Indians, history records that from the arrival of William Markham, Deputy of William Penn, until the year 1792, a period of one hundred and ten years, the whole right of soil of the Indians within the charter bounds of Pennsylvania, was extinguished by the following thirty-three treaties and purchases:

1.	1682, JULY 15.	Deed for lands between the Falls of Delaware and Neshammonys Creek, confirmed by William Penn, October 24, 1682.
2.	1683, JUNE 23.	Deed for "lands lying betwixt Pemmapecka and Nesheminek Creek *** and backward of the same, and to run two days journey with an horse, up into the country as the said River doth go."
3.	1683, JUNE 25.	Wingebone's release for lands "lying on the west side of the Schuylkill, beginning from the first falls *** and backward of the same as far as my right goeth."
4.	1683, JULY 14.	Deed for lands between Schuylkill and Chester Rivers.
5.	1683, JULY 14.	Deed for lands between Schuylkill and Pemmapecka Creeks.
6.	1683, SEPTEMBER 10.	Keketappan's deed "for his half of all his lands betwixt Susquehanna and Delaware which lieth on the Susquehanna side."
7.	1683, OCTOBER 18.	Machaloha's deed "for lands from the Delaware River and Chesapeak Bay, and up to the Falls of the Susquehanna."
8.	1684, JUNE 3.	Manghougsin's release "for all his land on Perkioming."
9.	1684, JUNE 7.	Richard Mettamicont's release "for lands on both sides Pemmapecka Creek on the Delaware."
10.	1685, JULY 30.	Deed for lands "between Pemmapecka and Chester Creeks, and back *** as far as a man can go in two days" from a point on Conshohockin Hill.
11.	1685, OCTOBER 2.	Deed for lands between Duck and Chester Creeks, and backward from Delaware, "as far as a man could ride in two days with a horse.
12.	1692, JUNE 15.	Acknowledgment of satisfaction for land "lying between Neshamina and Poquessing *** and extending backwards to the utmost bounds of the Province."
13.	1696, JANUARY 13.	Col. Thomas Dongan's, formerly Governor of New York, deed to William Penn for lands on both sides of Susquehanna, from the lakes to the "Chesapeak Bay."
14.	1697, JULY 5.	Taminy's deed for the lands between Pemmopeck and Neshaminy, and "as far back as a horse can travel in two summer days."
15.	1700, SEPTEMBER 13.	Deed of the Susquehanna Indians for the lands on "both sides of the Susquehanna and next adjoining the same, and comprising Dongan's Deed." (No. 13).
16.	1701, APRIL 23.	Ratification of Dongan's Deed and the Deed of September 13, 1700 (No. 14), "by the Susquehanna, Shawona, Potowmack, and Conestogoe Indians."
17.	1718, SEPTEMBER 17.	Deed of release by the Delaware Indians for "the lands between the Delaware and Susquehanna Rivers, from Duck Creek *** to the Lehigh Hills."

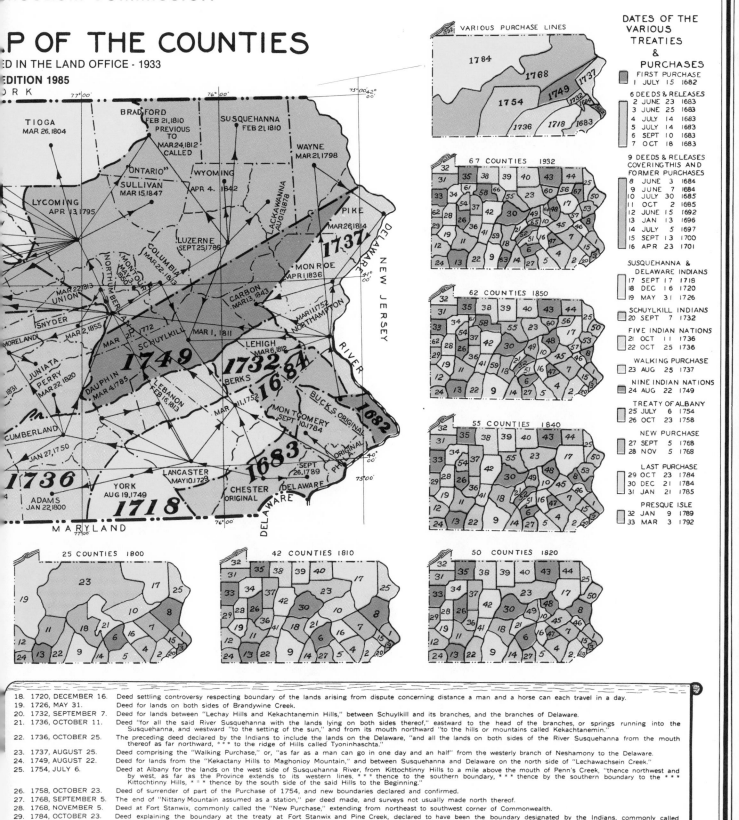

OF PENNSYLVANIA

MUSEUM COMMISSION

P OF THE COUNTIES
ED IN THE LAND OFFICE - 1933
EDITION 1985

VARIOUS PURCHASE LINES

67 COUNTIES 1932

62 COUNTIES 1850

55 COUNTIES 1840

25 COUNTIES 1800

42 COUNTIES 1810

50 COUNTIES 1820

18. 1720, DECEMBER 16.   Deed settling controversy respecting boundary of the lands arising from dispute concerning distance a man and a horse can each travel in a day.

19. 1726, MAY 31.   Deed for lands on both sides of Brandywine Creek.

20. 1732, SEPTEMBER 7.   Deed for lands between "Lechay Hills and Kekachtanemin Hills," between Schuylkill and its branches, and the branches of Delaware.

21. 1736, OCTOBER 11.   Deed "for all the said River Susquehanna with the lands lying on both sides thereof," eastward to the head of the branches, or springs running into the Susquehanna, and westward "to the setting of the sun," and from its mouth northward "to the hills or mountains called Kekachtanemin."

22. 1736, OCTOBER 25.   The preceding deed declared by the Indians to include the lands on the Delaware, "and all the lands on both sides of the River Susquehanna from the mouth thereof as far northward, * * * to the ridge of Hills called Tyoninhaschta."

23. 1737, AUGUST 25.   Deed comprising the "Walking Purchase," or, "as far as a man can go in one day and an half" from the westerly branch of Neshamony to the Delaware.

24. 1749, AUGUST 22.   Deed for lands from the "Kekactany Hills to Maghonioy Mountain," and between Susquehanna and Delaware on the north side of "Lechawachsein Creek."

25. 1754, JULY 6.   Deed at Albany for the lands on the west side of Susquehanna River, from Kittochtinny Hills to a mile above the mouth of Penn's Creek, "thence northwest and by west, as far as the Province extends to its western lines, * * * thence to the southern boundary, * * * thence by the southern boundary to the * * * Kittochtinny Hills, * * * thence by the south side of the said Hills to the Beginning."

26. 1758, OCTOBER 23.   Deed of surrender of part of the Purchase of 1754, and new boundaries declared and confirmed.

27. 1768, SEPTEMBER 5.   The end of "Nittany Mountain assumed as a station," per deed made, and surveys not usually made north thereof.

28. 1768, NOVEMBER 5.   Deed at Fort Stanwix, commonly called the "New Purchase," extending from northeast to southwest corner of Commonwealth.

29. 1784, OCTOBER 23.   Deed explaining the boundary at the treaty at Fort Stanwix and Pine Creek, declared to have been the boundary designated by the Indians, commonly called the "Last Purchase."

30. 1784, DECEMBER 21.   Deed declaring Lycoming to be the boundary.

31. 1785, JANUARY 21.   Deed at Fort Stanwix and Fort McIntosh for the residue of the lands within the Commonwealth, made October 23, 1784, and January 21, 1785.

32. 1789, JANUARY 9.   Indian cession of lands at Presque Isle including the Triangle.

33. 1792, MARCH 3   On October 3, 1788, an Act was passed authorizing the Supreme Executive Council to draw on the State Treasurer for a sum of money for defraying the expense of purchasing from the Indians lands on Lake Erie. It is usually called the "Purchase of the Triangle." It contains 202,187 acres.

Pennsylvania Land Records

A History and Guide for Research

by Donna Bingham Munger

Published in cooperation with the
Pennsylvania Historical and Museum Commission

Scholarly Resources Inc.
Wilmington, Delaware

Frontispiece: Genealogical Map of the Counties. (*Pennsylvania Historical and Museum Commission*)

© 1991 by Scholarly Resources Inc.
All rights reserved
First published 1991
Printed and bound in the United States of America
Second printing 1993
Third printing 1996

Scholarly Resources Inc.
104 Greenhill Avenue
Wilmington, DE 19805-1897

Library of Congress Cataloging-in-Publication Data

Munger, Donna B.
    Pennsylvania land records : a history and guide for research / Donna Bingham Munger.
        p.   cm.
    Includes bibliographical references and index.
    ISBN 0-8420-2377-1. — ISBN 0-8420-2497-2 (pbk.)
    1. Land settlement—Pennsylvania—History—Archival resources. 2. Pennsylvania—History—Archival resources. 3. Pennsylvania—Genealogy—Archival resources. I. Title.
Z1329.M85   1991
[F149]
                                                                    90-21384
                                                                        CIP

About the Author

A resident of Pennsylvania for twenty-five years, Donna Bingham Munger is a native of Washington State. She was educated at the University of Washington, where she received an M.A. in American colonial history in 1956. She has also done extensive research and graduate study in history at the University of Maryland, Washington University in Saint Louis, and the Pennsylvania State University. Previous publications have dealt with the history of medicine in twentieth-century America and the Connecticut settlers in Pennsylvania. Since 1982 she has been an associate historian with the Pennsylvania Historical and Museum Commission, and she was the final chief of the Division of Land Records, 1986–1989.

Contents

Tables of Selected Historical Research Aids

Charts

Maps and Illustrations

Abbreviations and Short Titles

Annals
Samuel Hazard. *Annals of Pennsylvania, from the Discovery of the Delaware, 1609–82.* Philadelphia, 1850.

Brief Account
William Penn. *A Brief Account of the Province of Pennsylvania in America.* London, issued in at least three versions 1681–82. In *PWP* 5:271.

Chester Co.
J. Smith Futhey and Gilbert Cope. *History of Chester County, Pennsylvania.* Philadelphia, 1881.

Com. Bk.
Commission Book

CR
Samuel Hazard, ed. *Colonial Records.* 16 vols. Harrisburg, 1851–1853.

Exem. Rec.
Exemplification Record. A perfect copy of a record or office book lawfully kept.

General Cash Accounts
"General Cash Accounts for William Penn from Ledgers A–H, 10 Sep't. 1701–28 March 1778," original, Penn-Physick Mss. Copy entitled "Pennsylvania Cash Accounts, 1701–78," Penn Papers, HSP.

HSP
Historical Society of Pennsylvania, Philadelphia

Inv.
Inventory

LDS micro.
Microfilm prepared by the Church of Jesus Christ of Latter-day Saints

LO micro.
   Land Office microfilm

Min. Bd. Prop.
   Minutes of the Board of Property

Min. Com. Prop.
   Minutes of the Commissioners of Property

Min. Prov. Coun.
   Minutes of the Provincial Council of Pennsylvania. Harrisburg, 1838–1840.

NGSQ
   National Genealogical Society Quarterly

PA (1)
   Samuel Hazard, ed. *Pennsylvania Archives.* 1st ser. 12 vols. Philadelphia, 1856.

PA (2)
   John B. Linn and William H. Egle, eds. *Pennsylvania Archives.* 2d ser. 19 vols. Harrisburg, 1874–1893.

PA (3)
   William H. Egle and George Edward Reed, eds. *Pennsylvania Archives.* 3d ser. 30 vols. Harrisburg, 1894–1899.

PA (4)
   George Edward Reed, ed. *Pennsylvania Archives.* 4th ser. 12 vols. Harrisburg, 1900–1902.

PA (5)
   Thomas Lynch Montgomery, ed. *Pennsylvania Archives.* 5th ser. 8 vols. Harrisburg, 1906.

Pa. Hist.
   Pennsylvania History

PaL
   Laws of the General Assembly of the Commonwealth of Pennsylvania, 1700–   . Harrisburg, 1829–

Pat. Bk.
   Patent Book

Penn-Logan Corres.
   Correspondence between William Penn and James Logan, 1700–1750. Memoirs of the Historical Society of Pennsylvania, vols. 9–10. Philadelphia, 1870.

Penn-Physick Mss
Penn-Physick Manuscripts. Penn Papers. HSP.

PGM
Pennsylvania Genealogical Magazine

PHMC
Pennsylvania Historical and Museum Commission

PMHB
Pennsylvania Magazine of History and Biography

PSA
Pennsylvania State Archives, Harrisburg

Purdon
Purdon's Pennsylvania Consolidated Statutes Annotated. Philadelphia, 1930– .

PWP micro.
The Papers of William Penn. Philadelphia, 1975. Microfilm. (Fourteen reels plus guide; references are to reel and frame.)

PWP 1
Mary Maples Dunn and Richard S. Dunn, eds. *The Papers of William Penn.* Vol. 1. Philadelphia, 1981.

PWP 2
Richard S. Dunn and Mary Maples Dunn, eds. *The Papers of William Penn.* Vol. 2. Philadelphia, 1982.

PWP 3
Marianne S. Wokeck, Joy Wiltenburg, Alison Duncan Hirsch, and Craig W. Horle, eds. *The Papers of William Penn.* Vol. 3. Philadelphia, 1986.

PWP 4
Craig W. Horle, Alison Duncan Hirsch, Marianne S. Wokeck, and Joy Wiltenburg, eds. *The Papers of William Penn.* Vol. 4. Philadelphia, 1987.

PWP 5
Edwin B. Bronner and David Fraser. *The Papers of William Penn.* Vol. 5, *William Penn's Published Writings, 1660–1726: An Interpretive Bibliography.* Philadelphia, 1986.

RG-4
Records of the Office of the Comptroller General, PSA

RG-8
Records of the General Loan Office and State Treasurer, PSA

RG-12
Records of the Department of Highways, PSA

RG-14
Records of the Department of Internal Affairs, PSA

RG-17
Records of the Land Office, PSA

RG-21
Records of the Proprietary Government, PSA

RG-26
Records of the Department of State, PSA

RG-28
Records of the Treasury Department, PSA

SmL
Laws of the Commonwealth of Pennsylvania, 1700–1829 [Smith's Laws]. 10 vols. Philadelphia, 1810– .

Some Account
William Penn. *Some Account of the Province of Pennsilvania in America.* London, 1681. In *PWP* micro. 3:132.

Statutes 1
Gail McKnight Beckman, comp. *The Statutes at Large of Pennsylvania in the Time of William Penn.* Vol. 1, *1680–1700.* New York, 1976.

Statutes 2–18
James T. Mitchell and Henry Flanders, comps. *The Statutes at Large of Pennsylvania.* Vols. 2–18 [1700–1809]. Harrisburg, 1896–1919.

Sur. Bk.
Survey Book

Susq. Co. Papers 1–4
Julian P. Boyd, ed. *The Susquehanna Company Papers.* Vols. 1–4. 1932. Reprint. Ithaca, NY, 1962.

Susq. Co. Papers 5–11
Robert J. Taylor, ed. *The Susquehanna Company Papers.* Vols. 5–11. Ithaca, NY, 1967–1971.

TPP
John D. Kilbourne, ed. *The Thomas Penn Papers.* Wilmington, DE, 1972. Microfilm.

W&S

Allen Weinberg and Thomas E. Slattery, comps. *Warrants and Surveys of the Province of Pennsylvania Including the Three Lower Counties, 1759.* Philadelphia, 1965.

WPHM

Western Pennsylvania Historical Magazine

Wt. Bk.

Warrant Book

Acknowledgments

Research for this GUIDE began in an effort to decipher the transcripts prepared under the 1759 law to record warrants and surveys. Popularly called the Green Books due to the color of their binding, these volumes had become an enigma to the current generation of researchers. I owe a special debt to the late William A. Hunter, who first encouraged this project by sharing with me his analysis of the Green Books and the many boxes of historically valuable land records retrieved from storage in the attic of the capitol building. The two and one-half years that I have spent as chief of the Division of Land Records have afforded me the opportunity to study the documentation in depth. During this period, Edward Price, James Arnold, Dorothy Weiser, Lee Engle, and Hertha Williams provided invaluable assistance, giving me time to translate my research into writing. Jonathan Stayer, Lillian Ulrich, James Arnold, Lee Engle, and Marianne Wokeck read a draft of the GUIDE and made valuable suggestions, thus preventing me from citing many inaccuracies. Ward Weiss and R. Kent Stuetz generously contributed the fruits of their research on the 1735 Lottery Land and the receiver general's office, and Louis Waddell called my attention to related documents. My most valuable critic, my husband, Bryce L. Munger, approached the topic as a neophyte and provided many needed comments concerning interpretation and clarity.

The archival background of the GUIDE is the body of land records in the Pennsylvania State Archives. In the late 1950s the Bureau of Land Records undertook an overall records management program, which included a complete inventory, lamination, and microfilming. For some reason, the projected publication of a catalog or guide to the records failed to happen. Twenty years later, when attempting to use the documents for historical research, I more than once noticed the absence of any type of finding aid available for public use. The production of this work was undertaken when my position shifted from patron to chief. Infrequently are we given the opportunity to act when we boldly exclaim: "If I were to be in charge. . . ." But, as events unfolded, such a situation materialized. I am especially indebted to John B. B. Trussell, Harry E. Whipkey, Larry E. Tise, and Brent D. Glass for permitting me, a public historian, to pursue original research. It is intended that this GUIDE will benefit the public as much as the staff and will form the bibliographic base for my projected study of land policy and politics in Pennsylvania.

Users who find errors are encouraged to contact me so that corrections can be made in subsequent editions: Donna Bingham Munger, Pennsylvania Historical and Museum Commission, Box 1026, Harrisburg, PA 17108-1026.

Introduction

Origin and Type of Records

The records described in this GUIDE document the process of land settlement in Pennsylvania. Dating from before the establishment of Pennsylvania as a colony and continuing to the present time, they record the first transfer of land from William Penn, the proprietor; from his heirs, the proprietaries; and from the Commonwealth to purchasers. The records may be classified under two categories: 1) those whose function is basically legal—applications, warrants, surveys, return of surveys, patents, and the minutes, caveats, and depositions of the commissioners of property and Board of Property; and 2) those whose original function and present age make them primarily of historical interest, such as exoneration certificates, proof of settlement certificates, and special records of purchasers who obtained land in other than normal ways. Examples of the second category are Donation and Depreciation land grants, certified Connecticut Claimants, East Side and West Side applications, and Virginia Entries. Virtually all records of the proprietary offices of the secretary of the province, surveyor general, receiver general, and master of the rolls, and the Commonwealth offices embodied in the Land Office are involved.

First title to land in Pennsylvania usually was and is acquired through a five-step process of application, warrant, survey, return of survey, and patent.

> The APPLICATION is a request for land, usually a certain amount in a particular place.

> The WARRANT is a written order to survey and usually restates the amount and location requested in the application.

> The SURVEY is the actual process of going upon the land, measuring and marking the courses and distances, and drawing a tract diagram.

> The RETURN OF SURVEY is a written restatement combining the warrant and survey and signifies that the purchase price and all fees have been paid.

> The PATENT is the final deed from the proprietor or the state passing ownership of the particular tract of land to its initial purchaser.

As a proprietary colony, Pennsylvania was owned independently of government control. The proprietor, William Penn, and his sons and heirs, the proprietaries, operated their own Land Office. Although certain regulations existed, tracts were surveyed in indiscriminate courses and distances after they were sold. This practice created a jigsaw-puzzle effect on the Pennsylvania countryside.

As a state-land state, Pennsylvania not only continued many of the proprietary procedures but also adapted several federal land policies. The Land Office became part of the state government and was controlled by acts of assembly. Surveying districts were established, and tracts within the newly opened areas of the state were surveyed in rectangular configurations before they were sold. Eventually the disposal of vacant land was handled partially through the Deputy or County Surveyor's Office.

All original records generated in the initial transfer of land to an individual are in the custody of the Pennsylvania State Archives located in Harrisburg, Pennsylvania. Previously the records were located in the Department of Community Affairs, formerly called the Department of Internal Affairs. Since 1981 they have been housed in the Bureau of Archives and History of the Pennsylvania Historical and Museum Commission.

Structure of the Guide

This GUIDE is designed to be used as a history that can be read straight through from beginning to end or as a series of reference sections about specific topics, each complete in itself. To accomplish this design, each section begins with a historical explanation of the events that led to the creation of the pertinent records. Then follows an annotated inventory of original loose records and bound volumes where applicable. In cases where two or more original volumes have since been bound together, the original volumes are cited singly, as appropriate. Only records specific to the time frame of the section are discussed in each section. Whenever similar records or record series cross periods, they are discussed in each section as they apply.

Section Organization

This GUIDE is divided into five main sections. Sections II, III, and IV are separated into subsections as follows: A) introduction to the section; B) basic policies of the period; C) regions open for settlement, including purchase treaties and county formation; D) categories of purchasers and the special records pertaining thereto; E) categories of land and the relevant records; F) composition of the Land Office and the records pertaining to it; and G) basic land records of the period.

Section I briefly discusses pre-Penn land settlement and the Pennsylvania land records dealing with the period before 1682.

Section II presents a lengthy discussion of land settlement from 1682 to 1732, during the proprietorship of Penn. The main body of land records generated during this era is extant in the original and in one or more copied versions. Researchers usually find these early records confusing because it is not easy to detect a recording system. This GUIDE will outline the system and explain how it and the specific records developed.

Section III describes the changing policies and procedures followed by the sons and heirs of William Penn from 1732 to 1776. The proprietaries, as they were called, relied upon the provincial secretary to run their land business, much as the first proprietor had done. Many irregular practices developed during this period, especially

between 1732 and 1765. After 1765 a more systematic procedure for the transfer of lands was established, beginning with the East Side and the West Side application programs.

Section IV centers on land settlement procedures and records as they were established under the authority of the Commonwealth from 1776 to 1990. The period up to 1905 did not differ greatly from the colonial era. Although proprietary land became public land under legislative control, procedures and records for titling land changed little.

Section V briefly explains Commonwealth land policy and titling procedures since 1905.

Selected Historical Research Aids and Endnotes

This GUIDE combines original research with a compilation of the records. A great deal of detective work among the records, backed by the realization that for every law there is a set of records, provided the backbone for the enterprise. Earlier publications dealing with land settlement in Pennsylvania lent their hints, clues, facts, and interpretations, as did numerous articles and books devoted to specific individuals and other related topics. The annual reports of the Department of Internal Affairs were especially helpful. The most valuable of these sources are cited in the Tables of Selected Historical Research Aids located throughout the GUIDE. Endnotes following the subsections usually reference only sources not included in the tables. When an original dated document is cited, the date is given exactly as it was written to facilitate finding the relevant passage. New Style equivalents are supplied in brackets where necessary.

Microfilm

All land records generated before 1957 are available on microfilm. The annotated inventories of records provided in the sections correlate microfilm reels with original loose papers and bound volumes. The code "LO micro." for "Land Office microfilm" is followed by the appropriate reel number. The number preceding the decimal point refers to the series, and the number following the point refers to the roll within the series. In a few situations, reference is made to micro-

Table 1. Research Aids: Land Settlement in Pennsylvania

Huston, Charles. *An Essay on the History and Nature of Original Titles to Land in the Province and State of Pennsylvania.* Philadelphia, 1849.

Lewis, Lawrence, Jr. *An Essay on Original Land Titles in Philadelphia.* Philadelphia, 1880.

Rineer, A. Hunter. "This Land Is Your Land, This Land Is My Land: A Brief Introduction to Historic Pennsylvania Land Records." *Journal of the Lancaster County Historical Society* 89 (September 1987): 99–105.

Sergeant, Thomas. *View of the Land Laws of Pennsylvania.* Philadelphia, 1838.

Shepherd, William Robert. *History of Proprietary Government in Pennsylvania.* New York, 1896.

Smith, Charles. "Note." In *SmL* 2:105–261. Philadelphia, 1810.

Wilkinson, Norman B., comp. *Bibliography of Pennsylvania History.* Harrisburg, 1957. See also Carol Wall, ed., *Bibliography of Pennsylvania History: A Supplement* (Harrisburg, 1976); and John B. B. Trussell, Jr., comp., *Pennsylvania Historical Bibliography: Additions through 1985,* 6 vols. (Harrisburg, 1979–1989).

film of other collections. In those instances, "Reel" is followed by the number of the microfilm reel within the general state archives collection. Appendix C offers a complete numerical listing of Land Office microfilm reels and corresponding descriptions.

Microfilm is available for use at the state archives in Harrisburg or by purchase. The Family History Library of the Church of Jesus Christ of Latter-day Saints also has microfilm of many of the original loose land records but not of bound volumes

Research Methods

Researchers focusing on a particular individual should start by carefully identifying the name of the individual to be searched for (with variant spellings), the appropriate era, the name of the county at the time of the individual's residence, and, if possible, the name of his or her township. Usually the place to begin is among the county deeds, with a regular title search backward. Often the deed of conveyance between the second and first owner of a tract will repeat the warrant and patent information. If such information is not given, at least the pertinent county and period will be identified. The researcher will then be able to move to the appropriate state land record indexes and continue the investigation.

Warrant and Patent Registers

The warrant registers serve as a master index for warrants, surveys, and patents. They give the number of the warrant; name of the warrantee; type of the warrant; quantity of land warranted; location warranted; date of the warrant; date of the return of survey; acres returned; name of the patentee; patent volume, number, and page; and survey volume, number, and page. The warrant number and the survey volume, number, and page apply to both the original individual document and the book copy. Surveys are not indexed separately.

When the patentee is known but not the warrantee, separate patent registers may be consulted to locate the volume and book where the patent is copied. The patent registers are divided into three series by date. Each volume is organized also by date and then by name of patentee.

Special Registers

Several special registers either augment or substitute for the regular warrant and patent registers. It is important to know which special registers should be consulted for each period. For example, the Old Rights registers substitute for the warrant registers of the pre-1733 period, and the East Side and the West Side application registers, the New and Last purchase registers, the Depreciation and Donation land registers, and the Certified Townships Luzerne register all contain references to information that cannot be found through the regular warrant registers.

Guide to the Registers

Pre-1733

Old Rights, Philadelphia
   Warrants, surveys, and returns of survey
Old Rights, Bucks and Chester
   Warrants, surveys, and returns of survey
Original Purchases
   Warrants, surveys, and returns of survey for
   First Purchasers and their Under Purchasers
Patent Register, Series A and AA
   Patent volumes
Proprietary Rights Index
   Warrants and surveys

1733–1781

Warrant Registers
   Warrants, surveys, and patents
Patent Registers, Series A and AA
   Patent volumes
East Side (Susquehanna) Applications
   Surveys 1765–1769
West Side (Susquehanna) Applications
   Surveys 1766–1769
Baynton and Wharton Warrants
   Warrants, surveys, and patents
New Purchase 1768
   Surveys
Proprietary Rights Index
   Warrants and surveys

1781–Present

Warrant Registers
   Warrants, surveys, and patents
Patent Register, Series P, 1781–1809
   Patents
Patent Register, Series H, 1809–Present
   Patents
Northumberland Lottery
   Warrants, surveys, and patents
Last Purchase 1784
   Surveys
Depreciation Lands
   Surveys and Patents
Donation Lands
   Surveys and patents
Certified Townships Luzerne
   Surveys and patents

A Note about Delaware Records

Original loose records in the Pennsylvania Land Office apply only to the area encompassed by the current state boundaries. They do not include land records relating to colonial Delaware, although land distribution in colonial Delaware was originally under Pennsylvania's jurisdiction. During colonial times the three Delaware counties were referred to as Pennsylvania's Lower Counties. Penn had negotiated with the duke of York for the grant of the three Lower Counties to ensure Pennsylvania's control of the Delaware River. Although the legislatures of Delaware and Pennsylvania were separate after 1701, land transactions were conducted under the control of both Pennsylvania and the local county courts until well into the eighteenth century.

Pennsylvania land records relating to the Lower Counties, namely, New Castle, Kent, and Sussex, were transferred to Delaware in 1801. The loose warrants, surveys, and copies (exemplifications) of patents were traded for Delaware's support of the Chesapeake and Delaware Canal Company project. An accounting of the records given to Delaware is contained in two volumes in the Pennsylvania Land Office collection and cited in the sources below.

Many other Delaware records were inextricably mixed with records of Pennsylvania and could not be transcribed or transferred. These were applications for warrants; petitions, caveats, and minutes of the early commissioners of property and the later Board of Property; certain proprietary papers; and warrant registers. Under the Delaware Fugitive Records Project of the late 1970s the Delaware Bureau of Archives and Records purchased microfilm of these Pennsylvania records. In addition, Delaware bought microfilm of the transcripts of the original records by Provincial Assembly member John Hughes in 1759 under the Pennsylvania law to record warrants and surveys.

Thus, the Delaware State Archives have three sets of Pennsylvania land records pertaining to New Castle, Kent, and Sussex counties: 1) the original papers, 2) the microfilm of other legal papers generated in the process of transferring land from proprietary to private ownership, and 3) the microfilm of the 1759 transcripts of the loose papers.

RECORDS: BOUND VOLUMES

LIST OF PAPERS TRANSFERRED TO THE STATE OF DELAWARE, 1801   (Binding No. 141).

Divided into separate sections for the three counties—New Castle, Kent, and Sussex—the contents of this volume cite 7,208 warrants, surveys, and miscellaneous papers. Warrants are listed alphabetically, with warrant number, warrantee, warrant date, quantity warranted, and date returned. Surveys give warrantee and acreage. Miscellaneous papers include proprietary papers; lands fallen to Maryland; papers relating to the dispute between Penn and the Maryland proprietor, Charles Calvert, third baron Baltimore; and papers on New Castle County relating to James Steel, deputy receiver general and collector of quitrents for the Delaware counties.

LIST OF LANDS TRANSFERRED TO THE STATE OF DELAWARE   ACT OF FEBRUARY 19, 1801   (Binding No. 170)   LO micro.: 25.36.

Lists 1,656 records, including patents, petitions, returns of survey, depositions, and miscellaneous papers pertaining to land that lay within the Lower Counties and later became part of the state of Delaware.

Pre-Penn Land Settlement

I.A. Introduction

Colonial settlement in the area that was to become Pennsylvania began long before William Penn received his proprietary grant from the king of England in 1681. The Swedes, the Dutch, and the English, in turn, each established authority along the Delaware River. Land records, usually entered among court records, resulted from these successive periods of settlement. The original deeds granted to individual settlers were maintained in the archives of the respective colonizing countries and in the New York Colonial Archives. The Pennsylvania State Archives and its Land Office hold bound copies of many of these records. The records are also available on microfilm, and some have been published in book form.

I.B. Lower Delaware Region

The Pennsylvania land records date from the beginning of English authority along the west side of the Delaware River. Long vying with the Dutch for dominance in the North American trade, the English emerged supreme in 1664 by defeating the Dutch in New York and, at the same time, seizing the Dutch-controlled Delaware River region.

The work of transforming the government of the Delaware region to conform to English law progressed systematically until the Dutch unexpectedly regained control in 1673. Quickly initiating comprehensive procedures for governing the area, the new administration established three jurisdictional areas: one centered at New Amstel (present-day New Castle, Delaware), one at Upland (Chester, Pennsylvania), and one at Whorekill, or Hoornkill (Lewes, Delaware).

The short-lived Dutch government soon reverted to English control. Retaining the three jurisdictional regions established by the Dutch, the English created a fourth district, Saint Jones, by dividing Whorekill in 1680. Four years earlier, in 1676, they had extended the duke of York's laws —which were in effect in New York since 1664—to the Delaware region. The introduction of the duke's laws signified the end of Dutch control. Ordinances for governing both New York proper and the Delaware region were promulgated by the English governor and the council of New York. Old land patents issued under the Swedish and Dutch were renewed and recorded, and settlers holding unpatented land were permitted to obtain patents. These were signed by the royal governors, Richard Nicolls (1664–1668), Francis Lovelace (1668–1673), and Edmund Andros (1674–1681). Book copies cited in the sources below form the earliest body of Pennsylvania land records.

The four jurisdictional areas eventually became counties under Penn's proprietorship. The Upland region became Chester County; Whorekill, whose name had been changed to Deal, became Sussex County; Saint Jones became Kent County; and the town of New Castle gave its name to New Castle County. During the entire colonial period, the power to grant land in the three Lower Counties, Kent, Sussex, and New Castle, remained with the Penn family or with the local courts, although the Annexed Territories, as they were often called, had their own colonial government after 1701. In 1776

Table 2. Research Aids: Pre-Penn Records

Annals. *

The Duke of York Record, 1646–1679. Original Land Titles in Delaware. Wilmington, 1903.

Memoirs of the Historical Society of Pennsylvania. Vol. 7, *The Record of the Court at Upland, 1676–1681.* Philadelphia, 1860.

Munroe, John A., and John C. Dann. "Benjamin Eastburn, Thomas Noxon, and the Earliest Map of the Lower Counties." *Delaware History* 21 (Fall-Winter 1985): 217–32.

Myers, Albert Cook, ed. *Walter Wharton's Land Survey Register, 1675–1679.* Wilmington, DE, 1955.

"Papers Relating to Colonies on the Delaware, 1614–1682." In *PA* (2) 5.

"Papers Relating to the Dutch and Swedish Settlements on the Delaware River." In *PA* (2) 7:485–873.

PWP 2.

Records of the Court of New Castle on Delaware, 1671–1681. Lancaster, 1904.

Soderlund, Jean R., ed. *William Penn and the Founding of Pennsylvania, 1680–1684: A Documentary History.* Philadelphia, 1983.

*For full citations of shortened titles in the tables of research aids, see Abbreviations and Short Titles, pp. xxi–xxv.

the Lower Counties became the state of Delaware.

I.C. Upland Records

Only the Upland jurisdictional area remained a part of Pennsylvania. Official pre-Penn Pennsylvania land records, therefore, are concerned only with transactions pertaining to Upland. Originally, the Upland court jurisdiction extended from the mouth of Christiana Creek (present-day Wilmington, Delaware) northward to the limits of European settlement near the falls of the Delaware River at Trenton. References within the Upland court proceedings indicate that as early as 1672 questions of land title were referred to the court for decision. The court also entertained applications for land settlement, granted warrants to survey, received returns of surveys, and required that real estate transfers be made before it. A 1677 tax list included in the court records gives the names of men ages sixteen to sixty living within the Upland area at that time. Court proceedings for Upland from 1676 to the close of the administration of the duke of York and the transfer of the territory to Penn in 1682 are not part of Pennsylvania's official land records but have been published and are cited in Table 2.

Using pre-Penn land records can be a confusing task. Geographic names have changed, making a historical atlas or map of the Delaware River region a necessary adjunct to reading the descriptive surveys. Researchers can find maps of the area and drawings of some of the pre-Penn land grants in secondary sources such as some of those given in Table 2. In tracing deeds, researchers should be aware that a patent issued during the English pre-Penn period may be the oldest legal title to a parcel of Pennsylvania land.

RECORDS: BOUND VOLUMES

PATENTS BY ROYAL GOVERNORS OF NEW YORK   LO micro.: 25.32; 1759 transcript: PATENTS 1677–1682   (Binding No. 26)   LO micro.: 25.5.

Two forms of the earliest volume of land records covering the territory that was to become Pennsylvania. The first patent is dated 1667 despite the transcript title of 1677. The thirty-eight entries include several patents to land currently lying in the Passyunk section of

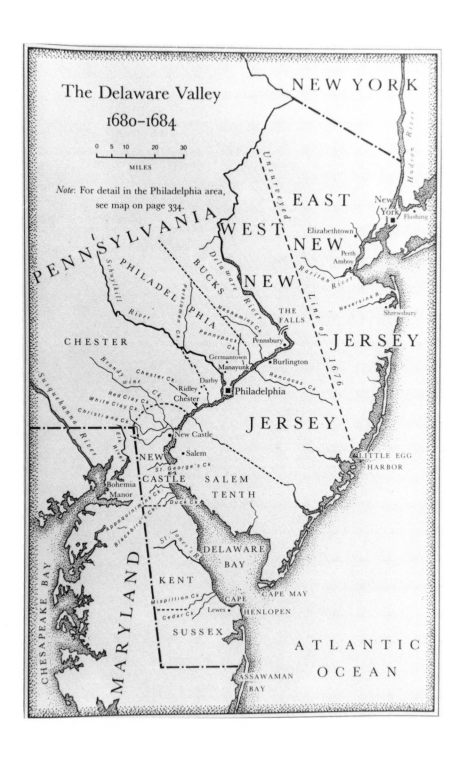

Map 1. The Delaware Valley, 1680—1684. (*University of Pennsylvania Press*)

south Philadelphia and the surrounding area. Transcripts of these patents are also in Philadelphia County deed records under *Exemplification Records* (8:423–54) and are available on microfilm as part of the Philadelphia County recorder of deeds records.

NEW CASTLE COUNTY SURVEY NOTES, 1675–1679   Reel 471.

Contents of the original volume from which Albert Cook Myers prepared *Walter Wharton's Land Survey Register, 1675–1679* (see Table 2). The volume contains fifty descriptive surveys Wharton made of land in present-day Pennsylvania and Delaware preparatory to issuance of patents by the governor of New York. Lovelace first appointed Wharton surveyor general in 1671, and he conducted his duties under both English and Dutch governments until his death in 1679. The area of his surveys extends from modern New Castle County, Delaware, into Bucks County, Pennsylvania.

Land Settlement, 1682–1732: The Proprietorship of William Penn

II.A. Introduction

This section discusses the land policies, regions open for settlement, categories of settlers, categories of land, Land Office, and records during the proprietorship of William Penn. The period extends from 1682, shortly after Penn received his charter for Pennsylvania, to 1732, after his will was finally settled and the proprietorship of the province passed to his sons.

During these fifty-one years, Penn resided in America for only two short periods. He spent nearly two years in the province between October 1682 and August 1684 overseeing the beginning of the new society and the establishment of his land policies. He returned to England to try to settle his dispute with Lord Baltimore over the Maryland boundary. In 1699, Penn journeyed to Pennsylvania again, hoping to solve a myriad of problems that had arisen during his fifteen-year absence. One of his new revenue-generating schemes was a settlement along the Susquehanna River on land that had not been freed of all Indian claims. In a letter to his brother-in-law, Sir John Lowther, Penn describes the Susquehanna as a "glorious river" and notes that the best land in the province is seventy miles into the interior.[1] His second visit, cut short by the threat of

Pennsylvania's becoming a royal colony, ended in 1701. He was never to return to Pennsylvania again.

Before leaving in 1701, Penn modified his policies but failed to respond positively to many land-related concerns brought forward by the colonists. In particular, settlers wanted the elimination of quitrents in Philadelphia, the opening of all unsold lots in the city to general sale, an automatic 10 percent surplus permitted on all surveys, and an adherence to old rents despite the rise in land values.[2] Penn considered these requests unreasonable, ordered a general resurvey of all tracts granted, and asked for a complete and accurate rent-roll.[3] He was most insistent on adhering to his land policies because he was deeply in debt and desperate to receive a profit from his investment in the colony.

When Penn returned to England, he tried to keep in close contact with the province. Problems such as the collection of quitrents, inaccurate and overplus surveys, and disputed grants are frequent topics in his correspondence. Operational practicalities usually modified the execution of his instructions, however. As Penn's years of absence wore on, he gradually lost control of his land affairs. When, in 1708, he was forced to mortgage his province, responsibility for land distribution passed to the commissioners

5

of property, who were authorized to dispose of land on behalf of the mortgagees.

After Penn's death in 1718, his second wife, Hannah, assumed the proprietorship, but the management of the province passed to his commissioners of property acting as trustees. Upon Hannah's death in 1726, her three sons, John, Thomas, and Richard Penn, became the proprietors, but the commissioners of property continued to sell land on behalf of the mortgagees until the mortgage debt was settled in 1730 and Thomas Penn arrived in Pennsylvania, shortly thereafter.

---

[1]Pennsbury, August 16, 1701, *PWP* 4:65.
[2]From the Pennsylvania Assembly, September 20, 1701, ibid., 91–92; to the Pennsylvania Assembly, September 29, 1701, ibid., 95–97; *CR* 2:41–43.
[3]To James Logan, November 3, 1701, *PWP* 4:119–20.

II.B. Basic Policies

II.B.1. Charter Rights

William Penn received his charter to Pennsylvania in 1681 in payment of a debt the king owed to his father, Admiral Sir William Penn, who had died in 1670. The grant made Penn the sole owner of forty-five thousand square miles of colonial real estate, the largest land area in the North American colonies to be held by a private citizen. His grant covered the entire present limits of Pennsylvania, except for a triangular piece of land along the northwest border added in 1792.

As absolute owner of a proprietary colony, Penn had the authority to dispose of the land. His charter permitted him to charge both a fee of sale and a yearly rent for lands he granted, feudal practices still followed in England at the time. Penn also had the right to reserve parcels of land for his own use and to organize them into manors. Beyond these two provisions, his charter left the distribution of land unspecified.

II.B.2. Annexed Counties

To help make his provincial enterprise profitable, Penn sought to control the navigation of the Delaware River. This goal involved annexing land south of Pennsylvania on the western side

---

Table 3. Research Aids: William Penn and Pennsylvania

Bronner, Edwin B. "Penn's Charter of Property of 1701." *Pa. Hist.* 24 (1957): 267–92.

Dunn, Richard S., and Mary Maples Dunn, eds. *The World of William Penn.* Philadelphia, 1986.

Nash, Gary B., ed. "The First Decade in Pennsylvania: Letters of William Markham and Thomas Holme to William Penn." *PMHB* 90 (1966): 314–52, 491–516.

PWP 1–5.

Soderlund, Jean R., ed. *William Penn and the Founding of Pennsylvania, 1680–1684: A Documentary History.* Philadelphia, 1983.

Trussell, John B. B. *William Penn, Architect of a Nation.* Harrisburg, 1980.

---

of the river and along the Delaware Bay. The owner, the duke of York, conveyed the land to Penn in August 1682 following considerable negotiation. Called the country of Newcastle, the area was already heavily settled compared to the province of Pennsylvania. Soon, it unofficially took on the name Lower Counties or Annexed Territories on the Delaware. The three counties, known by the same names today, were New Castle, Kent, and Sussex.

The three Lower Counties and the three upper counties of Chester, Philadelphia, and Bucks formed one Provincial Assembly. Differences between the two areas proved too great for sufficient cooperation, however, and the Lower Counties broke away in 1701 to form their own assembly. Nevertheless, land distribution in the Lower Counties was handled by the proprietary government, and records were kept in one unified system.

II.B.3. Purchases from Earlier Inhabitants

Penn accepted his charter with the understanding that all earlier land grants made by the English government at New York were valid. He extended this policy to previous land grants made by the Swedish and Dutch governors. Calling all those who held such grants *old* settlers, Penn usually required a resurvey before he issued them a patent and claimed the quitrent. Pre-Penn inhabitants who failed to apply for a new patent were covered by laws passed by the Pennsylvania Assembly in 1700 and again in 1711. Although the laws were repealed by the Crown, the policy of recognizing the land claims of earlier settlers had been established.

Adopting a similar policy toward the Indians, Penn recognized their right to the lands they occupied and, in a series of treaties with them, purchased title to prescribed areas before offering settlers the same land. Penn's first promotional tract, *Some Account*, specifically states that land sold will be free from any "Indian" encumbrance.[1] He and his heirs adhered to this policy in an ever-expanding series of purchases, as reference to the Genealogical Map of the Counties (front.) will show.

Since the Lower Counties had been settled much earlier than Pennsylvania, it was not necessary for Penn to extinguish the Indian titles there, and only one treaty affected that area. Recorded May 13, 1728, as confirmation of a grant from Sasoonan and other chiefs to William Penn, the treaty is copied in Pat. Bk. A-6-59.[2]

---

[1] *PWP* 5:264–69.

[2] See also *Min. Prov. Coun.*, June 5, 1728; and *Early American Indian Documents* 1:182–83 (see Table 4).

II.B.4. Terms of Settlement

To dispose of his land in a profitable fashion, Penn attempted to draw investors and colonists who would purchase shares in the province and agree upon a set of rules and regulations for settlement. By the time he had devised a land distribution system that was attractive to all concerned and profitable, Penn had modified his original ideas several times. But, once established, his system continued in operation until his death in 1718.

Penn's terms included provisions for several different categories of purchasers. He intended to rely upon wealthy Quakers in England and Ireland to be the mainstay of his settlement. These investors would purchase large tracts of land and subdivide and resell them in smaller parcels. Acting as miniproprietors, the investors would encourage more colonists to settle. Penn also planned to attract yeomen, craftsmen, and farmers who could afford to purchase or rent only small tracts. Finally, he provided for servants by offering small tracts of headright land to both servant and master.

Penn's system also included provisions for the distribution of different categories of land. Common land composed of country tracts and town lots was to be available on general terms. Certain portions of common land carried restrictions, however. Choice lots in the first great town, and liberty land, initially were intended for Original Purchasers only. Proprietary land composed of manors and smaller tracts was reserved for special allocation.

Penn expected country tracts to be surveyed in regular configurations of not more than 500 acres and occupied within a two- to three-year period by settlers. According to a statement made by his commissioners in 1701, "The Proprietary would never grant above 500 Acres to any one person and no faster than it could be improved."[1] Penn repeatedly admonished his commissioners: "Whatever is Irregular vacate; for I shall be very strict."[2] Aware of the large amount of warranted but unoccupied land, he called upon the purchasers to settle their acreage or run the risk of forfeiture.[3]

Finally, Penn's land distribution system included recording procedures that reflected a combination of English land law and the proprietary nature of the colony. As an example, Penn's appointees handled the sale and transfer of land in their private offices, but council and assembly appointees recorded deeds and conveyances in the public record office and local courts.

---

[1] Min. Com. Prop. Bk. G, 1st 10ber [December] 1701.

[2] Ibid. Bk. C, Instructions to William Markham, Thomas Ellis, and John Goodson, Worminghurst, 8th 12th Mo. 1686 [February 1687].

[3] Ibid., "A Proclamation concerning Seating of Land," Worminghurst, 24th 11th Mo 1686 [January 1687], and Philadelphia, 26th 5 Mo [July] 1687.

II.B.5 Modifications

During the interval between Penn's death in 1718 and the formal assumption of the proprietorship by his heirs in 1732, his land distribution system underwent several modifications. Although James Logan, secretary for proprietary affairs, and the commissioners of property attempted to continue the established policies, they were without clear direction when unprecedented issues arose. As a result, three distinct developments occurred during this interim: 1) the sale of new land was limited to the income necessary to pay the colony's mortgagees, 2) more warrants on old rights were therefore granted than new warrants, and 3) it became common for settlers to occupy land before obtaining a warrant.

Meanwhile, simultaneous pressure on three frontiers was more than Penn's land system could handle. Irish and German immigrants were pushing west to the Susquehanna River. Indians were insisting on their claim to land north of the Lehigh Mountains. In the south, uncertainty over the location of the Maryland boundary brought many intruders into Pennsylvania.

Beginning with the settlement about 1710 of the township of Donegal in Chester County (currently in Lancaster County), many more families settled without warrants than with them. Within a decade the rapid immigration of large numbers of Germans and new waves of Irish had made it impractical to use the established but cumbersome procedures of obtaining warrant, survey, and patent in order to secure land title.

In 1722, Governor William Keith established a proprietary foothold on the west side of the Susquehanna River on land not clear of Indian title. Under his right to survey land for the proprietors, Keith laid out his version of Springettsbury Manor and also surveyed land for himself.[1] It was no coincidence that the land he had chosen for himself supposedly contained a copper mine. Few settlers actually moved across the river, but Keith used his settlement to create a buffer between the older portions of the province and the frontier.[2] Employing similar tactics in 1723, he granted land in the Tulpehocken Valley to a group of Germans from the Schoharie River Valley in New York. To encourage Indians to move from the yet unpurchased area, the governor permitted the Germans to settle without the necessary warrants. Although Keith was forced from office for his high-handed approach, the stage had been set for land ownership simply by settlement and improvement.

[1] Min. Com. Prop. Bk. I, 16th 2d mo [April] 1722; Sur. Bk. B-23-231.
[2] See also III.E.1.a, Licensed Land.

II.C. Regions Open for Settlement

At the beginning of Penn's proprietorship in 1682, provincial territory open for legal settlement lay within a circumscribed area composed of the three original Pennsylvania counties and the three Lower Counties on the Delaware. A series of purchase treaties with the Indians gradually extended the legal area for settlement to the north and west. In this way, Penn cemented his friendship with the Indians and paid them with "Goods, merchandizes, and utensills," including wampum and guns.[1] By the formal end of Penn's proprietorship in 1732, settlement was legal as far north as the Lehigh hills and as far west as the watershed of the lower Susquehanna River.

[1] *Early American Indian Documents* 1:51–108.

II.C.1. Purchase Treaties, 1682–1732

Before Penn landed in the province, Deputy Governor William Markham negotiated the first purchase treaty with the Indians. In preparation, Penn had sent three letters to the Indians telling of his desire to live in harmony with them. By the terms of the treaty, the Delaware Indians sold their lands between Neshammonys Creek and the falls of the Delaware River. Purchased on July 15, 1682, this area soon became part of Bucks County.

In 1683, through several more purchase treaties, Penn acquired land along the lower Delaware River. One group of deeds—all dated June 23—transferred land between Neshaminy and Pennypack creeks and as far into the country as a two days' journey on horseback. Another deed, dated June 25, gave Penn land, formerly owned by an Indian named Wingebone, west of the Schuylkill River and above the falls. Two purchases on July 14 gained the acreage between the Schuylkill and Chester rivers and between the Schuylkill and Pemmapecka creeks. Following these initial treaties, subsequent purchases extended farther inland. On September 10,

Penn bought half of the area between the Delaware and Susquehanna rivers. He added to this on October 18 with the purchase of land from the Delaware River and the Chesapeake Bay to the falls of the Susquehanna. The 1683 purchases added a sizable area to what was already available for legal settlement. Together with the 1682 purchase, they created an arch of land open for settlement extending from the Maryland border to the Delaware River.

Between 1684 and 1701 nine additional purchase treaties were negotiated to confirm former treaties or add new land. In 1684, on June 3 and 7, two treaties opened land on Perkiomen and Pennypack creeks. One year later a purchase covered land that extended westward as far as a man could travel in two days. When this distance was measured in 1688, it was found to reach the Susquehanna River. Lands on both sides of the Susquehanna, beginning at the head of the river and extending to the Chesapeake Bay, were deeded to Penn in 1696 by Colonel Thomas Dongan, former governor of New York. This treaty was confirmed in 1700, but the Indians did not interpret it as confirming rights to the west side of the Susquehanna or the north side of the Lehigh hills. The remaining treaties either covered land purchased earlier, provided additional compensation to Indian chiefs who believed that payment had been inadequate, or confirmed friendly and peaceful relations between Indians and European settlers.

In 1718 the final treaty of Penn's proprietorship confirmed all the previous deeds for the land between the Delaware and Susquehanna rivers and from Duck Creek (Dover River in present Delaware) to the Lehigh hills.

The Genealogical Map of the Counties (front.) refers to each treaty mentioned in this section, and transcripts of the treaties appear in CR and PA (1).

II.C.2. County Formation, 1682–1732

Land within the area open for settlement was originally divided into six political subdivisions, or counties. The lower Delaware area, composed of New Castle, Kent, and Sussex counties, had been defined and organized long before Penn annexed it to Pennsylvania. Perhaps to provide

Table 4. Research Aids: Indian Treaties, 1682–1732

Early American Indian Documents: Treaties and Laws, 1607–1789. Vol. 1, *Pennsylvania and Delaware Treaties, 1629–1737,* edited by Donald H. Kent. Washington, DC, 1979.

Jennings, Francis. "Brother Minquon: Good Lord!" In *The World of William Penn,* edited by Richard S. Dunn and Mary Maples Dunn. Philadelphia, 1986.

Kent, Donald H. *History of Pennsylvania Purchases from the Indians.* New York, 1974.

Wallace, Paul A. *Indians in Pennsylvania.* Harrisburg, 1964.

a political balance, he separated the province of Pennsylvania into three counties also: Chester, Philadelphia, and Bucks. At first, these six counties formed one governmental unit and sent representatives to the same General Assembly.

No record of the official formation of the Pennsylvania counties seems to be extant, but the counties were specifically named in the earliest provincial records in conjunction with the selection of council and assembly members. Their boundary lines were vague, however, until officially determined in 1685, two and one-half years after proprietary government began to function.[1]

Each of the three original Pennsylvania counties—Philadelphia, Bucks, and Chester—was bounded on the east by the Delaware River and on the north and west as far as negotiated Indian treaties permitted settlement. The line between Philadelphia and Bucks counties ran along the east side of Potquessin Creek from its mouth on the Delaware River northwest to near its source and continued in the same direction along the west side of Southampton and Warminster townships. Between Philadelphia and Chester counties the line began at the mouth of Bough Creek on the Delaware River, wound its way northwest up Bough and Mill creeks, turned northeast along the west side of the liberty lands, angled its way to the Schuylkill River, and then followed the Schuylkill northwest. The county lines as described here are best seen in detail on

Thomas Holme's *Map of the Improved Part of the Province of Pennsilvania in America* (see Table 6).

Lancaster was the fourth Pennsylvania county to be formed. Emerging in 1729 from the heavily populated western portion of Chester County, it faced special frontier problems. As with the original counties, Lancaster had no defined northwestern boundary. However, settlement under warrant seldom was permitted on the west side of the Susquehanna River until after 1736. On the east, Octoraro Creek and its extension to the Schuylkill River marked the Lancaster-Chester boundary.

_____

[1]*Min. Prov. Coun.*, 1st 2d Mo [April] 1685.

II.D. Categories of Purchasers

Penn's initial idea was to attract three categories of settlers to occupy his land: purchasers, renters, and servants. Purchasers would form the nucleus around which he would build his new society. To the first one hundred purchasers he planned to sell shares worth 5,000 acres each. A price set at one hundred pounds per share would permit Penn to begin his settlement with 500,000 acres sold and one hundred thousand pounds in his account. Penn called his initial nucleus of investors First Purchasers and expected them to function as miniproprietors, subdividing and re-selling portions of their land to Under Purchasers. Individuals who could not afford to buy shares would be accepted as renters. They could rent partial shares of not over 200 acres at a yearly fee per acre. Servants would be alloted 50 acres upon the completion of their term of indenture, and every purchaser on behalf of every servant enlisted would receive a 50-acre headright.

Penn quickly realized that few investors were willing to pay as much as one hundred pounds for 5,000 acres of Pennsylvania wilderness. He was therefore forced to modify his initial ideas. In the second version of his promotional tract *Brief Account* and in his published statement of agreement with his First Purchasers entitled *Certaine Conditions or Concessions . . .,*[1] he permitted the formation of joint purchasing arrangements in which as many as ten people would join together to buy one 5,000-acre share. He also agreed to sell and rent tracts of land as small as 125 acres and to allow purchasers a voice in determining the location of their land. Finally, Penn announced that each of the First Purchasers (and renters) would be allowed land within the first town or city in proportion to the total amount of land purchased. With these concessions made, sales in England, Scotland, and Ireland moved quickly.

_____

[1]*Brief Account* (July 1681); *Certaine Conditions or Concessions*, in *PWP* 2:98–102.

II.D.1. Purchasers

Of the three categories of people Penn sought to attract to Pennsylvania, purchasers were the most important. Classified into four different groups by the timing of their purchase, these investors became subproprietors. Purchasers of shares before Penn's settlement began in the province in 1682 were classed as First Purchasers. Penn added a few late purchasers to the list and created an enlarged group called Original

Chart 1. Areas of Settlement and County Formation, 1682–1732

Date*	Indian Deed Number*	County
1682	[annexed]	New Castle, Kent, Sussex (state of Delaware, 1776)
1682	1	Southeast corner Bucks
1683	2–7	Original **Bucks** (1), **Chester** (2), **Philadelphia** (3)
1684	8–16	Enlarged Bucks
1718	17–19	Enlarged Chester and Philadelphia
1729	—	**Lancaster** (4) from Chester

*Dates and deed numbers refer to the Genealogical Map of the Counties (front.).

Table 5. Research Aids: First Purchasers

"The First Purchasers of Pennsylvania, 1681–1685." In *PWP* 2: 630–64.

Pomfret, John E. "The First Purchasers of Pennsylvania." *PMHB* 80 (1956): 137–63.

Roach, Hannah Benner. "The First Purchasers of Pennsylvania." In *Passengers and Ships Prior to 1684,* edited by Walter Lee Sheppard. Vol. 1, *Penn's Colony* (Baltimore, 1970), 195–208.

Purchasers. Individuals who bought land from Original Purchasers were called Under Purchasers. All other settlers who bought land in Pennsylvania from William Penn were called After Purchasers or simply purchasers.

II.D.1.a. First Purchasers

The nucleus of Penn's settlement was a group of investors from England, Scotland, and Ireland who purchased the first one hundred shares, or rights to Pennsylvania land. Known as First Purchasers, they were primarily Quaker merchants, craftsmen, shopkeepers, and farmers. Penn granted land to them through deeds of lease and release that serve to identify First Purchasers in the records today.[1]

In purchasing their shares, or rights, First Purchasers agreed to a set of rules and regulations. Printed under the title *Certaine Conditions or Concessions agreed upon by William Penn . . . and those who are the adventurers and purchasers . . .* , these regulations enumerated twenty conditions.[2] One in particular set First Purchasers apart from other buyers. Penn agreed to allocate two acres in a large city or town for each one hundred acres a First Purchaser bought.

Although Philadelphia, as it was laid out, was not large enough for this provision to be enforced, Penn designated land adjacent to the city where First Purchasers would have their 2 percent.[3] They also agreed to survey no more than 1,000 acres of land in any one location unless they placed a family on each 1,000 acres within three years. This condition marked an effort to prevent purchasers from holding vast amounts of land for speculative purposes. Yet, despite this requirement, the most common complaint about Penn's land policies revolved around the ill effects of large tracts of unseated land. At the time of divestiture in 1779, Edmund Physick, the Penn family agent in Pennsylvania, calculated that, between March 1681 and October 1682, Pennsylvania's First Purchasers bought approximately 874,550 acres of land.[4]

Three catalogs of First Purchasers can be identified in the Land Office collection and are contained in the records cited below. Each is titled similarly, "An Account of Lands in Pennsylvania Granted by William Penn to Several Purchasers in England, Scotland, Ireland," and each uses the same cataloging system. In the catalogs, First Purchasers are grouped in sections of 10,000 acres consecutively numbered with roman numerals. Each catalog contains more sections than the previous one, and sections do not correspond exactly between the catalogs. Regrouping and errors in copying account for the slight discrepancies. The catalogs are also printed, with their numbering systems corrected, on John Reed's *Map of the City and Liberties of Philadelphia* (see Table 7).

Another list of First Purchasers is included in an early warrant book cited below. This may have been considered the official list, since it is entered in a volume generated at the time. Proprietary correspondence sometimes refers to such a list of First Purchasers.

Reconstructed lists of First Purchasers may be found in the sources listed in Table 5.

RECORDS: LOOSE PAPERS

AN ACCOUNT OF THE LAND IN PENNSYLVANIA GRANTED BY WILLIAM PENN . . . TO SEVERAL PURCHASERS WITHIN THE KINGDOM OF ENGLAND (Pat. Bk. AA-5-130-39) LO micro.: 12.

The earliest catalog, containing 259 purchasers grouped into thirty-two sections, which account for sixty-four of the one hundred shares Penn planned to sell. It is dated October 25, 1681, and was apparently sent with the earliest shipload of settlers who set out for Pennsylvania. It includes Penn's appointment of commissioners of property and a statement of his instructions to them to allot ten thousand acres for a town in which the purchasers of every five thousand acres shall have one hundred acres. This catalog was copied into Pat. Bk. AA-5, pp. 130–39, in 1763 from the original three pieces of parchment.

AN ACCO[UN]T OF THE LANDS IN PENNSYLVANIA GRANTED BY WILLIAM PENN . . . TO SEVERAL PURCHASERS WITHIN THE KINGDOM OF ENGLAND (Proprietary Papers, folder 2, item 4)   LO micro.: 23.1.

The second catalog of purchasers, an eleven-page handwritten original draft or copy containing fifty-three purchaser groups and accounting for the sale of all of the original one hundred shares. However, it skips section XXXIII in its numbering of purchaser groups and leaves section XLIV blank. The Free Society of Traders in Pennsylvania accounts for two purchaser groups of ten thousand acres each. This catalog includes Penn's reappointment of commissioners of property to supervise the laying out of lots according to three sets of previous instructions and, apparently in error, is dated the 31st of the second month [April] 1682.

SALES IN ENGLAND BY WILLIAM PENN OF LANDS IN PENNSYLVANIA   (RG-21, item 15)   Reel 600.

The third catalog of purchasers in England, containing fifty-seven purchaser groups. Some purchasers' names appear more than once as they acquired additional shares. The catalog, marked "Copia" (Copy), is dated the "22 Day of the 3rd month [May] 1682" and was sent with Philip Ford, William Penn's business manager, to Thomas Holme, surveyor general in Pennsylvania. The handwritten note on the manuscript "Left by Isaac Brown" refers to Isaac B. Brown, secretary of internal affairs in 1895 and 1903–7. The catalog is reprinted in *Annals*, 637–42; and *PA* (1) 1:40–46.

RECORDS: BOUND VOLUMES

WARRANT BOOK NO. 3   1682–1684   (Binding No. 15)   LO micro.: 25.3; 1759 transcript in PROPRIETARY WARRANTS   (Binding No. 26)   LO micro.: 25.5.

The first six pages of Wt. Bk. 3 contain an alphabetized list titled "An Account of Lands in Pennsylvania Granted by William Penn to Several Purchasers in England, Scotland, Ireland." The list gives purchasers' names, amounts of land purchased, and, for some purchasers, the general location. This may have been considered the official list, for it is entered in a volume containing papers generated at the time, and a list of First Purchasers is frequently referred to in proprietary correspondence.

[1]See II.G.1, Deeds of Lease and Release.
[2]*PWP* 2:98–102.
[3]See II.E.1.c, Liberty Land.
[4]General Cash Accounts, 242–49.

II.D.1.b. Original Purchasers

The term Original Purchasers is applied to an expanded list of First Purchasers. Penn added names to the First Purchaser list for several reasons. First, he sold more shares, or rights, than his intended one hundred, accepting the purchases of several individuals who had been slow to respond to the initial offer. These people he called Late Purchasers. Second, Penn also accepted the money of new buyers, either investors in England or settlers who arrived in Pennsylvania. To new purchasers who would buy the rights to one thousand acres, he extended the privileges given to First Purchasers, particularly choice lots in the first city.[1] Third, Penn resold the rights that many First Purchasers had not activated by taking up land in Pennsylvania.

Shortly after divestiture in 1779, the names of new and Late Purchasers were extracted from information given in warrants and added to the list of First Purchasers. This created an enlarged list entered in a register titled "Original Purchases," which applies to the three original counties of the province of Pennsylvania only and not to the three Lower Counties. To each of the individuals listed in this register, Penn had extended the terms of *Certaine Conditions or Concessions*, granting them old rights as if they were First Purchasers.

All Original Purchasers, including First Purchasers, were required to register a deed of lease and release or a special order from Penn before they could request a warrant to survey. After 1685 the request was made before the commissioners of property and recorded in their minute book. Warrants were usually requested for only a portion of the total purchase; thus, each Original Purchaser may have several requests and several warrants made out in his name. Although the sequence of receiving a warrant did not always occur in the preferred order, usually a deed of lease and release or a special order should be on record for each Original Purchaser who settled in Pennsylvania.

The amount of land that Original Purchasers warranted did not always match the amount of land they purchased. In some cases it was much more and in some cases less. Original Purchasers who brought servants received additional land beyond the amount they had purchased. For each servant they sponsored they received fifty additional acres called headright land. Other Original Purchasers who exhibited a marked amount of overplus land simply took more than they were entitled to take. However, since not all Original Purchasers claimed all their rights, the sale of unclaimed rights proved to be a good business, and warrants emanating from such rights are dated as late as 1794.

The official group of Original Purchasers is listed alphabetically in the Original Purchases register cited below. It includes Under Purchasers who bought land from Original Purchasers or claimed land in their right. The amounts and locations of Under Purchasers' land are also included.

RECORDS: BOUND VOLUMES

ORIGINAL PURCHASES   LO micro.: 1.21.

An alphabetical list of First and Late purchasers, giving the disposition of their land in the three original counties of Pennsylvania and in the city liberties. Letters and numbers refer to the 1759 Transcripts (see III.G.6, 1759 Transcripts, and Appendix A). For each purchaser the following information is given: 1) his name and quantity of land; 2) to whom granted (himself or an Under Purchaser) and the quantity; 3) where taken up and the quantity; 4) the date of warrant, letter, and number; 5) the date of survey, letter, and number; and 6) the date of return, book, and page. The letter and number following the date of warrant refer to the letter and number listed in the left-hand column of each Old Rights register. The letter is the first letter of the last name of the warrantee, and the number is the assigned placement of the warrantee within his group of last names. Thus, "B 21" means the twenty-first individual in the list whose last name starts with B.

WARRANT BOOK 1682–1762   (Binding No. 114).

An older version of the Original Purchases register containing many notes (for example, assessed rent) not transferred to the newer register cited above.

[1]Min. Com. Prop. Bk. G, 8th 10th Mo [December] 1701.

II.D.1.c. Under Purchasers

Under Purchasers were individuals who bought land in the right of Original Purchasers rather than directly from Penn. Their purchase was not intended to carry with it any of the rights granted to Original Purchasers in *Certaine Conditions or Concessions.* Instead, Under Purchasers bought land allocated to Original Purchasers but on which Original Purchasers had not settled.

The transfer of land from Original Purchaser to Under Purchaser was usually accomplished in one of two ways. First, if an Under Purchaser bought rights to land that the Original Purchaser had not yet warranted, the Original Purchaser submitted the request for a warrant to survey the land in the name of the Under Purchaser, and the Under Purchaser paid for the warrant.[1] Second, if an Under Purchaser bought land already warranted but not yet surveyed, the Under Purchaser paid the expense of the survey, the Original Purchaser withdrew his warrant, and a new warrant was recorded in the name of the Under Purchaser. This latter procedure was the forerunner of the warrant to accept, which was introduced by Penn's heirs and also applied to subdivisions of land previously warranted.

Despite Penn's policies, some Under Purchasers were granted rights similar to Original Purchasers. For example, purchasers in the Welsh Tract who bought directly from agents were granted rights to lots in the city and the city liberties. Due to such variances, it was very difficult to keep track of the amount of land warranted in an Original Purchaser's right, and the total amount often exceeded the amount actually purchased.

The names of Under Purchasers are listed in the Original Purchases register under the name of the person in whose right they bought land, and their warrant and survey information is referenced. To avoid confusion when researching early purchasers, check this register to see if the purchaser is warranting in his own right or in the right of an Original Purchaser.

RECORDS: BOUND VOLUME

ORIGINAL PURCHASES   LO micro.: 1.21.

For a description see II.D.1.b, Original Purchasers.

[1]Min. Com. Prop. Bk. G, 17th 10th mo [December] 1701.

II.D.1.d. After Purchasers

After Purchasers, a term used by Penn, were settlers or speculators who warranted land in their own name and were neither First Purchasers, Original Purchasers, nor Under Purchasers. Some historians have called them subsequent purchasers, but early registers and minutes simply designate them "purchasers" as opposed to First Purchasers. Penn did not make provision for After Purchasers as a separate category because he expected them to buy land in the right of Original Purchasers. Instead, After Purchasers received their land by applying directly to the commissioners of property or to the governor of the province or by leasing or purchasing land within proprietary manors. Not covered by the old rights granted to First Purchasers in *Certaine*

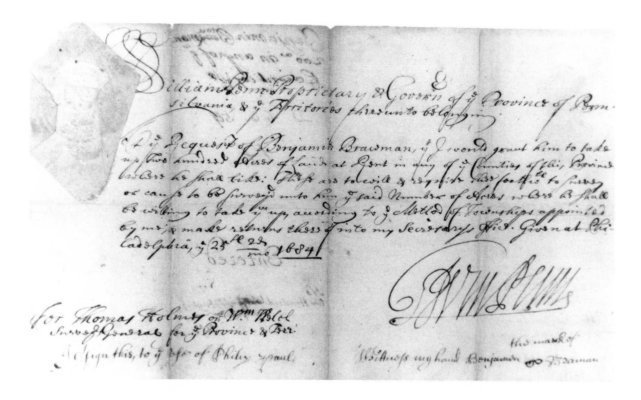

Warrant signed by William Penn to survey two hundred acres of land at rent. (Sur. Bk. D-66-59)

Conditions or Concessions, many After Purchasers nevertheless were permitted to buy Philadelphia city lots.

The phrasing of the warrant, not the date, identifies After Purchasers. Their warrants omit the reference to purchasing in the right of some-one else. Although After Purchasers did not have old rights, their warrants were grouped with all pre-1733 warrants under the rubric "old rights" when the original records were copied in 1759. Therefore, After Purchasers and Original Purchasers are mixed together in the Old Rights registers.

Many colonists who would have fallen into the category of After Purchasers, such as early Scots-Irish and Palatine settlers, did not warrant land during the Penn era. After the death of William Penn in 1718, the proprietary agents refused to sell more land than would pay off the proprietor's mortgage debt on the colony. At issue

was who held the proprietary power and whether the commissioners of property were empowered to grant clear title to land. Settlers who took the risk and paid the price of ten pounds per one hundred acres were granted warrants and surveys. Most prospective purchasers simply selected land on their own and squatted. In part, the policy of encouraging groups of Germans and Scots-Irish to settle on the frontier beyond the line of legal settlement bought the commissioners of property extra time. Later, when Penn's heirs made an effort to warrant and patent all the land that actually had been settled, many would-be After Purchasers were added to the records.

II.D.2. Renters

Renters, the second category of people Penn wanted to attract as settlers, were prospective colonists who could afford passage for themselves and their families but, upon arrival in Pennsylvania, had no money to buy land.

Initially, they were permitted to rent fifty acres of country land for each person in the family, male and female alike, over sixteen years of age.[1] This policy quickly changed, however, and the proprietor rented out larger tracts of one hundred to five hundred acres.[2] Terms for renting country land were usually one penny per acre per year in areas close to navigable rivers.[3] This amounted to eight shillings four pence per year for one hundred acres.[4] Some colonists found this very expensive and preferred to purchase at the usual rate of five pounds per one hundred acres.[5] Rent for land more distant from navigable rivers was often set in bushels of wheat.[6] Occasionally, special conditions, usually involving location, called for special terms of rent. For instance, Ellis Jones leased eight acres for twenty-one years at the annual rent of twelve pence, and Joshua Tillery rented fifty acres above the falls of the Schuylkill at three pence per year for one hundred years.[7] By the late 1680s renting country land had become quite common, although the original warrant register indicates that renting country land in the Lower Counties was more common than in the three Pennsylvania counties.[8]

According to the terms of *Certaine Conditions or Concessions*, renters were eligible also to lease lots or squares in the city.[9] Lots for rent were usually located inland from the Delaware or Schuylkill River and in less desirable locations than those designated for Original Purchasers. Richard Turner, for instance, leased three lots between Seventh and Eighth streets (contiguous to a lot he already rented) for three shillings per year for twenty-one years. Terms to rent city lots varied but usually ran between eight and ten shillings per year for one hundred feet of frontage or an entire square bounded by four streets.[10]

By making land available to settlers through rent, Penn created a class of mortgagees. Settlers who paid rent in perpetuity had claim to their tract as if they had been purchasers. The tract could not be warranted to others, and renters could request permission to purchase their land at any time.[11]

Renters went through the same process of locating their tract as did purchasers. They submitted a request to the commissioners of property, who authorized a warrant to survey. Renters'

warrants appear intermixed with purchasers' warrants in the original records; only the phraseology of the warrant identifies renters (see p. 15).

Renters can be found easily by consulting two of the original volumes of land records. In the volume Returns [of Survey] Philadelphia City Lots No. 2 (Binding No. 93), an *R* in the margin identifies a renter. In Wt. Bk. 1685–1691 (Binding No. 14), the word "Rent" or "Renter" is entered beside the individual's name in the lists of warrants granted. The requests for these warrants can usually be found in the minute books of the commissioners of property under the corresponding dates. While many of these warrants are referenced under the individuals' names in the Old Rights register, many others are only available in the original warrant books. Warrants for renters in the Lower Counties were transferred to Delaware and are not referenced in the Old Rights register.

---

[1]*Certain Conditions or Concessions . . .*, in *PWP* 2:98–102. See, for example, Wt. Bk. 3 (Binding No. 15), 188.

[2]See, for example, Sur. Bks. D-66-59, D-76-87, and D-75-14.

[3]Min. Com. Prop. Bk. D, 15th 12 Mo [February] 1689–90; ibid., 5th 2nd Mo [April] 1690; ibid., 25th 8thber [October] 1690.

[4]*PWP* 4:119, n. 16.

[5]Min. Com. Prop. Bk. D, 17th 11th mo [January] 1690/1.

[6]Ibid., 28th 4th Mo [June] 1690; ibid., 20th 7th [September] 1690; ibid., 10th 11 Mo [January], 1690/1; ibid., 22d 1st Month [March], 1689–90.

[7]Ibid., 14th 12th mo [February] 1690/1; ibid., 8th 12 mo [February] 1690/1.

[8]Wt. Bk. 1685–1691 (Binding No. 14).

[9]Min. Com. Prop. Bk. D, 22nd 1st Mo [March] 1689–90; ibid., 3rd 3rd Mo [May] 1690.

[10]Ibid., 25th 8thber [October] 1690/1; ibid., 30th 6th Mo: [August] 1690.

[11]Ibid., 25th 8thber [October] 1690.

II.D.3. Servants

The third category of people Penn sought to attract as settlers was composed of indentured servants, whom he looked upon as the labor force for the province. At first, he granted special rewards to Original Purchasers who would act as sponsors and to the servants they brought.[1] Similar terms were offered later to other purchasers, renters, and their servants.[2]

After their term of indenture was complete, servants were granted full citizenship and fifty acres of land at an annual rent of two shillings. Servants obtained this acreage, called headright land, by following the same procedures as renters and purchasers. When they were ready to claim their land, they submitted a formal request and received a warrant to survey. Servants can be identified by the phrasing of the warrants, which state that they were formerly servants. Those who had worked together under one sponsor were sometimes granted one warrant for the total amount of land they were eligible to receive. In this way, they could continue to live and work together.[3]

The urgency of setting aside headright land came to the attention of Deputy Governor William Markham, Penn's first land agent, even before the proprietor arrived in Pennsylvania. Markham feared that servants who were totally dependent upon their headright land for support might need to wait too long if all of the First Purchasers were accommodated first. He therefore drew up a general warrant to locate and lay out a sufficient quantity of land to satisfy the needs of servants.[4] No evidence indicates that this warrant was ever executed, but one of the earliest warrants granted on a headright was for land in the same area as the Servants' Township that Penn later authorized.[5]

In 1701, acting upon his earlier plans, Penn set aside one particular township for servants.[6] The tract contained about 6,000 acres and was located in the northern part of Bucks County immediately north of Hilltown Township and east of Perkasie Manor. Although Penn wanted to call the township Freeman-Town or Freetown, many original warrants refer to the tract as the Servants' Township. Only a few servants seem to have located their headright land in the township. By 1740 the area had been renamed Rockhill Township and was no longer designated entirely for servants. At the time of divestiture in 1779, Edmund Physick calculated that 4,571 3/4 acres had been granted to former servants of Original Purchasers.[7]

[1]*Certaine Conditions or Concessions . . .*, in *PWP* 2:98–102. See especially p. 99.
[2]Sur. Bk. D-77-155; Wt. Bk. 3 (Binding No. 15), 210.
[3]Min. Com. Prop. Bk. G, 21st 11th Mo 1701 [January 1702].

[4]Sur. Bk. D-85-81.
[5]Sur. Bks. D-68-196 and D-68-246.
[6]Sur. Bk. D-85-68.
[7]General Cash Accounts, 235.

II.E. Categories of Land

As in the feudal system, where the king kept some of the land and distributed the rest among his lords, William Penn kept some of the province and sold the rest to the people. Penn's charter, based upon English feudal land law, permitted him to establish special tracts of proprietary land, which he could handle as he wished. The charter also assumed that the majority of the province would be common land available to all settlers alike. These provisions thus divided Pennsylvania land into two categories: proprietary and common.

Due to Penn's special concessions to Original Purchasers, common land was separated automatically into country land, city lots, and liberty land. The vast majority was country land, which comprised all land in the province purchased from the Indians except Philadelphia lots and liberty land. Original Purchasers and other purchasers had equal access to country land and were able to buy it at generally uniform prices. The smallest portion of common land was the Philadelphia city lot. City lots were available only to Original Purchasers and renters, although Penn reserved a section of the town for his right to make special grants to anyone. Many city lots were never claimed, and shortly after divestiture in 1779 the Commonwealth offered them for open sale. The third portion of common land, liberty land, was located in a specific area immediately north of the city of Philadelphia and only available to Original Purchasers.

Penn reserved a small amount of land for his own use. Although he planned to set aside one tenth of every township as proprietary land, he did not strictly follow this practice. Usually his land officers selected the best tract within a township or a given area. Consequently, proprietary tracts varied in size. The larger were called manors; the smaller were simply termed tracts or lots. Penn kept little proprietary land for his own and his family's estates. The rest he sold to other individuals at a higher rate than normal.

Table 6. Research Aids: Early Pennsylvania Maps

Garrison, Hazel Shields. "Cartography of Pennsylvania before 1800." *PMHB* 59 (1935):255–83.

Holme, Thomas. *A Map of the Improved Part of the Province of Pennsilvania in America Begun by Wil: Penn Proprietary & Governor thereof Anno 1681*. In *PA* (3) Appendix 1-10, No. 23. Also in *PWP* 3:636–56.

Kleinfelter, Walter. "Surveyor General Thomas Holme's 'Map of the Improved Part of the Province of Pennsylvania.' " *Winterthur Portfolio* 6 (1970):41–74.

Rosenberger, Homer. "Early Maps of Pennsylvania." *Pa. Hist.* 11 (1944):103–17.

II.E.1. Common Land

Common land in Pennsylvania, consisting mainly of country land, was generally available to all purchasers, but the city lots and liberty land that made up the remainder of common land were bonuses available only to Original Purchasers. Exceptions were made, however, especially when Penn was in need of money, and many After Purchasers were able to buy city lots and liberty land.

II.E.1.a. Country Land

The bulk of the land in the province was country land. Comprising all common land but Philadelphia city lots and liberty land, country land was available to anyone who would follow the proper warranting procedures. Penn had no fixed price for it but charged whatever the market would bring. At times, country land sold for as much as twenty to thirty pounds per 100 acres, but studies indicate that the average price was ten pounds per 100 acres.[1] First Purchasers were required to locate 98 percent of their acreage in country land. After Purchasers usually had no choice but to locate all of their parcels in country land.

The amount of country land that could be purchased in any one name varied. Originally,

Penn had sold 5,000-acre shares, but with the restriction that only 1,000 acres could be located in a single area. He later agreed to sell tracts as large as 10,000 and as small as 125 acres.

Penn proclaimed in 1686 that each township of 5,000 acres should have at least ten families, and he included the phrase "according to the method of townships" in every warrant. To him this meant that tracts would adjoin each other "yᵗ yᵉ Province might not lie like a Wilderness as some others yett doe by vast vacant tracts of Land but be Regularly Improved for ye benefitt of socyety in helpe [of] Trade Education Govermᵗ. Also Roads Travell Entertainement &c."[2] Penn apparently believed that townships should "lie square" with a village in the center, and in 1685 he explained two versions of this concept in *A Further Account of the Province of Pennsylvania.*[3]

If Penn's plan had been carried out, Pennsylvania would be composed of neat square and rectangular townships similar to the New England style, but his idea was never widely implemented. Only two townships, Newtown and Wrightstown in Bucks County, were laid out according to his plan.[4] Both were surveyed with tracts radiating out from a center square like spokes on a wheel. Penn's insistence on placing tracts next to each other had some impact, however, for the townships in the three original counties appear orderly in their configuration when compared to those laid out farther inland at a later date.

Under the political system established for the province, each county was responsible for forming its own townships. Chester County court records indicate townships in the early 1680s, but, in Bucks County, court records show that townships were not officially designated until 1692.[5] Surveys of some of the township boundaries in Bucks and Chester counties are on file with the land records and cited below. A few surveys indicate warrantee tracts within the townships and may well be the earliest warrantee township maps on record.

Country land was mapped only once during Penn's proprietorship, although several editions of the map were produced. Penn needed the document as promotional literature for his colonial venture. Before he left the province in 1684, he asked Surveyor General Thomas Holme to prepare a map from surveys that had been completed and returned to the Land Office. The project languished while the deputy surveyors procrastinated in returning their drafts. Holme finally completed the map in 1687. This version was published the same year under the title *A Map of the Improved Part of the Province of Pennsilvania in America*, with the subtitle *A Map of the Province of Pennsilvania, Containing the Three Countyes of Chester, Philadelphia, & Bucks as far as yet surveyed and Laid out, ye Divisions or distinctions made by ye different Coullers, respects the Settlements by way of Townships*. The bottom margin of this first edition contained a 4,000-word "General Description of the Province of Pennsylvania in America." The advertisement announced that the map gave "the Figure of every particular Persons piece or parcels of Land taken up." An examination of the land records corroborates the theory that the Holme map is the first warrantee tract map for the three original counties.

A second edition of the Holme map, incorporating grants made during Penn's second stay but deleting many earlier ones, was published sometime between 1701 and 1705 shortly after Penn returned to England. A reproduction of the second edition was published in 1846. Modern published versions of the Holme map are usually based upon this 1846 reproduction.[6]

The amount of country land sold during Penn's proprietorship was calculated by Edmund Physick after the divestiture in 1779. Physick's figures indicated that approximately 83,003 acres were sold between October 1682 and November 1701. Because there was no accounting of receipts during this early period, the income derived is unknown. The income from land sales for the remainder of the period, November 1701 to December 1732, was £12,610. At an average price of £10 per 100 acres, Physick calculated that 126,000 acres were sold. These two amounts, added to that of the First Purchasers' acreage, give a total of 1,183,653 acres sold between 1681 and 1732, or one fourteenth of the total province.[7]

RECORDS: LOOSE PAPERS

RETURN OF SURVEY   TOWNSHIPS   LO micro.: 20.5.

Four folders containing surveys of several of the townships in Bucks and Chester counties. Some of the surveys include tracts within the townships.

---

[1]*Chester Co.*, 150.

[2]"Instructions to Wm Markham 1687—A Proclamation by the Prop^y Deputy 26th 5th month [July] 1687," Wt. Bk. 1685–1691 (Binding No. 14) LO micro.: 25.2; *PA* (2) 19:5–6.

[3]Cited in *PWP* 5:320–23. For a transcript see Albert Cook Myers, ed., *Narratives of Early Pennsylvania, West New Jersey and Delaware, 1630–1707* (New York, 1912), 257–78.

[4]See Holme, *A Map of the Improved Part of the Province of Pennsilvania,* cited in Table 6. See also Wt. Bk. 3 (Binding No. 15), 208.

[5]See 1687 edition of Holme map.

[6]See especially *PA* (3) Appendix 1-10.

[7]"Affidavit, Penn Property in the Province," Accounts, Penn-Physick Mss 4:91–95.

II.E.1.b. Philadelphia City Lots

The most important modification in Penn's original land plans involved the granting of city lots. According to *Certaine Conditions or Concessions*, purchasers were to receive lots in the first city laid out.[1] These lots were to equal ten acres for every five hundred acres purchased, if the site selected was large enough. By allowing joint purchase arrangements, however, Penn increased the total number of settlers eligible for city lots beyond the number originally intended. This situation, compounded by insufficient land in the location chosen for the city, created a problem that was solved by reducing the size of the city lots and creating a second area, called the city liberties, where lots could be laid out as originally proportioned.

Table 7. Research Aids: Philadelphia City Lots

"Early Philadelphia Residents." Pennsylvania Department of Internal Affairs *Monthly Bulletin* 22, nos. 4, 5 (March, April 1954): 13–21, 27–29.

Holme, Thomas. A *Portraiture of the City of Philadelphia in the Province of Pennsylvania in America, 1683.* In PA (3) 4.

Lewis, Lawrence, Jr. *An Essay on Original Land Titles in Philadelphia.* Philadelphia, 1880.

Reed, John. *An Explanation of the Map of the City and Liberties of Philadelphia.* Philadelphia, 1774. In PA (3) 3:295–401. For the map itself see *PA* (3) 4.

Roach, Hannah Benner. "The Planting of Philadelphia—A Seventeenth-Century Real Estate Development." *PMHB* 92 (1968): 3–47, 143–94.

Snyder, Martin P. *City of Independence: Views of Philadelphia before 1800.* New York, 1975.

This shift in Penn's plans for the city made it difficult to know exactly who was eligible for lots. Original Purchasers claimed their right to city lots as part of the terms of their agreement with Penn, and he set aside specific streets where they were to have their lots. The early commissioners of property denied city lots to those who were not Original Purchasers. But, as settlement in the city moved more slowly than desired, After Purchasers and renters were encouraged to buy or rent city lots or to apply for lots using the unclaimed rights of Original Purchasers.

The site selected for the city contained twelve hundred acres between the Delaware and Schuylkill rivers. The tract formed a near rectangle two miles across, while two miles of waterfront extended north and south on the Delaware River, and one mile of waterfront stretched north and south on the Schuylkill River. The commissioners appointed to select a site for the city settled upon the location in early 1682. Three Swedish settlers occupied part of the site, but they were granted larger tracts in the liberty land and encouraged to move.

Preliminary plans and surveying began soon after the site for the city was selected. Settlers urgently needed to move from the caves along the bank of the Delaware River into regular homes. The commissioners held a drawing for the city lots in September 1682, shortly after the surveyor general, Thomas Holme, arrived. Only the fifty-four First Purchasers present were included in the drawing. The lots drawn were located along Second Street, Fourth Street, Broad Street, and Back Street, and each purchaser drew a lot on each street. Many settlers refused to wait for an official survey based upon the results of the drawing before they started to clear their tracts. The original or a handwritten copy of the drawing is filed in the Land Office and cited below. No existing titles can be traced to this first drawing, which Penn seems to have vetoed after his arrival in October, but it serves as an indication of exactly which purchasers had arrived by September 1682.

Penn also altered the original plan for the city and changed the names of the streets. He then had Holme draw up a map of the new plan, entitled A *Portraiture of the City of Philadelphia,* and published it in London in 1683 as part of a book advertising the province. Holme's plan divided the city into lots and included the names of most of the First Purchasers and the numbers of the lots allocated to them. In August 1683, Penn wrote that "[Philadelp]hia, . . . is at last Laid [out to the great Content of] those here that [are any wayes Interested therein; . . .]."[2] A manuscript of the list of purchasers and the numbers of their lots as they appear on Holme's *Portraiture* is cited in the records at the end of this section.

The new plan did not remain in effect long. Topography and other considerations necessitated changes almost immediately. Warrants and returns of survey show that city lots as finally granted did not correspond exactly to Holme's plan. Several returns of survey indicate instead that the current layout of the city developed from surveys that began as early as the latter part of 1684.

To obtain his city lot an Original Purchaser ordinarily took the usual step of requesting a warrant to survey. In most instances the lots were laid out with no reference to Holme's plan but rather in entirely different locations. Original Purchasers who arrived late and had not been included in the first allotment were given their choice of location. Other Original Purchasers sold their shares in the province to Under Purchasers and either passed their rights in city lots on to them also or sold the rights to others. The secretary for proprietary affairs entered warrants to survey city lots in the regular warrant book, along with all other warrants. Likewise, the returns of survey and patents to city lots were entered in the regular return of survey and patent books. The records on file can be accessed by using the Old Rights register for Philadelphia.

Land in the town not laid out for Original Purchasers was reserved for After Purchasers. Most of the vacant land lay upon the back streets or the banks of the Delaware and Schuylkill rivers. Bank lots could only be obtained upon special application, and a patent issued in that case contained many special stipulations.

The city of Philadelphia was incorporated in 1701, but city lots remained the private property of the Penn family until the time of sale.

RECORDS: LOOSE PAPERS

ORIGINAL SURVEYS   LO micro.: 6.189–90.

Original warrants, surveys, and returns of survey for Philadelphia city lots for the period 1682–1732 interfiled with the original loose surveys and numbered by the volume, book, and page. Indexes are in two separate volumes: the Philadelphia Old Rights register cited below under Bound Volumes and an unpublished in-house index. Warrants, surveys, and return of surveys referenced in the in-house index have not been copied into the copied survey volumes but are in volume D, books 112–14.

LOTTS OF THE 4 STREETS &c. A CERTIFICATE OF THE DRAWING OF ORIGINAL PURCHASERS LOTS   LO micro.: 21.1; transcript in WARRANTS AND SURVEYS 2, Philadelphia City Archives, LO micro.: 25.128.

Filed in the Philadelphia City Lots folders, this certificate is on two sheets of paper dated the "19th of the 7th month [September] 1682" and signed by Commissioners of Property William Markham, Thomas Holme, William Haig [or Haige], and Griffith Jones.

DIRECTIONS OF REFERENCE IN THE CITY DRAUGHT OF PHILADELPHIA TO THE LOTTS etc.   LO micro.: 21.1; copy in ACCOUNT OF LOTS RETURNED 1698   (Binding No. 61)   LO micro.: 25.14; transcript in WARRANTS AND SURVEYS 2, Philadelphia City Archives, LO micro.: 25.128.

Filed in the Philadelphia City Lots folders, this is the listing of the lots as they are numbered on Thomas Holme's map, A *Portraiture of the City of Philadelphia in . . . America*. The loose copy is not complete.

RECORDS: BOUND VOLUMES

PHILADELPHIA OLD RIGHTS   LO micro.: 1.10, 1.21.

A register of individuals who warranted and surveyed land in Philadelphia city and county. The same volume number and page refer to both the original loose survey paper and the copied survey.

WARRANT BOOK 1683   (Binding No. 115).

The inside label reads "List of Original Purchasers and Disposition of their Land—City Lot Book." This volume seems to be the original copy of the city lot counterpart of the Original Purchases register. The table of contents contains an alphabetical list of purchaser names, giving for each the following: 1) the lot number in the old plan; 2) to whom it was granted (Under Purchaser); 3) its location; 4) its warrant date, letter, and number; 5) its survey date, letter, and number; and 6) its return date, book, and page. The letters and numbers refer to the filing system represented in the 1759 transcripts. Unfortunately, the 1759 transcript of the Philadelphia city warrants is missing. However, the same original loose warrants can be accessed through the Old Rights register.

WARRANT BOOK 1683   (Binding No. 116)   LO micro.: 25.108.

A newer copy of Binding No. 115, giving the same information but also including references to Holme's plan of the city.

RETURNS OF PHILADELPHIA CITY LOTS NO. 2   (Binding No. 93)   LO micro.: 25.36.

An original volume in Surveyor General Holme's handwriting of copies of certificates for lots in Philadelphia that he returned to the secretary's office. The dates run from the "19th of the 4th month [June] 1683" to the "13th of the 5th month [July] 1684."

STEEL'S RENT ROLL FOR PHILADELPHIA   1731   (Binding No. 6b)   LO micro.: 25.1.

A rent roll prepared by James Steel for both the city and county of Philadelphia, organized by township and giving each purchaser's name, acreage, assessed quitrent, years due up to 1731, and amount paid.

---

[1]*Certaine Conditions or Concessions . . .*, in *PWP* 2:98–102.
[2]To the Free Society of Traders, August 16, 1683, *PWP* 2:455.

II.E.1.c. Liberty Land

The third category of common land, liberty land, was created to satisfy the terms of the original agreement between Penn and the First Purchasers.[1] According to this agreement, *Certaine Conditions or Concessions*, one of every fifty acres, or 2 percent, of the land bought by a First Purchaser was to be laid out in the first great town.[2] After the acreage necessary was calculated, the site chosen for the town turned out to be too small. Therefore, an area immediately north of the town was selected for the 2 percent tracts and set aside specifically for the "good and benefit" of the First Purchasers and others who qualified as Original Purchasers.[3] Referred to as the city liberties or the liberties of the city, the area adjoined the city on the north and west on both sides of the Schuylkill River and lay entirely within Philadelphia County.

The perimeter of the city liberties was originally surveyed by Deputy Surveyor Richard Noble during the early part of 1683.[4] The total amount of land within his survey was slightly over sixteen thousand acres. A portion was occupied by pre-Penn settlers and certain other colonists within townships abutting the northern border of the city. Consequently, the amount of land available to Original Purchasers was reduced to slightly less than enough for each to have his full 2 percent. Noble's survey was lost, but in 1703 the area was resurveyed, providing a second survey from which the description of the liberty lands is taken. A very early map, not dated, showing several Original Purchasers' liberty lots is listed in the Land Office Map Inventory, filed in Land Office Drawer 0006 as Item 6.

The first map of the boundaries of the liberty lands was produced by Thomas Holme and is titled *A Map of the Improved Part of the Province of Pennsilvania in America Begun by Wil: Penn Proprietary & Governor thereof Anno 1681*, with the subtitle *A Map of the Province of Pennsilvania, Containing the three Countyes of Chester Philadelphia & Bucks as far as yet surveyed and Laid out. . . .* The map was first published in 1687, followed by several later editions.[5]

The layout of the lots within the liberty lands was first mapped in 1774 by John Reed, who also published a small book titled *An Explanation of the Map of the City and Liberties of Philadelphia* to accompany the map (see Table 7). Included in the book is a section devoted to Noble's first survey of the liberties. Reed's map essentially serves as a warrantee tract map of the liberties, and the book recites in detail the courses and distances of all the surveys within the liberties and the Original Purchaser's name under which each liberty lot was claimed.

Although liberty land was specifically created for First Purchasers, other purchasers also were permitted to buy it. Whenever a purchaser decided to take up his liberty land, he submitted a request to the commissioners of property. Using the same procedures as with country land and city lots, the commissioners granted a warrant to survey after checking the Original Purchasers

list. Requests and warrants to survey containing the phrase "liberty land" or "city liberties" are seen throughout the early records.

A purchaser's 2 percent in the liberties was deducted from the total purchase, although the amount was not necessarily an exact 2 percent. Because liberty land on the east side of the Schuylkill River was thought to be superior in quality to that on the west side, the two areas were granted at different ratios. Eight acres in the eastern liberties was equivalent to ten acres in the western liberties.

No special register of lots within the liberty land exists in the Land Office collection. However, in addition to Reed's *Explanation*, both the Old Rights register to Philadelphia County and the Original Purchases register furnish other ways to locate a purchaser's liberty lots.

---

[1]Min. Com. Prop. Bk. G, 26th of the 11th Month 1701 [January 1702]; ibid. Bk. H, 21st 11 mo. [January] 1712–3.

[2]*Certaine Conditions or Concessions . . .*, in *PWP* 2:98–102.

[3]John Reed, *An Explanation of the Map of the City and Liberties of Philadelphia*, in *PA* (3) 3:311.

[4]On Richard Noble, see *PWP* 2:268, n. 26.

[5]See *PA* (3) Appendix 1-10. See also II.E.1.a, Country Land.

II.E.2. Proprietary Land

Under one of his proprietary rights, Penn reserved a portion of the land in Pennsylvania for his own use. He kept a small amount of this proprietary land for his private estates, and the rest he surveyed in both large tracts, often called manors, and smaller tracts, simply called tracts, lots, or lands.

Penn's charter permitted him to designate parcels of any size as manors and to govern them with courts baron and view of frank pledge, feudal features that were never instituted in Pennsylvania. He reconfirmed his charter right to proprietary land in *Certaine Conditions or Concessions* by stating that "In Every hundred thousand Acres the Governor & Proprietary by Lott reservall Tenn to himselfe which shall Lye but in One place."[1] From this statement historians conclude that Penn intended to take one tenth of the land for himself. Warrants and commissioners of property records during Penn's active years as proprietor indicate that his land

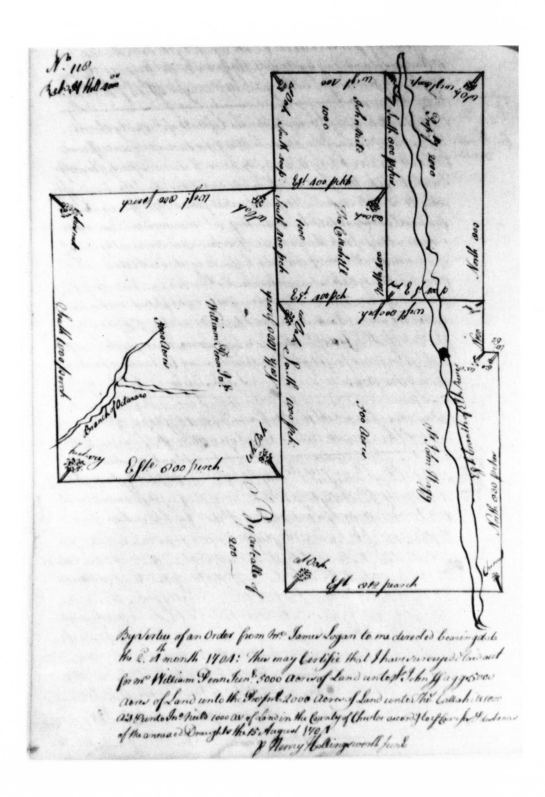

Five contiguous proprietary surveys, Chester County. (Returns—Chester A to P-15, p. 116)

officers made every effort to locate and survey the best 10 percent for proprietary land.

Penn granted far and away the largest amount of proprietary land to himself and his family. His first private preemption of land took place in 1683 when he set up Pennsbury Manor for himself. Within the next few years he assigned the Manor of Springfield to his first wife, Gulielma Maria; the Manor of Williamstadt to his son William, Jr.; and the Manor of Gilberts to himself. These manors, together with the Manor of Mount Joy assigned to Letitia Penn Aubrey and a large grant made to William, Jr., included a considerable extent of frontage on both the eastern and western sides of the Schuylkill River.[2] By 1686, Penn had authorized his commissioners of property to survey four more manors of 3,000 acres each for his sister Margaret's children and a 10,000-acre manor for his own daughter Gulielma Maria the younger.[3]

The Penn family maintained residences on very few of their manors, subdividing and leasing most of the land to others. Land within the family manors was to be rented in 150-acre tracts for eleven years, thereby creating a major source of steady income.[4] The family sold some manor land to individuals who were willing to pay more than the going rate in order to invest in choice real estate.

The special reserve that proprietary manors created caused certain problems. Purchasers, all of whom were required to settle their land within three years, complained of unfairness. The proprietor could reserve his manor land and later claim a higher price, while they were not permitted to hold theirs vacant. Purchasers looking for tracts along navigable rivers close to Philadelphia also complained that the proprietor held all the best land. Penn countered by claiming that he had not appropriated the total of his rightful tenth so as to avoid holes of unsettled land.[5]

To make up for acquiring less than his one-tenth proprietary share of land, Penn willed 60,000 acres of land to his second wife, Hannah, and her children. His heirs claimed their inheritance after his will was settled; consequently the sites were not selected until after 1730. When this land was added to the 51,250 acres Penn had granted to his first wife and her children, the total amount of land Penn allocated to family members amounted to 111,250 acres.[6]

Table 8. Research Aids: Proprietary Land

Browning, Charles H. *Welsh Settlement of Pennsylvania.* Philadelphia, 1912.

"Draughts of the Proprietary Manors in the Province of Pennsylvania." In *PA* (3) 4.

Gorman, Fred J. "Map of Penn's Manors." *PMHB* 67 (1943): 92–93.

Nash, Gary B. "The Free Society of Traders and the Early Politics of Pennsylvania." *PMHB* 89 (1965): 147–73.

In a few cases, Penn granted entire manors to individuals who represented land companies. The Free Society of Traders was the first such company; Penn sold it 20,000 acres in 1682.[7] The incorporation charter stated that all rents, services, and dues, and the usual manorial jurisdiction and privileges came directly under the governance of the society rather than under Penn. In return for settling the land with agricultural, manufacturing, and fishing enterprises, three officers of the society were to sit on the Provincial Council. Nicholas More, the society's president, built a house on the land but did nothing further to organize the manor. The society's venture failed, and in 1721 the Provincial Assembly confiscated its remaining land to be sold for the payment of debts.

A tally based upon entries in the Proprietary Rights register shows that during Penn's proprietorship he granted at least a dozen manors that were actually surveyed. Some manors have been studied extensively, resulting in publications with the name of the manor in the title. Regular bibliographic works in Table 1 and sources in Table 8 will assist in locating such publications.

In addition to manors, Penn used another type of proprietary grant as the source of a special discretionary fund. Setting aside small tracts or lots, he granted them for particular purposes. Many of Penn's Quaker friends received pieces of the most valuable land on the navigable rivers. Penn also leased or sold such tracts to his friends for the best terms the market would bring. Other parcels were granted as payment for services rendered, and from these he received no income.

Many special grants are entered in the Proprietary Rights register; others appear under the name of the recipient in the warrant registers.

Penn also authorized a few special grants to groups of purchasers who wished to settle together. The Welsh purchasers received a warrant permitting them to locate forty thousand acres within the province.[8] Dated March 13, 1684, the warrant accounts for tracts surveyed in several different locations within Chester County and caused innumerable problems.[9] A copy of some of the original minutes of the Welsh purchasers is filed with the loose Proprietary Papers, Folder 5 (LO micro.: 23.1). Other copies of minutes will be found in Commissioners of Property G-7 1701–1709 and in *PA* (3) 1:3–24.

The records listed below contain references to warrants and surveys made under Penn's proprietary right.

RECORDS: LOOSE PAPERS

ORIGINAL SURVEYS   LO micro.: 6.1–190.

Original surveys of proprietary rights tracts, including manors, are filed with the regular original surveys. Many have been hand transcribed into the copied survey books. The Proprietary Rights register cited below should be consulted for reference to volume, book, and page numbers of both original and copied versions. Other original surveys, not copied, may be accessed through a separate set of indexed Land Office notebooks containing search sheets.

RECORDS: BOUND VOLUMES

COPIED SURVEYS   SERIES A, B, BB, C, D   LO micro.: 28.1– .

Hand-drawn book copies of the loose warrants and surveys, including proprietary land. For access the proper index to use is the Proprietary Rights register.

PROPRIETARY RIGHTS INDEX.

The index to the warrants and surveys, both loose and copied, of most of the land granted by proprietary right. Arranged by county, entries give the name of the grantee, the warrant date, and the survey volume, book, and page. A copy of the index is in *PA* (3) 3:217–93 but does not include the citation of the survey volume, book, and page.

---

[1]*Certaine Conditions or Concessions . . .,* in *PWP* 2:98–102.
[2]To Thomas Fairman, *PWP* 2:483–84. See also Holme, *A Map of the Improved Part of the Province of Pennsilvania,* in *PA* (3) Appendix 1-10, No. 23.
[3]From Wm Penn, 8th 12th Mo 1686 [February 1687], Min. Com. Prop. Bk. C.
[4]Ibid.
[5]Ibid.
[6]General Cash Accounts, 240–41. See also drafts of some of the manors in *PA* (3) 4.
[7]Sur. Bk. D-88-173-74.
[8]Wt. Bk. 3 (Binding No. 15), 142.
[9]*PWP* 3:313–16.

II.F. Land Office

The basic procedures used to transfer Pennsylvania land to private ownership were established during the proprietorship of William Penn. For the sale of land and record processing, Penn established a set of independent offices: the commissioners of property, a secretary for proprietary affairs, a surveyor general and deputies, a master of the rolls, and a receiver general. The men who filled these positions were responsible directly to Penn and did not fall under the control of the Provincial Assembly. The officials wereresponsible for maintaining and preserving the records of their own offices.

The functions they performed, by tradition, have been grouped together under the term Land Office, although no such single office actually existed during Penn's proprietorship. Penn used the term Office of Propriety in referring to all the positions necessary to run his land business.

The first Land Office was located in Samuel Carpenter's Philadelphia residence, which came to be known as the Slate Roof House. James Logan, secretary for proprietary affairs, and Penn lived there after they arrived in Pennsylvania in 1699. Logan kept the minutes of the commissioners of property, the warrant books, and the returns of survey in his office. Jacob Taylor, who superintended the surveyor general's business, used Penn's old "closet," or private chamber, for his office. Apparently, the loose papers on which warrants were written and surveys were drawn were stored in the "next room" just above Taylor's.[1] Logan and Taylor left the Slate Roof House in 1704 and moved to Clark's Hall when Governor John Evans arrived.[2]

Patents and deeds were recorded in the Public Records Office by the master of the rolls. At first, the only provincial records office was in Philadelphia. Eventually each county created a records office,but the Philadelphia County office and the provincial office continued to share the same staff and facilities throughout the entire colonial period.

---

[1]James Logan to Wm Penn, Philadelphia, 7th 3rd [May] 1702, Penn-Logan Corres. 1:101.

[2]Clark's Hall also was called "William Clark's great-house in Chestnut Street." James Logan to Wm Penn, Philadelphia, 25th 3d-Mo [May] 1704, ibid., 284.

II.F.1. Commissioners of Property

Penn's primary assistants in his land business were the commissioners of property. Their basic duty was to oversee the distribution of land in the proprietor's absence. When Penn was not in the province, the commissioners were the only officials with authority to grant and sign warrants and patents. Three to five commissioners usually held office at the same time. They met as a group to receive special requests for land or applications for warrants and to hear cases involving infractions of land procedures and regulations.

One of the commissioners was usually Penn's chief business agent. Carrying the title of secretary for proprietary affairs, this commissioner often served also as secretary of the Provincial Council and as receiver general at the same time. Such doubling or tripling in positions kept the land business squarely in the hands of the proprietor through his chief agent.

The first commissioners of property were appointed in October 1681 while they were still in England,[1] and they were to travel to Pennsylvania to oversee the distribution of land before Penn arrived. One of the commissioners, Penn's cousin William Crispin, died en route; Thomas Holme was appointed in his place in April 1682, before the commissioners actually began their duties in Pennsylvania. It is probable that these first commissioners did not function as a board. On April 10, 1681, before they had been selected, Penn appointed another cousin, William Markham, as his deputy in land affairs. Markham sailed for Pennsylvania ahead of the first settlers in order "to Survey Sett out, Rent, or Sell lands."[2]

When Penn arrived in Pennsylvania in October 1682, he assumed control of his own land affairs. He signed warrants, emphasized procedures, and settled land disputes. Shortly before he returned to England, he appointed another group of commissioners to act in his absence. In 1683 the signatures of this second group of commissioners, Thomas Lloyd, James Claypoole, and Robert Turner, began to appear on warrants.[3] The date of the commissioners' official appointment, however, seems to have been August 1684, coinciding with Penn's return to England.

The commissioners kept no minute book of their actions during these early years. Extant

Chart 2. Commissioners of Property, 1681–1732

Commissioners	Appointment Date
William Crispin, William Haige [or Haig], John Bezar, Nathaniel Allen (First catalog of First Purchasers)	October 25, 1681
Thomas Holme, William Haige, John Bezar, Nathaniel Allen (Second catalog of First Purchasers)	April 31, 1682
Thomas Lloyd, James Claypoole, Robert Turner (CR 1:66)	August 19, 1684
William Markham, Thomas Ellis, John Goodson (Min. Com. Prop. Bk. C, 1; PA (2) 19:3)	January 21, 1687
William Markham, Robert Turner, John Goodson, Samuel Carpenter (Min. Com. Prop. Bk. D, 1; Pat. Bk. A-1-271; Philadelphia County Exem. Rec. I, 187)	April 16, 1689
Robert Turner, Thomas Holme, Arthur Cook, Samuel Carpenter, John Goodson, Francis Rawle, Phineas Pemberton (Min. Com. Prop. Bk. F, 72)	April 21, 1694
James Logan, Edward Shippen, Griffith Owen, Thomas Story (Min. Com. Prop. Bk. G, 1)	October 28, 1701
James Logan, Edward Shippen, Samuel Carpenter, Isaac Norris, Richard Hill (Min. Com. Prop. Bk. H, 1)	November 9, 1711
James Logan, Isaac Norris, Richard Hill, Robert Asheton, Thomas Griffiths (Min. Com. Prop. Bk. I, 63*)	April 30, 1724

*According to Charles Huston (p. 224; see Table 1), the appointment date was April 30, 1724. Minute Book I shows attendance at commissioners' meetings by May 20, 1725.

records consist of warrants to survey signed by either Penn or two of the commissioners but no requests to take up land or minutes of meetings. The earliest warrants, mainly those granted to First Purchasers, may be traced in the first warrant book, now called Wt. Bk. 3 (Binding No. 15).

In 1687, Penn replaced his commissioners with another set of appointees to be governed by a specific set of instructions. Over the years the same themes ran through his instructions. He was very concerned about the common practice of surveying overplus land, that is, more acreage than was called for in the warrant. In particular, Penn believed that his commissioners were selling overplus land at prices more favorable to purchasers than to the proprietor. To forestall purchasers from claiming choice overplus land, the commissioners were to grant no warrant to resurvey land within five miles of any navigable river, and any overplus land that was returned on a survey was not to be sold but reserved for proprietary use. Penn also repeatedly admonished his commissioners to be more diligent in surveying his proprietary share of land in each township. Too frequently the commissioners had sold choice land to settlers before the proprietary tenth had been surveyed. Most important to Penn, his commissioners were to see that the quitrents were collected.

The new commissioners of property began to meet weekly as a board in 1687 and to record their proceedings in a minute book.[4] Although meetings became less frequent as the years progressed, the plan seems to have been to begin a new minute book each time a new group of commissioners was appointed. The minute books were inventoried and labeled in 1759 in compliance with the law to record warrants and surveys. At that time, the first minute book was lettered C, apparently to follow Pat. Bk. A and Wt. Bk. B. Minute books D, E, G, H, and I followed. Book F, recently identified as a Philadelphia County letter of attorney book, was correctly labeled a record book in the 1759 inventory but was erroneously called a minute book in the published PA. The minute books and transcripts are cited below.

At each meeting the commissioners of property received settlers' requests for warrants to survey land. Requests from Original Purchasers were to be accompanied by a processing fee but no purchase money, since Original Purchasers had paid for their land before arriving in Pennsylvania. The commissioners verified the Original Purchaser's deed of lease and release or special order from Penn before authorizing the warrant.[5] Requests from After Purchasers were to be accompanied by the processing fee and a portion of the payment, but this regulation was not always enforced. The commissioners also received requests from settlers desiring to rent land, renters asking to purchase land, and servants and sponsors asking to take up their headright land. In addition, they handled land disputes.

Upon Penn's death the management of his colonial estate was left to the commissioners of property acting on behalf of the mortgage trustees. The commissioners were instructed to manage the proprietary land until the mortgage against the estate was discharged. As the records show, they met infrequently.

RECORDS: BOUND VOLUMES

MINUTES OF PROPERTY [Book C of the Commissioners of Property]   (Bound in Wt. Bk. 1685–1691, Binding No. 14)   LO micro.: 25.2; 1759 transcript: OLD RIGHTS—PHILADELPHIA, CHESTER, BUCKS, NEW CASTLE, KENT AND SUSSEX   (Binding No. 23)   LO micro.: 25.5; *PA* (2) 19:3–21.

MINUTES OF PROPERTY [Book D of the Commissioners of Property, 1689–1691]   (Filed in Proprietary Papers, folder 3; with index)   LO micro.: 23.1; 1759 transcript: MINUTES OF COMMISSIONERS OF PROPERTY   1689–1692   (Binding No. 21)   LO micro.: 25.4; *PA* (2) 19:22–64.

MINUTES OF PROPERTY [Book E of the Commissioners of Property, 1691–1692]   (Filed in Proprietary Papers, folders 3, 4)   LO micro.: 23.1; 1759 transcript: MINUTES OF COMMISSIONERS OF PROPERTY   1689–1692   (Binding No. 21)   LO micro.: 25.4; *PA* (2) 19:65–92.

MINUTE BOOK F NO. 6 [of the Commissioners of Property]; 1759 transcript: MINUTES OF COMMISSIONERS OF PROPERTY   1689–1692   (Binding No. 21)   LO micro.: 25.4; and RECORDS MISCELLANEOUS WITH INDEX   (Binding No. 39)   LO micro.: 25.8; *PA* (2) 19:93–184.

This is actually not a minute book but a book of deeds and other records and probably a letter of attorney volume for Philadelphia County. No minutes appear to have been recorded between October 12, 1692, and November 19, 1701. Only a portion of this volume is printed in *PA*; the original must be consulted for the remainder.

MINUTES OF PROPERTY [Book G of the Commissioners of Property]   (Bound under the title COMMISSIONERS OF PROPERTY G-7   1701–1709; Binding No. 20; with index)   LO micro.: 25.20; 1759 transcript: MINUTES OF COMMISSIONERS OF PROPERTY   1701–1709   (Binding No. 20)   LO micro.: 25.4; *PA* (2) 19:185–502.

Two separate volumes, although the binding numbers are the same for the original and the copy. The original includes a book of minutes of the Welsh purchasers and a listing of

First Purchasers and other grantees. For a transcript of Welsh purchasers see Warrant Register 1700–1705 (Binding No. 22; LO micro.: 25.4; PA [2] 19:674–766).

COMMISSIONERS OF PROPERTY H-8   1712–1720 [Minute Book H of the Commissioners of Property]   (Binding No. 21)   LO micro.: 25.20; index in LO micro.: 25.1; 1759 transcript in OLD RIGHTS—PHILADELPHIA, CHESTER, BUCKS, NEW CASTLE, KENT AND SUSSEX   (Binding No. 23)   LO micro.: 25.5; PA (2) 19:503–673.

COMMISSIONERS OF PROPERTY I-9   1716–1732 [Minute Book I of the Commissioners of Property]   (Binding No. 22)   LO micro.: 25.20; 1759 transcript: WARRANT REGISTER 1700–1705   (Binding No. 22)   LO micro.: 25.4; PA (2) 19:674–766.

---

[1] Pat. Bk. AA-5-130–39.
[2] PWP 2:85–86; Annals, 503.
[3] See Wt. Bk. 3 (Binding No. 15).
[4] Min. Com. Prop. Bk. C, 13th. 3 Mo [May], 1687.
[5] See, for example, Min. Com. Prop. Bk. D, 14th 4th Month [June] 1690.

II.F.2. Secretary for Proprietary Affairs

Penn's chief agent in his land business was his secretary for proprietary affairs. Usually serving as one of the commissioners of property, the secretary was responsible for conducting the meetings and keeping the minutes. He also processed all requests to purchase land, overseeing the steps through the stages of warrant, survey, and patent. Issuing warrants to survey, he affixed to them the lesser seal of the province and sent them to the surveyor general. Receiving return of surveys from the surveyor general, the secretary drew up patents and sent them to the master of the rolls to be recorded.

Two men seem to have shared the task of land agent during the earliest years of settlement. One of them, William Markham, was Penn's first proprietary secretary. Appointed on April 10, 1681, while still in England, Markham was to proceed to Pennsylvania ahead of the first settlers in order "to Survey Sett out, Rent, or Sell lands."[1] The other agent, Nicholas More, became secretary of the Provincial Council on May 2, 1683. The handwriting of both More and Markham appears in the warrant books until 1685, when More was removed from office.

Penn then set the precedent for vesting three interlocking positions in his proprietary secretary. First, he appointed Markham to More's vacated position as secretary of the council.[2]

Then he gave Markham a third assignment in January 1687 by appointing him a "Commissioner of Land."[3] Markham retained all three positions until 1694 when he became lieutenant governor under newly appointed Governor Benjamin Fletcher.

In the five more years until Penn returned to Pennsylvania at the end of 1699, Patrick Robinson served as secretary of the province and master of the rolls.[4] Robinson was responsible for processing and recording warrants and patents, as well as recording the minutes of the Provincial Council.

When Penn returned to America he brought James Logan and soon appointed him secretary for proprietary affairs. Penn instructed Logan to gather together all books, papers, commissions, instructions, and other materials belonging to the office of property.[5] After one year of learning the land business, Logan, like Mark-

---

Table 9. Research Aids: James Logan

"Papers Relating to Provincial Affairs in Pennsylvania, 1682–1750." In PA (2) 7:3–300.

Penn-Logan Corres.

Tolles, Frederick B. *James Logan and the Culture of Provincial America.* Boston, 1957.

ham before him, took on the responsibilities of several interlocking positions. At Penn's parting in the later months of 1701, the proprietor appointed Logan receiver general and sent him a long list of instructions.[6] Shortly thereafter, Logan received his appointment as one of the new commissioners of property. A few months later, he was admitted to the Provincial Council and added the job of provincial secretary to his duties.[7] He served year after year as secretary of the province and as proprietary secretary, issuing warrants to survey and resurvey, receiving returns of survey from the surveyor general, and confirming patents. He continued in these positions, except for a short period during Governor William Keith's administration, until Penn's sons and other heirs became the proprietors. Some of Logan's account books and correspondence about land affairs were preserved with the land records and are cited below, but the majority of his material is at the Historical Society of Pennsylvania.

RECORDS: LOOSE PAPERS

JAMES LOGAN'S CORRESPONDENCE   LO micro.: 21.1

Only one folder of miscellaneous letters to Logan dated 1712–1722, concerning quitrents, requests for land, and petitions, and including a few statements of accounts Logan carried on behalf of others.

MISCELLANEOUS PAPERS   BOX 24   LO micro.: 24.4.

Contains Logan's account books with the proprietors and trustees for the period 1712–1734.

GENERAL CORRESPONDENCE 1713–1775   (RG-17)   Reel 3982.

Contains several letters from Isaac Taylor, surveyor, to Logan, 1713–1720.

SECRETARY AND CLERK OF THE PROVINCIAL COUNCIL, GENERAL CORRESPONDENCE, 1700–1722   (RG-21).

Includes many Logan papers.

RECORDS: BOUND VOLUME

MARKHAM'S BOOK   (Binding No. 17)   LO micro.: 25.3.

Includes a list of 844 warrants granted between 1682 and 1685, arithmetic and geometric problems in surveying, and instructions on how to survey a manor.

---

[1]*PWP* 2:85–86; *Annals,* 503.
[2]*CR* 1:142.
[3]Pat. Bk. A-1-295.
[4]Record Book F No. 6, p. 60. See II.F.5, Master of the Rolls
[5]*Penn-Logan Corres.* 1:48.
[6]Ibid., 59.
[7]*Min. Prov. Coun.,* April 21, 1702.

Table 10. Research Aids: Surveyors General, 1682–1732

Cummings, Hubertis. "The Surveyors General of the Province of Pennsylvania." Pennsylvania Department of Internal Affairs *Monthly Bulletin* 29, nos. 2, 3, 5, 7, 9 (February, March, May, July, September 1961): 14–15, 22–27, 24–26, 22–25, 24–26.

Hough, Oliver. "Captain Thomas Holme, Surveyor-General of Pennsylvania and Provincial Councillor." *PMHB* 19, 20 (1895, 1896): 413–27, 248–56.

The Jacob and Isaac Taylor Papers, 1683–1750. Collection No. 651. HSP.

II.F.3. Surveyor General and Deputies

The surveyor general of the province worked hand in hand with the secretary for proprietary affairs in the operation of the Land Office. Receiving warrants to survey from the secretary, the surveyor general was responsible for recording and forwarding the warrants to the deputy surveyors of the counties. The deputies usually performed the on-site survey and collected two thirds of the surveying fee as their pay.[1] The three Lower Counties were served by their own surveyors general, and the secretary sent warrants to survey directly to them. When the survey was returned to his office, the surveyor general certified the accuracy of the survey and prepared a return of survey report for the secretary. He filed the original survey in his office, along with the original warrant.

Four surveyors general held office during William Penn's proprietorship, but only three actually served. The first, Penn's cousin William Crispin, was appointed in England but died en route to Pennsylvania. The second, Thomas Holme, was commissioned to take Crispin's place on April 18, 1682.[2] Holme worked as surveyor general for the next fifteen years. Many important duties were entrusted to him and his staff, which consisted of a deputy surveyor general and a deputy surveyor for each county. They laid out plans for Philadelphia, the first large city; surveyed the lots within the city and the liberty land; and surveyed tracts, townships, and manors within the province. A further part of Holme's job was to produce the first detailed maps of both the city of Philadelphia and the province of Pennsylvania (see Table 6). Holme became a highly respected landowner of considerable fortune and lived until 1695.

After Holme's death the province was without a surveyor general for three years while the secretary worked directly with the deputy surveyors of each county. In 1698, Penn selected a mathematically talented relative, Edward Pennington, to be the third surveyor general. Commissioned on February 26, he served a scant two years, dying of smallpox in January 1702 at age thirty-four.[3] Penn, busy in England, failed to appoint a replacement.

Lacking direction, the commissioners of property took all the books, records, warrants, and papers of the surveyor general into their own care. They asked the secretary, James Logan, to superintend the surveyor general's office with the assistance of Jacob Taylor, "an able fitt hand well skilled in Surveying."[4] Taylor, a schoolteacher in Abington, had been favored for the position by Logan. He worked as a clerk under Logan, learning the office duties, until he was formally appointed surveyor general in March 1707.[5]

Taylor served as surveyor general until 1733, making the position an office job while he relied upon the field services of his deputy surveyors. Although he also surveyed many properties, drafts of his work are far less numerous than those made by the county surveyors. Taylor's office life permitted him the time to publish an annual almanac and write poetry; a few of his verses are scattered among the land records.

Deputy surveyors, the fieldmen who were responsible for actually conducting the survey, wielded a considerable amount of power. Frequently surveying more land than was authorized in the warrant, presumably for the benefit of the purchaser, deputies often refused to return completed surveys or collected fees. That the province could function without a surveyor general for even a short period bears testimony to the political influence and strength of the early deputies. Thomas Fairman was a particularly influential deputy. Because he served as deputy surveyor before Penn arrived, he captured the early business. After the proprietor arrived, Fairman continued as deputy surveyor for Philadelphia County. Although he may have been a good surveyor, he was guilty of surveying more land than was ordered in the warrant (overplus land) and of failing to return many of his surveys.

The names of deputy surveyors appear on the surveys that they returned to the surveyor general or to the secretary. Among the earliest deputies were Charles Ashcombe in Chester County and Israel Taylor in Bucks County. Other deputy surveyors were Robert Longshore, Henry Hollingsworth, and Isaac Taylor. Like Fairman, Ashcombe and Israel Taylor were often sources of irritation to the surveyor general. Guilty of malpractice in office, they refused to return surveys and remit fees, and they invariably surveyed large amounts of overplus land. Disclosure of their irresponsibility resulted in the first law setting standard surveyors' fees. Passed in 1690, the law observed that the money collected from deputy surveyors' fees was the principal source of profit for the young government.[6]

Beginning in 1701, a set of regulations governed deputy surveyors' professional behavior. The regulations grew out of the 1700 Law of Property, which never went into effect.[7] At issue

was Penn's general order to resurvey all tracts in the province. Because many of the early surveys had been executed in a careless manner, more land had been included within the tracts than was purchased. The new regulations required deputy surveyors to take an oath of office and post bond and also spelled out specific business procedures. After recording the warrant in a registry book, the deputy surveyor was to conduct the survey by going upon the land and then to record his fieldwork in a field book. He was to send the surveyor general a formal drawing of the survey, with the fieldwork attached. The formal drafts are the original surveys on file in the Land Office collection.

The deputy surveyor's field notebooks remained in his possession until he left office. The new deputy surveyor usually inherited the books and used them as long as they were of value or law required them to be available to the public. Local historical societies now hold some deputy surveyors' field notebooks; the books were not, by law, returned to the Land Office.

RECORDS: LOOSE PAPERS

GENERAL CORRESPONDENCE OF THE SURVEYOR GENERAL   1682–1873   LO micro.: 21.3.

Correspondence for the period 1682–1732 is contained within one folder.

RECORDS: BOUND VOLUME

LIST OF DEP[UTY] SURVEYORS   [1713–1850]   LO micro.: 25.29.

Lists deputy surveyors by name in chronological order, giving the date of commission, the original district, the district as altered, and remarks.

---

[1]Min. Com. Prop. Bk. C, 13: 3 Mo. [May] 1687.
[2]Pat. Bk. A-1-7.
[3]Min. Com. Prop. Bk. G, 19th 11th Mo 1701 [January 1702].
[4]Ibid.
[5]Min. Com. Prop. Bk. H, 26 11 mo 1707 [January 1708].
[6]*Statutes* 1:175–76.
[7]Ibid. 2:118–23. See also Edwin B. Bronner, "Penn's Charter of Property of 1701," *Pa. Hist.* 24 (1957): 267–92.

II.F.4. Receiver General

The office of receiver general was formally instituted in 1689, principally to collect purchase

money and quitrents on land but also to handle the proprietor's other accounts.[1] Prior to 1689 the commissioners of property had handled the task of collecting both quitrents and the purchase price on land sales. Acting as inspectors or overseers, the commissioners had delegated the job of collecting quitrents to James Harrison, William Penn's steward at Pennsbury Manor. Harrison and his understewards received ten bushels of English wheat annually for their efforts, but no records survive to testify to their effectiveness as collectors.[2] In fact, Penn complained to Thomas Lloyd in 1686 that, although his quitrents were in value at least five hundred pounds per year, he could not get one penny.[3]

The quitrent system, initiated by Penn to provide his family with a steady income, placed a nominal ground rent upon all land whether purchased or rented. Although the quitrent was figured from the time of the return of survey, the money was not collected until the land was patented. The idea, accepted in principle by the First Purchasers, swiftly became a sore issue when the payments were due. Since Penn had established no particular system for regulation and collection of quitrents and had assessed varied amounts according to the terms of the sales or leases, purchasers clamored for uniformity. Furthermore, after 1685 they resisted the requirement that quitrents be paid in money or silver, not produce.

Each patent stated the amount of annual quitrent. First Purchasers were to pay one shilling sterling annually for every one hundred acres. The quitrents on city lots depended upon the size and location of the lots. For example, commercial lots along the Delaware River brought a higher sale price and a higher quitrent than less desirable locations within the city. Headright land had still another scale: former servants paid two shillings per fifty acres, and their masters paid four shillings per fifty acres. Old purchasers, that is, the pre-Penn inhabitants, and After Purchasers, or those who were not Original Purchasers, also paid at different rates. Old purchasers paid in bushels of wheat; everyone else, in silver at varying rates.

Eager to collect the quitrents due him, Penn appointed former Governor John Blackwell to the newly created position of receiver general in 1689.[4] Penn's instructions commanded Blackwell to assign the task of collecting the quitrents to the county sheriffs, as was the practice in England.[5] The receiver general quickly learned that no one knew how much quitrent had been paid or how much was actually due. An accounting system for recording the monies collected

from the sale of land and collection of the quitrents had never been established, despite Penn's 1687 instructions to his commissioners of property.[6]

Anticipating a relief from his problems as governor, Blackwell instead found the colonists to be as uncooperative in paying quitrents as they had been in solving their factional disputes. Doing his utmost to follow instructions, the receiver general constructed a true rent-roll and attempted to collect the quitrents. He later complained, however, that he was tried beyond his patience and had not collected enough to pay for his horse's board, let alone his own.[7] Unhappy, he resigned a few months after he was appointed and left the colony.

Blackwell's rent-roll of 1689, the earliest for the province, covers Philadelphia City and County and also Chester, Kent, and Sussex counties. It lists the category of each purchaser, the size of the tract, the amount of rent, and the number of years for which the rent was to be collected. The original rent-roll is in the Logan Papers at the Historical Society of Pennsylvania. Printed portions are cited in Table 11.

Little is known of the work accomplished by the receivers general in the ten years after Blackwell. Samuel Jennings was appointed in July 1690.[8] Within a few months he had named a deputy, Benjamin Chambers, to assist in collecting rents in the city and county of Philadelphia.[9] Apparently, Chambers had some success, for he remained in his post for about ten years. Jennings did not appreciate the responsibility, however, and in 1693 gave up the receiver generalship. In desperation the commissioners of property talked one of their own members, Robert Turner, into taking the job.

Realizing that the quitrent issue generated antiproprietary sentiments, Penn consolidated his land business in one position during his second stay in the province, 1699–1701. His new secretary for proprietary affairs, James Logan, became the receiver general also. Logan made new rent-rolls "with great pains and Labour" and sent them to the proprietor in 1706.[10] The contents of the portion of this rent-roll for Philadelphia seem to fit the Extract of a Rent Roll cited in the records below and published in the Pennsylvania Department of Internal Affairs *Monthly Bulletin* 22, nos. 4, 5 (March, April 1954): 13–21, 27–29. Logan was no more optimistic about his success as receiver general than

Table 11. Research Aids: Quitrent

"The Blackwell Rent Roll," *PWP* 3:679–737.

Bond, Beverly, Jr. *The Quit Rent System in the American Colonies*. New Haven, 1919.

Cadwallader, Richard. *A Practical Treatise on the Law of Ground Rents in Pennsylvania*. Philadelphia, 1879.

Roach, Hannah Benner. "The Blackwell Rent Roll, 1689." *PGM* 23 (1963): 68–94.

his predecessors had been. After one year in the position he wrote to Penn explaining that he did not expect to realize anything from rent and that land, in general, was moving slowly. However, account journals dating from 1701 and rent-rolls dating from 1703 indicate that Logan made considerable headway in collecting quitrents. Between 1701 and 1705 he was able to send more than four thousand pounds to Penn in England and to pay an additional three thousand pounds on Penn's account in Pennsylvania.[11]

Legislation passed in 1705 also assisted in quitrent collection.[12] Specifying the times, places, and means of collecting the quitrents, the law created a uniform process that shaped quitrent administration for the remainder of the colonial era. The law also stated the landowner's right to examine the accounts of the receiver general or his deputies and established guidelines regarding unpaid quitrents. All too frequently, the liability for unpaid quitrents was passed along to unsuspecting buyers because the land had not been patented.

The rent-rolls, daybooks, journals, and ledgers created by the implementation of the 1705 law mark the beginning of a series of records that lasted throughout the proprietary era. The series indicates a pattern of collection and record keeping commensurate with the requirements outlined in the law. The receiver general or his deputy visited every county at a publicized time in March or April of each year. Notices were published in the *Pennsylvania Gazette* prior to the visit, and places of attendance were specified. The deputy receivers took small rent-roll books with them in which to record quitrent collections. Upon their return to Philadelphia the amounts collected were transferred into the daybooks of the receiver general in chronological order along with other forms of receipts. These figures were also entered into the journals and ledgers that served as the master account books of the office.

After Penn was forced to mortgage his province, the collection of quitrents became more difficult. Logan continued to serve as receiver general, but he was joined by Isaac Norris.[13] Deputy receivers had success only in the more populated areas of the province and not at all in the Lower Counties. Inhabitants of New Castle, Kent, and Sussex declined to pay because land titles in those counties were constantly in dispute. Logan was of the opinion that it might take an armed force to make the landholders pay.[14] One of Logan's deputy receivers reported in 1712 "spight and mallice" and "Much Rediccule" and "hypocritticall Laughter" and wonder at his "Insolance to demand Quitt Rents."[15]

Tiring of the duties of receiver general after serving as proprietary agent for ten years, Logan hired James Steel as his assistant. After returning from his trip to England in 1712, Logan appointed Steel collector of the proprietor's quitrent for Kent County.[16] Steel performed so well in his collection duties that, in 1714, Logan made him office manager and deputy receiver general for quitrents for the entire province and the Lower Counties.[17] Year after year, the journals document Steel's salary, house rent, and office expense allowance. Steel's Rent Roll for Philadelphia, prepared in 1731 and cited in the records below, gives a fairly complete listing of the original property owners for both the city and county.

The records cited below explain how the receiver general's office operated. City and county rent-roll books were compiled from the records in the secretary's office. These small books were carried by a deputy receiver to central locations, such as Chester, Darby, and Pennsbury, and on a particular previously announced day in March or April landowners and renters appeared to pay their rent. The rent was recorded on the spot in the rent-roll books. Back in Philadelphia the accounts were entered in the proprietary journals. Other accounts paid in the receiver's office in Philadelphia or at particular nearby locations were entered in the daybooks. Summaries of the daybook transactions also were copied into the journals. Information from the daybooks was entered also into master ledgers in the receiver's office. The ledgers contained a block of space for each payer; all payments credited to a payer's account were entered in that space, and the page number of the daybook entry was given. The journals and ledgers give a fairly complete picture of proprietary land affairs, while the rent-rolls and daybooks are good sources for locating property owners and renters.

RECORDS: LOOSE PAPERS

PHILADELPHIA RENT ROLL.

The inside title indicates that this rent-roll was made by Governor John Blackwell. Although an incomplete version of the rent-roll, it relates directly to that document and gives each lot's warrant and survey dates. Filed in the Philadelphia City Lots folders, it is not microfilmed.

EXTRACT OF A RENT ROLL FOR YE CITY OF PHILADELPHIA   LO micro.: 21.1.

Probably prepared by James Logan in 1703, this rent-roll is filed in the Philadelphia City Lots folders and gives each purchaser's name, lot size, and yearly rent, and the present owner of the lot. Partially microfilmed. The original is reprinted under the title "Early Philadelphia Residents," cited in Table 7.

RECORDS: BOUND VOLUMES

STEEL'S RENT ROLL FOR PHILADELPHIA   1731   (Binding No. 6b)   LO micro.: 25.1.

See II.E.1.b, Philadelphia City Lots.

QUIT RENT ROLLS   1703–1744   (With index)   Reel 468.

A series of individual quitrent books used by deputy receivers. The maximum years due for quitrent in the books being nineteen, the earliest books were prepared in 1703, or nineteen years after 1684, the year when the first patents were granted. Contents of the rolls vary. The most complete give the following information: the First Purchaser or renter, the present possessor, when the land was laid out, the patent date, the yearly rent in sterling, the year from which rent was due, the year it was paid and to whom, the remaining years, the sum due in 1703, the amount now paid, where the survey was recorded, and a description.

RENT ROLLS   1683–1776   (With index).

Master rent-roll books kept in the receiver general's office. Prepared by county, they are arranged within by township. Information includes the resident's name, the date residency began, the acreage, and the amount collected. Not all listings are complete.

DAY BOOKS [of the Receiver General]   LO micro.: 25.37.

Volume 1 covers the period 1720–1738 and contains chronological entries of the amounts collected for land sales, quitrents, and other proprietary income. For each entry the following information is given: the individual's name, to whom or what account payment was directed, and the amount received. For quitrents, entries are grouped by the town where the receiver collected.

JOURNALS [of the Receiver General]: A NO.1, 1701–1710; B NO.1, 1712–1733 Reel 469.

Master journals of proprietary accounts, containing information from the rent-rolls and the receiver general's daybooks. Entries are in chronological order and include accounts of land and quitrents collected by location, giving the name of the payer, acres, township, and amount paid.

LEDGERS [of the Receiver General]: A NO.1, 1701–1710; B NO.1, 1712–1732 (With index) LO micro.: 25.80.5.

Volumes organized by the first listing of a payer in the daybook for the time period of each volume. A block of space for each person includes a listing of all amounts paid. The information given includes the payer's name, the date paid, the page in the daybook, and which account was credited.

[1]CR 1:313.
[2]Min. Com. Prop. Bk. C, 13th 3mo [May] 1687.
[3]*Chester Co.,* 155.
[4]Pat. Bk. A-1-252.
[5]*PWP* 3:259–61.
[6]Min. Com. Prop. Bk. C, 13: 3 mo [May] 1687.
[7]From John Blackwell [May 15, 1690], *PWP* 3:279.
[8]Min. Com. Prop. Bk. D, 28th 4th Mo. [June], 1690; Pat. Bk. A-1-271.
[9]Pat. Bk. A-1-272.
[10]James Logan to Samuel Clement, May 13, 1719, PA (2) 7:70.
[11]From Logan, 4th 5th moth [July] 1705, PA (2) 8:65; *PWP* 4:365.
[12]*Statutes* 2:223.
[13]Trustees to Logan, 30th, 9th mo [November] 1711, PA (2) 7:27.
[14]Logan to Clement, May 13, 1719, ibid., 70.
[15]Jonas Greenwood to Logan, April 19, 1712, ibid., 38.
[16]Min. Com. Prop. Bk. H, 27th 8ber [October], 1712. See also Logan to Clement, Philadelphia, May 5, 1719, PA (2) 7:68.
[17]Min. Com. Prop. Bk. H, 13th 6 mo [August] 1714.

II.F.5. Master of the Rolls

The master of the rolls was responsible for recording patents as part of his duty to enroll the provincial laws and preserve the public records. The position of master of the rolls was created by the Laws Agreed Upon in England in 1682 and confirmed later the same year at Chester, Pennsylvania, in the Great Law. The acts required that all charters, gifts, grants, and conveyances of land, including deeds of lease and release, bills, bonds, and specialties, be recorded in a public enrollment office within two months if made inside the province and six months if made outside.[1]

On December 24, 1683, Penn appointed Thomas Lloyd to be master of rolls and records and to execute the law.[2] Lloyd opened the provincial Rolls Office in Philadelphia in January 1684. He seems to have created two different record series, one for patents and one for all other types of legal records. Patent volumes began with the letter A, followed by the number of the volume within the series, for example, A-1 or A-2. Legal volumes began with a different letter depending upon the type of document. Deeds of lease and release were recorded in A and B volumes, the C volumes contained conveyances between Original Purchasers and Under Purchasers, the D volumes usually contained letters of attorney, and the E through H volumes contained Philadelphia County land transfers between Under Purchasers and others or simply between others.

Despite the recording law the regulations were not enforceable and were generally ignored from the beginning. Few Original Purchasers who settled in Pennsylvania bothered to record their deeds of lease and release within the initial six-month time limit. Since the buyers had already paid the total purchase price and obtained warrants and surveys to cover at least a portion of their land, they resisted the law and the extra fee involved. Their attitude gave rise to an argument over the legality of forcing the registration of deeds and controversy over whether a recorded deed carried more force of law than an unrecorded deed.

Interests in favor of a provincial public registry were strong, however, and the assembly passed a provincial law in 1688 attempting to force deed registration. The law provided for the validation of all unrecorded conveyances brought in for recording within certain time limits. Exempted from the provisions were bonds, bills, and specialties; the law abolished the requirement that they be recorded.

A new law in 1693 offering enticements to record deeds replaced the attempt to force registration. Henceforth, exemplifications, or legal office copies, of deeds that were recorded were to be as valid in a court of law as original deeds.

Between 1684 and 1715 only three men served as fully commissioned masters of the rolls. Lloyd held the position for ten years (1684–1694), except for a ten-month period in 1688 when William Markham substituted for him. Lloyd also served as president of the Provincial Council and keeper of the great seal.[3] Upon Lloyd's death in 1694, Patrick Robinson was commissioned master of the rolls. He served for six years with David Lloyd as his clerk and

deputy. Thomas Story, commissioned in 1700, succeeded Robinson.[4] Griffith Owen, Maurice Lisle, and Charles Brockden served as deputies under Story.

To encourage deed recording, the Rolls Office was eventually decentralized. While Story was master of the rolls, a law in 1706 provided for a recorder of deeds in each county but failed to provide for a method of appointment. This oversight was corrected in 1715, and a recorder was added to the county offices. Each county was required to maintain an office for recording deeds, mortgages, and conveyances.[5] In Philadelphia County, however, the position of recorder of deeds was given to the master of the rolls. This official had been recording Philadelphia deeds for the past thirty years and would continue to do so until 1777. Brockden was appointed to the two positions in 1715 and remained both master of the rolls and recorder of deeds for a remarkable fifty-two years.[6]

The master of the rolls recorded letters of attorney, bills of exchange, indentures, bankruptcies, and other like documents in a series of volumes called Letter of Attorney. Before 1715 these volumes contain records for the three original Pennsylvania counties and the three Lower Counties. Letter of Attorney volumes for the post-1715 period are devoted mainly to Philadelphia County.

Apparently, when the state offices moved to Lancaster in 1799, the Letter of Attorney volumes moved also. To facilitate access to the records for Philadelphia County, the county office of the recorder of deeds made legal copies of Philadelphia records. Called exemplifications, the volumes contain copies of patents, deeds of lease and release, letters of attorney, and regular deeds. The exemplification volumes became part of the Philadelphia County deed records and can be accessed by referring to the Philadelphia County records.

RECORDS: BOUND VOLUMES

LETTER OF ATTORNEY   D-2   VOL. 4   LO micro.: 25.124.

Contains recording dates for 1684–1691. The entries include affidavits, agreements, awards, bills, bonds, certificates, letters of attorney, and similar legal records. An index is bound separately.

RECORD BOOK F NO. 6   LO micro.: 25.126–27.

Contains recording dates for 1693–1695. The entries include deeds, letters of attorney, patents, letters, mortgages, and similar records. Originally thought to be a commissioners of property minute book, a portion of this volume was printed in *PA* (2) 19:93–184. By the contents of the volume and a recently found comment in another volume titled "Hughes' List" (Binding No. 62) concerning the original location of Record Book F in the master of the rolls office, I conclude that the Record Book more correctly belongs with the Letter of Attorney volumes. (See also II.G.2, Applications.)

BILLS, BONDS, RELEASES   D-2, NO. 4: 1697–1702   (Binding No. 78).

Includes letters of attorney, assignments, deeds, and other similar legal records. Although the entries were recorded beginning in 1697, the instruments themselves were drawn as early as 1690.

INDEX FOR LETTERS OF ATTORNEY, ETC.   D-2, VOL. 4   1697–1702   (Binding No. 24)   LO micro.: 25.21.

Index for Bills, Bonds, Releases D-2, No. 4.

LETTER OF ATTORNEY   E-3   VOL. 5   1696–1705   LO micro.: 25.126.

Devoted mainly to Philadelphia County deeds.

LETTER OF ATTORNEY   NO-2   [D-2, Vol. 5]   1701–1712   (With index)   LO micro.: 25.124.

Contains legal documents such as indentures, bankruptcies, bills of lading, and awards.

LETTER OF ATTORNEY   D-3   No. 5   LO micro.: 25.126.

Contains recording dates for the period 1711–1728 and includes letters of attorney and Philadelphia business and shipping dealings.

LETTER OF ATTORNEY   D-2   No. [Vol.] 2   LO micro.: 25.123.

Contains recording dates for the period 1728–1745.

---

[1]For a discussion of the Frame of Government of Pennsylvania see especially *PWP* 2:137–238. See also *PA* (4) 1:27–44.

[2]Pat. Bk. A-1-2.

[3]*Min. Prov. Coun.*, 19th 6 mo [August] 1684.

[4]Pat. Bk. A-1-373.

[5]*SmL* 1:94.

[6]Appointed May 28, 1715, *Statutes* 3:53–57; removed September 28, 1767, *CR* 9:397. See also *SmL* 1:443–45.

II.G. Records

Although proprietary officials followed inferior recording methods by today's standards, and many aberrations of the system developed with use, the vast majority of land records is still in existence in either original or copied form. With an understanding of the system's organization and a complete record search, it is possible to know with some degree of certainty which records for each original land transaction have or have not survived.

For Original Purchasers a sixfold series of documents effected the transfer of land from proprietary to private ownership: 1) deed of lease and release, 2) informal oral or written application, 3) warrant to survey, 4) survey, 5) return of survey, and 6) patent. For all other purchasers only steps 2 through 5 were required. Each of the necessary records has survived in either original or copied form for some purchasers. For others only one or more records may be extant.

The original loose warrants, surveys, and returns of survey for the period 1682–1732 are called old rights. The reason for this arrangement is explained in II.G.7, Old Rights. Indexes devoted to old rights for Philadelphia, Bucks, and Chester counties were later prepared and serve as warrant registers for the period. The registers were printed in PA (3) 2:662–769, and 3:3–214, but the volume, book, and page references are omitted.

In the early 1900s the original warrants, surveys, and returns of survey for 1682–1732 were hand copied and bound into volumes labeled "Copied Surveys Old Rights." As the loose original warrants and returns of survey were copied, the originals were refiled with the loose original surveys using the same filing numbers as the bound volumes of the copied surveys in which the copies appear. A few loose returns of survey were not copied and remain with the returns of survey for the later periods.

The following brief summary of each record indicates its major function. A more detailed discussion will be found on the subsequent pages.

1. A DEED OF LEASE AND RELEASE, the first document in the series for an Original Purchaser, was evidence of his right to a given amount of unlocated land.

2. An APPLICATION, the first document in the series for renters, servants, and After Purchasers, was an informal request to rent or purchase a given amount of land. For Original Purchasers the application was a request to take up land already purchased.

3. A WARRANT, granted if the application was approved, was an order to survey the amount of land requested and was required for all purchasers and renters.

4. A SURVEY, conducted by a deputy surveyor, followed the warrant. Usually the survey was drawn on paper as a protracted figure with corner markers and adjoining owners named, but sometimes the survey was only a verbal description.

5. A RETURN OF SURVEY, or written rendering of the combined warrant and survey information, was prepared after the survey was conducted and any outstanding purchase fee paid.

6. A PATENT, or final deed to the land, completed the transfer of ownership and was issued after the warrantee had satisfied the fee and purchase requirements.

II.G.1. Deeds of Lease and Release

William Penn transferred land to Original Purchasers by deeds of lease and release. Occasionally, Original Purchasers also used deeds of lease and release to transfer land to Under Purchasers. The documents stated the total amount of land involved in the transaction but did not describe specific locations of land in Pennsylvania.

The use of deeds of lease and release extends back to the English feudal system. In receiving the grant of Pennsylvania from the king of England, Penn became the feudal seignior, or lord of the province. He held his land in free and common socage of the king, which meant that Penn was absolute proprietor and was required only to pay a yearly token rent to the Crown. He was not required to perform or provide annual service as was the older feudal custom. Penn's charter to Pennsylvania provided for a similar relationship between himself and his purchasers. All purchasers owned their land outright but also in the right of Penn, making them subject to quitrents, forfeiture, and escheat.

A deed of lease and release passed effective ownership from the Crown to Penn and to the purchaser. For this two-step transfer the deed actually consisted of a pair of indentures acting as one conveyance. The first indenture was a lease, or statement of intention to sell, and placed the land in the hands of the purchaser for a specified period of time, usually one year. The second indenture, a release, dated the day after the lease, removed the land from the jurisdiction of the Crown and placed it under the jurisdiction of the proprietor. The release began with a restatement of the charter bounds of the province, its formation into a seigniory, and the power given to Penn to make grants of land. The main part of the release stated the amount of acreage sold, that the land was to be held in the right of Penn, and that it would be surveyed as agreed upon in *Certaine Conditions or Concessions* (cited in II.D.1.a, First Purchasers) or some later agreement. A third document, or formal statement of receipt, followed the deed of lease and release and completed the land transaction. In the statement, Penn acknowledges payment of the purchase price in return for "one paire of Indentures of Release and Confirmation."

The original deeds of lease and release were drawn up in England and usually given to the purchasers themselves. Copies were not entered in a master register, and apparently Penn did not keep a current and accurate list. After arriving in Pennsylvania, each purchaser was responsible for recording his own deed within six months or as soon as a public registry was established.

Nearly three years passed between the time the earliest of the First Purchasers received deeds and a rolls office was opened for business. On December 23, 1683, a year after actual surveying, land clearing, and settlement began, Penn appointed Thomas Lloyd master of rolls and records. Lloyd opened his office in January 1684. He used just one book for recording both deeds of lease and release and conveyances between parties.

Years later the deeds of lease and release, the deeds of conveyance between first and second parties, and other documents down the chain of title for Philadelphia County were copied from the proprietary records. Entered in the Philadelphia County records, they were called exemplifications, meaning legal copies of original records. Thus, many deeds of lease and release also appear among the Philadelphia County deed books in volumes titled "Exemplifications."

RECORDS: BOUND VOLUMES

LEASE AND RELEASES-A-1   (Binding No. 79)   LO micro.: 25.33.

The earliest book, containing copies of original deeds of lease and release covering the period 1684–1706, although not in strict chronological order. The volume also includes some letters of attorney, bills, bonds, and certificates. For regular letter of attorney books see II.F.5, Master of the Rolls.

LEASE AND RELEASES BOOK B [No. 2]   (Binding No. 80; with index)   LO micro.: 25.33–34.

Copies of original deeds of lease and release, begun in 1706. Slightly repaginated, the contents do not correspond exactly with the small index bound in the front; see General Index below. The volume also includes conveyances, certificates, bills, and bonds.

RELEASE BOOK B, NO. 3   (Binding No. 81)   LO micro.: 25.34.

Deeds between second and third parties or further along the chain of title, not leases and releases. Entries are dated mainly 1704–1706.

BILLS, BONDS, RELEASES   D-2, NO. 4: 1697–1702   (Binding No. 78).

A Philadelphia County Letter of Attorney volume containing a few deeds of lease and release.

GENERAL INDEX LEASES AND RELEASES   (Binding No. 77)   LO micro.: 25.33.

Contains several different indexes: 1) pages AB–351a constitute a grantor index to the volumes in the master of the rolls office, that is, the Lease and Release volumes, the Letter of Attorney volumes, and the Philadelphia County deed books through H; 2) pages 355–90a, a grantor index of minutes of deeds acknowledged or passed in court; 3) pages 395–459, an index to the H volumes of Philadelphia County deeds; 4) pages 460–95, an index to patentees in the AA series of patent books; 5) pages 497–503, an index to Lease and Release Book B No. 2; 6) page 505, an index to Letter of Attorney D volumes for some last names beginning with A.

II.G.2. Applications

During William Penn's administration an application was an oral request to locate, rent, or buy a particular piece of land. Anyone—an Original Purchaser, renter, servant, or new purchaser—could present the request to the commissioners of property or to Penn if he was in the province.

Requests submitted during the years 1682–1687 were not recorded. After 1687, however, requests were recorded in the minute books of the commissioners of property. Usually the entry simply reads "Upon request of . . ., granted a piece of land, quantity . . . Acres."

To locate the surviving applications, or requests to take up land, refer to the printed minute books of the commissioners of property in *PA* (2) 19. The name index should be checked for applications submitted between 1687 and 1732, but the researcher should be aware that all years are not covered. For a complete discussion of the minute books see II.F.1, Commissioners of Property.

II.G.3. Warrants

A warrant was an order to survey. The secretary wrote the warrant after the proprietor or commissioners of property approved the purchaser's request. Some warrants were written by William Penn himself. The warrant specified the amount of land to be surveyed and whether the warrantee was an Original Purchaser, Under Purchaser, After Purchaser, renter, or servant. If the warrantee was an Original Purchaser, the warrant often stated the total amount of land originally purchased, although any one warrant was limited to five hundred to one thousand acres. If the warrantee was an Under Purchaser, the chain of title was recited. Finally, if the warrantee was an After Purchaser, renter, or servant, the sale price or terms of rent and the amount of quitrent were stated.

Warrants also included standard phrases covering general land policy. In particular the early warrants stated that surveys were to be made according to the "plan of townships." This phrase meant that new tracts were to adjoin older tracts leaving no pockets of vacant land. Many warrants also stated that the surveyed land was to be clear of Indian claim and the tract settled and improved within six months.

The custom of requiring warrants to survey developed after settlement began. The earliest of the Original Purchasers simply had their city lots and country acreage surveyed after they arrived. But by 1685 the commissioners of property had devised a system of warrants, probably in an effort to keep track of the amount of land being surveyed.

Consequently, whenever an Original Purchaser claimed a portion of his purchase after 1685, he had to obtain a warrant. This meant

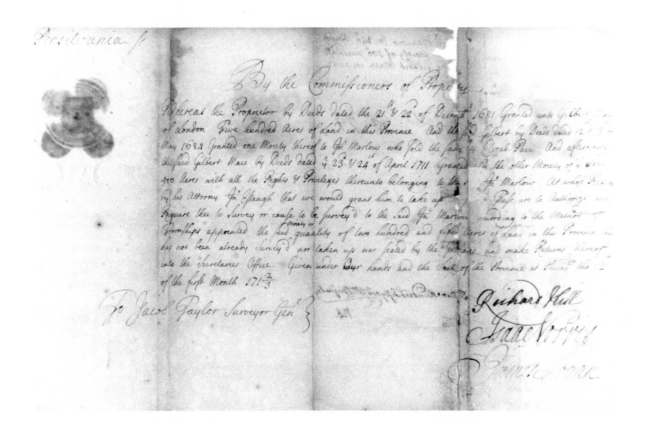

Warrant to survey country land for an Under Purchaser. (Sur. Bk. D-69-79)

separate warrants for city lots, liberty land, and country land. Upon learning of this system, Penn expressed grave concern because he undoubtedly feared it would have a negative impact on the Original Purchasers. Since the warrant system was not part of his final agreement with them, Penn wrote to Thomas Lloyd in 1685 saying that "It is an abominable thing to have three warrants for one purchase 'tis oppression that my soul loathes. . . . why not one warrant for all, at least for liberty lott & remainder."[1] At issue was the amount of surplus, or overplus, land being surveyed and the extra fees and expenses involved. The entire situation led to one of the major controversies between Penn and the colonists.

By 1701 procedures for handling the warrant system had been carefully worked out. The secretary wrote the warrant and affixed the lesser seal of the province. Then two or more commissioners of property or Penn signed the warrant. The secretary entered a copy of the warrant in a warrant book and sent the original to the surveyor general. The surveyor general kept the original warrant in his office and sent a copy to the deputy surveyor of the county where the land was to be surveyed.[2]

Over time, warrants took on different forms. Most of the warrants for the period 1682–1732 were not descriptive. They stated in general terms the desired location for the acreage requested. The other common type of warrant for this period was the warrant to resurvey, which was issued if the original survey was in question. In 1700, Penn introduced a general program to resurvey all large tracts in the province with the intention of finding revenue from payments for overplus land. Although the act that authorized warrants to resurvey was repealed by the king in council, the provisions were generally carried out.

Most of the original warrants from the period 1682–1732 have survived and are part of the Land Office collection. Individuals who received warrants during this period of time are listed in the Old Rights registers.[3] Prepared in two volumes, one for Philadelphia City and County and one for Bucks and Chester counties, the Old Rights registers are the place to begin research for this period. They indicate whether the information pertaining to the warrantee was taken from a surviving warrant, survey, or return of survey.

Transcripts of the original warrants were made in 1759 under the law to record warrants and surveys. Bound into books, the transcribed warrants can be accessed by the book and page number in the Original Purchases register as well as through the Old Rights registers.[4]

Original warrants were copied again in the early 1900s and bound into the copied survey books. Both the original warrants and the hand-copied warrants in the copied survey books can be accessed through the Old Rights registers. The same volume, book, and page numbers refer to the copied warrants and the original warrants.

RECORDS: LOOSE PAPERS

ORIGINAL WARRANTS   LO micro.: 6.158–68, 6.180.

Original warrants for the period 1682–1732 are interfiled with the loose original surveys and numbered by the volume, book, and page. Most of the warrants are in volumes D-65 through D-114 (Old Rights), B-22, and B-23. The warrants are indexed in the Old Rights registers and hand copied into the copied survey volumes under the same volume, book, and page numbers. However, warrants in volume D-91 through D-114 have not been copied, although the search sheets and a separate in-house index have been prepared.

RECORDS: BOUND VOLUMES

WARRANTS   PETER GROVENDIKE   (Binding Volume 152).

The inside title of this volume is more descriptive: "A list of Warrants Renewed of Peter Grovendike by the Governors Warrant bearing Date the 31st Day of the 5th Month 1684." It is an alphabetical listing of seven handwritten pages, giving the names of pre-Penn settlers who took out warrants between 1675 and 1684, with the dates and acreage.

WARRANT BOOK NO. 3   1682–1684   (Binding No. 15)   LO micro.: 25.3; 1759 transcript in PROPRIETARY WARRANTS   (Binding No. 26)   LO micro.: 25.5, and WARRANTS PROPRIETARIES 1–113 WITH INDEX   (Binding No. 41)   LO micro.: 25.9.

The proprietary secretary's earliest book copy of warrants. The warrants were signed by Penn during his first stay in Pennsylvania (1682–1684) and were directed to the surveyor general, Thomas Holme.

WARRANTS 1682–1684 (Binding No. 16) LO micro.: 25.3; 1759 transcript: OLD RIGHTS WITH INDEX 1682–1685 (Binding No. 58) LO micro.: 25.13.

An original volume containing abstracts of warrants sent to the surveyor general. It is divided into two sections, each with an index. Section one, 118 pages, refers to purchasers. Section two, 43 pages, refers mainly to renters.

WARRANT BOOK 1685–1691 (Binding No. 14) LO micro.: 25.2; 1759 transcript: OLD RIGHTS—PHILADELPHIA, CHESTER, BUCKS, NEW CASTLE, KENT AND SUS-SEX (Binding No. 23) LO micro.: 25.5; *PA* (2) 19:3–21.

An original volume, basically a warrant register consisting of three lists of warrants: 1) 354 warrants in the counties; 2) warrants granted by commissioners of property William Markham, Thomas Ellis, and John Goodson; 3) 133 warrants for town lots. Information includes the name, date of warrant, quantity of land ordered, county, amount of the whole purchase, date of return, date of survey, and to whom and when the land was patented.

WARRANT BOOK 1700–1715 (Binding No. 117) LO micro.: 25.108; 1759 transcript: WARRANTS—PROPRIETARIES AND COMMISSIONERS 1700–1704 (Binding No. 36) LO micro.: 25.8, and WARRANTS 1704–1715 WITH INDEX (Binding No. 37) LO micro.: 25.8.

An original volume containing book copies of original warrants showing that the lesser seal had been affixed. All warrants are directed to the surveyor general.

WARRANT BOOK 1715–1741 (Binding No. 118) LO micro.: 25.108; index separately bound as WARRANT BOOK INDEX 1715–1741; 1759 transcript: WARRANTS OF PROP-ERTY 1715–1735 (Binding No. 28) LO micro.: 25.6.

An original volume. Warrants during William Penn's proprietorship cover pages 1–129. The 1759 transcript contains only part of the original but includes the period of Penn's proprietorship.

OLD RIGHTS—BUCKS NO. 1A TO 21A [21P] (Binding No. 24) LO micro.: 25.5. OLD RIGHTS—BUCKS NO. 22 P TO Z (Binding No. 25) LO micro.: 25.5.

The 1759 transcripts of original warrants and surveys for Bucks County. The index is the Original Purchases register.

OLD RIGHTS, CHESTER A-1 TO H-106 (Binding No. 31) LO micro.: 25.6–7.

A 1759 transcript of original warrants and surveys for Chester County. The index is the Original Purchases register.

OLD RIGHTS, CHESTER H-107 TO T-55 LDS micro.: 0020886.

A 1759 transcript in the Chester County Historical Society as manuscript no. 37180.

OLD RIGHTS, CHESTER   T-56 TO Y-4   (Binding No. 34)   LO micro.: 25.7.

A 1759 transcript of original warrants and surveys for Chester County. The index is the Original Purchases register.

PHILADELPHIA COUNTY   [Old Rights F-769 to H-1203, P-2421 to S-2441]   (Bound in WARRANTS AND SURVEYS 1, Philadelphia City Archives)   LO micro.: 25.128.

A 1759 transcript of original warrants and surveys.

OLD RIGHTS PHILADELPHIA   I-1225–P2420   (Binding No. 38)   LO micro.: 25.8.

A 1759 transcript of original warrants and surveys for Philadelphia County. The index is the Original Purchases register.

---

[1] 15th 6 mo. [August] 1685, *PWP* 3:50.
[2] Min. Com. Prop. Bk. G, 19th 11th mo 1701 [January 1702].
[3] See II.G.7, Old Rights.
[4] See III.G.6, 1759 Transcripts (Green Books).

II.G.4. Surveys

A survey was the actual process of going upon the land and measuring and marking the particular tract. According to William Penn's stated policy, surveys were to be made in regular configurations adjoining previously surveyed tracts.[1] Penn reasoned that such a method would prevent large spaces of unsettled land and make it easier to develop the province. If his policy had been followed, Pennsylvania's original warrant tracts would have been as regular as in the New England colonies. In practice, however, most purchasers took up land where they wished. The result is a jigsaw-puzzle effect for researchers piecing together the Pennsylvania warrant tracts.

The responsibility for executing the survey lay with the surveyor general. Upon receiving the warrant, or order to survey, from the secretary for proprietary affairs, the surveyor general filed the warrant in his office in Philadelphia and sent a copy to the deputy surveyor of the county where the survey was to be made. During the period 1702–1706, when there was no surveyor general, the secretary sent the copy of the warrant directly to the deputy surveyor. The deputy surveyor copied the order to survey in his registry book. He had the choice of conducting the actual survey with or without the purchaser in attendance. Usually the purchaser showed the surveyor the location to be surveyed and directed the courses and distances and shape of the survey.

Devious surveying practices abounded and prompted Penn to standardize instructions to deputy surveyors in 1701. The following requirements enumerated in the instructions indicate the areas most flagrantly mismanaged: 1) Surveys were to be made upon the land, not in the office; 2) tracts were to be as nearly contiguous to previously surveyed tracts as possible, unless the warrant stated otherwise; 3) tracts were not to be surveyed on lands specifically laid out for the proprietor; 4) tracts fronting creeks were to follow the rule of twenty perches by the creek to every one hundred acres if the distance back permitted;[2] 5) tracts were not to exceed a 10 percent overplus allowance for roads and barrens; and 6) tract boundaries were to be clearly marked by using natural objects, such as trees or rocks, or by posts or stones.[3]

When completed, the survey, drawn on paper as a protracted figure and with the field work attached, was returned to the surveyor general's office. Filed beside the warrant and arrayed by county, the survey remained in the surveyor general's office until the buyer paid the remaining purchase money and patent fees. A copy of the survey was not given to the purchaser, although the purchaser was to have paid the surveying fees and the cost of preparing the draft. After the purchaser met all payments the surveyor general examined the survey and the deputy's calculations.[4] If the survey matched the warrant, the surveyor general prepared the return of survey.

These procedures were not always followed. Many deviations occurred. Before 1701, when the deputy surveyors were operating without explicit instructions, many surveys were not sent back to the surveyor general. Even after 1701 the survey might have been drawn on the deputy surveyor's copy of the warrant, so that the survey on file in the secretary's office might include warrant information.

Another common problem was the surveying of more land than was called for in the warrant. The excess, called overplus land, was then sold to the purchaser at a more favorable rate than the primary purchase. Surveyor General Thomas Holme claimed that it was not uncommon to find that his deputies had surveyed 300 to 400 acres of overplus land in a 1,500-acre purchase.[5] The minute books of the commissioners of property carry many references to warrants that were to be executed on other warrantees' overplus land.

To put a stop to surveying more land than was called for in the warrant and to generate badly needed revenue, Penn ordered a resurvey of all of the province and territories in 1701.[6] Overplus land was to be limited to a total of 10 percent: 4 percent for differences in surveys and 6 percent for roads and highways that might be built.[7] All remaining overplus land found upon resurvey was to be reserved for the proprietor rather than sold.

Many original surveys from the period 1682–1732 have survived as loose papers and are stored in the Land Office collection. To locate a survey made for a warrantee, consult the Old Rights registers.

The original surveys have also been microfilmed and hand copied twice into books. The first book copies were made in 1759 under the law to record warrants and surveys. Some of the 1759 volumes are in the Land Office collection, some are in the Philadelphia City Archives, but all are cited below and are available on microfilm. The second book copies were made beginning in 1833 under a law to copy all old and mutilated records in the Land Office. These are the working copies used today and referred to as copied survey books. The surveys from William Penn's proprietorship are in a portion of the copied survey books labeled "Old Rights." The old rights part of the copying project was never completed, but the search sheets and an in-house index for the incomplete portion are on file.

RECORDS: LOOSE PAPERS

ORIGINAL SURVEYS   LO micro.: 6.158–68, 6.181–90.

Original surveys are on individual sheets of paper, laminated, and filed in the same random order as the copied survey books (see volume numbers below). The surviving surveys from the period 1682–1732 are filed mainly in volumes D-65 through D-114 (Old Rights) and can be accessed through the Old Rights registers. They are microfilmed as indicated above. The same volume, book, and page numbers refer to the loose survey and the copied survey.

RECORDS: BOUND VOLUMES

COPIED SURVEYS   [Series A to Z, A-1 to A-89, B-1 to B-23, BB-1 to BB-4, C-1 to C-234, D-1 to D-90]   LO micro.: 28.1–.

Volumes consisting of hand-drawn copies of original surveys. Most of the surveys from the proprietary period were copied into volumes D-65 through D-90 and B-22 through B-23.

These volumes were labeled "Old Rights" (original surveys filed as volumes D-91 through D-114 have not been copied). Within each volume there is no particular order, but the Old Rights registers serve as the index and cite the volume, book, and page for each name indexed.

DEPUTY SURVEYORS ORDER BOOK 1682–1693   (With index); 1759 transcript: OLD RIGHTS 1682–1693 WITH INDEX   (Binding No. 50)   LO micro.: 25.11.

The entries in this book are the copies of the warrants to survey sent to the deputy surveyors. Thus, they are a shortened form of the original warrant statement.

NEW CASTLE, KENT, AND SUSSEX SURVEYS   LO micro.: 25.31.

A deputy surveyors' book containing copies of warrants and surveys for land mainly in Kent and Sussex counties. The first 76 pages covering the period 1683–1686 are entries signed by J. Barkstead; the remaining pages are entries signed by Robert and William Shankland. An entry on page 29 by William Shankland indicates the book as his on "30 Aug 1735."

COPIES OF SURVEYOR GENERALS WARRANTS—1700   (Binding No. 1)   LO micro.: 25.1; index bound in PATENT REGISTER 1701–1728   (Binding No. 5)   LO micro.: 25.4.

Copies of warrants to survey sent to deputy surveyors from Edward Pennington, surveyor general. Entries are in paragraph form and dated 1700 and 1701.

1759 TRANSCRIPTS.

See the volumes of transcribed warrants listed under II.G.3, Warrants. Original warrants and surveys are entered next to each other in the volumes.

---

[1]Min. Com. Prop. Bk. C, from Wm Penn, 8th 12th mo 1687 [February 1688]. See also II.B.4, Terms of Settlement, n.3.
[2]Sur. Bk. D-71-150.
[3]Thomas Sergeant, *View of the Land Laws of Pennsylvania* (Philadelphia, 1838), 264–66.
[4]Min. Com. Prop. Bk. G, 19th 11th mo 1701 [January 1702].
[5]From Thomas Holme, 24th 3 mo [May] 1687, *PWP* 3:158.
[6]*PWP* 4:119. See also Sur. Bk. D-73-262 for warrant to resurvey Christiana Hundred in New Castle County and Darby, Ridley, Springfield, Marple, and Newtown townships in Chester County.
[7]*Statutes* 2:118–23.

II.G.5. Returns of Survey

The return of survey was an internal record of the surveyor general's office used to certify the authenticity of the survey. Consisting of a narrative description, the return of survey served as a notice of record that the particular piece of land had been purchased and all fees were paid. At one time, failure to find a return of survey on record could negate a claim to land.

Return of survey for a tract on Brandywine Creek. (Sur. Bk. D-69-300)

The surveyor general prepared the return of survey from the warrant and survey information on file in his office. He entered a copy of the return of survey in a book and sent the original to the secretary's office. The return of survey stated the date of the warrant, name of the warrantee, date of the survey, description of the survey, and date the return of survey was sent to the secretary's office. Essentially, the return of survey was an abstract of the combined warrant and survey.

Many of the original returns of survey from the period 1678–1732 have survived. Some are filed with the surveys and can be accessed through the Old Rights registers. Others are filed chronologically with the loose returns of survey and can be accessed by the date of patent. Many were copied in 1759 under the law to record warrants and surveys and are indexed in the Original Purchases register. In the early 1900s some of the returns of survey were copied, and the transcripts were bound in the Old Rights copied survey volumes. The originals were filed with the surveys. All returns of survey are cited below.

RECORDS: LOOSE PAPERS

RETURN OF SURVEY   1682–1732   LO micro.: 5.115–17.

Filed chronologically by date of patent in fifty-one folders. The earliest of these returns are copies of Upland court records dating from 1678. The collection also includes many returns of survey for Philadelphia city lots. There is no separate index.

ORIGINAL SURVEYS   LO micro.: 6.181–90.

Many original returns of survey for the period 1682–1732 have been copied and refiled with the original surveys. They are filed mainly in volumes D-65 through D-114 (Old Rights) and can be accessed through the Old Rights registers. The same volume, book, and page numbers refer to the loose returns of survey and the copied returns of survey.

RECORDS: BOUND VOLUMES

COPIED SURVEYS   LO micro.: 28.1–.

Copied returns of survey for the period 1682–1732 are bound in volumes D-65 through D-90 of the copied surveys; D-91 through D-114 have not been copied. Within each volume there is no particular order, but the Old Rights registers serve as the index.

RETURNS OF SURVEYS-A-1   1684–1693   (Binding No. 68; with index)   LO micro.: 25.31.

Contains two books bound back to back, each with an index. They are thought to be the earliest books generated in the surveyor general's office. The contents are the surveyor general's book copies of returns of survey, with narrative descriptions giving the date of warrant, name of the warrantee, description of the survey, and date the return was sent to the secretary. Many are signed by Deputy Surveyor General Robert Longshore.

REGISTER OF SURVEYS—1684   (Binding No. 7; with index)   LO micro.: 25.1–2; 1759 transcript in WARRANTS AND SURVEYS 3, Philadelphia City Archives, LO micro.: 25.128.

Also a return of survey book; entries cover the period 1684–1700, with a few at the end for 1716–1724. They are not in chronological order and are in two or three different handwritings.

RECORDED SURVEYS 1684 NO. 32   (Binding No. 6d)   LO micro.: 25.1.

Contains returns of survey. The inscription "Secretaries Copies into Book B" on an inside page indicates that this volume might have been prepared in the secretary's office as a record of receipt.

CAPT WM MARKHAM LIST OF PAPERS RECEIVED   PP. 1–70   (Binding No. 61)   LO micro.: 25.14.

An account of papers that Surveyor General Edward Pennington received from William Markham in 1698.

RETURN OF SURVEYS 1701   (Binding No. 18; with partial index)   LO micro.: 25.3; 1759 transcript of first part in WARRANTS AND SURVEYS 4, Philadelphia City Archives, LO micro.: 25.128.

The inside title of this volume reads "The Copies of the Surveyor General's Returns 1700." The first part contains 113 pages covering the period 1700–1720; the second part contains 128 pages beginning with an index and covers the period 1733–1736. Warrants and Surveys 4 contains an index to the first part.

PHILADELPHIA CITY [Old Rights, Returns A–W]   (Bound in WARRANTS AND SURVEYS 2, Philadelphia City Archives)   LO micro.: 25.128.

A 1759 transcript of original returns of survey for Philadelphia City.

PHILADELPHIA COUNTY [Old Rights, Returns A–Y]   (Bound in WARRANTS AND SURVEYS 6, Philadelphia City Archives)   LO micro.: 25.129.

A 1759 transcript of original returns of survey for Philadelphia County.

RETURNS—CHESTER [Old Rights] A TO P-15   [Bucks Old Rights] A TO Z   (Binding No. 32)   LO micro.: 25.6–7.

A 1759 transcript of original returns of survey for Chester and Bucks counties.

RETURNS   CHESTER [Old Rights] P14 TO Z   (Binding No. 53)   LO micro.: 25.11.

A 1759 transcript of original returns of survey for Chester County and a continuation of Returns—Chester [Old Rights] A to P-15. It also contains returns on new warrants for the period after 1732.

PAPERS IN OFFICE OF SURVEYOR GENERAL—1730   (Binding Volume 155).

An inventory, arranged by county, of warrants and surveys on file in the surveyor general's office as of 1730 on which no returns of survey had been made. The papers of several large landholders are listed by name and independently of county.

II.G.6. Patents

A patent was a deed from the proprietor conveying legal title to the land described in the return of survey, subject to quitrents. The document represented the final step in the transfer of land to individual ownership. Some purchasers patented their land as soon as the tract was surveyed, others waited several years, and some did not patent their land at all. Frequently the warrantee and the patentee were different individuals. Sometimes one or more generations of

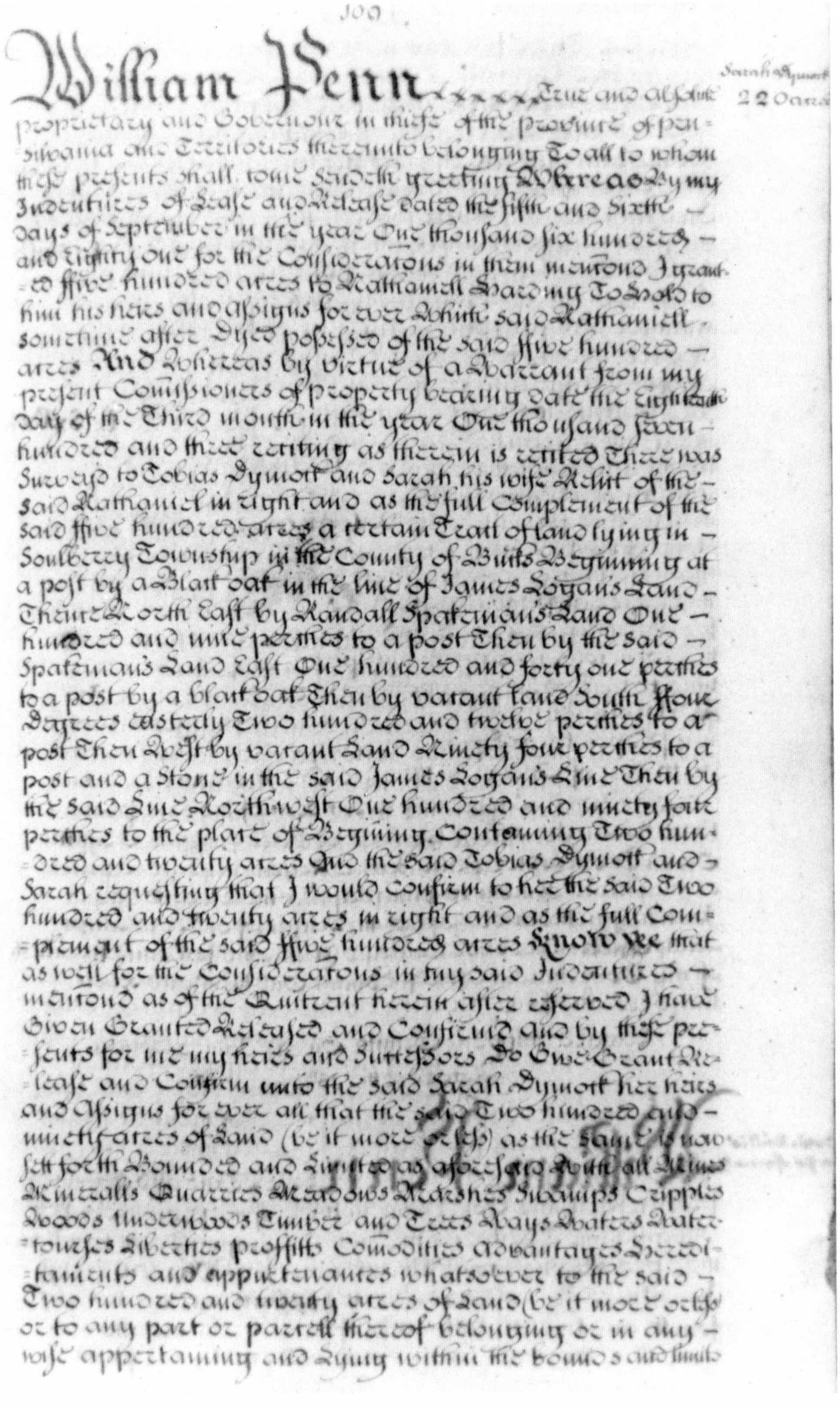

100

Sarah Dymock 220 acres

William Penn ×××× True and absolute proprietary and Governour in chiefe of the province of Pennsilvania and Territories thereunto belonging To all to whom these presents shall come Sendeth greeting Whereas by my Indentures of Lease and Release dated the fifth and sixth days of September in the year One thousand six hundred and eighty one for the Considerations in them mentioned I granted ffive hundred acres to Nathaniell Harding To hold to him his heirs and assigns for ever Which said Nathaniell sometime after Dyed possessed of the said ffive hundred acres And Whereas by virtue of a Warrant from my present Commissioners of property bearing date the Eighteenth day of the Third month in the year One thousand seven hundred and three reciting as therein is recited There was Surveyed to Tobias Dymock and Sarah his wife Relict of the said Nathaniell in right and as the full Complement of the said ffive hundred acres a certain Tract of land lying in Soulberry Township in the County of Bucks Beginning at a post by a Black oak in the line of James Logan's Land Thence North East by Randall Spakeman's Land One hundred and nine perches to a post Then by the said Spakeman's Land East One hundred and forty one perches to a post by a black oak Then by vacant land South ffour degrees easterly Two hundred and twelve perches to a post Then West by vacant Land Ninety four perches to a post and a Stone in the said James Logan's Line Then by the said Line Northwest One hundred and ninety four perches to the place of Beginning Containing Two hundred and twenty acres And the said Tobias Dymock and Sarah requesting that I would confirm to her the said Two hundred and twenty acres in right and as the full Complement of the said ffive hundred acres Know Yee that as well for the Considerations in my said Indentures mentioned as of the Quitrent hereinafter reserved I have Given Granted Released and Confirmed and by these presents for me my heirs and Successors Do Give Grant Release and Confirm unto the said Sarah Dymock her heirs and Assigns for ever all that the said Two hundred and ninety acres of Land (be it more or less) as the same is now sett forth Bounded and Limited as aforesaid With all Mines Minerals Quarries Meadows Marshes Swamps Cripples Woods Underwoods Timber and Trees Ways Waters Water-courses Liberties proffitts Comodities advantages Hereditaments and appurtenances whatsoever to the said Two hundred and twenty acres of Land (be it more or less) or to any part or parcell thereof belonging or in any wise appertaining and lying within the bounds and limits

Portion of a patent for an Original Purchaser. (Pat. Bk. A-3-109)

owners intervened between the dates when the warrant and the patent were issued.

Patents granted during William Penn's proprietorship were prepared in longhand on parchment. The document recited the information contained in the warrant and survey, including the terms of purchase and the amount of quitrent that was owed. Affixed with the greater seal of the province, the patent was signed by either Penn or the commissioners of property, depending upon who was in the province at the time.

The process of obtaining a patent to a tract of land differed slightly between Original Purchasers and other purchasers. Because Original Purchasers had paid for their land by buying shares, there were no further charges for a patent except a small recording fee and the annual quitrent. The surveyor general sent the return of survey to the secretary, who wrote the patent from the description therein. After recording the patent in a patent register, the secretary had the document signed by the proprietor or commissioners of property and then sent it to the master of the rolls. There the patent received the greater seal of the province and was copied into a patent book. The original copy was given to the patentee.

All other purchasers were required to pay the remainder of the purchase price to the receiver general before the secretary would prepare the patent. Consequently, Penn's system of appointing the secretary to serve as receiver general meant that fewer steps were involved in the patenting process. The inability to pay the complete purchase price contributed to the reluctance of many After Purchasers to patent their land.

The earliest patents were recorded in 1684 after the Rolls Office opened. Patent registers for the period 1684–1732 prepared in the secretary's office have survived. They were copied, as were the other records, under the 1759 recording law. Both the original volumes and the copies are cited below.

The patent books prepared in the Rolls Office have also survived and form the first seven volumes of the A series of patents. However, patents on warrants initiated during this period might have been granted much later and consequently may be found in the AA patent series or even the P patent series. The patent books are large ledger-sized volumes, and entries from the 1684–1732 period are in the original longhand of the master of the rolls or his clerk. The patent books have been microfilmed. A master index for the A series is in its own volume. These volumes are cited below.

The original loose patent has always been the property of the patentee.

RECORDS: BOUND VOLUMES

PATENT BOOKS   [Series A and AA]   (Index bound separately)   LO micro.: 3–17.

Series covering the period 1684–1781 and indexed in the same master volume. Most of the entries for the 1684–1732 period are in series A, books 1 through 7, but some early patents were recorded at later dates and are thus entered in later volumes. The A series also includes some patents from the pre-Penn era. The Patent Index to the A and AA series should be used to locate an entry, but several volumes have their own indexes.

PATENT INDEX   [Series] A & AA   LO micro.: 1.16.

Arranged alphabetically by last name and grouped by volume; thus all Es for series A, book 2 (A-2), are followed by all Es for series A, book 3 (A-3). For each name the index gives the date of patent, page, number of acres, warrantee, date of warrant, and county.

TRACT PATENT NAME INDEX   PATENT BOOKS A–AA   LO micro.: 1.20.

An alphabetical index of tracts by their patent name. The following information is given: the tract name, patent book, patent date, patentee, area, warrantee, warrant date, and county.

WARRANT BOOK 1685–1691   (Binding No. 14)   LO micro.: 25.2; 1759 transcript: OLD RIGHTS—PHILADELPHIA, CHESTER, BUCKS, NEW CASTLE, KENT AND SUSSEX   (Binding No. 23)   LO micro.: 25.5; PA (2) 19:3–21.

Contains a list of patents and may well be the patent register for the dates cited.

PATENT REGISTER   1701–1728   (Binding No. 5)   LO micro.: 25.1; 1759 transcript: PATENTS 1701–1728   (Binding No. 22)   LO micro.: 25.4.

Includes: 1) A long narrow book titled "Alphabet to the Old Patent Book"; and 2) Patent Register 1701–1728, which contains 548 patents for 1707–1709, no patents for 1710–11, and approximately 270 patents for 1712–1728.

II.G.7. Old Rights

The term old rights as it is used today refers to all pre-1732 warrants, surveys, and returns of survey. The Old Rights registers serve as warrant registers for the period 1682–1732, and all research for this period should begin with them.

Old rights did not always have such a sweeping definition, however. Originally the term referred to the land rights of First Purchasers. The shares they bought gave them the right to an equivalent amount of country land. Country land was not surveyed before it was purchased but could be laid out in any location contingent on two restrictions: 1) The tract was to be within the region purchased from the Indians, and 2) adjoining tracts owned by the same person were to be less than one thousand acres unless a family was settled on each one thousand acres within three years. A First Purchaser's only obligation before claiming a portion of his right was to produce a deed of lease and release or a special warrant from William Penn. As generally practiced, First Purchasers' land rights equaled the amount of their purchase distributed 98 percent in country land and 2 percent in liberty land. They also received a bonus of one or more lots in the city of Philadelphia, depending upon the amount of their purchase. A First Purchaser could also claim fifty acres of headright land for each servant sponsored.

The number of purchasers eligible to claim land under old rights gradually grew. Penn added several Late Purchasers to his list of First Purchasers, thereby creating a group called Original Purchasers. Most Original Purchasers claimed only a small portion of their land rights in their own names. The remaining land they sold to settlers whom they attracted from Europe or who arrived in Pennsylvania without purchasing land beforehand. These settlers became Under Purchasers, who claimed land in the right of Original Purchasers. Under Purchasers received warrants to survey their tracts in their own names, even if the Original Purchaser had already been granted a warrant for the same tract or a larger portion including the tract. In many instances the Original Purchaser then claimed a like amount of land in another location.

This system created a great deal of confusion. Soon it became difficult to know when an Original Purchaser had warranted and surveyed his total purchase. Frequently the total amount of land warranted in the right of an Original Purchaser equaled more than the total shares purchased. Furthermore, in many instances duplicate warrants and surveys covered the same tract of land.

The practice of claiming land in the right of an Original Purchaser began to break down with the pressure of rapid settlement. New purchasers arrived so fast that warrants to survey land outside of Original Purchasers' surveys had to be granted. By the 1740s land officers could not easily separate the warrants and surveys granted under old rights from the rest of the warrants and surveys granted during Penn's proprietorship. In 1759 the assembly authorized a major project of copying all the proprietary land records (see III.G.6, 1759 Transcripts [Green Books]). The men in charge, John Hughes and Richard Peters, simply grouped all warrants and surveys granted before 1732 together under the rubric "old rights" and began the administration of Penn's heirs with new warrants.

A cautionary point must be added. Claims to land under Original Purchasers' old rights were honored throughout colonial times. The claimant had only to produce an authentic deed of lease and release or a special warrant from William Penn and prove that the total amount of acreage originally purchased had never been claimed, and a warrant to survey the proper size of tract would be granted. Since the land claimed could be located anywhere in the province, surveys authorized under old rights may be found in places as far inland as Mifflin County.

The Old Rights registers for locating the original warrant and survey records for land claimed before 1732 are cited below. The same volume, book, and page numbers refer to the loose records and the hand-copied records in the copied survey books.

RECORDS: LOOSE PAPERS

ORIGINAL SURVEYS   LO micro.: 6.158–68, 6.180.

All original old rights warrants and surveys are filed as original surveys and indexed in the Old Rights registers cited below. Most of them are in volumes D-65 through D-114. Those numbered D-65 through D-90 and B-22 through B-23 have been hand copied into the copied survey books. Those numbered D-91 through D-114 are not copied. The filing system for the original surveys uses the same numbering system as the copied survey books.

RECORDS: BOUND VOLUMES

PHILADELPHIA OLD RIGHTS   LO micro.: 1.10, 1.21.

Serves as the warrant register for pre-1732 Philadelphia City and County. It references the volume, book, and page of the original and copied surveys. Names are grouped alphabetically by the first letter of the last name, then numbered consecutively through the letter S. Beginning with the letter T, they are numbered consecutively by each letter. For each name the following information is given: the type of document from which the survey information was taken (warrant, return, draft, or resurvey), acres, date, and volume, book, and page of the original and copied surveys. At the end of the volume is a listing of several large landholders and their papers held by the Land Office.

OLD RIGHTS 1682   [Bucks and Chester]   LO micro.: 1.9–10, 1.21.

Serves as the warrant register for pre-1732 Bucks and Chester counties. It references the volume, book, and page of the original and copied surveys. Names are grouped alphabetically by the first letter of the last name, then numbered consecutively for each letter. For each individual the following information is given: the type of document from which the survey information was taken (warrant, return, draft, or resurvey), acres, date, and volume, book, and page of the original and copied surveys.

OLD RIGHTS   (Binding No. 157)   PA (3) 2:662–769, 3:3–214.

Prepared in 1759 by John Hughes as an inventory of old rights records in the secretary's office. It serves as an index to the 1759 bound volumes of copies of original warrants, surveys, and returns of survey. Because the volume was prepared in 1759, there is no cross-reference to the current filing system; consequently, the *PA* reprint contains no reference to the current filing system.

REGISTER OF OLD RIGHTS   (Binding No. 138).

A copy of the volume titled "Old Rights" (Binding No. 157) but incomplete. Prepared by Hughes as part of the 1759 inventory of Land Office records, the volume includes a catalog or list of papers and books in the surveyor general's office as of 1759.

OLD RIGHTS 1682–1684   (Binding No. 151).

An incomplete index, from A to part of *D* only, of purchasers, to whom they granted land, and when it was warranted, surveyed, and returned.

COPIED SURVEYS   OLD RIGHTS   Volumes D-65 to D-90; B-22 to B-23   LO micro.: 28.1– .

Contain hand copies of original old rights papers. Access is through the Old Rights registers.

Land Settlement, 1732–1776: The Proprietorship of the Penn Heirs

III.A. Introduction

This section discusses land policies, practices, and recording procedures during the proprietorship of the heirs of William Penn: his three sons, John, Thomas, and Richard, and Richard's sons, John and Richard. For the remainder of the colonial era, 1732–1776, the Penn family owned all the unappropriated land in the province of Pennsylvania and was responsible for its orderly disposal.

Land management under the heirs of William Penn followed closely the patterns originally established in the colony. Although Thomas Penn oversaw proprietary affairs as a resident of Pennsylvania from 1732 to 1741, the affairs of property thereafter until 1763 were largely in the hands of agents while the Penn heirs resided in England.

The first Penn heir to establish a permanent residence in Pennsylvania was John Penn, Richard's son. John Penn served as governor of Pennsylvania and watched over proprietary interests from 1763 to 1771 and from 1773 to 1776. His brother, Richard, substituted for him during the years 1771–1773. John continued to live in Philadelphia even after Pennsylvania joined with the other American colonies in declaring independence, and he died there in 1795.

Spurred by the rapid influx of European immigrants throughout the proprietary era, the proprietors periodically opened additional portions of the province to settlement. In so doing they continued William Penn's policy of purchasing the land from the natives before permitting legal settlement. The purchase of a vast tract of land in 1754 (modified in 1758) permitted legal settlement as far west as the Allegheny Mountains. Another large purchase in 1768 added a wide swath of land extending diagonally across the colony from northeast to southwest. By the end of the proprietary era, settlement was legal in the south and eastern two thirds of the colony.

In land affairs the young proprietors' main objective was to encourage rapid settlement of the colony. To accomplish this goal they reorganized proprietary offices and introduced new land schemes. They set their agents to work collecting quitrents and laying out new proprietary manors and towns. They also raised the price of land to fifteen pounds ten shillings per one hundred acres and set the quitrent at a uniform one halfpenny sterling per year per acre, but they offered to sell large tracts at reduced rates.

Evidence of a transition in proprietary attitude, these activities led to the development of many irregular practices. Most of them were

Table 12. Research Aids: The Penn Heirs and Pennsylvania

Smith, Edward O., Jr. "Thomas Penn, Chief Proprietor of Pennsylvania: A Study of His Public Governmental Activities from 1763 to 1775." Ph.D. diss., Lehigh University, 1966.

TPP.

Tully, Alan. "Proprietary Affairs in Colonial Pennsylvania 1726–1739." *Journal of the Lancaster County Historical Society* 82 (Easter 1978): 94–122.

Wainwright, Nicholas B. "The Penn Collection." *PMHB* 87 (1963): 393–419.

brought about through reaction to uncontrolled settlement. The introduction of the application system in 1765 legalized ownership by settlement and improvement and set the policy for all future land distribution. New categories of purchasers, new categories of land, and new records developed as a result of the younger Penns' policies.

III.B. Basic Policies

When John, Thomas, and Richard Penn became the owners of Pennsylvania, they inherited a land distribution system based upon proprietary principles. As proprietors the young Penns had absolute authority to dispose of land. In addition, they inherited a Land Office, an established record-keeping process, and an obligation to continue purchase treaties with the Indians. During their administration the Penn heirs made fundamental changes to their land settlement system while retaining the established framework.

In the early years of their proprietorship, 1732–1765, the brothers permitted many irregular practices to develop. Reacting to a rapidly expanding population, their overriding concern seemed to be to settle as many people as possible. Yet the young proprietors also managed to look out for their own financial interests. The latter part of their proprietorship, 1765–1779, brought a marked change in policy. After several years of experience they understood the necessity of

legalizing the practice of ownership by settlement and improvement.

III.B.1. Proprietary Interests

From the proprietary viewpoint the most important land policies were those that provided the Penn family with a steady income. Financial circumstances dictated the absolute necessity of continuing to set aside for their own use one tenth of all the land surveyed. The proprietors attempted to rent this reserve, usually termed manor land, in farm-sized tracts. Lacking great success, they nevertheless pursued the policy throughout the proprietary era.

Adding towns to their list of proprietary land, the Penns sought to increase their holdings and give direction to the political and economic development of the province. They extended William Penn's idea of founding his settlement around the one great town of Philadelphia by establishing a proprietary town as the seat for each new county. Retaining some of the town lots for rental, they sold the rest.

Regulation of quitrents was also of "utmost consequence" to the Penns.[1] The income derived from quitrents was calculated as a permanent part of their assets. To be able to collect their money was more important to the Penns than to turn people off the land. Consequently the proprietaries used every method they thought proper to encourage squatters to warrant and patent their land. This attitude eventually led to the legalization of ownership by settlement and improvement.

[1]"Letter from Thomas Penn to James Tilghman, November 7, 1766," *WPHM* 57 (1974): 242.

III.B.2. Presumptive Settlement

The practice of occupying vacant land without obtaining approval from the proprietors began as soon as settlement extended more than a few days' walk beyond the Land Office in Philadelphia. The situation was aggravated by a rapid rate of European immigration that coincided with the inability of the proprietary trustees to grant more land than would pay the Penns' mortgage debt. As a result, very few warrants to survey land were issued between 1720 and 1733.[1] In fact, most people thought the Land Office was "shut up from 1718 to 1732."[2] To bypass their inability to grant more than a few warrants, the commissioners of property or the secretary of the Land Office granted tickets to select individuals. The tickets had the same validity as warrants in ordering surveys. However, the survey drawings were not returned to the Land Office, and later warrants were written to resurvey the original tracts.

Other settlers, especially Irish and German immigrants, encouraged by a seemingly lenient proprietary attitude, simply took it upon themselves to locate and improve their own plot of ground on the frontier. Many settlers went beyond the treaty lines although token efforts were made to enforce the law. Purchase treaties usually resulted from the pressure these frontiersmen exerted. Despite their lawless behavior such settlers seemed to expect to pay for the land at the going rate whenever the system caught up with them.

One of the overriding desires of John, Thomas, and Richard Penn's proprietary administration was that squatters obtain titles to their land. The proprietors began by using enticements such as the lottery scheme of 1735. Winners would be able to obtain warrants to survey the land they were already settled upon.[3] This scheme may have been the first public acknowledgment of an evolving law of ownership by settlement and improvement. However, the lottery proved to be unsuccessful, and the Penns turned to coercion. In several public announcements, Richard Peters, proprietary secretary, advertised dates by which all delinquent accounts for settled lands were to be paid, but with enforcement impossible and the removal of frontier families impracticable, coercion proved fruitless. In the few cases where squatters applied for warrants, the documents were issued retroactively using language to the effect that the original warrant could not be found. Later in the application system these became known as warrants of acceptance.

---

[1]"Letter of Instructions of James Logan to James Steel, 1727," *PMHB* 24 (1900): 495.

[2]Peter Wilson Coldham, "Pennsylvania Land Company," *NGSQ* 74 (December 1986): 290–92.

[3]See III.E.1.b, Lottery Land.

III.B.3. Vacating Warrants

Another irregular practice encouraged by the Penns' land system was paying a portion of the purchase price and then avoiding payment of the outstanding balance. The secured warrant created a unique quasi title, but payment of the outstanding balance and the grant of a patent were the only steps to an absolute title.

For owners who held deeds to unpatented land, Richard Peters, secretary of the Land Office, devised what was called a vacating warrant. This transferred the rights of the original warrantee to the new owner by claiming noncompliance with the original terms of sale. The Land Office sometimes directed a new survey; at other times the original survey was accepted. Whichever the case, the patenting process then proceeded. Under a vacating warrant the original warrantee occasionally received some remuneration from the next owner and actually transferred his interest. More often than not, however, original warrantees had simply taken flight and left no traceable transaction.

III.B.4. Survey without Warrant

Some settlers were creative enough to find a surveyor who would conduct a survey without a warrant and return the draft to the Land Office, where it was usually accepted. This aberration in Land Office practice resulted in several provincial court cases. Lawyers argued that surveys made without a warrant or order from the surveyor general's office could have no enforceable basis. Such surveys constituted unauthorized private acts of individuals.

Associated with private surveys was the Land Office practice of asserting that warrants had been issued to survey land when in reality they had not, nor had purchase money been received. Apparently the Land Office adopted such action to accommodate people who did not have sufficient money to make the required down payment of one half of the purchase price.

III.B.5. Application System

Over the years individual settlers encountered increasing difficulty in obtaining warrants and surveys. The Land Office and the deputy surveyors favored speculators, politicians, and their own interests above legitimate settlers. Often using fictitious names, speculators warranted thousands of acres of choice land and sometimes retained a deputy surveyor for his service. Settlers were simply forced to squat and occupy.

To obtain land, many settlers moved west beyond the treaty line of the Allegheny Mountains after the French abandoned Fort Duquesne in 1758. But the Pennsylvania frontier was not secure from Indian attack, and the assembly failed to respond to frontiersmen's demands for protection. In keeping with the proprietary Indian policy, the Land Office had no authority to grant land west of the Allegheny Mountains, and deputy surveyors had little interest in venturing into Indian territory.

Peace in 1763 brought security to the Pennsylvania frontier. Squatters who had abandoned their settlements quickly returned. They prospered and sought to protect their valuable improvements by securing title to them. The proprietaries, on their part, were anxious to learn how much land had actually been settled and to collect the purchase monies and back interest.

Consequently the proprietors instituted a major policy change in 1765. Settlers who could certify improvement of unwarranted land and were willing to accept the results of a survey would be granted a warrant provided they submitted an application and paid the purchase price with back interest. In other words, the application would lead directly to the survey, and the warrant would be prepared after the survey was returned to the Land Office. Called the application system, the new procedure created a new type of warrant called a warrant to accept.

III.C. Regions Open for Settlement

During the period 1732–1776, Pennsylvania's land area open for legal settlement was significantly enlarged. Through a series of six major purchase treaties with the Indians, increasingly larger amounts of land were added to the regions already open for settlement. By the end of the proprietary era, settlement was legal in the eastern, southern, and western two thirds of the province.

The younger Penns supported the earlier proprietary policy of purchasing land from the

---

Table 13. Research Aids: Pennsylvania Maps, 1732–1776

Evans, Lewis. *A General Map of the Middle British Colonies in America.* 1755. In PA (3) Appendix 1-10.

———. *A Map of Pennsylvania, New Jersey, New York, And the Three Delaware Counties.* 1749. In PA (3) Appendix 1-10.

Scull, Nicholas. *Map of the Improved Part of the Province of Pennsylvania.* 1759. In PA (3) Appendix 1-10.

Native Americans and understood how this policy contributed to peaceful colonization and sustained development. However, they lacked the ability to anticipate settlement pressures and failed to clear the land of Indian claims ahead of time. Consequently purchase treaties were made as a reaction to settlement that had already occurred. As the new colony repeatedly outgrew its artificial boundaries, squatters continuously intruded upon unpurchased Indian territory. When confronted regarding such illegal settlement, James Logan, William Penn's secretary for proprietary affairs, had insisted that the commissioners of property would never consent to settlement on lands that the Indians still owned.[1] Regardless of this high ideal, Indian relations in the province were often strained as a result of uncontrolled westward expansion, and hostilities ultimately flared in the French and Indian War. Not until the end of the war were the proprietors able to negotiate a purchase treaty that made the western portion of the province relatively safe and available for settlement.

---

[1]To John, Thomas, and Richard Penn, 17th 9br [November] 1729, PA (2) 7: 129–32.

III.C.1. Purchase Treaties, 1732–1758

Before the French and Indian War a set of five purchase treaties with the Indians extended legal settlement to the Allegheny Mountains in the west and the Pocono Mountains in the north. Each of these treaties came about as a direct result of settlers' encroaching on the unpurchased Indian land. Out of this territory four new counties came into existence, York, Cumberland, Berks, and Northampton, making eight counties in all by 1758.

The upper Schuylkill and Delaware rivers region presented the first concern to the new proprietors. The lands at Tulpehocken were especially of interest. Within months of his arrival in Pennsylvania, Thomas Penn negotiated a purchase treaty with the Indians who claimed the area. The treaty, signed September 7, 1732, opened land along the Schuylkill River watershed between the Lehigh hills and the Kittatinny Mountains and enlarged Bucks, Philadelphia, and Lancaster counties.[1]

The land west of the Susquehanna River presented the next area for purchase treaties. A grant from New York's former Governor Thomas Dongan in 1696 and treaties in 1700 and 1701 lacked territorial definition. They were interpreted as transferring claim to the land, not settlement rights. Relying upon these early treaties, both Governor William Keith of Pennsylvania and the young Penns surveyed land for themselves and granted licenses to settle on the west side of the Susquehanna River. But the proprietors refused to interpret the treaties as opening the area to general settlement.

To open the Susquehanna River watershed to legal settlement, the proprietaries negotiated a new purchase treaty with the Six Nations of the Iroquois Confederation. Dated October 11, 1736, the treaty defined the new northern and western settlement boundary as the crest of the Kittatinny Mountains.[2] The entire purchase area fell within what was then Lancaster County.

The only land in eastern Pennsylvania still not purchased from the Indians was the upper Delaware River region. The famous Walking Purchase of 1737 changed that situation.[3] Instead of traveling the expected thirty miles, one walker raced sixty miles to the foot of the Kittatinny Mountains and then turned northeast toward the Delaware Water Gap. The territory he covered outlined a tract much larger than the Indians had anticipated when they agreed to sell as much land as a man could cover in one and one-half days. Land as far north as the mouth of Lackawaxen Creek was transferred to proprietary ownership and opened to legal settlement. To insist that the Delaware Indians leave the Forks of the Delaware, the proprietors were

Table 14. Research Aids: Indian Treaties, 1732–1776

Early American Indian Documents: Treaties and Laws, 1607–1789. Vol. 2, *Pennsylvania Treaties, 1737–1756,* edited by Donald H. Kent. Washington, DC, 1984.

Kent, Donald H. *History of Pennsylvania Purchases from the Indians.* New York, 1974.

forced to arrange a second treaty with the Six Nations in 1742.[4] The newly added territory enlarged Bucks County.

Settlers in western Pennsylvania continued to press beyond established boundaries into prized Indian hunting and trapping grounds. Although the Indians registered complaints, they reluctantly sold another tract to the proprietors on August 22, 1749. This land lay north of the previous purchases but south of the northeast branch of the Susquehanna River. Mahanoy Creek and a line running northeast to the mouth of Lackawaxen Creek marked the northern boundary. In return for this territory the proprietors agreed that all illegally settled persons in the Juniata Valley to the west would be removed.[5] This 1749 purchase enlarged Bucks, Philadelphia, and Lancaster counties.

The proprietors negotiated another purchase treaty in 1754 just before the French and Indian War. The purchase resulted from a conference at Albany with the Six Nations. Held by order of the British Crown, the conference was to produce a general treaty marking the western bounds of settlement for all the American colonies. As initially agreed upon, the 1754 treaty opened a broad patch of Pennsylvania land lying to the west and northwest as far as the charter bounds of the province extended and left only a small part of the colony for Indian use.[6] The Indians' dissatisfaction with the treaty and the threat of French hostility forced the British government to intercede and reduce the size of the area purchased. The western bounds of settlement became the Allegheny Mountains. The transaction to correct the treaty was completed on October 23, 1758.[7] All the land included in the purchase lay within Cumberland County.

---

[1]PA (1) 1:344–47.
[2]The Five Nations (Mohawk, Seneca, Oneida, Onondaga, and Cayuga) became the Six Nations

about 1715 by the addition of the Tuscarora. *PA* (1) 1:494–98.

³*PA* (1) 1:541–43.

⁴For lengthy discussions see *Early American Indian Documents: Treaties and Laws, 1607–1789,* vol. 2, *Pennsylvania Treaties, 1737–1756,* edited by Donald H. Kent (Washington, DC, 1984), 1–51; *CR* 4:559–86.

⁵*PA* (1) 2:33–37.

⁶Manuscript copy, RG-26, PHMC; *Early American Indian Documents* 2:339–42.

⁷*SmL* 2:122.

III.C.2. County Formation, 1732–1758

By 1758 four counties had been carved out of all the new areas open for legal settlement. York and Cumberland counties were established in the west, and Berks and Northampton in the east. York (1749) and Cumberland (1750) were formed from the western portion of Lancaster County. The Susquehanna River served as the dividing line between Lancaster County and the two new counties. York had a western boundary that ran along the ridge of the South Mountains. Its northern boundary was the Yellow Breeches Creek from its mouth at the Susquehanna River to Dogwood Run. York's southern boundary was the Maryland line.

In 1750, Cumberland County was created to the north and west of York County. Cumberland's western and northern boundary was set at the ridge of the Kittatinny Mountains, the old 1736 treaty limits. Many settlers preferred to believe that the boundary was the western line of the province, as stated in Penn's charter. They moved west of the Kittatinny Mountains and angered the Indians and the proprietors alike. In the episode known as Burnt Cabins, the proprietors' agents forcefully removed several settlers. After the treaty of 1754 the Cumberland County boundary was moved farther west, but under the 1758 treaty the western boundary was set at the Allegheny Mountains.

Berks and Northampton were the next counties to be formed. By 1752 the so-called back inhabitants of Philadelphia, Chester, Lancaster, and Bucks counties had grown numerous enough to petition for the creation of their own counties. Berks County was created in 1752 to extend northwest to the extremity of the prov-

ince. It was bounded on the southeast by Chester and Philadelphia counties, on the west by Lancaster County, and on the east by Bucks County. Northampton also was formed in 1752. It encompassed the region north of Bucks County and east of Berks County to the provincial boundaries.

III.C.3. Purchase Treaties, 1763–1776

At the end of the French and Indian War a vast new section of provincial land was opened for legal settlement. Purchased from the Indians in 1768, the region was called the New Purchase, or the Purchase of 1768. The entire territory formed a wide swath running diagonally across the colony from northeast to southwest. The western boundary formed part of a longer line beyond which the middle colonies had agreed to prohibit settlement. The proprietors paid $10,000 for the settlement rights.¹ The agreement, reached at Fort Stanwix (Rome, New York), was the last purchase treaty between the proprietors and the Indians. Three new counties were formed within the region purchased: Bedford, Northumberland, and Westmoreland. By the end of the proprietary era, Pennsylvania was composed of eleven counties and a northwest quadrant that was still unavailable for legal settlement.

The new western boundary line is illustrated in the Genealogical Map of the Counties (front.). Beginning at Owego on the Susquehanna River in present New York State, the boundary followed the east side of the Susquehanna River to Towanda, then crossed the river and followed the south side of Towanda Creek to its headwaters. The boundary next ran along the north side of Burnett's Hills to a creek given only by its Indian name, then down the creek's south side to the West Branch of the Susquehanna River. The boundary then followed the south side of the West Branch of the Susquehanna to the forks in the river located east of the shortest straight overland route to Kittanning on the Ohio River. From Kittanning the boundary followed the Ohio River to the western boundary of the province, where the diagonal line ended.

Confusion over a few of the boundary's geographic features caused some problems. The

Chart 3. Areas of Settlement and County Formation, 1732–1758

Date	Indian Deed Number*	County
1732	20	Bucks, Philadelphia, and Lancaster enlarged
1736	21–22	Lancaster enlarged
1737	23	Bucks enlarged
1749	24	Bucks, Philadelphia, and Lancaster enlarged; **York** (5) formed from Lancaster
1750	—	**Cumberland** (6) formed from Lancaster
1752	—	**Berks** (7) formed from Philadelphia, Chester, and Lancaster; **Northampton** (8) formed from Bucks
1754, 1758	25–26	Cumberland enlarged

*Deed numbers refer to the Genealogical Map of the Counties (front.).

location of Burnett's Hills was imprecisely identified, and no English translation existed for the creek given only by its Indian name, making unclear whether it was Pine Creek or Lycoming Creek. Consequently the proprietaries were reluctant to permit settlement in that particular region for fear of continued Indian problems. Otherwise the Purchase of 1768 more than doubled the provincial area open for legal settlement.

---

[1]CR 9:554–55.

III.C.4. County Formation, 1763–1776

The three new counties formed between 1765 and 1776 came mainly from territory within the Purchase of 1768. At first, the region was divided into two counties: Bedford and Northumberland. Settlement moved westward so rapidly, however, that the county of Westmoreland was soon formed from the western portion of Bedford County.

Bedford County, the first of the three new counties to be established, was formed in 1771. It encompassed the area between Cumberland County and the western boundary of the province. The dividing line between Cumberland and Bedford counties ran along the summit of the Blue and Tuscarora mountains to the gap

near the head of Path Valley. From the gap the line ran north to the Juniata River, then up the Juniata River and along the summit of the mountain to the head of Standing Stone Creek. The line then ran northeast to Berks County and turned west along the Berks line to the western bounds of the province.

Northumberland, established in 1772, was the second of the three new counties to be formed from the Purchase of 1768. Taking territory from every contiguous county, Northumberland was formed from Northampton, Berks, Lancaster, Cumberland, and Bedford, as well as the entire northeastern portion of the New Purchase. Beginning at the confluence of the Mohontongo Creek and the Susquehanna River, the Northumberland County boundary ran up the Susquehanna to the head of the Little Juniata Creek. From there the boundary ran north to the Berks County line and then northwest to the Pennsylvania-New York line. The boundary then extended east along the provincial line to a point due north of the Great Swamp. Turning due south, the county line ran to the headwaters of the Lehigh Creek and down the creek to a straight west-southwest line to Spread Eagle Creek. The boundary then followed this creek to the Susquehanna River at the point of origin.

Westmoreland, established in 1773, was the last of the three new counties. Formed entirely from territory that had been part of Bedford County, Westmoreland's north, west, and south

Chart 4. Areas of Settlement and County Formation, 1763–1776

Date	Indian Deed Number*	County
1768	27–28	Cumberland, Berks, and Northampton enlarged
1771	—	**Bedford** (9) formed from Cumberland
1772	—	**Northumberland** (10) formed from Northampton, Berks, Lancaster, Cumberland, and Bedford
1773	—	**Westmoreland** (11) formed from Bedford

*Deed numbers refer to the Genealogical Map of the Counties (front.).

boundaries were the same as Bedford's had been. The dividing line between Bedford and Westmoreland counties ran along the ridge of the Laurel Hills and then along the ridge between the watersheds of the Susquehanna and Allegheny rivers to the 1768 purchase line at the headwaters of the West Branch of the Susquehanna River.

III.D. Categories of Purchasers

New categories of purchasers had begun to emerge by the time John, Thomas, and Richard Penn became the proprietors of Pennsylvania. In place of Original Purchasers were speculators who bought unclaimed old rights as desirable investments. After Purchasers were replaced by new purchasers who were arriving in ever increasing numbers. Finally, forming a new category were presumptive settlers, commonly called squatters.

III.D.1. New Purchasers

New purchasers formed the greatest continuity between the administration of William Penn and that of his sons. Essentially, new purchasers were the same as After Purchasers. They warranted and surveyed their land before they settled; consequently, new purchasers (or, more simply, purchasers) can be identified by a warrant to survey.

Signifying partial payment of the purchase price, the warrant to survey was usually inter-

preted as representing ownership. During the early years of their proprietorship the young Penns granted as many warrants to survey as their land officers could process. Estimates from the warrant register for the period 1733–1738 point to over one thousand warrants granted per year. Nevertheless the amount was insufficient to keep up with the rapid rate of settlement. The annual number of actual purchasers soon became significantly less than the annual number of squatters.

Before 1754 purchasers were restricted to tracts located within the purchases of 1754 and earlier. After the Purchase of 1768, buyers were permitted to apply for land within the newly added territory. Regardless of tract location, purchasers were required to submit an application for the warrant as the first formal document. Consequently a warrantee who purchased land before he settled should have an application in his name on file.

In addition to the current warrant registers, which are arranged by county, an earlier set of warrant registers, cited in the sources, is arranged chronologically. Covering the period 1733–1759, these registers almost exclusively list purchasers who partially paid for and surveyed their land before they settled. If a settlement date is known but not the location, these warrant registers are helpful. To study the progression of settlement or make any kind of statistical analysis, these early warrant registers are also of value.

RECORDS: BOUND VOLUMES

WARRANT REGISTER   1733–1738   (Binding No. 51)   LO micro.: 25.11.

Pages 86–315 of this volume contain a chronological register of warrants granted for the above time period. For many entries a notation indicates the approximate date of settlement.

FRAGMENTS OF WARRANT BOOK 1a-1b   LO micro.: 25.1; 1759 transcript in [Warrants Copies 1729–1733]   WARRANT REGISTER   1733–1738   (Binding No. 51)   LO micro.: 25.11.

The transcript is more nearly complete than the original. Section 1a corresponds to Warrants Copies 1729–1733, and Section 1b is the remaining fragment of Warrant Register 1739–1741.

WARRANT REGISTER   1741 TO 1752   PART 1 OF 2   PG. 1–300   (Binding No. 57)   LO micro.: 25.12–13.
WARRANT REGISTER   1741 TO 1752   PART 2 OF 2   PG. 301–558   INDEX (Binding No. 57)   LO micro.: 25.13.
WARRANT REGISTER   1752–1759   WITH INDEX   (Binding No. 54)   LO micro.: 25.12.

Chronological listings giving the warrantee, situation, county, acres, and date settled.

III.D.2. Presumptive Settlers

Presumptive settlers, otherwise known as squatters, were the product of a land settlement system unable to cope with the rapid rate of immigration. As opposed to purchasers, presumptive settlers located and improved a tract without first obtaining a warrant. By simply finding a desirable tract of land, clearing a few acres for a crop, and building a cabin, they pretended legal ownership, but in actuality they had no legal claim to their land. After several years in one place they frequently sold their improvement and moved on.

Presumptive settlers were usually immigrants with little money. By 1760 their presence dominated the Pennsylvania countryside. Even as early as 1726, James Logan, William Penn's proprietary secretary, noted the consequence of their settlement when he wrote to Hannah Penn: "I doubt not but there are at this time near a hund[d] thous[d] Acres possess'd by persons who resolutely sett down and improve without any manner of Right or Pretence to it."[1]

Whether squatters were "expressly encouraged" by the proprietors or only "connived at" has been a long-standing question.[2] Nevertheless, squatters formed a large segment of the landed yeomanry, and the Land Office specifically directed several programs toward encouraging them to warrant and patent their land.

The land lottery of 1735 was perhaps the first official program aimed at squatters.[3] Families who had "inadvertently" settled upon land to which they had no legal claim were given the opportunity to secure their land "at an easy rate." Tracts won in the lottery could be located "anywhere within the Province" except on manor land and land that had been improved by others.[4] Under these circumstances the presumptive settler could choose to obtain a warrant and be assured that his land would not be taken by others.

Because the lottery attracted few squatters, the proprietaries next attempted a program of coercion. The Land Office promised eviction for everyone who had not obtained a warrant or paid their purchase price by March 1739.[5] Again, however, through failure on the part of the proprietors to carry through, presumptive settlers did not comply with the threat in significant numbers.[6] Only when Indians complained about squatters upon land not yet sold to the proprietors did the Land Office take action. The episode at Burnt Cabins in 1750, when Richard Peters forcibly removed white settlers from the Juniata Valley, was a token effort to appease the Indians.

Lacking the resources or desire to remove the presumptive settler, the Land Office ultimately accepted the practice of ownership by settlement and improvement. The proprietaries devised a procedure known as the application system, which allowed all squatters within the purchases of 1754 and earlier to title land directly from a survey. Under the application system the survey was conducted after the application was submitted and before the purchase price was paid. The warrant was then prepared for the exact number of acres in the survey, and the entire purchase price was collected at once. Most presumptive settlers responded positively to the application system and warranted and patented their land. Exactly who these squatters were and where they were settled can be studied by reference to the East Side and West Side application registers.[7]

Presumptive settlers within the Purchase of 1768 were also treated to a version of the application system. Although relatively few squatters had settled on the frontier prior to the French and Indian War, the number increased dramatically as soon as active hostilities ceased. After the Purchase of 1768, settlers already there were given special preference before the region was opened to general settlement. Frontier traders and military officers were included, and the application system with a lottery variation was adapted to their needs. Presumptive settlers within the Purchase of 1768 can be studied by referring to the New Purchase register.

While special programs certainly assisted presumptive settlers, more was needed. For the first time in over twenty years the Board of Property convened as a body in 1765. The board began to give special consideration to presumptive settlers. In virtually every case of conflicting rights between squatter and absent warrantee, preference went to the individual who could demonstrate improvements to the land. These decisions cemented the foundation of the policy of ownership by settlement and improvement.

---

[1] 1 11 mo [January] 1725/6, Official Correspondence, 1, Penn Papers, HSP. Reprinted in *PMHB* 33 (1909): 347–52.

[2] *SmL* 2:159.

[3] See III.E.1.b, Lottery Land.

[4] A copy of the lottery advertisement is in Pat. Bk. A-7-224–26.

[5] Sur. Bk. B-23-157.

[6] Vacating warrants were prepared for a few tracts that squatters vacated. See, for example, Philadelphia County Warrants S-64 and S-127.

[7] See III.E.1.c, Settled Unwarranted Land.

Table 15. Research Aids: Speculators

Cohen, Norman. "William Allen: Chief Justice of Pennsylvania, 1704–1780." Ph.D. diss., University of California, Berkeley, 1966.

Guide to the Microfilm of the Baynton, Wharton, and Morgan Papers. Harrisburg, 1967.

Savelle, Max. *George Morgan: Colony Builder.* New York, 1932.

III.D.3. Speculators

Although Original Purchasers were the first land speculators in Pennsylvania, large-scale speculation did not flourish until the young Penns took over the province. During their administration, several individuals with strong proprietary connections became active speculators. Some began their business by buying up old rights that had not been claimed. Others purchased large amounts of proprietary manor land with an eye toward resale.

Foremost among the early speculators was William Allen. Philadelphia merchant and friend of the proprietors, Allen served as chief justice of the provincial supreme court from 1751 to 1774. He began to amass large amounts of land after inheriting his father's fortune in 1725. Allen invested a portion of his inheritance in the warrant rights to the ten thousand acres left to William Penn's grandson William Penn.[1] Allen bought other warrant rights from the Penn family, many in the years before 1733, but he continued to deal in land until the Revolution cut his activities short. In his land dealings, Allen favored tracts rich in iron ore and timber in order to support his mining and trading interests, but he also speculated heavily in tracts surrounding the city of Philadelphia. So well known was Allen to the Land Office that even as early as 1730 his papers were filed separately.[2] When the Land Office records were microfilmed after 1957, many of Allen's warrants, surveys, and returns of survey—totaling over 180—were filed with the original surveys, where they can be accessed through the Old Rights registers. One additional folder cited in the records below remains filed under Allen's name.

The papers of other active speculators who were proprietary friends were also filed separately by the Land Office. Among the speculators were Andrew Hamilton and Casper Wistar. A native of Germany, Wistar amassed a fortune as a brass button maker and invested much of his profits in land. Through loans to the Penn family he acquired such parcels as Fells Manor and many of the tracts involved in the lottery of 1735. Over 80 warrants, surveys, and returns of survey are recorded under his name in the Old Rights registers.

Governor Andrew Hamilton, another active speculator, dealt mainly in town tracts, purchasing many acres immediately north of Philadelphia in Springettsbury Manor. He also owned the tract on which the town of Lancaster was laid out, and only by virtue of his ownership was it not a proprietary town. Over 50 of Hamilton's warrants, returns, and surveys were filed separately and can be accessed through the Old Rights registers.

Speculators also dealt in land to protect their other business interests. John Baynton and Samuel Wharton, owners of a trading company formed about 1757, warranted many tracts of western land. Importing and exporting goods between foreign countries and the Indians and settlers on the western frontier, Baynton and Wharton needed to protect their trade routes through the province and so secured warrants to numerous tracts of land adjoining the Kittanning and Indian paths over which their wagon trains traveled. They took some of the warrants in their name and some in the names of others.[3] Failing to patent the tracts, Baynton and Wharton later lost them to the Commonwealth.[4] The Baynton and Wharton warrants are filed separately among the warrants and cited below.

RECORDS: LOOSE PAPERS

WILLIAM ALLEN'S PAPERS   LO micro.: 21.1.

A collection of several different accounts of Allen's landholdings.

WARRANTS   BAYNTON AND WHARTON   LO micro.: 3.7.

Contains one folder of forty warrants in the names of John Baynton and Samuel Wharton and four folders of eighty-four warrants in the names of other individuals. The collection can be accessed through a special index in the back of Warrant Register 14: Franklin, Fulton, Juniata, Mifflin, Perry, Snyder, Union [Counties].

---

[1]Sur. Bk. D-113-162; James Logan to John, Thomas, and Richard Penn, 17th 9br [November 1729], *PA* (2) 7:123.

[2]Papers in Office of Surveyor General—1730 Volume 155. See II.G.5, Returns of Survey.

[3]Warrants dated 1762–1765 were in the names of others, warrants dated 1766 were in John Baynton's and Samuel Wharton's names. A map of the Kittanning and Indian paths (Land Office Drawer 9, Item 21) shows Baynton and Wharton tracts. See the Land Office Map Inventory.

[4]*Guide to the Microfilm of the Baynton, Wharton, and Morgan Papers* (Harrisburg, 1967): 26.

III.E. Categories of Land

Policy changes under the proprietaries, especially the gradual acceptance of ownership by settlement and improvement, brought changes in the procedures for distributing land. These changes came about gradually; they were not initiated as part of a comprehensive plan but rather developed in reaction to events as they occurred. The results in turn modified the categories of land.

The Land Office began to think about land as either improved or unimproved. The new categories more accurately reflected the actual situation of land settlement. Unimproved land remained vacant before it was warranted and surveyed. Improved land was settled, cultivated, and then surveyed, purchased, and warranted.

Proprietary land continued as a separate category of land but took on a new dimension. The younger Penns made a better effort to reserve their allotted tenth. They surveyed sizable portions of the best land in each new purchase prior to opening the area to general sale. Imbued with greater business acuity than the first proprietor, William Penn's heirs also set aside the choice tracts in each new county for proprietary towns.

Eventually the Land Office handled country land according to the purchase in which it was located. To accommodate the large number of presumptive settlers who had simply squatted upon the land, the proprietors developed a special program called the application system. Although the application system went into effect in 1765, the program only applied to improved land within the purchases of 1754 and earlier, since no other land was legally available for settlement. Improved land within the Purchase of 1768 was later distributed under a modified application system.

To explain the changing land categories, this subsection categorizes land by purchase treaty and designates subcategories for the different distribution programs. Divided into two major parts, the subsection first discusses land within the purchases of 1754 and earlier and the programs for licensed land, lottery land, application system land, and vacant land. The second part of this subsection discusses land within the Purchase of 1768 and the programs for military tracts, gentlemen's tracts, and settlers' tracts.

III.E.1. Land within the Purchases of 1754 and Earlier

Anxious to encourage settlement in Pennsylvania, the young Penns and their land agents devised several new programs for distributing land. They first experimented with granting licenses to settle upon land not yet purchased from the Indians. They next devised a lottery scheme to sell the remaining land within the purchases of 1732 and earlier. Finding neither of these approaches satisfactory, John and Thomas Penn eventually gave official sanction to the practice of ownership by settlement and

improvement. By permitting tracts to be surveyed after they were settled, they enabled land to be distributed more rapidly.

III.E.1.a. Licensed Land

The practice of granting licenses to settle on land not purchased from the Indians created the first new category of country land. Licenses not only helped to keep track of settlers who went beyond the treaty line but also carried the promise that warrants would be granted as soon as the land was purchased from the Indians.

The idea of granting licenses was not entirely new with the young Penns. Before licenses were introduced, many immigrant groups received special sanction to settle near the frontier. As early as 1718 or 1719, James Logan permitted a group of Scots-Irish immigrants to settle together along the Susquehanna River in West Conestoga Township and on Chickasalunga Creek in what was then Chester County. Logan used the Scots-Irish as a barrier against any possible disturbance from the Marylanders or Indians and renamed the township Donegal in the settlers' honor. Although Logan granted warrants to a few of the Scots-Irish, many more settled without warrants.[1]

Governor William Keith also granted certain immigrants special permission to settle. Secretly he brought a group of Germans from Schoharie, New York, to the Tulpehocken Valley in 1723. They settled on a very good tract of land that had not been purchased from the Indians. By his own admission, Logan had connived at the surveying of the tract in 1722, presumably to hold it. He used part of the inheritance right of Letitia Penn Aubrey to justify the warrant.[2]

By 1727 immigration had reached such proportions that large groups who wanted to settle together were handled by being sent to the back parts of the province. No application to the commissioners of property or warrant to survey was required. Palatine Germans and Scots-Irish were particularly involved.[3]

Actual licenses, however, began with the settlement of a group of Germans and others on the west side of the lower Susquehanna River. The west side was then beyond the settlement line. Although a purchase treaty had been negotiated with the Delaware and Susquehanna

Whereas upon the Application of John & James Hendricks, & some others, Inhabitants of Pensilvania, the Comissioners of Property did in the Year 1728 order Samuel Blunston to lay out a Tract of Land of Twelve hundred Acres lying on the West Side of Susquehannah opposite to Hempfield; which Land was then settled by the said Parties, and is now in the Posession of the said John Hendricks and of Joshua Minshall, who holds in right of the said James Hendricks; and it appearing to me that the said John Hendricks & Joshua Minshall are settled upon the said Land by regular Surveys orderd to be made in the Year 1728 of which I approve and will order a Patent or Patents to be drawn for that share of the said Laid out to the said James Hendricks to John Hendricks & Joshua Minshall as soon as the Indian Claim thereon shall be satisfied on the same Terms other Lands in the County of Lancaster shall be granted ———

Philadelphia,
20. March 173⅔

License to settle granted by Thomas Penn on a Blunston survey. (Sur. Bk. D-113-181) tribes in 1718, the stronger Five Nations of the Iroquois Confederation still claimed title. Intruding Maryland claimants in the same area also presented a nagging problem to Pennsylvania settlers and officials. Thinking a copper-mine lay near the west bank of the Susquehanna, Governor Keith claimed proprietary prerogative and in 1722 issued orders to survey a tract for himself and a tract for a proprietary manor. Employing the unused land rights of Springett Penn, William Penn's grandson, Keith named the area Springettsbury Manor.[4] Controversy between Keith and the commissioners of property ensued, but by the late 1720s several German settlers had moved onto the manor.[5] Keith's survey of Springettsbury Manor was not recorded by the Land Office, but, when the land was secured by purchase from the Five Nations in 1736, Thomas Penn signed licenses dated October 30, 1736, confirming occupancy by the settlers. A record of the Springettsbury licenses is cited below.

In spite of Pennsylvania settlements on the west side of the Susquehanna River, Maryland encroachments continued. To protect Pennsylvania's territorial interests, proprietary officials lent their formal support to German settlers who wanted to cross the Susquehanna River. Defiantly and openly they broke with the established Penn policy of first buying the land from the Indians. Knowing that the west side of the Susquehanna soon would be released by the Indians, the proprietors granted Samuel Blunston a commission to issue "licenses to settle."[6] Blunston, a trained surveyor and deputy register for Lancaster County, had been an active correspondent with Thomas Penn. Many of Blunston's letters dealing with the licensing issue can be found in TPP. Blunston Licenses, dated between January 24, 1734, and October 31, 1737, were granted to both new and older residents in the troubled region. Settlement and improvement would give the licensees first rights to warrants when the territory was officially purchased from the Indians.

The Blunston Licenses resembled warrants in many respects and contained essentially the same information: the settler's name, desired acreage, and location. Like warrants they carried more weight than applications and were always upheld in courts of law. Granted to adventurers, however, the great majority of Blunston Licenses were held by men who did not remain to warrant their land.[7] Since the licensee was not required

to make a down payment on the purchase price before the license was issued, he had nothing to lose in moving on. A record of the Blunston Licenses is cited below.

The policy of granting licenses or certificates to settle was also applied in other situations. In particular, licenses were granted to traders who assisted in the military occupation of the frontier and in securing the western fur trade. Apparently certain deputy surveyors were granted powers to give licenses or certificates to settlers to locate along the major roads or Indian paths.[8] Examples of this practice can be found among the gentlemen's tracts applications in the East Side Applications register. In all cases where settlement occurred by license, regular warrants could not be granted until the land had been purchased from the Indians. Essentially licenses or certificates to settle were the forerunners of the application system.

To locate a warrant issued on the basis of a license or certificate, consult the warrant register of the county with jurisdiction at the time. For example, most of the warrants issued on Blunston Licenses will be found in the Lancaster County warrant register. Lancaster County had jurisdiction on the west side of the Susquehanna River until 1749, thirteen years after the last Blunston Licenses were issued.

Table 16. Research Aids: Licenses to Settle

Bair, Robert C. "Early Developments and Surveys West of Susquehanna River in York County, Pennsylvania." Pennsylvania Department of Internal Affairs *Annual Report of the Secretary of Internal Affairs* (1906): A.61–A.199.

Donehoo, George P. A *History of the Cumberland Valley.* 2 vols. Harrisburg, 1930. See 1:39–72.

Flower, Lenore Embick. *Blunston Licenses and Their Background.* Carlisle, PA, 1961.

Kain, William H. "The Penn Manorial System and the Manors of Springettsbury and Maske," *Pa. Hist.* 10 (1943): 225–42.

Prowell, George R. *History of York County Pennsylvania.* 2 vols. Chicago, 1907. 1:19–35.

Rupp, I. D. A *Collection of 30,000 Names of Immigrants in Pennsylvania.* Philadelphia, 1875.

RECORDS: LOOSE PAPERS

WARRANTS   YORK COUNTY   SPRINGETTSBURY MANOR   LO micro.: 3.156.

One folder containing a certificate listing names of settlers in the manor of Springettsbury to whom the Commonwealth granted warrants after 1800.

A RECORD OF LICENSES GRANTED TO SUNDRY PERSONS TO SETTLE & TAKE UP LAND ON THE WEST SIDE OF SUSQUEHANNA RIVER   (Proprietary Papers, folder 12; with index; for photocopy and hand copy see Land Office Map Inventory)   LO micro.: 23.1.

Contains two lists: 1) a handwritten chronological list of settlers who obtained licenses after they had settled within Springettsbury Manor; and 2) a list of licenses to settle granted by Samuel Blunston, which gives the date, name, acreage, and location.

---

[1]"Terms For Ye Donnegallians," Thomas Penn to James Logan, Philadelphia, 23d Jany, 1733, PA (2) 7:172–73; "Letter of Instructions of James Logan to James Steel, 1727," PMHB 24 (1900): 495.

[2]Logan to John, Thomas, and Richard Penn, 17th 9br [November], 1729, PA (2) 7:129–32.

[3]Min. Prov. Coun., Sep't. 14, 1727; CR 3:282.

[4]Robert C. Bair, "Early Developments and Surveys West of Susquehanna," Pennsylvania Department of Internal Affairs Annual Report of the Secretary of Internal Affairs (1906): A.86; Sur. Bk. D-113-125.

[5]Sur. Bks. D-113-176, B-23-231; Min. Com. Prop. Bk. I, 16th day of ye 2d mo. [April], anno 1722.

[6]Thomas Penn to Samuel Blunston, August 8, 1734, roll 4, frames 708–10, TPP.

[7]Min. Bd. Prop. Bk. 1, Oct. 27, 1766, PA (3) 1:155–56.

[8]Ibid., March 20, 1766, PA (3) 1:121.

III.E.1.b. Lottery Land

The lottery scheme of 1735 created the second new category of country land and distinctly placed the young proprietors' stamp upon land distribution in Pennsylvania. Deviating from all previous procedures, this scheme was used to encourage the sale of vacant land within the existing counties of Bucks, Chester, Philadelphia, and Lancaster. Much of the land designated for the lottery was swampy or barren and not suitable for cultivation, but the proprietors were anxious to sell as much land as possible within the older areas before negotiating another purchase treaty and opening a new area to settlement.

Although a 1730 act of the Provincial Assembly prohibited both public and private lotteries, legal clarification permitted the young Penns to proceed with the "Scheme of a Lottery."[1] To help the scheme succeed, proprietary agents closed the Land Office so that no warrants to survey could be issued while the lottery was being offered.

Advertisements for the lottery appeared as broadsides and in newspapers. They announced the special sale of one hundred thousand acres of land and used a twofold rationale for the "adventure": 1) the settlement of lands would bring increased income and trade to the province, and 2) families who had inadvertently settled on property to which they had no legal claim could secure their lands "at an easy rate."[2] The latter point seems to be the first open recognition of ownership by settlement and improvement.

The lottery proposed to sell 7,750 tickets at forty shillings each. If all tickets had been purchased, the income would have covered the normal cost of the one hundred thousand acres as if the land had sold at the going rate of fifteen pounds ten shillings per one hundred acres. A portion of the tickets drawn, numbering 1,293, was worth tracts ranging in size from twenty-five to three thousand acres. The remaining 6,457 tickets were worth no land. To encourage purchasers, the quitrent on Lottery Land was reduced from the going rate of one halfpenny

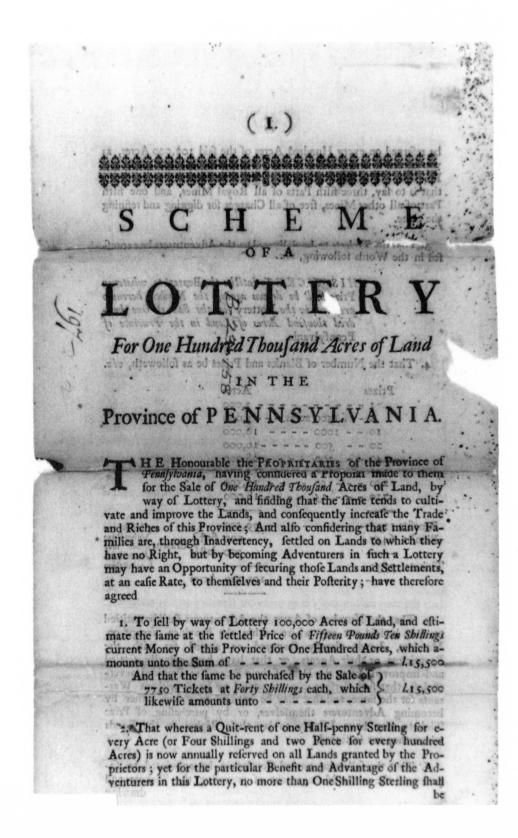

(I.)

SCHEME
OF A
LOTTERY
For One Hundred Thousand Acres of Land
IN THE
Province of PENNSYLVANIA.

THE Honourable the PROPRIETARIES of the Province of *Pennsylvania*, having considered a Proposal made to them for the Sale of *One Hundred Thousand* Acres of Land, by way of Lottery, and finding that the same tends to cultivate and improve the Lands, and consequently increase the Trade and Riches of this Province; And also considering that many Families are, through Inadvertency, settled on Lands to which they have no Right, but by becoming Adventurers in such a Lottery may have an Opportunity of securing those Lands and Settlements, at an easie Rate, to themselves and their Posterity; have therefore agreed

1. To sell by way of Lottery 100,000 Acres of Land, and estimate the same at the settled Price of *Fifteen Pounds Ten Shillings* current Money of this Province for One Hundred Acres, which amounts unto the Sum of - - - - - - - - - - *l.*15,500

And that the same be purchased by the Sale of 7750 Tickets at *Forty Shillings* each, which likewise amounts unto - - - - - - - } *l.*15,500

2. That whereas a Quit-rent of one Half-penny Sterling for every Acre (or Four Shillings and two Pence for every hundred Acres) is now annually reserved on all Lands granted by the Proprietors; yet for the particular Benefit and Advantage of the Adventurers in this Lottery, no more than One Shilling Sterling shall be

Announcement of the land lottery of 1735. (Sur. Bk. B-23-158)

Table 17. Research Aids: Lottery Land

Weiss, Ward E. "Lotteries and Lottery Land in Pennsylvania." Bucks County Genealogical Society *Newsletter* 3 (Summer 1984): 33–35.

———. "The 1735 Land Lottery in Pennsylvania." 1988. Unpublished paper in author's possession.

sterling (amounting to four shillings two pence per one hundred acres) to the original rate of one shilling sterling per one hundred acres. Tracts won could be located anywhere within the province except on manor land, land improved by others, and land that had not been released by the Indians.[3]

The requisite number of lottery tickets was never sold, and there is no record that the lottery was ever drawn. An unknown number of tickets became the basis for a limited number of land sales, however. A manuscript volume in the Land Office titled "Abstract of Lists of Warrants for the Province and Counties," cited in the records below, includes an entry dated August 20, 1741, which indicates that 16,851 acres had been sold and warranted as Lottery Land, a far cry from the 100,000 acres that the proprietors wanted to sell. The warranted Lottery Land lay primarily in Bucks County, although small amounts were also claimed in Lancaster, Chester, and Philadelphia counties. As late as 1770, lottery tickets were still being used to secure land in Pennsylvania.

Land claimed under the 1735 lottery scheme can be identified by the statement to that effect in the original warrant or survey. These records can be located through the regular warrant registers, but the registers will not mention the lottery scheme. Each record must be checked individually.

RECORDS: LOOSE PAPERS

ABSTRACT OF LISTS OF WARRANTS FOR THE PROVINCE AND COUNTIES.

A collection of reports for the years 1706–1740, with an addendum for 1756. See Land Office Map Inventory.

MISCELLANEOUS PAPERS   BOX 36 NUMBER 14   LO micro.: 24.25.

Contains miscellaneous manuscript papers pertaining to the 1735 land lottery.

---

[1]*Statutes* 4:143–44.
[2]A copy of the lottery advertisement appears in Pat. Bk. A-7-224–26.
[3]Ibid.

III.E.1.c. Settled Unwarranted Land

Land claimed by settlement and improvement created the third new category of country land. Legally recognizing this method of obtaining land was another way in which the young Penns deviated from their predecessor's plan of settlement. Proprietary land officers developed new procedures aimed solely at encouraging settlers to warrant land they had already settled and improved. Called the application system, the new procedures marked the final acknowledgment that the practice of ownership by settlement and improvement had become a proprietary policy.

By the early 1760s the assumption that all unwarranted country land within the purchases of 1754 and earlier was vacant and unimproved had given way to the realization that thousands of squatters were settled upon the land. Admitting that it had lost track of the amount of occupied land, the Land Office was forced to develop new procedures. One of the main goals was to increase the Penn family's annual income by collecting the large number of outstanding quitrents.

The new procedures introduced a formal application as the required starting document in the patenting process. Because the application stated the location of the land, by common use the document tended to be called a location. The new procedures also introduced a new type of warrant, called a warrant to accept. This was granted after the survey was conducted. The object was to accelerate the patenting process by going directly from an application to a survey. The warrant to accept was drawn only after the occupant paid for his land and produced a certified statement of his date of settlement so that interest in arrears could be collected.

The procedures and regulations of the application system were announced to the public on June 17, 1765. The applicant was to appear in person at the Land Office in Philadelphia, where his name, the date of application, and the description of the land were entered in a special application book set aside for that purpose. To curb speculation, each applicant was limited to a maximum of three hundred acres. At the end of each day or week, depending upon the number of applications, the secretary of the Land Office sent copies of the applications to the surveyor general. The surveyor general registered the receipt of the copies in his application book and sent the copies directly to a deputy surveyor with orders to survey. The survey was to be completed within six months and a drawing showing courses, distances, and adjoining owners returned to the surveyor general. The applicant had another six months to produce a certified statement of his settlement date and the nature of his improvement and to pay the receiver general for the land. The rate was five pounds sterling or the equivalent in Pennsylvania money per one hundred acres and one penny sterling per acre quitrent per year. After payment was received, a warrant was sent to the surveyor general telling him to accept the survey and to send a return of survey to the secretary's office. The secretary made out the patent from the return of survey form.

To avoid an overload in the Land Office, the new application system was first used for settled unwarranted land on the east side of the Susquehanna River. Begun in 1765, this was called the East Side Application program. The following year, 1766, the application system was extended to the west side of the Susquehanna River and was there called the West Side Application program.

III.E.1.c(1) East Side Applications

The application system was first used to title settled unwarranted land on the east side of the Susquehanna River within the purchases of 1754 (as corrected in 1758) and earlier. All land applied for was to lie east of the Susquehanna River and south of a line drawn between Mahanoy Creek and Lackawaxen Creek. The resulting records are collectively called East Side Applications. The program was in effect from August 5, 1765, through September 6, 1769. During that time, 4,160 applications were recorded.

Examination of the records shows that the Land Office followed the application system procedures described above quite faithfully. The secretary received the application, usually on a small piece of paper, entered a copy in a special book set aside for East Side Applications, and filed the loose piece of paper in his office. The applicant paid no purchase money at this time. The secretary prepared a certified copy of the application and either gave the copy to the applicant to carry to the surveyor general or sent it with a batch at the end of the week. The surveyor general certified the receipt of the applications and entered them in a book. Thus, there are two original East Side Application books, one from the secretary's office and the other from the surveyor general's office, and one set of original loose applications. These books and records are cited below.

A former receiver general, Lynford Lardner, was the first East Side applicant. He submitted three applications for a total of 250 acres and so set the precedent for one of the most serious problems with the application system: splitting one settled tract into two or more portions. The tract with the buildings became the improved portion to be purchased with interest and quitrent from the date of settlement, and the remaining land was taken as vacant, hence with no retroactive fees.

East Side Applications could be taken out for settled unwarranted land in any of the seven Pennsylvania counties in existence on the east side of the Susquehanna River. However, the majority of applications were for land in the

Warrant to accept a survey on East Side Application no. 2078, Berks County. (Berks County Wt. N-7)

northwestern areas of Berks and Northampton counties.

East Side applicants are listed in the East Side Applications register. If the applicant completed a survey and paid for his land, and a warrant to accept was completed in his name, he will also be listed in the warrant register of the county of jurisdiction at the date of the warrant. The warrant could be dated several years after the application date; consequently the county of jurisdiction might have changed. If someone else paid for the land, the warrant to accept was completed in that individual's name, and he is listed in the warrant register as the warrantee.

Care must be taken in searching for East Side applicants because the East Side Applications register translates the location of the applications into their present-day counties and townships.

RECORDS: LOOSE PAPERS

APPLICATIONS FOR WARRANT   [East Side]   LO micro.: 7.10–20.

The loose, original East Side Application papers date between August 5, 1765, and September 6, 1769, and are interfiled with the regular applications for the same period. Some are labeled "ES" for East Side and numbered. Applications are filed chronologically and then by the first letter of the last name.

RECORDS: BOUND VOLUMES

EAST SIDE APPLICATIONS   LO micro.: 1.8.

Prepared in 1949 and in current use. Several indexes are contained in this volume: 1) alphabetical by the first letter of the last name and then grouped by the first vowel, for example, Aa, Ae, Ai, Ao, Au; 2) alphabetical within current counties, for example, Berks, Bucks, Carbon, Chester, Dauphin, Lancaster, Lebanon, Lehigh, Monroe, Montgomery, Northampton, Northumberland, Pike, Schuylkill, Wayne; 3) alphabetical within townships of current counties; and 4) alphabetical within the township, citing copied survey volume, book, and page. Following the indexes, the register contains the complete abstract of the 4,160 East Side Applications, giving information under the categories of date, application number, acres, copied survey volume, description, township, and county. The end of the register contains a complete alphabetical listing of names with application numbers.

EAST SIDE OF SUSQUEHANNA APPLICATION BOOK   (Binding No. 63)   LO micro.: 25.30–31.

Notations in red seem to indicate that this was the register used by the Land Office staff before the 1949 version was prepared. Categories listed are date, number, name, acres, and description. All 4,160 applications and a few additional applications numbered as half numbers are included.

APPLICATION BOOK   1765–1768   EAST SIDE NO. 1   (Binding No. 108)   LO micro.: 25.117.

Appears to be the secretary's East Side Application book. The first two pages are missing. The volume is arranged in columns for the following categories: the number of the application, name, acres, and description including the township and county. On every few pages a notation occurs that the previous applications were copied and sent to the surveyor general's office. The last date for this volume is July 29, 1768, application number 3,499.

APPLICATION FOR SURVEY EAST [Side] NO. 2   1768–1769   (Binding No. 109)   LO micro.: 25.117.

A continuation of Binding No. 108 above. The first entry is application number 3,500, August 1, 1768; the last entry is number 4,160, September 6, 1769. Volumes 108 and 109 therefore comprise a complete set of East Side Applications.

APPLICATION BOOK   1765–1766   EAST SIDE   (Binding No. 107)   LO micro.: 25.117.

The distinctive feature of this volume is the sealed and certified statements by the secretary every few pages that the contents are true transcripts of entries for applications, accompanied by the surveyor general's statement that he has received all his fees up to the given date. Entries are for applications number 1 through number 2,240 only.

APPLICATIONS   EAST SIDE   1765–1766   (Binding No. 105)   LO micro.: 25.117.

An incomplete volume that is a register of applications received by John Lukens, surveyor general. The contents give incomplete information for applications number 1 through number 1,644, dated June 8, 1766. Categories listed are as follows: number of the application, quantity, "applyer's name," date, survey received, returned, acres, and perches.

INDEX A–Z   NOS. 1 TO 3267   EAST SIDE APPLICATIONS   (Binding No. 131).

Contains an alphabetical listing of applicants by the first letter of the last name and then grouped by the first vowel (for example, Aa, Ae, Ai, Ao, Au) and gives the application number only. Incomplete.

INDEX TO EAST SIDE APPLICATIONS   (Binding No. 106)   LO micro.: 25.117.

A complete listing of the 4,160 applications, arranged alphabetically by the first letter of the last name and then grouped by the first vowel.

EAST SIDE APPLICATIONS REGISTER   1765–1769   RG-17.

An earlier set of registers. Volume 1 is organized alphabetically by last name, and volume 2 is organized by application number.

III.E.1.c(2)   West Side Applications

Applications for settled unwarranted land on the west side of the Susquehanna River within the purchases of 1754 (as adjusted in 1758) and earlier were accepted beginning August 1, 1766. All land applied for was to lie west of the Susquehanna River, east of the Allegheny Mountain range, and south of the West Branch of the Susquehanna River. Settlers who had built and resided within this area could apply for the land they had improved.

Procedures for the West Side Application program were the same as those for the East Side Application program. Applicants were required to show proof of the nature of their improvement and the date of first settlement. Interest and quitrents were figured from that date.

Surveying more land than was requested on the application was common. Many warrants to accept issued during 1766 and the first quarter of 1767 reveal surveys for two or three times as much land as the application requested. An effort to prevent the surveying of excess land led to new regulations limiting the overplus survey to 10 percent. These regulations were often dispensed with, however, when adjoining owners were not affected.

During the three-year period when West Side Applications were accepted, from August 1766 to August 1769, a total of 5,595 applications were recorded. If the usual allowance of 300 acres had been surveyed on each application, a total of 1,678,500 acres could have been warranted.

West Side applicants are listed in the West Side Applications register. If the applicant completed a survey and paid for his land, and a warrant to accept was completed on his behalf, his name will also be listed in the warrant register of the county of jurisdiction at the date of the warrant. The warrant, being a warrant to accept, could be dated several years after the application date; consequently the county of jurisdiction might have changed. If someone else paid for the land, the warrant to accept was completed in that individual's name, and his name is listed in the warrant register as the warrantee.

RECORDS: LOOSE PAPERS

APPLICATIONS FOR WARRANT   [West Side]   LO micro.: 7.11–20.

The loose, original West Side Application papers are interfiled with the regular applications for the same time period. Some are labeled "WS" for West Side and numbered. Applications are filed by date and then by the first letter of the last name.

RECORDS: BOUND VOLUMES

WEST SIDE APPLICATIONS   1766–1769   (With index)   LO micro.: 1.8–9.

The current register in use and the one from which the microfilm was prepared. The contents give the date, application number, applicant's name, acreage, copied survey number, and description or location of the land. The county and township have been added to most of the entries. The index giving the applicant's name and number must be used.

WEST SIDE APPLICATIONS REGISTER   1766–1769.

A register formerly in use.

WEST SIDE APPLICATIONS   (Binding No. 64).

The inside title of this volume states that it is "The Book of Entries of the Applications taken in the Office for Vacant Land on the West Side of Susquehanna River. . . ." The volume is a complete book of all 5,595 West Side Applications, giving for each the following: date, number, to whom granted, quantity, and situation. The volume appears to be too neat to be the original application book, but the entries are in several different handwritings.

APPLICATION BOOK 1767–1769   WEST SIDE   (Binding No. 110; with index)   LO micro.: 25.117.

The first application in this volume is number 3,037, dated March 1, 1767. The entries continue through number 5,595, the last West Side Application. This is then the second half of a set of two volumes, but the first volume is missing. For each application the following information is given: date, number, name of applicant, acres, and situation. A certified statement entered at the end of every week or two indicates that a batch of applications had been sent to the surveyor general.

III.E.1.d. Vacant Unwarranted Land

Vacant unwarranted land was the fourth category of country land within the purchases of 1754 and earlier. The only category of land that was not new, vacant unwarranted land was the same as William Penn's country land. The same procedures used to transfer country land to private ownership under Penn's proprietorship were used to transfer vacant unwarranted land. Before 1765 four main documents were involved: the warrant, survey, return of survey, and patent. A fifth document, the application for the warrant, gradually came into use and after 1765 was required.

Vacant unwarranted land was available in every county formed out of the purchases of 1754 and earlier: Bucks, Chester, Philadelphia, Lancaster, York, Cumberland, Berks, Northampton, and Bedford. Settlers with sufficient funds to protect their investments usually selected their land before settlement, submitted an application, received a warrant to survey, and surveyed and patented their land.

Even during and after the East Side and West Side application programs, vacant unwarranted country land was available. The identifying element was the type of warrant. Settlers who obtained warrants for vacant unwarranted land received warrants to survey. Information concerning the amount of vacant country land warranted in each county between 1733 and 1776 can be found by consulting the regular warrant registers. For example, about 50 percent of the warrants granted in Cumberland County between 1770 and 1776 were for vacant unwarranted land identifiable by the warrant to survey.

The sources for locating settlers who purchased vacant unwarranted land are the basic records discussed in III.G, Records. The warrant register of the county of jurisdiction at the time the warrant was granted is the starting point and serves as a master index for locating warrants, surveys, returns of survey, and patents. Applications may be located by date, usually the same date as the warrant. If the patentee is known, the patent index will provide warrant and survey information.

III.E.2. Land within the Purchase of 1768

A new purchase of land from the Indians and the last by the Pennsylvania proprietary government was negotiated in the fall of 1768. Creating a broad diagonal strip of land from northeast to southwest across the colony, the purchase extended the lands legally open to settlement. The new settlement boundaries became the West Branch of the Susquehanna River, the Ohio and Allegheny rivers, and the western limits of the province. The boundary line began at Owego on the Susquehanna River in present New York

State, followed the east side of the Susquehanna River to Towanda Creek, ran up Towanda Creek to its headwaters, then went along Burnett's Hills to the headwaters of Pine Creek, and ran down Pine Creek to the West Branch of the Susquehanna River. From there the boundary ran along the West Branch of the Susquehanna River to the forks closest to the shortest straight overland route to Kittanning on the Allegheny River and down the Allegheny River to the western boundary of the province (see the Genealogical Map of the Counties, front.).

Frequently called the New Purchase, the Purchase of 1768 occurred shortly after the end of the French and Indian War. Negotiated partly to legitimize established settlements in the west, the purchase treaty was part of a broader agreement with the Indians reached at Fort Stanwix (Rome, New York). The proprietors' interest in the treaty signaled their interest in populating the province. The $10,000 that Thomas and Richard Penn paid for the New Purchase seemed to be a good investment.[1] They could open western land to permanent settlements that would be located nearer to the Indian trade in the Illinois Territory. They could also establish buffer settlements along the Susquehanna River to prevent the Connecticut settlers of the Susquehanna Company from moving farther west.[2]

The purchase treaty of 1768 was originally recorded in New York State. Later, in 1781, a copy was entered in the Rolls Office in Philadelphia, in Philadelphia County Deed Book D-3, p. 23. Another copy was entered in Lancaster County Deed Book U, p. 68, because one of the provisions conveyed Conestoga Indian land in Lancaster County to the proprietors.

---

[1]John Penn, their brother, died in 1746.
[2]See IV.D.3, Connecticut Claimants.

III.E.2.a. Settled Unwarranted Land (New Purchase Applications)

Before opening land within the Purchase of 1768 to regular settlers, proprietary officials planned to accomplish two important objectives. The first objective entailed planting a buffer settlement at the forks of the Susquehanna River. Composed of zealous Pennsylvanians, this settlement was designed to prevent the westward spread of Connecticut colonists of the

Table 18. Research Aids: Pennsylvania Maps, Purchase of 1768

Gant, John C. *Map of the Frontiers of the Northern Colonies with the Boundary Line established Between them and the Indians at the Treaty held by S. Will Johnson at Ft Stanwix in Novr 1768.* Albany, 1768. In *PA* (3) Appendix 1-10.

Scull, William. *Map of the Province of Pennsylvania.* Philadelphia, 1770. In *PA* (3) Appendix 1-10.

Susquehanna Company.[1] The second objective entailed recognizing the claims of squatters who were already settled within the newly purchased area. These plans produced three distinct subcategories of land within the Purchase of 1768: 1) officers' tracts, 2) gentlemen's tracts, and 3) settlers' tracts.

To accomplish their objectives, the land officers used a modification of the application system for the initial disbursement of land within the Purchase of 1768. For five months in 1769, settlers already on the land could participate in a lottery to determine the priority rating of their application. But, before the Land Office was willing to accept applications from settlers already on the land, the proprietors made special grants to military and civilian personnel who had assisted in the recent war against the French and their Indian allies.

---

[1]John Lukens to Thomas Penn, February 21, 1769, General Correspondence of the Land Office, 1713–1771, reel 3982, PSA; Edmund Physick to Thomas Penn, February 4, 1769, Penn-Physick Mss 3:5. Also in roll 9, frames 602–4, *TPP.*.

III.E.2.a(1) Officers' Tracts

Anxious for a settlement at the forks of the Susquehanna River as an impediment to Connecticut settlers of the Susquehanna Company, the proprietors encouraged a group of officers who had served in the French and Indian War to apply for a special application for land.[1] Leading the group was Colonel Turbott Francis, the brother-in-law of James Tilghman, secretary of the Land Office and secretary to the Board of Property. The group itself was composed of officers who had served under Colonel Henry Bouquet in the First and Second Battalions of the Pennsylvania Regiment of 1764. Expressing an interest in forming an estate in Pennsylvania, Bouquet might have planted the idea of a special settlement in the minds of his men. He had hoped to secure a grant for as much as 100,000 acres in the New Purchase as soon as the land was available.[2]

The officers' special application was submitted and approved on February 3, 1769, several months before the Land Office was officially open to accept applications.[3] Their grant for 24,000 acres was to be laid out in not less than three 8,000-acre contiguous segments. Application number 1 in the New Purchase 1768 register covers the twenty-six officers who were involved and lists their names, amounts of land, and tract locations.[4] Several officers took more than one tract. Agreeing to settle a family on each 300 acres within two years from the time of survey and to pay five pounds sterling per 100 acres and one penny sterling quitrent, the officers were granted the same terms as all other settlers within the New Purchase.[5]

Surveys for the officers' tracts took place before the Land Office accepted applications from new settlers. One of the three 8,000-acre segments was located along the south side of the West Branch of the Susquehanna River near Bald Eagle Creek. At the time it was surveyed, it was in the jurisdiction of Cumberland and Berks counties; but, by the time warrants to accept were prepared, the tract was in Northumberland County. A copy of the original survey can be found in Survey Book BB-1-2.

---

[1]Thomas Penn to James Tilghman, January 31, 1769, Letter Book 9:324–27, roll 3, *TPP.*

[2]Henry Bouquet to Captain Rudolph Bentinck, April 29, 1765, U.S. Army Military History Institute, Carlisle, PA. Also in Louis M. Waddell, ed., *The Papers of Henry Bouquet,* vol. 6, forthcoming.

[3]For the original application see Muster Rolls, LO micro.: 21.2.

[4]Colonel Asher Clayton's claim was disallowed. See New Purchase register.

[5]Min. Bd. Prop. Bk. 1:163.

III.E.2.a(2) Gentlemen's Tracts

A second group of French and Indian War officers from Pennsylvania regiments of the years

1756–1760 also received special consideration for New Purchase lands. To distinguish them from Colonel Francis and the officers of 1764, the Land Office called these officers of earlier years gentlemen. On February 22, 1769, just two weeks after the officers' grant, the gentlemen received permission to take up a maximum of eighty thousand acres within the Purchase of 1768 under the same conditions as the officers'.[1]

Forty-five gentlemen were involved in this scheme, and their applications are numbered 2 through 46 in the New Purchase register. Many of the applications, as with the other officers, were for tracts at the forks of the Susquehanna River. James Tilghman, the secretary of the Land Office, was among the applicants. He received five thousand acres on the West Branch of the Susquehanna River within the area also claimed by the Susquehanna Company. Tilghman's land was to be surveyed "next after the officers are served."[2] Other applications were submitted on behalf of men who had been settled in the far western part of the province for many years before the Purchase of 1768. The last several gentlemen's applications were granted to men such as Andrew Byerly of Bushy Run, who had received licenses from the commander in chief at Fort Pitt to settle along Braddock's Road as a sort of peacekeeping force.

Surveys of the gentlemen's tracts also were made before the Land Office opened the area to regular settlers. According to Edmund Physick, receiver general, the gentlemen rushed the surveyors from town in order to make the surveys and took the precaution of employing other persons to go along to assist in finding the best land possible.[3]

---

[1]Min. Bd. Prop. Bk. 1:164–65.
[2]*Susq. Co. Papers* 3:xvi.
[3]Penn-Physick Mss 3:9–13.

III.E.2.a(3) Settlers' Tracts

Under the guise of permitting the "back inhabitants . . . sufficient time to bring in their Applications," the Land Office did not accept settlers' applications to take up land in the Purchase of 1768 until April 3, 1769.[1] The people were "exceedingly exasperated," wrote Edmund

Physick. He thought that the gentlemen's grants had brought "unhappy effects" on the affairs of Thomas Penn.[2] Even before settlers' applications were accepted, back inhabitants petitioned Governor John Penn, Richard Penn's son, in protest about the amount of land in the New Purchase taken up by officers and other private gentlemen.[3] Some presumptive settlers filed caveats against officers who surveyed tracts overlapping earlier improvements. The main question was one of priority: Were surveys to be made on settlers' improvements first or for those who drew earlier numbers in the lottery?

Settlers' applications were numbered independently, beginning over again with number 1. Due to the large number anticipated, a lottery scheme was used in determining priority. When the applications were received, they were placed in a box, mixed together, drawn out, and numbered in the order they were drawn.[4] Drawings took place every day or every other day from April 3 through September 5, 1769. The first 2,802 applications were drawn and dated April 3.

Records and procedures were in keeping with the method used for the sale of settled improved land. Each applicant was limited to three hundred acres at a cost of five pounds sterling per one hundred acres. No purchase money was required when the application was submitted, but the entire amount was to be paid within a year after the survey. Since the survey was conducted on the authority of the application, a warrant to accept was prepared after the surveyor general sent the return of survey document to the secretary. Interest and quitrent accrued from the date of the return of survey, which was to be within six months of the application date. The patent was issued after the entire purchase price was paid. Thus the usual document series on a New Purchase application was application, survey, return of survey, and patent.

New Purchase applicants usually did not complete the patenting process. Many did not even bother with a survey. The requirement to pay for the land within one year of the survey was not enforced, and so there seemed to be no good reason to continue the patenting process and obtain a warrant to accept and a patent. The application system thus contributed to the large amount of settled and improved but unwarranted and unpatented land inherited by the

Warrant to accept a survey on a New Purchase 1768 Application, Bedford County. (Bedford County Wt. B-29)

Commonwealth government years later. For a discussion of how this problem was handled see IV.E.1.a, Land Granted by the Proprietary Government.

New Purchase applications are listed in the New Purchase register. In all they number 3,853 and date mainly between April 3 and September 5, 1769, although a few are dated as late as 1773. The original applications, written on small pieces of paper, are filed under Applications, New Purchase.

If the applicant completed a survey and paid for his land, and a warrant to accept was completed in his name, he also will be listed in the warrant register of the county of jurisdiction at the date of the warrant. The warrant could be dated several years after the date of the application; consequently the county of jurisdiction might have changed. If someone else paid for the land, a warrant to accept was completed in the new owner's name, and that person will be listed in the warrant register as the warrantee.

RECORDS: LOOSE PAPERS

NEW PURCHASE APPLICATIONS   LO micro.: 7.1–4.

Each original application is written individually on a small piece of paper and filed in chronological order in a series of folders. The applications are copied verbatim in the New Purchase register.

RECORDS: BOUND VOLUMES

NEW PURCHASE—1769   (With indexes)   LO micro.: 1.9.

The most recent register of New Purchase applications. Entries are in numerical order and give the following information: the date of the application; number of the application; name of the applicant; acres; description of the location; survey volume, book, and page; and current location. The volume includes indexes by county and township and an alphabetical index by name.

NEW PURCHASE REGISTER, 1769.

An earlier version of the volume above.

APPLICATIONS FOR SURVEY   LAST PURCHASE   1769–1773   NOS. 1–3849   (Binding No. 113)   LO micro.: 25.118.

The inside title reads "The Book of Entries of Applications taken in the Land Office." The term Last Purchase in the title refers to the most recent purchase made by the proprietaries, this being the Purchase of 1768. Information entered gives the application date, application number, applicant's name, acres applied for, and location.

INDEX OF NEW PURCHASE REGISTER   (Proprietary Papers, folder 6, item 1)   LO micro.: 23.1.

A complete index to the bound volume Applications for Survey Last Purchase 1769–1773 Nos. 1–3849 (cited above). It is arranged alphabetically by the first letter of the last name and then grouped by the first vowel.

INDEX TO NEW PURCHASE APPLICATIONS   (Binding No. 111)   LO micro.: 25.117.

Applicants' names are grouped by the first letter of the last name, and the only information cited is the application number.

APPLICATIONS   NEW PURCHASE   NOS 1–3683   (Binding No. 112)   LO micro.: 25.118.

A book prepared in the secretary's office. It includes a copy of the printed advertisement and statements with the Land Office seal affixed referring to the periodic transmittal of the applications to the surveyor general. The information in columnar form gives the date received, application number, applicant's name, and acres requested. Notations entered at a later date indicate return of survey or warrant to another individual.

[1]Min. Bd. Prop., *PA* (3) 1:255.
[2]Penn-Physick Mss 3:29–37.
[3]Ibid., 18.
[4]Ibid., 9–13.

III.E.2.b. Vacant Unwarranted Land

Vacant unwarranted land within the Purchase of 1768 continued to be transferred to private ownership using procedures similar to those of William Penn's proprietorship. The significant differences between his administration and that of his heirs were the requirements that an application be submitted as a formal document and that the purchase price be paid in full at the time of application. The warrant to survey became the second document in the series of records necessary to title land and indicated that the tract had not been settled by the applicant prior to the warrant date.

Although the Purchase of 1768 covered a vast territory running diagonally across the state from northeast to southwest, no new counties were formed immediately. As a result of the purchase, Cumberland County extended its jurisdiction to the western border of the province; Northampton County, to the northern border; and Berks County, to a strip of land situated between the two. After three years the new territory was divided into its own counties: Bedford in 1771, Northumberland in 1772, and Westmoreland in 1773. No other counties were formed during the Penns' administration. Thus all vacant unimproved land transferred from proprietary to private ownership within the Purchase of 1768 will be found in the warrant registers for Cumberland, Berks, Northampton, Bedford, Northumberland, or Westmoreland counties.

III.E.3. Proprietary Land

When John, Thomas, and Richard Penn became the proprietors of Pennsylvania, they expected to follow their father's practice of appropriating proprietary land for themselves and leasing it for steady, long-term income. The young Penns expanded the concept, however, to include not only manors but also proprietary towns and islands.[1] Thomas Penn's instructions from his brothers shortly before he sailed for Pennsylvania in 1732 ordered him to reserve every "5th: 7th: or 10th part in all fresh settlements" for the family and call them "Proprietors Lotts." The brothers anticipated a continual increase in the value of the lots as the settlements surrounding the proprietary tracts enlarged.[2] The Penns saw their true wealth coming from leasehold rents, not outright land sales or difficult-to-collect quitrents.

[1]For roads see State Road and Turnpike Maps, 1706–1873, RG-12.
[2]May 20, 1732, Letter Book 1:54, roll 1, *TPP.*

III.E.3.a. Proprietary Manors

Between 1732, when Thomas Penn arrived in Pennsylvania, and 1776, when the colonies declared independence, the proprietors warranted and surveyed approximately sixty proprietary manors and many smaller tracts. Varying in size from a few acres to over sixty-four thousand acres, all were located within the purchases of 1768 and earlier. Many, such as Sunbury, Kittanning, and Pittsburgh, occupied strategic locations along major waterways. Several other proprietary tracts were not surveyed until after the Revolutionary War began.[1] In a rush to grab land, the proprietors had warranted vast tracts in Northampton County only months before the war broke out. The Commonwealth government honored the surveys made on the warrants, and the tracts formed a significant part of the land that remained in the Penn family after the end of the war.

The proprietors often failed to understand the colonists' reluctance to lease proprietary

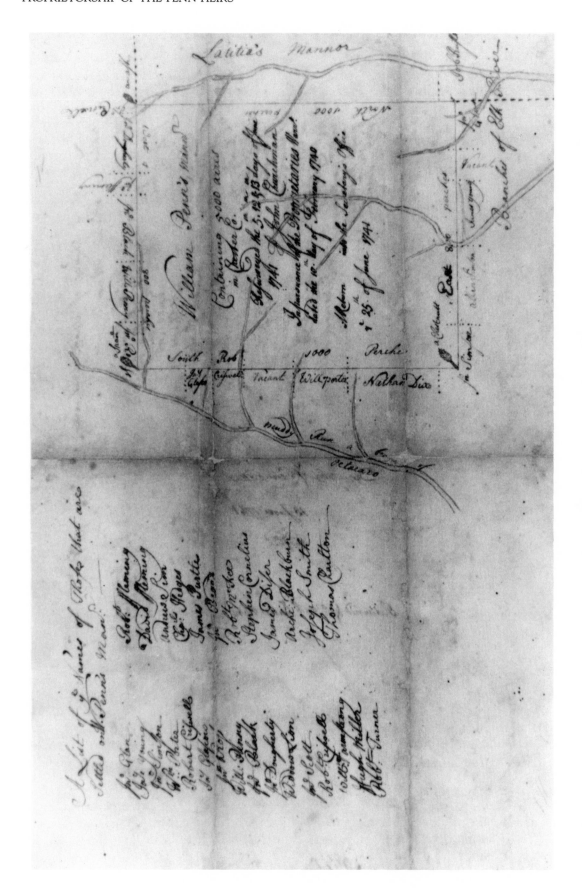

Draught of William Penn's manor, Chester County, as resurveyed in 1741, giving the names of those settled in the manor. (Sur. Bk. D-69-284)

land, but the Penns quickly grasped the strategic role that manor land could play in the development of the province. Using their proprietary prerogative to survey tracts, the Penns established manor land as a bulkhead on the frontier, especially in areas not purchased from the Indians. Even before Thomas Penn arrived, the trustees of the province, in conjunction with the young proprietors, issued several warrants to survey proprietary tracts. The warrants were based upon William Penn's bequest of ten thousand acres of land in Pennsylvania to each of his son William's three children and to his youngest daughter from his first marriage.[2] Records between 1717 and 1732 include warrants to survey tracts in each of the children's names. Richard and Thomas Penn also initiated warrants to lay out tracts for themselves based on their inheritance as soon as William Penn's will was decided in their favor.[3]

Each of these proprietary manors was surveyed in frontier locations of strategic importance and on land not yet purchased from the Indians. Located on the west side of the Susquehanna River and in the Lehigh and Tulpehocken valleys, the manors were surveyed in response to pressure to extend settlement into these regions. The manors were subdivided and leased or sold in total, but the main reason for their existence was to induce groups of immigrants to settle on the frontier.[4]

During the remainder of the colonial era the Penns continued to locate choice land for themselves. Shortly after Richard Peters became proprietary secretary in 1737, Thomas Penn directed him to look for good parcels of land that could be laid out for the proprietors' tenths.[5] Correspondence between Penn and Peters shows that Penn repeatedly admonished the secretary to lease these lands to tenant farmers. Even as late as the 1750s the proprietors expected to make four or six times the income they could in England from leasing land.[6] Again, when James Tilghman became secretary of the Land Office in 1765, Thomas Penn reminded him that the proprietors desired "only one-tenth" to be surveyed to themselves. They asked that it be located in one tract rather than several small tracts as had come to be the practice.[7]

Unfortunately the Land Office kept no continually updated list of manor land. On an order from Thomas Penn, John Georges, proprietary secretary for the years 1733–1737, at-

tempted to prepare a list of all the old proprietary warrants for only Philadelphia County, but he found the task difficult to accomplish because there are numerous irregularities in the old warrant books.[8] Later, in 1741, Penn asked Peters to prepare drafts of proprietary lands, but he had not seen the results by 1749 when he wrote to Peters again requesting a complete list and draughts of the manors and land showing the subdivisions held by renters and purchasers.[9] A list prepared after 1752, including tracts in Berks and Northampton counties, seems to be the result.[10] Another list, prepared after 1773 probably by Edmund Physick in response to the divestiture law, is included in the Proprietary Papers in the Land Office. This list is probably accurate for its year. The most complete list of all manors ever surveyed appears in PA (3) 4, along with many reproduced survey maps. Unfortunately the list omits reference to the original survey on file in the Land Office. For the original survey the Proprietary Rights Index must be consulted. Another set of survey maps in the collection of the Historical Society of Pennsylvania includes subdivisions laid out within the manors. Apparently prepared by William Smith of Delaware County, the set is titled "Proprietary Manors and Lands in Pennsylvania of John Penn Jr. and John Penn."

Another major problem facing the Penn family during the colonial era was the taxation of their proprietary land. From earliest days proprietary land had been exempt from all forms of taxation, and the proprietors took the position that they were not legally liable to pay tax. However, when the defense of the province during the French and Indian War called for an increase in revenue, the Pennsylvania Assembly turned to the proprietary land for additional funds. After several abortive efforts the assembly succeeded in passing a law in 1759 to tax the proprietary land. By the terms of the law, township assessors were to draw up detailed lists of taxable property including proprietary land. To facilitate the assessment, the assembly passed the 1759 recording law requiring that the original land records, all in proprietary control, be transcribed. For a discussion of the impact of this law see III.G.6, 1759 Transcripts (Green Books). The new tax was levied fairly with the exception of lots in the town of Carlisle, and even Thomas Penn admitted that "Upon the whole" the tax did not seem great.[11]

A new law passed in 1769 established definite policies in assessing proprietary land.[12] Exempt from taxation was unoccupied and unlocated proprietary land. Located but not cultivated proprietary land, including borough and town lots, was not to be assessed at a higher rate than the lowest rate for regular settlers. From 1770, when the law went into effect, until 1776, proprietary land was taxed like any other Pennsylvania land.

Estimates of the total amount of proprietary land were prepared from time to time. "An Estimate of the Proprietary's appropriated Lands" prepared some time after 1752 but before 1760 indicates that at midcentury approximately 172,000 acres of proprietary land valued between twenty and two hundred pounds were available for sale.[13] Another list of "Land Surveyed for the Proprietary Family" prepared after 1773 but before 1776 shows approximately another 106,000 acres surveyed for the Penn family during the third quarter of the eighteenth century.[14] Physick, in his General Cash Accounts prepared at the time of divestiture, estimated the proprietary estates in Pennsylvania to have included nearly 522,784 acres of land between 1681 and 1776.

He claimed that a little over 111,250 of those acres were surveyed for members of the Penn family.[15]

Warrants and surveys of proprietary land were recorded in colonial provincial and county records under the Penn name as if the Penns were any other purchaser. The subdivisions of proprietary tracts, however, were private deals between the Penns and their renters or purchasers. Although some of the subdivided tracts were granted on warrant, survey, and patent, many were conveyed by deed poll and recorded on the county level.

Warrants and surveys of proprietary land may be located through the Proprietary Rights Index cited below. The index is also printed in *PA* (3) 3:217–93, but the references to volume, book, and page numbers were left out. A separate list of proprietary manors is also printed in *PA* (3) 4, and copies of the surveys of several of the more important tracts are reproduced in the volume. The list, however, does not include the reference to the original warrants or surveys on file in the Land Office. For that information consult the Proprietary Rights Index cited below.

RECORDS: LOOSE PAPERS

ORIGINAL SURVEYS   LO micro.: 6.1–190.

Original warrants and surveys for proprietary land, especially manors, are filed mainly in volumes D-88 and BB-4.

RETURNS   PROPRIETARY TRACTS   LO micro.: 5.119.

One folder containing a few of the returns of survey for proprietary manors.

A LIST OF LAND SURVEYED FOR THE HONBLE PROPRIETARY FAMILY IN THE COUNTY OF   (Proprietary Papers, folder 2)   LO micro.: 23.1.

Includes proprietary land surveyed in all counties formed through 1773.

AN ESTIMATE OF THE PROPRIETARY'S APPROPRIATED LANDS IN THE PROVINCE OF PENNSYLVANIA   (See Land Office Map Inventory).

Prepared after 1752, possibly by Richard Peters in response to Thomas Penn's request.

RECORDS: BOUND VOLUMES

PROPRIETARY RIGHTS INDEX   Partial transcript in *PA* (3) 3:217–93.

Organized by county and topic (Islands, Roads and Rivers, Towns), this index is a reference to some of the original and copied warrants and surveys for proprietary land. The copy in *PA* (3) does not include reference to the volume, book, and page numbers.

ORDERS TO SURVEY FOR USE OF PROPRIETARIES   1746   (Binding No. 120)   LO micro.: 25.108.

An incomplete volume of warrants.

---

[1]"Certificate of Surveyor General Concerning Lands Surveyed after 4 July 1776 for the proprietaries," Sur. Bk. D-80-296.

[2]Com. Bk. A-1-275.

[3]"An Account of the Honorable Thomas Penn's Lands in Pennsylvania, May 12. 1732," roll 4, frame 433, *TPP*; Accounts of Warrants and Surveys, May 12, 1732, Accounts 4:13 (microfilm), Penn-Physick Mss.

[4]See III.E.1.a, Licensed Land.

[5]Richard Peters to Edward Smout, Jan. 22, 1738 [1739], Peters Letter Books, HSP.

[6]Thomas Penn to Richard Peters, January 10, 1756, Letter Book 4:203–11, roll 1, *TPP*.

[7]"Thomas Penn to James Tilghman, Nov. 7, 1766," *WPHM* 57 (1974): 239.

[8]Proprietary Rights register, *PA* (3) 3:217.

[9]"An Abstract of the Proprietors Letter, Feb 13, 1749," Land Office Drawer 0006, Item 9. See Land Office Map Inventory.

[10]"An Estimate of the Proprietary's Appropriated Lands in the Province of Pennsylvania," Land Office Drawer 0006, Item 9. See Land Office Map Inventory.

[11]Thomas Penn to Richard Peters, March 8 and May 10, 1760, Letter Book 6:216–18, 223–39, roll 2, *TPP*.

[12]*Statutes* 7:307–9.

[13]Land Office Drawer 0006, Item 9. See Land Office Map Inventory.

[14]Proprietary Papers, folder 2; LO micro.: 23.1.

[15]Affidavit, Penn Property in the Province, Accounts 4:91–95 (microfilm), Penn-Physick Mss.

III.E.3.b. Proprietary Towns

In addition to manors the proprietors created six proprietary towns during their administration: York, Reading, Carlisle, Easton, Bedford, and Sunbury. All were laid out on manors or special tracts the proprietors had warranted in their own names or purchased from others. Portions of each town included land owned by others as well. The proprietors also attempted to control the land surrounding the towns by taking warrants to all vacant land within five miles of every town.

Thomas Penn played a very active role in the location and planning of the proprietary towns. His correspondence shows that he con-

ferred at length with his land officers and other interested landholders and supervised town planning and the sale of lots. The income from ground rent earned his family seven shillings sterling per lot per year.

While the layouts of these six towns were not identical, they followed a rectilinear plan similar to Philadelphia's. Each surrounded a central square and was composed of rectangular town lots, called in lots, and five- to ten-acre out lots. Open land designated for public buildings, a market place, and a burial ground was also a common feature. Most importantly, each proprietary town became a county seat with special privileges to hold weekly markets and annual fairs.

Chart 5. Proprietary Towns

Town	Laid Out	Surrounding County Formed
York	1741	1749
Reading	1748	1752
Carlisle	1751	1750
Easton	1752	1752
Bedford	1766	1771
Sunbury	1772	1772

The terms to purchase a lot differed slightly among the proprietary towns, but certain consistent features served as a sort of building code. In addition to paying ground rent, the purchaser was required to build a substantial dwelling, usually within one year. The minimum size of the dwelling varied from sixteen feet square in York to twenty feet square in Bedford, but the requirement of a good chimney of brick and stone remained the same for each town.

Procedures for acquiring lots in proprietary towns differed from those for acquiring country land. Tickets, or pieces of paper specifying the terms on which lots could be obtained, were issued to applicants by the surveyor laying out the lots on the site. The tickets served as a record showing the applicant's right to build upon and improve the lot he had selected. The surveyor sent the list of applicants to the secretary's office. If the terms of purchase were met, and the lot was located on proprietary or other privately owned land, the applicant received a deed that was recorded in the county record office. If the lot was located on country land, the applicant was issued a return of survey, a warrant to accept, and a patent, all of which were recorded in the Land Office.

Original town plans, instructions for surveying, and lists giving applicants' names are among the original loose land records and are cited below. Other town records and surveys may be located through the Proprietary Rights Index also cited below. If the lots were not on the proprietary reserve, the individuals who warranted them are listed in the warrant registers of the county at the time the lots were offered.

RECORDS: LOOSE PAPERS

PROPRIETARY TOWNS   LO micro.: 11.4.

Nine folders of records, including lists of applicants, instructions for surveying, and town plans for Bedford, Carlisle, Sunbury, Easton, Reading, Indiana (planned to be a proprietary town but surveyed too late), and York.

A GROUND PLAN OF READING IN 1750'S   FIRST PURCHASERS OF LOTS AS SHOWN BY LAND OFFICE RECORDS.

Filed in Land Office Drawer 0086, Item 43, a map of connected warrantee tracts of the first purchasers in Reading.

RECORDS: BOUND VOLUMES

PROPRIETARY RIGHTS INDEX   Partial transcript in PA (3) 3:217–93.

Surveys of the manors that later became towns may be accessed in this register under the current county in which they are located. The transcript in PA (3) does not include reference to survey books.

III.E.3.c. Islands

Islands had been set aside as a special type of land from the first days of the province. In his original instructions to his commissioners of property, William Penn wrote: "Let no Islands be disposed of to any Body, but all things remaine as they were in that respect till I come."[1] Once in Pennsylvania he permitted very few islands to be warranted as isolated tracts. Those that were granted were usually considered to be part of the land on the nearest shore.

Several factors may account for Penn's policy. He was certainly conscious of the public need for the right of use and passage of the navigable rivers within the province, a charter right granted to him. His lack of clear jurisdiction over islands in the Delaware River may also have led him to prefer a consistent policy and to permit the warranting only of islands that were close to the shore. Penn, however, did look upon islands as land to be granted as a special award. For instance, in 1701 he granted Thomas Fairman an island in the Delaware River in return for special services Fairman had performed as a surveyor.[2]

The later proprietors, following William Penn's policy, generally refrained from granting islands as separate tracts of land. It was not until the mid-1700s that developing industries made islands especially valuable. In 1760 the proprietors issued a general warrant to survey for their own use the unappropriated islands in the Delaware, Schuylkill, and Susquehanna rivers and the other rivers and creeks of the settled portions of the province. In the Schuylkill River alone, twenty-five islands were surveyed.[3] The proprietors made special grants of these islands to purchasers who paid the highest price. Islands surveyed under the proprietary warrant are listed in the Proprietary Rights Index.

RECORDS: BOUND VOLUMES

PROPRIETARY RIGHTS INDEX   Partial transcript in *PA* (3) 3:217–93.

Pages 246–65 of this register list islands warranted by the proprietors and cites references to the survey books and pages. The transcript in *PA* (3) does not include the survey references.

APPLICATIONS FOR ISLANDS   VOLUME 163   (With index)   Transcript in *PA* (3) 3:461–82.

Pages 1 and 2 of this volume contain a copy of the return of survey for the twenty-five islands in the Schuylkill River warranted to the proprietors in 1760 and surveyed in 1763.

---

[1]Wm Penn to William Crispin, John Bezar, and Nathaniel Allen, 30 Sep't. 1681, *PWP* 2:120.

[2]Pat. Bk. A-2-732.

[3]In addition to the application volume cited in the records see "Susquehanna and Schuylkill Island Survey, 1759–61," Mss Group 1100, HSP.

III.E.4. Philadelphia City Lots

During the 1740s, Thomas Penn devoted much attention to Philadelphia city lots. His interest was "in granting out the remainder of them and in preserving every foot" to which the proprietors had a right.[1]

Before Penn left Pennsylvania for England in 1741, he asked Benjamin Eastburn, his surveyor general, to construct a rent-roll and plan of the city.[2] In response, Eastburn mapped Philadelphia as it was actually plotted during Thomas Penn's stay in the province. None of the public squares as laid down in Thomas Holme's old plan were included, and few occupants were named. An accompanying document titled "Account of Lots in the City," cited in the records below, provided occupants' names and also first grantees or renters, dates when lots were laid out and patented, and quitrents. Fragmentary and torn copies of both Eastburn's map and his rent-roll are among the land records and are cited below.[3]

Apparently not satisfied with Eastburn's job, Penn wrote to Richard Peters for assistance.[4] Peters, the proprietary secretary, passed the request on to William Parsons, who had replaced Eastburn as surveyor general in 1741. Parsons studied the Original Purchasers' records and sometime during his term of office, 1741–1748, drafted a new map of Philadelphia. Penn was satisfied and in the years that followed referred to Parsons's map of the city as his authority on Philadelphia lots.

Parsons's map, titled *Plan of Philadelphia*, was reproduced as a book of city squares, or blocks, not as a flat map. The squares showed the oldest part of the city and its original surveys. Names of 381 individual and 9 corporate patentees and the width and depth of each lot were given in the squares. One of the copies of Parsons's original map is in the Cadwalader Collection at the Historical Society of Pennsylvania. Parsons's *Plan of Philadelphia* was also indexed, reproduced, and published by Nicholas B. Wain-

wright in *PMHB* 80 (1956): 164–226. Several loose original pages similar to those used in Parsons's plan but indicating the subdivisions of Original Purchasers' lots are part of the Land Office Philadelphia Lot Collection. Many of these pages appear to be work sheets for the Parsons project, but others are definitely updates. For instance, one such square for "City Lots below 7th & 8th Streets and Between H St & Chest Streets" carries the notation "copy sent to Proprietaries 22 Sept 1764," which would have been at least fifteen years after Parsons's map was completed.[5]

Thomas Penn did have some success in selling Philadelphia city lots. The Philadelphia warrant register shows approximately 260 lots surveyed between 1740 and 1776. Another list of "Appliers for Lotts at the North End of the Town" for the years 1742 through 1744 gives forty names applying for 97 lots.[6] As was the case with applications for all other categories of land, surveys for these north end lots were returned at random times over many following years.[7]

Records for individuals purchasing Philadelphia lots between 1732 and 1776 may be found through the Philadelphia County warrant register. In the column indicating the acreage returned in the survey, the notation "City Lot" or simply "Lot" will appear rather than an amount.

RECORDS: LOOSE PAPERS

BENJAMIN EASTBURN'S PLAN OF PHILADELPHIA   [1737–1741].

A map on linen, showing all lots surveyed to date, the width and depth of each lot, and a few owners' names. See Land Office Map Inventory.

[PHILADELPHIA CITY LOTS]   LO micro.: 21.1.

Miscellaneous papers and returns of survey for Philadelphia lots, 1682–1781, in five folders.

ORIGINAL SURVEYS   LO micro.: 6.189.

Many Philadelphia lot papers are filed in volume D-112-1–99. These have not been copied into the copied survey volumes.

RECORDS: BOUND VOLUMES

PHILADELPHIA CITY LOTS   NO. 31 HUGHES' LIST   (Binding No. 165).

Benjamin Eastburn's "Account of Lots in the City" of Philadelphia. The words "No. 31 Hughes' List" refer to the number John Hughes gave to the volume in his 1759 inventory of the records in the surveyor general's office. The account is organized by street and gives the original owner, front footage, current owner (1733–1741), date laid out, date patented, and quitrent.

---

[1]Thomas Penn to Richard Peters, May 14, 1746, Letter Book 2:156, roll 1, *TPP*.

[2]Nicholas Scull to Richard Peters, June 25, 1755, Philadelphia Land Grants 7:77, Penn Papers, HSP.

[3]See also Benjamin Eastburn, "Manuscript Plan showing Philadelphia & Environs," in Quarto Vol., Logan and Dickinson Mss, HSP.

[4]May 14, 1746, Letter Book 2:156, roll 1, *TPP*.

[5]Sur. Bk. D-112-20.

[6][Philadelphia] City Lots, LO micro.: 21.1.

[7]For a perspective view of the city, 1754–1756, see Martin P. Snyder, *City of Independence: Views of Philadelphia before 1800* (New York, 1975), 44–45.

III.F. Land Office

Under the direction of Thomas Penn and his brothers John and Richard, the day-to-day operation of land affairs changed little. Although no single office existed for conducting business, the term Land Office was widely used. Between 1733 and 1741, when acting as the commissioners of property, Thomas and John Penn conducted business in their own home. After they both returned to England, they abolished the positions of commissioners of property and delegated the responsibility for signing warrants and patents to their deputy, the governor. Land disputes were either settled by the secretary of the Land Office or referred to Thomas Penn in England. In the early 1740s the west wing of the State House, otherwise known as Provincial Hall, was completed; and, as indicated in Sur. Bk. D-86-264, the secretary of the Land Office moved into one of the rooms. Shortly after 1763, when John Penn (Richard's son) became governor, the proprietors reinstituted a Board of Property. To handle the everyday operation of land affairs, however, the Penns continued to use three appointed assistants: their proprietary secretary, the surveyor general, and the receiver general.

III.F.1. Commissioners of Property

When Thomas Penn arrived in Pennsylvania in August 1732, he had with him a commission from his brothers John and Richard appointing him to serve as the only commissioner of property.[1] Although the commissioners had previously functioned as a board of three to five members, Thomas Penn was now to have sole responsibility for granting land and hearing controversies concerning land. Holding meetings in his own home, he made decisions about conflicting land claims and signed all warrants and patents. Upon his brother John's arrival in October 1734, both Penns served as commissioners of property, sitting together and jointly signing warrants and patents. After John Penn's return to England in 1735, Thomas Penn again assumed duties as the sole commissioner of property. Minutes of commissioners of property proceedings under Thomas and John Penn have survived for the years 1733–1741 and are cited in the records below.

In 1741, when Thomas Penn returned to England, he transferred his official authority for granting lands to his deputy, Governor George Thomas. However, Penn also appointed James Steel, Richard Peters, and Lynford Lardner to be

Chart 6. Governors, 1733–1765

Governor	Years in Office
George Thomas (Pat. Bk. A-10-318)	1741–1746
Anthony Palmer (interim governor and president of council; *PA* (1) 1:745)	1747–1748
James Hamilton (Com. Bk. A-2-41)	1748–1754
Robert Hunter Morris (Com. Bk. A-2-175)	1754–1756
William Denny (Com. Bk. A-2-216)	1756–1759
James Hamilton (Com. Bk. A-2-297)	1759–1763
John Penn (Com. Bk. A-2-414)	1763–1771

proprietary agents for land affairs.[2] Under this new arrangement the three proprietary agents were to do the work of the Land Office. Even though the governor was the only person with authority to sign warrants and patents, the three agents assumed responsibility for settling all land controversies.

The secretary of the Land Office, Richard Peters, who was succeeded by his brother William Peters, accepted petitions and caveats that plaintiffs filed. He held hearings and made decisions by himself. Frequently he requested pertinent information from the surveyor general.

Historians have claimed that commissioners of property minutes for the period 1741–1765 have been lost, but this interpretation does not seem to be borne out by the records. Rather, the minutes ceased when Thomas Penn returned to England in 1741 and the secretary began to hold meetings and make the decisions. Although conferring with Penn via letter, the secretary frequently made unilateral decisions.[3] Journals or minute books documenting the secretary's activities in this regard are lacking; the only surviving records of decisions from these years are filed among the loose original Board of Property papers.[4]

In 1765, two years after John Penn became governor, the vestiges of the old commissioners of property were instituted as the Board of Property. Its membership consisted of Penn, acting as governor; James Tilghman, secretary for proprietary affairs; John Lukens, surveyor general; and Edmund Physick, receiver general. For better management of the Land Office and dispatch of business, the board met once or twice a month at the governor's house to hear controversies involving property. An escalation of caveats brought on by the application system for the titling of settled improved land had caused a considerable increase in the number of cases. Minutes of the meetings, beginning September 5, 1765, are a valuable resource for studying the operations of the Land Office and often contain genealogical information. Transcribed for ease of use and indexed, the minutes are published in *PA* (3) 1. The minutes are also available in their original form and as copies in bound volumes cited below.

RECORDS: LOOSE PAPERS

BOARD OF PROPERTY   PETITIONS.

Petitions for the period 1733–1765 are filed in one folder. Another four folders carry undated petitions. Petitions for the period 1765–1786 are filed in three folders.

BOARD OF PROPERTY   PAPERS   LO micro.: 22.6–8.

The first thirty-six folders contain correspondence and miscellaneous papers for the period 1733–1775. A few maps and miscellaneous papers are filed alphabetically or under the label "Maps" or "General" at the end of this collection.

CAVEATS   LO micro.: 13.1–2.

Original loose caveats, formal statements asking that action not be taken, are filed in eighteen folders for the period 1733–1765 and in forty-one folders for the period 1765–1776.

DEPOSITIONS   LO micro.: 18.1.

Statements submitted in evidence before the Board of Property, including copies of wills. The first five folders contain papers for the period 1732–1783.

RECORDS: BOUND VOLUMES

COMMISSIONERS OF PROPERTY 10-K   1732–1741   [Minute Book K of the Commissioners of Property]   (Binding No. 22)   LO micro.: 25.20–21; 1759 transcript in WARRANT REGISTER 1700–1705   (Binding No. 22)   LO micro.: 25.4–5; *PA* (3) 1:25–110.

The first entry is dated March 17, 1733, but the minutes give no indication of who is present at meetings until December 3, 1734, when the meetings are held "at the Proprietaries" and one or both of the proprietors (Thomas and John) are present. Most of the entries are then prefaced "Signed the following patents." The last entry is dated July 27, 1741.

MINUTE BOOK NUMBER 1   [Board of Property]   1765–1772   VOLUME 1   LO micro.: 25.21; *PA* (3) 1:111–344.

The first four pages are missing; the volume begins with the meeting of September 5, 1765, and ends with the meeting of July 28, 1772.

MINUTE BOOK NUMBER 2   [Board of Property]   1772–1776   VOLUME 2   LO micro.: 25.21; *PA* (3) 1:345–416.

Minutes of meetings cover the period from September 27, 1772, through October 30, 1776. However, the last few pages carry minutes from 1772 that must have been entered after the rest of the volume was completed. The transcripts follow the same order. No meetings were held in the period from November 1776 to 1782.

INDEX   CAVEAT BOOKS 1 TO 7   1748–1792   (Binding No. 1)   LO micro.: 25.14.

An index to seven caveat books dated as follows: 1) August 8, 1748–November 7, 1762; 2) November 3, 1762–June 27, 1766; 3) July 1, 1766–September 7, 1768; 4) September 7, 1768–June 29, 1771; 5) July 19, 1771–December 27, 1784; 6) December 29, 1784–May 30, 1787; and 7) May 30, 1787–May 19, 1792.

CAVEAT BOOKS 1, 2, 3 AND 4   1748–1769   (Binding No. 2)   LO micro.: 25.14; *PA* (3) 2:159–471.

Contains four books bound as one. Copies of original caveats for the period 1748–1765 are in books 1 and 2. Books 3 and 4 cover the period 1765–1769. Entries are not in strict chronological order.

CAVEATS   1748–1771   (Binding Volume 162).

Copies of original loose papers. Signed by the secretary, they contain notations as to when hearings are scheduled, and thus this volume may hold the secretary's book copies. The volume titled "Caveat Books 1, 2, 3 and 4" contains corresponding entries.

CAVEATS   1769   (Binding No. 154).

Copies of original loose papers.

CAVEAT BOOK   1766–1768   (Binding No. 3)   LO micro.: 25.15.

Contains hand-entered book copies of loose papers.

CAVEAT BOOK   JULY 19, 1771 TO DEC. 27, 1784   (Binding No. 4; with index)   LO micro.: 25.14–15; PA (3) 2:472–660.

Contains hand-entered book copies of loose papers. The PA transcript calls this volume Caveat Book No. 5.

CAVEAT BOOK NO. 5   (Binding No. 5; with index)   LO micro.: 25.14.

Contains hand copies of loose papers for the period October 23, 1769–December 31, 1785.

---

[1]Pat. Bk. A-6-170.
[2]Pat. Bks. A-10-318 and A-10-320.
[3]See, for example, Board of Property Papers (cited above), folder 5, Sep't, 26, 1759.
[4]See Board of Property Papers, LO micro.: 22.6–7.

III.F.2. Secretary for Proprietary Affairs

The chief agent in the land business under Thomas, John, and Richard Penn, as under William Penn, was the secretary for proprietary affairs. Responsible for encouraging the sale of land, the secretary managed the warranting and patenting process. He was required to give bond and take an oath to preserve the papers belonging to his office. As under William Penn, the proprietary secretary served as a commissioner of property and usually as secretary of the province, keeping the minutes of the Executive Council meetings.

Four men served in the position of proprietary secretary between 1733 and 1776. Soon after Thomas Penn arrived in Pennsylvania, James Logan, longtime proprietary secretary, resigned. Penn appointed John Georges to fill the

Table 19. Research Aids: Richard Peters

Cummings, Hubertis. *Richard Peters, Provincial Secretary and Cleric, 1704–1776.* Philadelphia, 1944.

Fairbanks, Joseph H., Jr. "Richard Peters (c. 1704–1776): Provincial Secretary of Pennsylvania." Ph.D. diss., University of Arizona, 1972.

"Penn Family's Papers." Pennsylvania Department of Internal Affairs *Monthly Bulletin* 25, no. 2 (February–March, 1957): 1–6.

---

position[1]; he remained in office only four years. In 1737, Richard Peters was offered the position. Although many publications do not credit him with the office as early as 1737, he accepted the job and held it for the next twenty-three years.

His commission called upon him "to prepare and draw up all writings and instruments relating to the Land Office."[2] For the first four years, Peters worked directly under Thomas and John Penn. He administered the provincial land as well as the proprietary estates and manors. In 1740, Thomas Penn, pleased with the performance of his secretary, gave Peters a £150 bonus and a salary of £50 per year over and above the profits the secretary derived from the fees charged for warrants and patents. Just one year later, in 1741, Thomas Penn returned to England and left land affairs totally under Peters's control.

Peters soon added another responsibility to his already important status. In February 1743 he accepted the position of provincial secretary and served directly under the governor.[3] The appointment continued the precedent set by Logan when he served as proprietary and provincial secretary simultaneously. Being both the governor's secretary and the proprietors' secretary obviously reduced the opportunity for conflict in proprietary affairs. Peters held these two positions for several years and became more and more involved in provincial politics.

The first complete inventory of the Penns' proprietary papers may owe its existence today to the joint positions that Peters held. The inventory dates from 1748, when James Hamilton was appointed lieutenant governor of the province and as a routine matter all other provincial appointments were reaffirmed or changed. Peters's recommission ordered him to receive from Hamilton "all the Minutes Records and other Papers" belonging to the council, "Together with an Exact Inventory of the same", for which Peters was to grant a receipt and enter into a bond of two hundred pounds to safeguard the papers.[4] They formed the bulk of the collection essential for documenting the Penns' titles to land. Having only one workplace, Peters brought the papers into the secretary's office in the State House and prepared the inventory. From then on valuable provincial papers and land records became part of the same collection. Many of the items listed in the inventory were transferred to the Pennsylvania State Archives long before the Land Office became a part of the archives.

The 1748 inventory is divided into four sections: A, E, I, and O. Section A lists the basic documents necessary to establish the Penns' titles to land as well as various rent rolls and maps. The section begins with the grant of Charles II to William Penn in 1681 and ends with several Logan papers dated as late as 1741. Section E lists the more important governmental papers and commissions and instructions to proprietary agents. Section I contains the many Indian purchase deeds, and section O, the many New Jersey deeds of the Penn family. The inventory, cited in the records below, gives us a good picture of the operation of proprietary affairs.

Peters officially resigned in 1760 but stayed on long enough to teach the new secretary, his brother, William Peters, how to manage proprietary affairs. Years of neglect during the French and Indian War, coupled with the 1759 recording law, meant many hours devoted to reorganization in the Land Office. Furthermore, the secretary's job had taken on an added dimension: Provincial taxation of the proprietary estates necessitated a close watch over the Penns' land.[5]

William Peters proved to be a poor choice for the post. He complained of overwork and lack of time to send business reports to the proprietor. To augment his income, Peters attempted to raise the warrant and patent fees charged by his office. Further taking advantage of his position, he was guilty of purchasing large tracts of land for himself under fictitious names. He was replaced in 1765.[6]

At the request of John Penn, who had recently taken over the governorship of the province, James Tilghman became the new secretary for proprietary affairs. Thoroughly familiar with the nature of proprietary land business from his experience in Maryland, Tilghman had moved to Philadelphia about 1760 to practice law. He accepted Penn's offer, insisting on three hundred pounds per year and the fees of the office, the highest salary yet paid for the position.[7] Tilghman apparently ran a well-organized office and abided by the spirit of the regulations, even though he practiced some favoritism in the distribution of the land within the Purchase of 1768.[8]

RECORDS: LOOSE PAPERS

1748 INVENTORY OF PENN PAPERS   (Miscellaneous Papers, RG-21)   Reel 600.

A fifteen-page manuscript list of proprietary papers relating to the Penns' titles to all of their land holdings. Prepared in 1748, the list is divided into four major sections: A and E, grants and charters; I, Indian deeds; and O, New Jersey deeds. The list ends with a short section of a few items appended by Richard Peters after 1748.

GENERAL CORRESPONDENCE   1687–1853   (RG-17)   Reel 3982.

A collection of letters filed chronologically. It includes a few letters written by the secretaries of the Land Office, especially James Tilghman. Only records from 1713 to 1775 have been microfilmed.

---

[1]Com. Bk. A-1-1.
[2]Pat. Bk. A-8-284–85.
[3]Com. Bk. A-1-317; CR 4:639.
[4]Com. Bk. A-2-48.
[5]For William Peters's commissions see Com. Bk. A-2-346, 402; PA (3) 9:384. See also III.G.6, 1759 Transcripts (Green Books).
[6]Thomas Penn to John Penn ("Nephew"), December 14, 1765, Letter Book 8:329–31, roll 2, *TPP*.
[7]Charles P. Keith, *Provincial Councillors of Pennsylvania, 1733–1776* (Philadelphia, 1883), 399–400.
[8]See III.E.2.a(1), Officers' Tracts, and III.E.2.a(2), Gentlemen's Tracts.

III.F.3. Surveyor General and Deputies

III.F.3.a. Surveyor General

The surveyors general under John, Thomas, and Richard Penn played a more significant role than their counterparts under William Penn. Absent proprietors and a governor burdened with political affairs placed the major responsibility for land decisions upon the land officers. A rapidly growing population made it impossible for the secretary to run the land business alone. An increasingly larger role fell to the surveyor general.

The several duties of the surveyor general were outlined in the appointment commissions that the proprietors offered. A typical commission required the official to keep all the "Records, Books, Maps, Draughts, Warrants, Orderd Returns" of his office in good order. He was to duplicate all official documents and have them

Chart 7. Surveyors General, 1733–1776

Surveyor General	Years in Office
Benjamin Eastburn (Com. Bk. A-1-4)	1733–1741
William Parsons (Com. Bk. A-1-273)	1741–1748
Nicholas Scull (Com. Bk. A-2-13)	1748–1761
John Lukens (Com. Bk. A-2-402)	1761–1776

readily available for the secretary at all times. Furthermore, he was to keep "distinct from other Surveys" an "exact Account" of proprietary land. In return for his services the surveyor general received all the "Fees, Perquisities, Emoluments and Advantages" of the office and a small salary.[1]

When John, Thomas, and Richard Penn took over the province in 1732, they appointed Benjamin Eastburn surveyor general. During

Eastburn's tenure in office he was involved in two historically significant surveying ventures. The first was the famous Walking Purchase of 1737, in which Eastburn accompanied the walkers and knew ahead of time just how much land the proprietors planned to secure. Several tracts above the falls of the Delaware within the proposed purchase area had been claimed by settlement and improvement, sometimes with the blessing of the proprietors, and the settlers were clamoring to purchase the land and claim their legal rights. Eastburn's 1737 sketch map of the purchased territory, then part of Bucks County, formed the basis for Lewis Evans's 1738 map of the same area.[2]

Eastburn was later involved in the 1738–39 survey of the temporary boundary between Pennsylvania and Maryland. Commissioners from both colonies surveyed without incident as far west as the Susquehanna River. Continuing alone, Pennsylvania commissioners surveyed to the far side of the Kittatinny Mountains. They stopped at this point because the land further west was not purchased from the Indians.[3]

According to Nicholas Scull, Eastburn also drew up a plan of the city of Philadelphia and an accompanying rent-roll.[4] Apparently produced for Thomas Penn just before he left Philadelphia in 1741, the map was Eastburn's last contribution. He died the same year.

William Parsons, a familiar figure in Philadelphia social and intellectual circles, was appointed as Eastburn's successor. Parsons and Secretary Peters soon discovered that Eastburn had kept few records. In particular they could find no account of land surveyed for the proprietor. Parsons's task was to rectify that situation. He provided an accurate plan of the Philadelphia city lots so that the proprietors could be "exceedingly exact in granting out the remainder, and in preserving every foot we have a right."[5] After seven years as surveyor general, Parsons resigned in 1748.

Table 20. Research Aids: Surveyors General, 1732–1776

Cummings, Hubertis. "The Surveyors General of the Province of Pennsylvania." Pennsylvania Department of Internal Affairs *Monthly Bulletin* 30, nos. 2, 4, 7, 8, 10, 12 (February, April, July, August, November, December 1962): 23–29, 24–28, 26–29, 2–4, 24–27, 24–29.

Jordan, John W. "William Parsons." *PMHB* 33 (1909): 340–46.

Nicholas Scull, a professional surveyor, became the next surveyor general of the province. He had been a deputy surveyor for Philadelphia and Bucks counties for nearly thirty years and had collaborated with both Eastburn and Parsons on most of their major assignments. Scull also seems to have participated in the planning and surveying of every proprietary town laid out during his long career from 1719 to 1761. Scull's *Map of the Improved Part of the Province of Pennsylvania*, published in 1759, accurately pictures the portion of Pennsylvania that lies east of the Allegheny Mountains and south of the West and North branches of the Susquehanna River.[6] Scull died in 1761.

John Lukens, Scull's successor as surveyor general, served until the Revolutionary War, and after the war he was reappointed by the Commonwealth. Between 1765 and 1769 a vast amount of surveying was required for the East Side, West Side, and New Purchase application programs. To accomplish this work, Lukens built up the largest staff of deputy surveyors the province had yet seen. His deputies ranged far and wide, surveying proprietary manors and warrant tracts. In so doing they began to establish a patronage network that eventually led to the supremacy of the land speculator during the early years of the Commonwealth.

RECORDS: LOOSE PAPERS

GENERAL CORRESPONDENCE OF THE SURVEYOR GENERAL   1682–1873   LO micro.: 21.3.

Correspondence for the period 1732–1768 is contained in two folders.

GENERAL CORRESPONDENCE, SECRETARY AND SURVEYOR GENERAL, 1713–1775 Reel 3982.

Contains much of the surviving correspondence of the surveyors general.

RECORDS: BOUND VOLUMES

LETTER BOOK OF THE SURVEYOR GENERAL, 1762–1764.

One volume from the first years of John Lukens's term as surveyor general.

---

[1]See, for example, Com. Bk. A-1-4.

[2]Hubertis Cummings, "The Surveyors General of the Province of Pennsylvania," *Pennsylvania Department of Internal Affairs Monthly Bulletin* 30, no. 2 (February 1962): 26.

[3]Ibid.

[4]See III.E.4, Philadelphia City Lots.

[5]Thomas Penn to Richard Peters, May 14, 1746, Letter Book 2:154–57, roll 1, *TPP*. See also III.E.4, Philadelphia City Lots.

[6]See Table 13.

III.F.3.b. Deputy Surveyors

Under the proprietors a deputy surveyor received a formal commission and a separate set of instructions outlining his district and duties. In return he posted bond, which by 1764 amounted to two hundred pounds. The only significant change in instructions made between 1701 and 1765 was the requirement to record warrants and surveys in field books that could be examined by the surveyor general at his will. This token effort to keep surveyors honest was seldom exercised by calling the books to the office.

New regulations and instructions were added after 1765 as a result of the application system and the Purchase of 1768. The regulations called upon the deputy surveyors to be more careful in locating and completing surveys. Deputies were given six months to complete each survey and ordered not to survey more than 10 percent over and above the quantity mentioned in the warrant. The regulations also required deputies to lay tracts contiguous to one another. Tracts along rivers and creeks were to be three times deeper than the length along the water. Finally, deputies were to record and report dates when improvements on settled tracts were first begun, so that interest on the purchase price could be assessed from the first date of settlement.[1]

A list describing deputy surveyors' districts and duplicate copies of their commissions and instructions are part of the land records collection cited below.

RECORDS: LOOSE PAPERS

DEPUTY SURVEYORS DUPLICATE COMMISSIONS AND INSTRUCTIONS   LO micro.: 19.2.

Ten folders of commissions and instructions in this collection apply to the period 1733–1776.

RECORDS: BOUND VOLUMES

DEPUTY SURVEYORS' LISTS OF RETURNS   [1762–1887]   LO micro.: 25.27.

The surveyor general's account books of deputy surveyors' returns and fees. For each deputy the books list the person for whom a survey was made and returned, the acreage, and the fees returned. Deputies list C-D covers the earliest period for which the lists exist, 1762–1783.

LIST OF DEP[UTY] SURVEYORS   [1713–1850]   LO micro.: 25.29.

Cites each deputy's name, date of commission, original district, and district as altered. An alphabetized card file prepared from the information in this volume is available in the Land Office.

---

[1]Min. Bd. Prop. Bk. 1:7–8.

III.F.4. Receiver General

John, Thomas, and Richard Penn made no immediate change in the office of receiver general. Instead, one of their first decisions was to recommission Receiver General James Steel,[1] who had held this position since 1714, first under James Logan. He worked closely with the new secretary for proprietary affairs, Richard Peters, but reported directly to the Penns.

Little change in the receiver general's office procedures occurred until August 1741 when the Penns created two positions from the one. Steel retained the responsibility for collecting quitrents from the owners of country land and city and town lots. The job of collecting quitrents due on the proprietary tracts and manors went to Lynford Lardner, a young Englishman and brother-in-law of Richard Penn.[2] Steel died within the year, however, leaving the entire receiver general's job in Lardner's hands. Since Lardner found few records on which to base his collections, he drew up new rent-rolls, but he changed little else.[3] Quit Rent Book A, 1741–1742, cited below, is probably one of Lardner's rent-rolls.[4]

In addition to collecting quitrents, the receiver general was to collect payments made on all other proprietary business including land purchases. Upon payment he apparently completed a receipt and made an entry in his daybook. A few of these receipts remain in the Land Office collection and are cited below. A complete set

of daybooks, the daily chronological accounts of money collected for land sales, quitrents, and other proprietary income, is also part of the Land Office collection and cited below.

Summaries of the daybook transactions were copied into master account books, both journals and ledgers. Ledgers were organized by the name of the payer, with a block of space devoted to each individual. All payments credited to a payer's account were entered in that block along with the page number of the daybook entry. Journal entries were made in chronological order. All four types of books of the receiver general's office—rent-rolls, daybooks, journals, and ledgers—can be checked to see when and how much a purchaser paid for his land and what quitrent he paid, if any.

In 1746, to place more stringent control over the granting of patents, Thomas Penn combined the positions of receiver general and keeper of the great seal. Lardner, like James Logan before him, held both positions.[5] This move gave Lardner the authority to approve or disapprove all land patents, a responsibility well placed with the proprietary officer in charge of collecting the payments for land. Lardner worked for the Penn family for several years until he resigned in 1753.

The Penns, deciding to keep the receiver general's responsibilities for collecting quitrents split, appointed two men to fill the position: Richard Hockley and Edmund Physick.[6] Hockley had been under Thomas Penn's virtual guardianship for several years and was a friend of

Proprietary Secretary Peters. Physick had also been closely associated with Penn, serving as a clerk before becoming receiver general. Physick and Hockley worked together until Hockley resigned in 1768 to be appointed to the newly created position of auditor general of the Penn "Accompts in and for" the province of Pennsylvania, a position more honorary than anything else.[7] Hockley died in 1774.[8] Physick continued as receiver general through the end of the proprietary era and helped to oversee the divestiture of the Penn estate.[9]

One contribution of Physick, Hockley, and Thomas Penn to record keeping was the system of naming the tracts of land. The collection of quitrents being a perennial problem, the three men hoped to follow a tract of land by its own name rather than through the names of a series of new owners. Although the practice of naming tracts dated from much earlier, beginning about 1766 tract names were required when the land was patented. The patent index includes the tract name. A separate tract name index makes it possible to locate the warrantee and patentee if only the tract name is known.[10]

A major problem facing the receiver general during the era 1732–1776 was the controversy over taxation of the proprietors' privately owned manors and tracts. After a protracted battle between the assembly and the proprietors, the assembly passed revenue laws in 1759 and 1764 that included taxation of the proprietary estates at the same rate as all other land.[11] The income was to go toward funds to supply the troops in the French and Indian War and Pontiac's War. To assess the effect of the law, Thomas Penn ordered the receiver general to prepare a report of all proprietary manors and other appropriated land and to send copies of the assessments levied on this land to him in England.[12] Penn expected the receiver general to be prepared to challenge any unfair county assessment. Apparently the only assessment problem occurred in the proprietary town of Carlisle, where the vacant proprietary lots were not properly assessed as uncultivated land.[13] Since all proprietary records concerning taxation were sent to England, they became private papers of the Penn family and now are part of the Penn Papers at the Historical Society of Pennsylvania.

RECORDS: LOOSE PAPERS

RECEIVER GENERAL CERTIFICATES   LO micro.: 20.3.

Record partial payments for land. The contents of only one folder refer to the period 1744–1785.

RECORDS: BOUND VOLUMES

QUIT RENT ROLLS   1703–1744   (With index)   Reel 468.

A series of books for Philadelphia, Bucks, and Chester counties used by the deputy receivers to record the payment of quitrents. Entries are by township or area, including certain manors, and give the patentee's name, patent date, acres, quitrent assessed, quitrent collected, and subdivision of tracts.

RENT ROLLS   1683–1776   (With index).

Master rent-roll books kept in the receiver's office. Prepared by county, they are arranged within by township and give the resident's name, date residency began, acreage, and amount collected. Not all entries are complete.

QUIT RENT BOOK A, 1741–1742; QUIT RENT BOOK C, 1757–1776   Reel 468.

Contain records of cash payments and give the payer, date paid, acres, location, and amount paid. Book B, 1743–[1757], now missing, was turned over to the Commonwealth according to a report in the minutes of the Supreme Executive Council for June 14, 1781 (CR 12:755–57).

DAY BOOKS [of the Receiver General, Nos. 1–14, 1720–1779]   LO micro.: 25.37–40, 25.57.

Daily chronological accounts of money collected for land sales, quitrents, and other proprietary income. Entries give the individual's name, to whom or what account payment was directed, and the amount received. For quitrents, entries are grouped by the town where the receiver sat.

JOURNALS [of the Receiver General, C–H, 1733–1779]   Reels 469, 470; LO micro.: 25.61, 25.63–65.

Master journals of proprietary accounts, containing information from the rent-rolls and the receiver general's daybooks. Entries are in chronological order and include accounts of land and quitrents collected by location, giving the name of the payer, acres, township, and amount paid.

LEDGERS [of the Receiver General, C–H, 1733–1779]   (With index)   LO micro.: 25.80–82.

Organized by the first appearance of a payer in the daybook for the period of the volume. A block for each person includes a listing of all amounts paid. The information given includes the payer's name, the date paid, the page in the daybook, and which account was credited.

---

[1]Com. Bk. A-1-21.
[2]Pat. Bk. A-10-321.
[3]Richard Peters to Thomas Penn, March 2, 1741/2, Peters Letter Books, HSP; Joseph H. Fairbanks, Jr., "Richard Peters (c. 1704–1776): Provincial Secretary of Pennsylvania" (Ph.D. diss., University of Arizona, 1972), 48.
[4]On quitrents see also II.F.4, Receiver General.
[5]Com. Bk. A-1-373.
[6]Com. Bk. A-2-145.
[7]Com. Bk. A-3-512–15.
[8]Richard Peters to Lady Juliana Penn, September 18, 1774, Official Correspondence 9, Penn Papers, HSP; Edward O. Smith, Jr., "Thomas Penn, Chief Proprietor of Pennsylvania: A Study of His Public Governmental Activities from 1763 to 1775" (Ph.D. diss., Lehigh University, 1966), 483.
[9]See, in particular, General Cash Accounts.
[10]See III.G.5, Patents.
[11]See III.G.6, 1759 Transcripts (Green Books).
[12]To Richard Hockley and Edmund Physick, October 12, 1764, Letter Book 8:151–55, roll 2, *TPP*.
[13]Thomas Penn to John Penn ("Nephew"), July 13, 1764, Letter Book 8:108–12, roll 2, *TPP*.

III.F.5. Master of the Rolls

When the younger Penns assumed the proprietorship of Pennsylvania, Charles Brockden was master of the rolls for the province and recorder of deeds for Philadelphia City and County. He had held both positions since 1715 and continued to hold them until 1767. When the

Philadelphia County justices of the peace removed him from office in 1767 for "age and Infirmities," they reported that "the Records appeared to be in disorder and irregularly kept."[1] The justices appointed William Parr, Brockden's assistant, to be his successor as recorder of deeds. John Penn quickly added his commission making Parr master of the rolls for the province. For the rest of the proprietary era, Parr functioned as both master of the rolls and recorder of deeds for Philadelphia County.[2]

Among his duties the master of the rolls was responsible for recording all land patents. The special books in which he entered the patents are part of the Land Office collection and are discussed in III.G.5, Patents. The original patent became the private property of the purchaser.

The master of the rolls also recorded appointments, charters, and commissions. Many of these documents had been recorded in the regular patent books prior to 1733, but a separate series of commission books was begun in that year. These volumes are an important adjunct to determining legal dates. They are cited below.

Other legal documents, such as letters of attorney, bills of exchange, and probates, were recorded by the master of the rolls. Such documents were entered in a series of volumes titled "Letter of Attorney," which are cited below. Many of the records deal with private legal situations between inhabitants of England and settlers in the province. Others have to do with shipping and business interests. Since each county had its own recorder of deeds, Philadelphia County alone shared its office with the proprietary rolls office. Therefore, most of the records in the letter of attorney books refer to residents of Philadelphia County.

Usually the patent books and the county deed books were distinguished from each other and entries were seldom made in the wrong set of volumes. However, exceptions exist. By 1732 the master of the rolls had also served as the Philadelphia County recorder of deeds for over fifteen years. During that time some patents were recorded in the Philadelphia County deed books, and some deeds were recorded in the provincial patent books.

A special set of books containing all the deeds from the patent books that applied to Philadelphia County was prepared sometime after 1799 when the Land Office moved to Lancaster. Called exemplifications because they were legal copies of deeds, the documents in these several volumes are part of the Philadelphia County deed records and can be accessed through the Philadelphia County Exemplifications Index.

RECORDS: BOUND VOLUMES

COMMISSION BOOK A-1   [1733–1752]   LO micro.: 1; PA (3) 8.

COMMISSION BOOK A-2   [1752–1764]   LO micro.: 2; PA (3) 9.

COMMISSION BOOK A-3   [1764–1772]   LO micro.: 2; PA (3) 9, 10.

COMMISSION BOOK A-4   [1772–1776]   LO micro.: 2; PA (3) 10.

LETTER OF ATTORNEY   D-2 NO. 2   [1728–1745]   LO micro.: 25.123.

LETTER OF ATTORNEY   D-2 VOL. 3   [1746–1755]   LO micro.: 25.123–24.

LETTER OF ATTORNEY   D-2 NO. 5   [1758–1764]   LO micro.: 25.124.

LETTER OF ATTORNEY   D-2 NO. 6   [1764–1768]   LO micro.: 25.124–25.

LETTER OF ATTORNEY   D-2 NO. 7   [1768–1773]   LO micro.: 25.125.

LETTER OF ATTORNEY   D-2 VOL. 8   [1774–1777]   LO micro.: 25.125.

[1]Com. Bk. A-3-498; PA (3) 10:353–54. On Charles Brockden see John Clement, "Charles Brockden," PMHB 12 (1888): 185–89.

[2]Com. Bk. A-3-499.

III.G. Records

During the course of the proprietaries' administration, two fundamental changes developed in the series of records used to transfer land to individual ownership. The first change occurred with the requirement of a formal written application addressed to the secretary of the Land Office instead of an informal request to the commissioners of property. The second change came about through the gradual acceptance of ownership by settlement and improvement and the resulting introduction of a warrant to accept drawn up after the survey was conducted and the purchase price paid.

The steps for titling vacant unimproved land remained the same as under William Penn's proprietorship. Geographer Lewis Evans, in "An answer to some Queries of a Gentleman in Europe," outlined the steps in 1753.[1] His explanation is corroborated by the records themselves. The prospective purchaser submitted a formal request, now called an application, directly to the proprietary secretary and paid the necessary office fees and a portion of the purchase price. Common land purchased after 1732 usually cost the buyer fifteen pounds ten shillings per one hundred acres. One half of the total, or at least five pounds, was due upon submission of the application. Many applications dating from this period carry a notation indicating the amount paid. If the secretary had no reason to believe the acreage was under warrant by anyone else, he issued a warrant to survey. The warrant, signed by the governor, one of the Penns, or their appointed deputy as commissioner of property, was sent to the surveyor general. The surveyor general logged the warrant in a register and filed the original warrant alphabetically and then chronologically within the proper county files in his office. He also sent a copy to his appropriate deputy surveyor ordering him to survey the tract.

After the deputy surveyor completed the survey and the purchaser paid the surveying fee,

the deputy surveyor sent the completed draft of the tract to the surveyor general. The surveyor general filed the survey with the warrant. Whenever the purchaser paid the balance of the money to the receiver general, by law within six months, the surveyor general completed a return of survey document. He then entered a copy of the return of survey in his books and sent the original to the secretary. The secretary copied the information from the return of survey into the body of the patent, registered the patent in a book, and sent the original to the Rolls Office to be recorded. The master of the rolls copied the patent into a patent book and affixed the great seal of the province on the original patent before giving it to the purchaser as proof of legal title to the land, subject to quitrents.[2]

A slightly different order of steps existed after 1765 for applicants who had already settled and improved the land.[3] The settler submitted an application to the secretary but did not pay any of the purchase price. The secretary recorded the receipt of the application and sent it directly to the surveyor general. The surveyor general filed the application chronologically and then alphabetically and sent a copy to the deputy surveyor ordering him to survey. After the deputy surveyor completed the survey and received his fees, he sent the draft of the survey to the surveyor general, who filed it with the application. At this point the settler sent a certificate of date of settlement to the secretary and paid the entire purchase price and back interest to the receiver general. The secretary then sent a warrant to accept the survey to the surveyor general, who as a result prepared the return of survey and sent it to the secretary. The patent resulted in the usual way.

The following subsections contain a more detailed discussion of the titling process and of each document involved.

[1]Lewis Evans, "A Brief Account of Pennsylvania in a Letter to Richard Peters, Esq," Lewis Evans Mss, HSP.

²CR 8:337.
³Land Office Procedure, LO micro.: 20.5.

III.G.1. Applications

During the proprietaries' administration the application for a warrant became a regular part of the series of records necessary to warrant and patent land. Originating in the requests for warrants that were submitted to the commissioners of property during the proprietorship of William Penn, the application became an integral part of the system with the official recognition of ownership by settlement and improvement. Between 1732 and 1765 an informal application was used to request a warrant to survey, usually for unimproved land but often for land already settled and improved. After 1765 the application was used in three special land distribution programs: East Side Applications, West Side Applications, and New Purchase Applications. In these programs the land to be surveyed was already settled and improved, and the application, rather than the warrant, was used to order a survey. Once the pattern had been set, it was a short step for the application to become the required first step in the patenting process for both improved and unimproved land.

III.G.1.a. Applications, 1732–1765

Between 1732 and 1765, applications consisted of an individual's request for a warrant. The request was either written on a small scrap of paper or listed on a longer sheet of paper together with several others from the same geographic area and was carried to the Land Office by a representative. Included in the information on the application was the number of acres and the general location desired. Often the reason for the application was also stated. Usually the application was for a warrant to survey a tract that was not yet settled and improved, but sometimes it was for a warrant to accept a survey of a tract that was already settled. As the warrant registers show, warrants to accept become more common as the period progressed.

Rather than enter the application into the minutes of the commissioners of property as had been done during William Penn's proprietorship, the secretary copied the application into a separate application book. Some of these books have been rebound and are cited below; others are filed with the original loose applications. Surviving original applications from 1732 to 1741 indicate that Thomas Penn, serving in his capacity as commissioner of property, reviewed the applications and accepted or rejected them.

After 1741, when Thomas Penn returned to England and the job of commissioner of property was given to the governor, applications changed again. Although the application was still phrased as a request for a warrant to survey unimproved land, most applications actually stated that the tract included an improvement. The application went directly to the secretary who, in his capacity as receiver general, marked on the application the amount paid, usually one half of the total purchase price; signed it; and completed the warrant.

Many original applications from the 1732–1765 period are extant. Others exist as copies in books. Since the application was the first step in the patenting process, it was dated the same day or earlier than the warrant. For the period 1734–1762, many others are contained within longer lists and filed separately. Applications have not been indexed but can be accessed by searching backward from the date of the warrant.

RECORDS: LOOSE PAPERS

APPLICATIONS LISTS 1742–1774.

Lists of applications for the years 1742–1774 are filed in five folders. What appears to be the unbound register of applications for the years 1757–1759 is filed in folder 3.

APPLICATIONS FOR WARRANT   1734–1762   LO micro.: 7.5–9.

Mainly small pieces of paper filed by year, stating the name of the applicant, amount of land requested, and general location. Many applications are signed by the secretary, Richard Peters, and directed to the surveyor general.

RECORDS: BOUND VOLUMES

APPLICATIONS   1732–1733   (Binding No. 123).

Covers the period December 22, 1732, through September 18, 1733.

APPLICATIONS   1741–1746   (Binding No. 121).

Covers the period September 1, 1741, through December 5, 1746.

APPLICATIONS   1755–1756   (Binding No. 125).

Covers the period April 10, 1755, through September 8, 1756.

APPLICATIONS   1762–1763   (Binding No. 126).

Covers the period September 8, 1762, through March 24, 1763.

APPLICATIONS   1763–1764   (Binding No. 127).

Covers the period July 1, 1763, through November 23, 1764.

SPECIAL APPLICATIONS   OCT. 14, 1760–OCT. 4, 1765   (Binding Volume 166).

Covers the dates indicated.

III.G.1.b. Applications, 1765–1776

In 1765 the Land Office introduced an alternative series of steps for transferring settled unwarranted land within the purchases of 1754 and earlier to individual ownership. In two special programs, one for the east side of the Susquehanna River and one for the west side, the application led directly to the survey. Called East Side Applications and West Side Applications, the processes bypassed the warrant to survey and substituted a warrant to accept when the survey was completed and the entire purchase price had been paid. Applications under this program usually state the date of first settlement from which interest and quitrent were due and, therefore, are particularly valuable to researchers.

Early historians of land settlement in Pennsylvania called the new procedure the application system. To continue to do so is confusing because the application system applied to these two programs only, while the procedure was later adopted for settled unwarranted land within the Purchase of 1768. Furthermore, the application document continued to be used as the first step in titling unsettled unwarranted land.

Original applications for the period 1762–1776, including East Side and West Side applications, are filed chronologically and then alphabetically within each year. New Purchase (Purchase of 1768) Applications are filed separately in numerical order. In this GUIDE the applications for these programs are discussed and cited under III.E.1.c(1), East Side Applications; III.E.1.c(2), West Side Applications; and

III.E.2.a, Settled Unwarranted Land (New Purchase Applications). Books containing copies of

the original applications are also part of the Land Office collection and cited below.

RECORDS: LOOSE PAPERS

APPLICATIONS FOR WARRANT 1762–1776   LO micro.: 7.9–27.

Filed alphabetically within each year and written on small scraps of paper or in lists. They state the applicant's name, amount of land requested, and general location.

APPLICATIONS FOR WARRANT   NEW PURCHASE   LO micro.: 7.1–4.

Filed in numerical order, giving the applicant's name, acres, location, and adjoining owners.

RECORDS: BOUND VOLUMES

APPLICATIONS FOR WARRANT   1768–1771   [1764–65]   (Binding Volume 124).

Covers the period December 3, 1764, through October 25, 1765. Information given includes the applicant's name, adjoining owners, location, and date of first settlement from which interest and quitrent are due.

APPLICATIONS   1765–1766   (Binding Volume 128).

Covers the period October 18, 1765, through January 20, 1767. Information given includes the applicant's name, adjoining owners, location, and date of first settlement from which interest and quitrent are due.

APPLICATIONS MARCH 26 TO DECEMBER 11, 1767   (Binding Volume 122).

Covers the period indicated. Information given includes the applicant's name, adjoining owners, location, and date of first settlement from which interest and quitrent are due.

III.G.2. Warrants

Warrants took on new forms between 1733 and 1776. Previous historians of land settlement have interpreted the different forms as different types of warrants, but the Land Office registers and indexes recognize only three types: 1) the warrant to survey, 2) the warrant to accept a survey, and 3) the warrant of entry. The warrant to survey was the same as that of William Penn's administration. The warrant to accept was developed to accommodate ownership by settlement and improvement, a policy of the later proprietary era. The warrant of entry acknowledged the private sale or transfer of a warrant right from one individual to another.[1]

Each of the three types of warrants could be descriptive or indescriptive. Descriptive warrants contained enough information to locate the tract by specific geographic features and adjoining owners and became more common as ownership by settlement and improvement was recognized. Indescriptive warrants permitted latitude in surveying and usually were granted to speculators rather than to settlers.

The warrant to survey was granted to purchasers buying vacant unimproved land. Prepared by the secretary after the buyer had paid

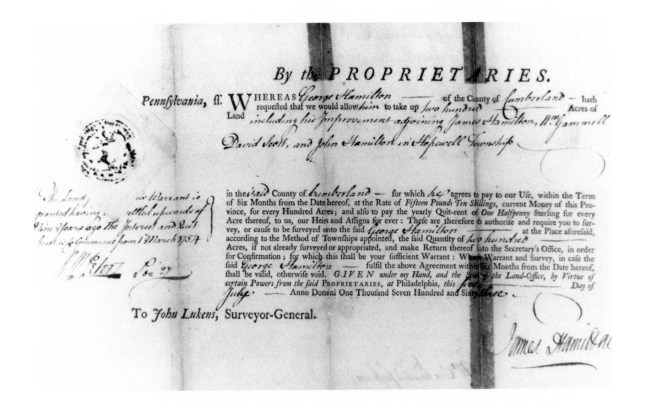

Warrant to accept a survey for George Hamilton, Cumberland County, 1763. Note the settlement and quitrent payment date. (Cumberland County Wt. H-141)

one half of the purchase price, the warrant to survey was essentially an order to the surveyor general telling him to survey a certain amount of land in a particular location. The warrant stated the warrantee's name, county, amount of land requested, location of the tract in general terms, purchase price, and amount of quitrent. It omitted the phraseology used under William Penn that the land surveyed was not to be seated by the Indians but retained the phrase that tracts were to be surveyed according to the method of townships, that is, contiguously. The warrant to survey also stated that the terms of sale were to be met within a given period, usually six months, or the warrant would be void.

The warrant to accept was usually granted to purchasers who were settled on the land before the survey was conducted. Prepared by the sec-

retary after the survey was completed and the exact acreage was known, the warrant to accept told the surveyor general to accept the survey and prepare the return of survey. This procedure had several advantages for the Land Office. Among others it eliminated duplicate paper work and assured the collection of the entire purchase price before the surveyor general prepared the return of survey. The warrant itself usually stated the warrantee's name; county; amount of land surveyed; location in general terms, perhaps giving the township; purchase rate; and quitrent. It often included the reason for the warrant.

The vacating warrant was a variation of the warrant to accept. The Land Office did not recognize the vacating warrant as a separate type of warrant but prepared one when the conditions of the original warrant had not been met. Thus the vacating warrant amounted to a second warrant for the same tract and was usually granted when the original warrantee had completed a warrant and survey but then sold or abandoned the tract. The Land Office would grant a warrant to accept to another individual who was willing to purchase the land as surveyed. This new warrant usually restated the original warrant, the fact that it was void, the new warrantee's name, and the new conditions, including the amount to be paid.[2]

The warrant of entry was granted as a special warrant to individuals who, by private arrangement, assumed a warrant previously granted to another person. Under these circumstances the Land Office did not issue a new warrant but copied the previous warrant and attached the new warrantee's name and date of warrant. Since the Land Office called the warrant book the book of entry, the rewritten warrant became the warrant of entry.

Procedures for handling and recording warrants under the proprietaries were similar to those under William Penn. Warrants to survey were prepared by the secretary and recorded in a warrant book before being sent to the surveyor general, who filed them and sent copies to the deputy surveyors. Warrants to accept were prepared by the secretary and recorded in a warrant book after the survey was completed and the fees were paid.

Warrants can be accessed by reference to the warrant registers cited in the records below. All warrants appearing in the warrant registers for the period 1732–1776 are available in either original or copied form. Original loose warrants were and still are filed by county of jurisdiction at the time the warrant was granted. Within each county, warrants are grouped alphabetically and then numbered chronologically. Under the 1759 law to record warrants and surveys, the original loose warrants were copied and bound into volumes for the first time.[3] These volumes are cited below. Original loose warrants were copied and bound into volumes a second time under the General Appropriation Act of 1911. These volumes are also cited below. The original warrants, the bound volumes, and the microfilm all follow the same order. Warrants were also copied into warrant books at the time the warrant was written; these book copies of the warrants are also cited below.

RECORDS: LOOSE PAPERS

ORIGINAL WARRANTS   LO micro.: 3.1–156.

Original warrants for the period 1732–1776 are filed alphabetically by county of jurisdiction at the time each warrant was granted. Within each county, warrants are grouped alphabetically and then numbered chronologically. Warrants are indexed in the warrant registers cited below.

RECORDS: BOUND VOLUMES

WARRANT REGISTERS   [1733–present]   LO micro.: 1.1–4; PA (3) 24–26.

Twenty-one volumes that function as master indexes to the original warrants. Each volume contains one or more of Pennsylvania's sixty-seven counties. Entries are grouped alphabetically by last name of warrantee, then listed chronologically by warrant date. For each warrantee the following information is cited: warrant number; warrantee's name; type of warrant; acres requested; warrant date; return date; acres returned; patentee's name; patent volume, number, and page; and survey book and page. See Appendix C for a correlation of warrants by county to microfilm reels; these registers have been microfilmed through 1957. The PA version published in 1898–99 is incomplete and omits survey, return of survey, and patent information.

WARRANT BOOK 1715–1741 (Binding No. 118) LO micro.: 25.108; index separately bound as WARRANT BOOK INDEX 1715–1741; 1759 transcript in WARRANTS OF PROPERTY 1715–1735 (Binding No. 28) LO micro.: 25.6; and WARRANTS 1735–1747 (Binding No. 29) LO micro.: 25.6.

Contains the secretary's book copies of warrants. Thomas Penn's signature begins to appear on warrants on page 130, dated November 3, 1733, and continues through 1741, with a few warrants appended at the end signed by Richard Peters and dated as late as 1744.

FRAGMENTS OF WARRANT BOOK 1a–1b LO micro.: 25.1; 1759 transcript in [Warrants Copies 1729–1733] WARRANT REGISTER 1733–1738 (Binding No. 51) LO micro.: 25.11.

In the 1759 transcript the *a* portion consists of 84 pages of warrants dated 1729–1733 and signed by Thomas, John, and Richard Penn. The *b* portion, pages 86–315 in the 1759 transcript, consists of a chronological warrant register for 1733–August 1741. The following information is listed: date of warrant, person's name and place of abode, situation of land granted, county, number of acres, comments, and in a few cases rate per acre, purchase money, and annual rent in sterling.

WARRANT REGISTER 1741 TO 1752 PART 1 OF 2 PG. 1–300 (Binding No. 57) LO micro.: 25.12–13.

Volume one of two volumes covering the indicated period. The volume is a copy of the missing original volume numbered 18S in the 1759 inventory of the secretary's office. The first entry is dated September 1, 1741; the last is dated November 22, 1748. For each entry the following information is given: date of warrant (in chronological order), to whom granted, situation, county (at time of warrant) and adjoining owner, acres, and comments.

WARRANT REGISTER 1741 TO 1752 PART 2 OF 2 PG. 301–558 INDEX (Binding No. 57) LO micro.: 25.13.

The second volume covering the indicated period and a continuation of the above volume. The first entry is dated November 22, 1748, and the last dated June 28, 1752.

INDEX TO WARRANT BOOK S 1741–1752 (Binding No. 4) LO micro.: 25.1.

The index to the missing original volume 18S in the secretary's office. It is also the original of the index that appears in the above volume.

WARRANT REGISTER 1752–1759 WITH INDEX (Binding No. 54) LO micro.: 25.12.

A copy of the missing original volume 19T in the 1759 inventory of the secretary's office. It is paginated 1–226 and continues the chronological listing of warrants as in the warrant registers for 1741–1752. The first entry is dated July 1, 1752, and the last, July 5, 1759.

INDEX TO BOOK T   1752–1772   (Binding Volume 153).

Seems to be the index to the missing original volume 19T in the secretary's office (see above). This index, however, covers a longer period of time and references pages into the mid-1770s, well beyond the last page, which is numbered 226 in the original according to the inventory list. This index gives names and page numbers only.

WARRANT BOOK NO. 27   1733–1734   (Binding No. 6f)   LO micro.: 25.1.

A warrant register for the period 1733–1736. Organized alphabetically by the first letter of the last name and then by county (Philadelphia, Bucks, Chester, Lancaster, New Castle, Kent, and Sussex), the register gives the warrantee, acres, and dates warranted, surveyed, and returned.

WARRANT BOOK   1733–1737   (Binding No. 6e)   LO micro.: 25.1.

Pages 1–59 of this volume are a repeat of Warrant Book No. 27 1733–1734. Dates for 1736–1737 begin on page 59, but the register is not complete for all letters of the alphabet. The volume is arranged alphabetically by the first letter of the last name and then by county.

WARRANT REGISTER   1741–1744   (Binding No. 119)   LO micro.: 25.108.

Covers the years indicated. The volume is arranged alphabetically and then by county (Philadelphia, Bucks, Chester, Lancaster, New Castle, Kent, and Sussex) and cites the warrantee, acres, and dates warranted, surveyed, and returned. The volume contains 92 of 128 original pages.

WARRANT BOOK NO. 9   1741–1748   (Binding No. 13)   LO micro.: 25.2.

Covers the years indicated. The volume is arranged alphabetically and then by county (Philadelphia, Bucks, Chester, Lancaster, New Castle, Kent, and Sussex) and cites the warrantee, acres, and dates warranted, surveyed, and returned. The information is not completed for many entries.

WARRANT BOOK NO. 18   1745–1746   (Binding No. 12)   LO micro.: 25.2.

Covers the years indicated. The volume is arranged by county (Philadelphia, Bucks, Chester, Lancaster, New Castle, Kent, and Sussex) within each letter of the alphabet and cites the warrantee, acres, and dates of warrant, order, copy warrant, and return paid.

WARRANT BOOK   1747–1748   (Binding No. 6c).

The inside cover bears the title "No. 24, Warrants commencing 6th June 1747, Anthony Palmer Esqr., Commissioner." The warrants cover the years indicated; the volume is arranged by county (Philadelphia, Bucks, Chester, Lancaster, New Castle, Kent, and Sussex) within each letter of the alphabet and cites the warrantee, acres, and date of warrant.

WARRANT BOOK NO. 22   1750–1751   (Binding No. 8)   LO micro.: 25.2.

Covers the years indicated. The volume is arranged by county (Philadelphia, Bucks, Chester, Lancaster, York, Cumberland, New Castle, Kent, and Sussex) and cites the warrantee, acres, and date of warrant.

INDEX NO. 21   1751 LIST   WARRANT BOOK   (Binding No. 9)   LO micro.: 25.2.

Covers the year indicated. The volume is arranged by county (Philadelphia, Bucks, Chester, Lancaster, York, Cumberland, New Castle, Kent, and Sussex) and cites the warrantee, acres, and date of warrant.

WARRANT BOOK   1752–1753   NO. 20   (Binding No. 10)   LO micro.: 25.2.

Covers the years indicated. The volume is arranged by county (Philadelphia, Bucks, Chester, Lancaster, York, Cumberland, New Castle, Kent, Sussex, Northampton, and Berks) and cites the warrantee, acres, and date, with comments.

WARRANTS   1753–1757   (Binding No. 11)   LO micro.: 25.2.

The inside title of this volume is "Warrants commencing 1st July 1753 James Hamilton Commissioner." The warrants cover the years indicated. The volume is arranged by county (Philadelphia, Bucks, Chester, Lancaster, York, Cumberland, Berks, Northampton, New Castle, Kent, and Sussex) and cites the warrantee, acres, and date of warrant.

ORDERS TO SURVEY FOR USE OF PROPRIETARIES   1746   (Binding No. 120)   LO micro.: 25.108.

Arranged by county and then alphabetized. The entries give the warrantee, acres, and date but seem to be incomplete for the year indicated.

WARRANTS—[Bucks]   NO. 1A TO 39C   (Binding No. 25)   LO micro.: 25.5.
WARRANTS—BUCKS   1737–1749   C TO H   (Binding No. 30)   LO micro.: 25.6.
WARRANTS BUCKS   H-141 TO M-241   (Binding No. 52)   LO micro.: 25.11
WARRANTS CHESTER   A-1 TO F-38   (Binding No. 34)   LO micro.: 25.7.
WARRANTS CHESTER   F-39 TO P-47   (Binding No. 35)   LO micro.: 25.7–8.
WARRANTS CHESTER   P-48 TO S-111   (Binding No. 47)   LO micro.: 25.10.
WARRANTS PHILADELPHIA   A-1 TO H-38   (Binding No. 42)   LO micro.: 25.9.
WARRANTS PHILADELPHIA   H-39 TO M96   (Binding No. 43)   LO micro.: 25.9.
WARRANTS PHILADELPHIA   M-97 TO S-262   (Binding No. 49)   LO micro.: 25.10–11.
WARRANTS LANCASTER   A-1 TO B386   (Binding No. 40)   LO micro.: 25.9.
WARRANTS LANCASTER   B-387 TO C-444   (Binding No. 56)   LO micro.: 25.12.
WARRANTS—BERKS   A-1 TO B-81   (Binding No. 44)   LO micro.: 25.9.

Transcripts made in 1759 of original loose warrants granted after 1732. The warrant registers serve as indexes.

COPIED WARRANTS (RG-14).

Copied warrants bound in oversized volumes. Authorized by the General Appropriation Act of 1911, the project was not completed. The set is composed of 175 bound volumes and 19 packages containing 313 booklets. It is organized by the same system as the original warrants; the warrant registers serve as an index.

---

[1]*SmL* 5:xiv–xvi.
[2]See, for example, Lancaster County Warrant B-248.
[3]See III.G.6, 1759 Transcripts (Green Books).

III.G.3. Surveys

Under the proprietaries little change in the method of conducting surveys or in the survey document occurred until 1765. Guidelines established in 1701 remained substantially the same through the early 1760s.[1] However, changes introduced in 1765 as a result of the application system set the surveying standard for the remainder of the proprietary era and the era of the Commonwealth as well.

The changes required deputy surveyors to make several modifications in their method of operation. After 1765, to control the practice of preferential treatment for certain purchasers, deputy surveyors were responsible for completing all surveys within six months or filing an explanation in the surveyor general's office. Other changes required deputy surveyors to report the initial date of settlement of every improvement that they surveyed and to keep a field book of "fair and regular entries in order of time" with a draught and field works, or all mathematical calculations, annexed.[2]

The most innovative change of all, however, was the requirement that all newly surveyed tracts be given a name.[3] The rationale was to make it easier to follow land for quitrent purposes. Finally, surveyors were to make sure that all tracts adjoining rivers or large creeks were at least three times deeper than the breadth along the water.

The normal surveying procedure was to begin at a corner of an adjoining tract or at an obvious topographical feature. Axmen worked ahead of the surveying crew to clear trees and underbrush. Chainmen measured distances by running horizontal lines, although sometimes a distance was incorrectly measured by running the chain along the ground. The surveyor kept the crew on line by using a compass. Corner markers were usually emblazoned on trees, preferably hardwoods such as hickory, chestnut, or oak, but stone piles and posts were not uncommon. An entire tract was to include a 6 percent allowance for roads and highways, so that an acre actually included 169.6 square perches rather than the standard 160 square perches. An overplus of more than 10 percent was not permitted.[4]

Using his own scale, the deputy surveyor drew the plat on a separate piece of paper and noted all adjoining owners and vacant land. These notations are valuable for constructing connected warrant tract maps. After pocketing one third of the surveying fee, the deputy surveyor signed the survey and sent it, along with two thirds of the fee, to the surveyor general. The surveyor general's office checked the calculations to make sure the acreage agreed with the warrant and then filed the survey with the warrant. These original surveys are part of the Land Office collection cited below.

The original surveys were later copied, and the copies were bound into books. The order was random, but the books were indexed in the warrant registers. The original loose surveys were refiled in the same order as they appeared in the copied survey books, so that the same volume, book, and page number applies to both the copied and the original surveys. The original surveys have also been microfilmed in the same order, and the copied survey books are in the process of being microfilmed.

RECORDS: LOOSE PAPERS

ORIGINAL SURVEYS   LO micro.: 6.1–190.

Original surveys are on individual sheets of paper, laminated, and filed in the same random order as the copied survey books (see volume numbers below). Volumes D-91 through D-114 are not in the copied survey books. Access is through the warrant registers.

RECORDS: BOUND VOLUMES

COPIED SURVEYS   LO micro.: 28.1– .

Original surveys have been hand copied in random order and bound into 466 volumes numbered as follows: A to Z, A-1 to A-89, B-1 to B-23, BB-1 to BB-4, C-1 to C-234, and D-1 to D-90. The warrant registers serve as the index.

---

[1]See II.G.4, Surveys.
[2]Min. Bd. Prop. Bk. 1:7–8. See III.F.3.b, Deputy Surveyors.
[3]See III.G.5, Patents.
[4]Min. Bd. Prop. Bk. 1, 13 Apr. 1767; PA (3) 1:171.

III.G.4. Returns of Survey

Under Thomas Penn the return of survey became the most important legal document in the Land Office, due to the many irregular practices that developed during this era, especially when surveys were made on an application without a warrant on record. The return of survey indicated that the entire purchase price had been paid. Completed in the surveyor general's office, the document restated in paragraph form the application or warrant and the survey and provided the information to fill out the patent. The return of survey also noted the consideration, or purchase money paid, any intermediary conveyance of the property, and the patentee and date.

Between 1737 and 1760 the surveyor general did not automatically send the return of survey to the secretary's office. Instead the secretary, Richard Peters, ordered the return after the purchaser applied for the patent. In this way, Peters could inspect the warrant and the applicant's right to the patent and determine the fees yet to be paid. He claimed that it was "frequently" necessary to write a second warrant, either a vacating warrant or a special warrant, to make the return of survey legal. When he

was satisfied, Peters sent an order, or ticket, to the surveyor general requesting the return of survey.[1] The ticket, written on a small scrap of paper, contained the basic warrant information and a notation concerning the amount required to settle the transaction. Called Richard Peters' Tickets, these papers constitute a separate collection in the Land Office and are cited below.

After the surveyor general prepared the return of survey he entered a copy in a return book and sent the original to the secretary's office. The secretary copied the information from the return of survey into the body of the patent. Beside the original return filed in the secretary's office, this procedure meant that there were "two 'Entries at Length' of all returns of survey; one in the surveyor general's office and the other in the body of the patent recorded in the Rolls Office."[2]

The original return of survey papers are part of the Land Office collection. They may be an especially valuable component to research in instances where the patentee is other than the warrantee. A chain of title and the date of conveyance may be recited. Available on microfilm, the returns are filed chronologically. The date of the return is given in the warrant registers. Returns dating from before 1760 have been copied three times, once in the original return books, once in the 1759 copies of the original return books, and once in the 1759 book copies of the loose papers. The last two copies were prepared under the 1759 law to record warrants and surveys. All the volumes are cited below.

RECORDS: LOOSE PAPERS

RETURNS OF SURVEYS   JAN., 1733–AUG., 1870   LO micro.: 5.1–114.

Original returns of survey for country land as opposed to city and town lots and proprietary tracts. The returns restate the warrant and survey information and often indicate the amount paid and to whom the land was patented.

RETURNS OF SURVEY   NOV., 1678–MARCH, 1800   LO micro.: 5.115–19.

Includes original returns of survey for proprietary tracts, Philadelphia city lots, and proprietary towns. The returns restate the warrant and survey information and often indicate the amount paid and to whom the land was patented.

RICHARD PETERS' TICKETS   1747–1756   LO micro.: 11.4–5.

Thirty folders containing Richard Peters's orders to the surveyor general to prepare the return of survey. Called tickets, the orders carry a brief statement of the warrant and amount remaining to be paid.

RECORDS: BOUND VOLUMES

COPIES OF THE SURVEYOR GENERAL'S RETURNS FROM OCTOBER 29, 1733   (Bound under the title RETURN OF SURVEYS 1701; Binding No. 18; with partial index)   LO micro.: 25.3; 1759 transcript in WARRANTS AND SURVEYS 5 (Index missing), Philadelphia City Archives, LO micro.: 25.129.

Contains the surveyor general's copies of returns of survey sent to the secretary. The returns recite in paragraph form the warrantee's name, date of warrant, chain of title, location and description of survey, number of acres, and date survey was returned. Entries are not in chronological order.

RETURNS, BUCKS, PHILADELPHIA   1719–1738   (Binding Volume 149; with index).

The contents appear to be copied entries of loose papers found after other return of survey books were made. Surveys date from 1719 through 1738, but dates are not given for many. Information included gives the name of warrantee, chain of title, description, acreage, and adjoining owners. Entries are not signed.

SURVEYOR GENERAL—RETURNS OF SURVEYS, NO. 5   1736–1740   (Binding No. 75)   LO micro.: 25.32; 1759 transcript in two parts: 1) WARRANTS AND SURVEYS

7, Philadelphia City Archives, LO micro.: 25.129; and 2) RETURNS INTO SECRETARY'S OFFICE WITH INDEX   (Binding No. 46)   LO micro.: 25.10.

Contains the surveyor general's copies of returns of survey sent to the secretary. Information given includes the date of warrant, date of survey, individual for whom the land was surveyed, location, description, acreage, and date of return. The index in the copy contains two columns; the first column refers to the original volume, while the second refers to the transcript.

RECORD OF RETURNS OF SURVEYS   1740–1747   (Binding No. 76; with index)   LO micro.: 25.32–33; 1759 transcript in RETURNS   1740–1747   (Binding No. 59; with index)   LO micro.: 25.13–14.

Contains the surveyor general's copies of returns of survey sent to the secretary. Information given includes the date of warrant, date of survey, individual for whom the land was surveyed, location, description, acreage, and date of return. Entries are not strictly chronological.

RETURN OF SURVEYS   1748–1753   (Binding No. 19)   LO micro.: 25.3–4; 1759 transcript in RETURN SURVEYS   JUNE 1748 TO JUNE 1753   WITH INDEX   (Binding No. 55)   LO micro.: 25.12.

Contains the surveyor general's copies of returns of survey sent to the secretary. Information given includes the date of warrant, date of survey, individual for whom the land was surveyed, location, description, acreage, and date of return. Not strictly chronological. The index bound in the transcript meshes with the original, not the transcript.

RETURNS   SURVEYS   1753–1759   (Bound in WARRANTS AND SURVEYS 8, Philadelphia City Archives)   LO micro.: 25.129.

A volume of general returns, marked "Book N in the Surveyor General's Office." It is probably a 1759 transcript of Book N, since it contains more pages than the original, and the index, complete for letters A–P, does not mesh with this volume. Entries are not in strict chronological order but give the date of warrant, date of survey, individual for whom the land was surveyed, location, description, acreage, and date of return.

PHILADELPHIA CITY NEW RETURNS   [A–W]   (Bound in WARRANTS AND SURVEYS 2, Philadelphia City Archives)   LO micro.: 25.128; LANCASTER COUNTY NEW RETURNS   [A–B69]   (Bound in WARRANTS AND SURVEYS 2, Philadelphia City Archives)   LO micro.: 25.128.

Two 1759 transcripts of original loose returns of survey for Philadelphia City and Lancaster County.

PHILADELPHIA COUNTY   NEW RETURNS   [B–S]   (Bound in WARRANTS AND SURVEYS 9, Philadelphia City Archives)   LO micro.: 25.129.

A 1759 transcript of original loose returns of survey for Philadelphia County.

RETURNS—LANCASTER B-70 TO H-66 (Binding No. 45) LO micro.: 25.9–10; RETURNS—LANCASTER H-67 TO M-41 (Bound with RETURNS—BUCKS L-23 TO Z; Binding No. 33) LO micro.: 25.7; RETURNS LANCASTER M 42 TO S 207 (Binding No. 48) LO micro.: 25.10.

The 1759 transcripts of original returns of survey for Lancaster County. They are successive continuations of Lancaster County New Returns [A–B69], cited above.

BUCKS NEW RETURNS [A–L] (Bound in WARRANTS AND SURVEYS 6, Philadelphia City Archives) LO micro.: 25.129.

A 1759 transcript of original returns of survey for Bucks County.

RETURNS—BUCKS L-23 TO Z LANCASTER H-67 TO M-41 (Binding No. 33) LO micro.: 25.7.

A 1759 transcript of original returns of survey for Bucks and Lancaster counties. It is a continuation of Bucks New Returns [A–L] and Returns—Lancaster B-70 to H-66, both of which are cited above.

RETURNS PHILADELPHIA A TO T CUMBERLAND A TO Z BERKS A TO Z CHESTER [Old Rights] P14 TO Z (Binding No. 53) LO micro.: 25.11. RETURNS YORK A TO Z NORTHAMPTON A TO Z WARRANTS 1735–1747 (Binding No. 29) LO micro.: 25.6.

The surveyor general's book copies of original returns of survey.

RETURNS 1734–1760 BERKS, BUCKS, CUMBERLAND, CHESTER, LANCASTER, NORTHAMPTON, YORK (Binding No. 27) LO micro.: 25.5.

A note on the inside cover of this volume indicates that all entries are completed returns of survey for which no patent was granted by the time the documents were copied in 1759 and 1760.

---

[1]PA (2) 8:270–71.
[2]CR 8:337.

III.G.5. Patents

No significant change in patents occurred during the period 1732–1776. Securing a patent was still the final step in the process of transferring land to individual ownership. The patent signified that the land had been purchased and conveyed legal title to the described tract.

The wording of the patent was taken from the return of survey document. Copied in longhand, the patent presented a verbal description of the tract's courses and distances, application and warrant information, purchase price, acreage, and quitrent. After September 1766 the standard portion of the patent, such as the reservation of one fifth of the ore from all nonroyal mines, was printed as a form, and spaces were left for filling in the pertinent information.[1]

Two copies of the patent were prepared, one on oversized paper and one on parchment. After the governor signed both copies, the parchment was affixed with the great seal and given to the purchaser. The paper copy was retained in the Rolls Office.

Periodically the Rolls Office copies of the patents were bound into books, and the books were indexed. The first set of patent volumes were lettered A and numbered 1 through 20. The last recording date in volume A-20 is May 31, 1760, shortly after Richard Peters resigned as secretary of the Land Office and his brother, William, became secretary. Historians know that record keeping had been neglected during the last several years of Richard Peters's administration, and the change in patent series may have been an effort to start afresh while

back recording went on at the same time. As indicated in the secretary's patent registers cited below, the proprietaries granted 2,659 patents between 1733 and 1760, the end of the A series.

The second set of patent volumes, the AA series, began in June 1760 and ended in 1776. Consisting of sixteen volumes, these patents incorporated the new feature of naming the patented tracts. For many years, Thomas Penn had suggested that tracts be named as a way of tracing them for quitrent purposes. Using the opportunity of the East Side and West Side application programs to send an updated set of instructions to the deputy surveyors, Surveyor General John Lukens appended to each set of instructions the requirement of giving some name to each survey returned to his office.[2] These survey names have been entered into a tract name index cited below, enabling the researcher to locate the patent or warrant if only the name of the tract is known.

RECORDS: BOUND VOLUMES

PATENT BOOKS   [Series A and AA]   (Index bound separately)   LO micro.: 2–15.

The A series covers the period 1733–1760, and the AA series covers 1760–1776. The two series are indexed together in one patent register. Several books also have individual indexes.

PATENT INDEX [Series] A & AA   LO micro.: 1.16.

Arranged alphabetically and grouped by volume and book. The following information is given: the patent date, page, acres, warrantee, warrant date, and county.

TRACT PATENT NAME INDEX   PATENT BOOKS A–AA   LO micro.: 1.20.

Arranged alphabetically by tract name, giving the following additional information: the patent volume, book, and page; patent date; patentee; acres; warrantee; warrant date; and county.

PATENT BOOK   1732–1741   (Binding No. 6)   LO micro.: 25.1; 1759 transcript in WARRANTS AND SURVEYS 2, Philadelphia City Archives, LO micro.: 25.128.

The inside title of this volume is "List of Patents Signed by the Proprietaries begun Anno 1732." The entries are not in strict chronological order but give the patentee, acres, location, rent, warrant, survey, date of patent, individual in whose right, and quantity, with remarks.

PATENT BOOK   1733–1744   (Binding No. 2)   LO micro.: 25.1; 1759 transcript in RETURNS OF SURVEYS   1733–1744   WITH INDEX   (Binding No. 39)   LO micro.: 25.9.

A patent register for the proprietaries' era beginning with no. 1 and ending with no. 595. Columns are headed: no., when returned, date warrant, quantity warranted, when surveyed, to whom surveyed, situation, county, quantity returned, date of patent, to whom granted, consideration money paid, date sent to the enrollment office, and remarks (Loan Office or quitrent).

PATENT BOOK   1745–1753   (Binding No. 3)   LO micro.: 25.1; 1759 transcript in MINUTES OF COMMISSIONERS OF PROPERTY   1701–1709   (Binding No. 20)   LO micro.: 25.4.

A continuation of Patent Book 1733–1744 (cited above), beginning with no. 595 (*sic*) and ending with no. 2011, December 23, 1752. Columns are headed the same in both volumes.

PATENTS   1753–1759   (Binding No. 60)   LO micro.: 25.14.

A continuation of Patent Book 1745–1753 (cited above). However, the numbering begins over again with no. 1, January 8, 1753, and ends with no. 648, July 2, 1759. The volume is columned and gives the same information as the earlier patent registers in the series.

---

[1]See Pat. Bk. AA-8-1.
[2]See, for example, "Deputy Surveyor's Duplicate Commissions and Instructions," folder 6, LO micro.: 19.2.

III.G.6. 1759 Transcripts (Green Books)

Original loose and bound land records were first copied in 1759. The project was the result of an act of the Provincial Assembly that provided for the copying of the proprietary land records with the intention of "preserving authentic duplicates."[1] Amounting to a complete inventory of both the secretary's and surveyor general's offices, the 1759 transcripts provide us with an invaluable historical tool. Although invalidated as official land records, these transcripts have assisted in interpreting proprietary land affairs.

One of the continuing sources of irritation and conflict between the citizens of the province and the proprietaries was the manner of recording warrants and ordering surveys. Claiming discrimination against small purchasers and favoritism for large landholders, the assembly made repeated efforts to pass legislation requiring proprietary land affairs to become public. Financial problems created by the French and Indian War brought the issue to a head. Success finally came following legislation permitting the assembly to tax proprietary estates. Once the proprietaries had agreed to allow their estates to be taxed, the assembly exerted its newly found power in an attempt to control the proprietary Land Office.

Legislation to record warrants and surveys passed the assembly on July 7, 1759. The essential features of the bill called for a new Public Records Office staffed by a recorder to be appointed by the assembly. The recorder was not to supplant the proprietary secretary and surveyor general but act as an impartial official, obligated by law to record all documents presented to him. The bill empowered the recorder to collect all the minutes of property, warrants, surveys, charts, maps, and other papers regardless of where they could be found; to number the records "in words at length"; to take an inventory; and then to transcribe them all. The bill outlined how the transcribing was to be done and the pay the clerks were to receive and appointed John Hughes, a member of the assembly, as the recorder.[2]

As soon as the bill took effect, Hughes employed a staff of clerks and began the task of transcribing the books and loose papers in the secretary's and surveyor general's offices. Careful study of the volumes shows that Hughes followed his instructions to the letter. Labeling each original book by office of origin and using a combination of numbers and letters, Hughes prepared a master list in which he recorded the number and letter; described the book; gave the number of pages written; cited the month, day, and year of the first and last entry; and recorded short identifying comments. After his staff had transcribed each book, Hughes checked the work and signed each volume, certifying its authenticity. He and his staff also numbered and signed or initialed each loose paper. They then copied the warrants and surveys for the period 1682–1732 into one set of volumes and the returns of survey into another set. For the period 1732–1759 they did not copy the surveys.

Meanwhile the proprietaries actively opposed the 1759 law and petitioned the king to nullify it on the ground that it impinged upon their proprietary rights. Despite the arguments of assembly representatives, including Benjamin Franklin, the Privy Council in September 1760 recommended a veto. The council used the argument that copies of legal records could not themselves also be legal records. By that time, however, most of the records had already been copied.

Although the project's results were invalidated as official land records, the work continued, and another year passed before the transcripts were returned to the assembly in two large trunks and Hughes was paid. The trunks contained twenty-five books of transcripts from the secretary's office records, forty-one books from the surveyor general's office, one unbound paper book of warrants and returns generated during the time the act was in force, and the inventory of papers and books transcribed. At this point the transcripts were numbered and certified, unfortunately creating yet another numbering system that had little rationale. The original books and loose papers remained in their respective offices.

Following a long and circuitous route, the transcripts, called Green Books for the color of their 1874 binding, eventually found their way in 1957 back into the Land Office but not without some mishaps and loss. Several of the Philadelphia City- and County-related volumes were sent to the Philadelphia City Archives. Other volumes have not been located. Furthermore, the rebinding does not present a sequential chronology of the volumes and makes their use difficult.

In this GUIDE the 1759 transcripts are cited in the records under the topic to which they apply, such as commissioners of property, warrants, surveys, and returns of survey. The original book is cited first, followed by the transcript. See Appendix A for the entire collection of original volumes and corresponding transcripts.

Individual records within the transcripts can be accessed by using one of several registers. For the period 1682–1732 the Old Rights registers reference all warrants, surveys, and returns of survey. Separated by county, the letter and number of the warrant, in some registers called the number of the paper, refer to the letter and number of the entry in the transcripts, whether for a warrant, survey, or return of survey. For the period 1733–1759 the two volumes Register of Old Rights (Binding No. 138) and Warrant Book Bucks, Chester, Philadelphia, Lancaster 1734–1759 (Binding No. 139) contain indexes to "new warrants," or those written between 1734 and 1759. These volumes are cited below in the records. No index to the return of survey volumes has been found, but the volumes are organized in the same way as the warrant volumes.

RECORDS: BOUND VOLUMES

HUGHES' LIST   (Binding No. 63); transcript: HUGHES' LIST   (Binding No. 62).

The original volume and copy differ slightly, but each contains an inventory of the bound volumes in the secretary's and surveyor general's offices in 1759 and an index to the bound volume copies of the loose papers in the secretary's office in the period 1682–1759.

REGISTER OF OLD RIGHTS   (Binding No. 138).

This and the volume cited below are the main indexes to the warrant volumes of the 1759 transcripts. The first pages (3–9) contain John Hughes's 1759 inventory of bound volumes in the surveyor general's office. The remaining pages are an old rights register ending with a few pages of a new warrants register for Philadelphia County.

WARRANT BOOK BUCKS, CHESTER, PHILADELPHIA, LANCASTER 1734–1759   (Binding No. 139).

A continuation of Register of Old Rights (cited above), containing an index to the new warrant volumes of the 1759 transcripts.

1759 Transcripts of Warrants, Surveys, and Returns of Survey for the Period 1684–1732 (Old Rights).

OLD RIGHTS—BUCKS   NO. 1A TO 21A [21P]   (Binding No. 24)   LO micro.: 25.5.

OLD RIGHTS—BUCKS   NO. 22 P TO Z   (Binding No. 25)   LO micro.: 25.5.

RETURNS— [Bucks]   A TO Z   (Binding No. 32)   LO micro.: 25.7.

OLD RIGHTS, CHESTER   A-1 TO H-106   (Binding No. 31)   LO micro.: 25.6–7.

OLD RIGHTS, CHESTER   H-107 TO T-55   (Chester County Historical Society, manuscript no. 37180)   LDS micro.: 0020886.

OLD RIGHTS, CHESTER   T-56 TO Y-4   (Binding No. 34)   LO micro.: 25.7.

RETURNS—CHESTER   A TO P-15   (Binding No. 32)   LO micro.: 25.6.

RETURNS   CHESTER   P14 TO Z   (Binding No. 53)   LO micro.: 25.11.

PHILADELPHIA COUNTY   [F-769 to H-1203, P-2421 to S-2441]   (Bound in WARRANTS AND SURVEYS 1, Philadelphia City Archives)   LO micro.: 25.128.

OLD RIGHTS PHILADELPHIA   I-1225–P2420   (Binding No. 38)   LO micro.: 25.8.

PHILADELPHIA CITY [Returns A–W]   (Bound in WARRANTS AND SURVEYS 2, Philadelphia City Archives)   LO micro.: 25.128.

PHILADELPHIA COUNTY [Returns A–Y]   (Bound in WARRANTS AND SURVEYS 6, Philadelphia City Archives)   LO micro.: 25.129.

1759 Transcripts of Warrants and Returns of Survey for the Period 1733–1759 (New Warrants)

WARRANTS—[Bucks]   NO. 1A TO 39C   (Binding No. 25)   LO micro.: 25.5.

WARRANTS—BUCKS   1737–1749   C TO H   (Binding No. 30)   LO micro.: 25.6.

WARRANTS BUCKS   H-141 TO M-241   (Binding No. 52)   LO micro.: 25.11.

BUCKS   NEW RETURNS   [A–L]   (Bound in WARRANTS AND SURVEYS 6, Philadelphia City Archives)   LO micro.: 25.129.

RETURNS—BUCKS L-23 TO Z   (Binding No. 33)   LO micro.: 25.7.

WARRANTS CHESTER   A-1 TO F-38   (Binding No. 34)   LO micro.: 25.7.

WARRANTS CHESTER   F-39 TO P-47   (Binding No. 35)   LO micro.: 25.7–8.

WARRANTS CHESTER   P-48 TO S-111   (Binding No. 47)   LO micro.: 25.10.

WARRANTS PHILADELPHIA   A-1 TO H-38   (Binding No. 42)   LO micro.: 25.9.

WARRANTS PHILADELPHIA   H-39 TO M96   (Binding No. 43)   LO micro.: 25.9.

WARRANTS PHILADELPHIA   M-97 TO S-262   (Binding No. 49)   LO micro.: 25.10–11.

PHILADELPHIA COUNTY   NEW RETURNS   [B–S]   (Bound in WARRANTS AND SURVEYS 9, Philadelphia City Archives)   LO micro.: 25.129.

RETURNS   PHILADELPHIA A TO T   (Binding No. 53)   LO micro.: 25.11.

PHILADELPHIA CITY NEW RETURNS   [A–W]   (Bound in WARRANTS AND SURVEYS 2, Philadelphia City Archives)   LO micro.: 25.128.

WARRANTS LANCASTER   A-1 TO B386   (Binding No. 40)   LO micro.: 25.9.

WARRANTS LANCASTER   B-387 TO C-444   (Binding No. 56)   LO micro.: 25.12.

LANCASTER COUNTY NEW RETURNS [A–B69]   (Bound in WARRANTS AND SURVEYS 2, Philadelphia City Archives)   LO micro.: 25.128.

RETURNS—LANCASTER   B-70 TO H-66   (Binding No. 45)   LO micro.: 25.9–10.

RETURNS—LANCASTER   H-67 TO M-41   (Binding No. 33)   LO micro.: 25.7.

RETURNS   LANCASTER   M 42 TO S 207   (Binding No. 48)   LO micro.: 25.10.

WARRANTS—BERKS   A-1 TO B-81   (Binding No. 44)   LO micro.: 25.9.

RETURNS   BERKS A TO Z   (Binding No. 53)   LO micro.: 25.11.

RETURNS   YORK A TO Z   (Binding No. 29)   LO micro.: 25.6.

RETURNS   CUMBERLAND A TO Z   (Binding No. 53)   LO micro.: 25.11.

RETURNS   NORTHAMPTON A TO Z   (Binding No. 29)   LO micro.: 25.6.

RETURNS   1734–1760   BERKS, BUCKS, CUMBERLAND, CHESTER, LANCASTER, NORTHAMPTON, YORK   (Binding No. 27)   LO micro.: 25.5.

---

[1]"An Act for Recording of Warrants and Surveys, and for Rendering the Real Estates and Property within this Province More Secure," July 7, 1759. In *Statutes* 5:448–55.

[2]Hughes was later the Pennsylvania Stamp Act commissioner.

SECTION IV

Land Settlement, 1776–1990: The Commonwealth

IV.A. Introduction

This section discusses land settlement in Pennsylvania under the government of the Commonwealth, 1776–1990. Formed during the American Revolution, the Commonwealth government suddenly became the owner of all unsold land in Pennsylvania. Totally unprepared for such responsibility, state leaders continued the land policies and record-keeping procedures established by the proprietary government. Many years elapsed before the state developed new land distribution policies and methods.

To gain administrative control of its vast domain, the new state government took three important steps. First, the legislature divested the Penns of their proprietary ownership; second, the Land Office completed titles to land granted by the proprietary government; and, third, the Commonwealth purchased the remaining land within the Pennsylvania charter bounds. Establishing a Land Office controlled by the legislature, the state proceeded to transfer its unsold land to private ownership as quickly as possible. For a government in need of income, land served as a medium of exchange as well as a basis for taxation. Conflict between squatter and speculator marred the early years of the state and was not brought under control until the majority of favorable land had passed into private hands. Incomplete titles and a nonexistent mapping system eventually placed the burden of proving the vacancy upon the applicant.

As the state disposed of its land, the land officers grew less and less important. Originally they were among the major appointed officials of the newly formed state government, and each one maintained his own office. Gradually, however, one office was merged with another until the Land Office became part of the Department of Internal Affairs in 1874. Remarkably the records of each office survived virtually in their entirety.

The questions of how and why the legislature and the Land Office developed new policies and procedures are answered in this section. New categories of purchasers are introduced, new land distribution programs are discussed, and the evolution of ownership by settlement and improvement is unfolded. Finally, this section presents the new Land Office of the Commonwealth and the records generated in the transfer of land from public to private ownership.

IV.B. Basic Policies

At first the newly formed state government adopted the proprietary government's land policies and procedures. Slowly, as the need arose, the legislature and the Land Office formed their own land policies and procedures for titling land. Their pragmatic approach to the business of land differed little from the proprietary era, although Commonwealth policies were more clearly stated in land legislation. From special considerations

125

for selected settlers through different programs for particular geographic regions, an orderly land policy gradually developed. By 1817 the sale of land in the entire state was on a uniform basis. Subsequent land policy simply readdressed the Commonwealth's role in relation to the amount of control it wished to exert over its most basic natural resource, its land.

IV.B.1. Divesting Law

One of the first orders of business of the newly created Commonwealth government was to gain legal control of its own land. Appointing a legislative committee to examine the claims of the proprietors, the Pennsylvania General Assembly sought a way to settle accounts with the Penns. The result was the Divesting Law of 1779. The law transferred all ungranted land within the bounds of William Penn's charter to the disposal of the legislature. The law also abolished quitrents and ordered all arrears in purchase money to be paid to the newly formed state government. In return the Penn family was to be reimbursed with £130,000 sterling of Great Britain and permitted to retain ownership of all private estates and proprietary manors that had been surveyed and returned to the Land Office before July 4, 1776. To complete the transfer of ownership, all loose land records and bound volumes belonging to the land officers were to be turned over to the Commonwealth.[1]

Compensation to the Penns failed to reflect the true value of Pennsylvania's unsold land. The amount was determined in recognition of the "enterprising spirit which distinguished the founder of Pennsylvania" and what the new state thought it could afford.[2] Paid in installments of £15,000 to £20,000 per year, the reimbursement was not due to begin until one year after the end of the Revolutionary War. Funds were first raised by selling the land on which the British barracks had been built in the northern liberties during the war. The total debt was finally discharged after 1791.[3]

The majority of property remaining in the Penn family lay in northeastern Pennsylvania, especially Northampton County, but the family also owned several other tracts throughout the state. In Philadelphia, for example, the Penn estate consisted of ground rent on several lots that had been within Springettsbury Manor.[4]

Much of the manor land the family claimed had actually been under private ownership for many years but never warranted and patented. In the years following the divestiture, various arrangements transferred legal ownership to the current residents. These records will be found in the county of jurisdiction at the time the transfer occurred. The grantor may be the Penns, an intermediate lawyer, or the Commonwealth. For a detailed map of Penn family holdings in Pennsylvania, consult John Hill, "A Map of Pennsylvania Divided into its Counties and Exhibiting the Property of John Penn Jun. Esq., 1787," HSP; a photocopy is in Land Office (Map Inventory), Drawer 0038, Item 1.

---

[1] *Purdon* 64 § 1, 1–8.
[2] *Statutes* 14:81–85.
[3] Ibid.
[4] Two manors named Springettsbury were surveyed. The first (before 1703) lay adjacent to Philadelphia. The second (1722) was located within Cumberland County.

IV.B.2. Commonwealth Interests
IV.B.2.a. Land as Raw Income

Land, long a source of revenue for the proprietary government, was no less so for the Commonwealth. In need of money to pay its Revolutionary War debts, the new state government immediately sought to collect all outstanding purchase money and fees due on titles begun under the proprietary government. With the same terms as had been offered in 1765, the only additional charge was the interest on the outstanding balance. Various mortgage programs encouraged warrantees who could not afford an immediate cash outlay. Others were granted an exoneration of interest for the years when they were unable to occupy their land during the war. Although the state did not collect the sums it needed, most of the titles to land granted under the proprietors were completed by the mid-1820s.

For an additional source of income the new government began to sell all unappropriated land to which Indian claims had been extinguished. This encompassed the southern and eastern portions of the state, all within the purchases of 1768 or earlier. Increasing the price for land east of the Allegheny Mountains and reducing the price for land west of the mountains, the legislature set a maximum size of four hundred acres per tract. An initial rush to obtain land brought many sales. This was followed by a dramatic reduction in price that brought land to its lowest rates ever. After remaining low for several years, the price of land returned to its old rate once most of the valuable sites had been sold.

The legislature also began to sell the land north and east of the Ohio, Allegheny, and Susquehanna rivers as soon as the Indian claims had been extinguished. In contrast to older portions of the state, land in this region was offered in tracts as large as one thousand acres and at an increased price. The state appeared to be solely interested in disposing of its northern wilderness and reaping the profit. Sluggish sales, however, contributed to the reduction of both tract size and cost. Land sold rapidly to speculators once the price was reduced, and little was left vacant after 1817.

While the state was busily selling its land, the legislature also gave away a portion. Devising ways to help pay its Revolutionary War debts, the legislature used land to pay loyal officers and soldiers of the Pennsylvania Line. Certificates given to them in lieu of depreciated currency represented land. The certificates could be used as legal tender in the purchase of land or could be redeemed for money raised through the sale of land, specifically, the Depreciation Land. In the Donation Land program, tracts instead of money were given to officers and soldiers of the Pennsylvania Line who served to the end of the war.

Following the Civil War, the state again turned to land for immediate income. The legislature passed a lien law to encourage the completion of titles on all unpatented land. Lien lists in each county pressured landowners into compliance. Favorable results enabled the state to realize a sizable income toward paying its war debt. The lien dockets were closed in 1899 signifying the passing of the vast majority of land into private hands and the end of the sale of land as a direct source of income.

IV.B.2.b. Reserved Land

Although not aware of the need for forestry reserves and land conservation, the early Com-

monwealth did set aside a small portion of land for its own use. Located entirely within the Purchase of 1784, the reserved tracts were selected for their strategic importance. Usually located at the confluence of two or more rivers, some of the tracts were reserved for their military importance; others were selected as possible town sites.

Following the proprietary model, the Commonwealth surveyed each town into lots and appointed a commissioner to sell them. Purchasers had to meet certain building and occupancy requirements before a patent could be granted. Such town planning in Pennsylvania had its inception in William Penn's ideas for his green country town of Philadelphia. Although the practice of reserving town sites was a short-lived policy, the early Commonwealth government benefited from the proprietary precedent.

IV.B.3. Ownership by Settlement and Improvement

Adopting the proprietary government's policy of ownership by settlement and improvement, the new Commonwealth government began by protecting the rights of squatters who had settled illegally beyond designated purchase boundaries. After consummating the Purchase of 1784, the Land Office first offered preemption certificates to settlers who occupied land that lay between Lycoming and Pine creeks, the disputed boundaries of the Purchase of 1768. Settlers in other areas of the Purchase of 1784 were given the opportunity to participate in the Northumberland Lottery. A successful drawing in the lottery enabled settlers to secure a warrant for the land they already claimed.

The Commonwealth also protected the rights of settlers who had obtained their land by extralegal means. Both Virginia Claimants and Connecticut Claimants who met certain requirements and who actually lived upon the land were given preference over absentee Pennsylvania landowners and new applicants. For the first time the Commonwealth actually disallowed Pennsylvania patents if they were found to be in conflict with settlement on the land.

The requirement of occupancy and cultivation as the only way to obtain a patent was introduced in the infamous land legislation of

1792. Designed to benefit settlers in the northwestern portion of the state, the law included sufficient loopholes to have just the opposite effect. Settlers and speculators could circumvent the Land Office and go directly to deputy surveyors for surveys. Although patents required proof of five years' occupancy and cultivation, an escape clause in the law permitted the waiver of the five-year requirement if dangerous Indian relations had prevented settlement. A boon to speculators, the prevention clause probably caused more problems than it solved. Nevertheless, the basic policy of ownership solely by settlement and improvement was established. Within a few years the same policy, minus the prevention clause, was extended to the eastern portion of the Purchase of 1784 and the rest of the state.

IV.B.4. Applicant Required to Prove the Vacancy

Stymied by the proprietary system that permitted surveying in random courses and distances, the Commonwealth Land Office had no way of knowing where warrantee tracts lay in relation to one another. Seeing a need for change, the new government attempted to apply the basics of the federal system of land surveying. In the area north and west of the Ohio, Allegheny, and Susquehanna rivers and in the Depreciation and Donation land, tracts were surveyed in neat squares and rectangles before they were sold or given away. Most of the other land in the same geographic region was surveyed into tracts whose length was not greater than twice its width.

Nevertheless, without warrantee tract maps, the surest way to eliminate overlapping surveys was to place the burden of proving the vacancy upon the applicant. Thus, beginning in 1807, the applicant was required to submit proof that no prior warrant for the same tract had been granted to him or to anyone under whom he claimed. Necessitating a title search on the part of the applicant, this policy was designed to inhibit the granting of more than one warrant for the same piece of land. Always the critical problem, duplicate warrants caused great confusion and many court battles.

A new law requiring applicants to go one step further in proving the vacancy was passed

in consequence of the land lien laws of 1864 and 1868. The flood of applicants for patents following the enforcement of these laws brought a marked increase in controversy over land ownership. Because most lien law applicants had purchased their land from the county at sheriffs' sale, they knew neither the warrantee nor if the land had ever been warranted. To avoid court battles and give descendants of the original warrantee an opportunity to claim title, applicants after 1874 were required to publish their application in the local newspaper. This requirement has remained an integral part of warranting and patenting land.

IV.C. Regions Open for Settlement

At the close of the Revolutionary War in 1783, not all of the territory within the charter boundaries of Pennsylvania was available for legal settlement. The Indians commonly known as the Six Nations of the Iroquois Confederation still claimed a large section of the state. Their claim included all land lying to the northwest of the Purchase of 1768. Anticipating a treaty with the Indians for the purchase of this region, the General Assembly passed acts appropriating certain sections for special programs. Some land was to be sold for the purpose of redeeming the depreciation pay certificates given to the Pennsylvania officers and soldiers who had served in the Continental Army and Navy during the Revolutionary War. Other land was to be donated to the officers and soldiers who served to the end of the war.

IV.C.1. Purchase Treaties, 1784–85

As soon as the Revolutionary War was over, the General Assembly authorized the Supreme Executive Council, Pennsylvania's executive branch, to appoint commissioners to meet with the Six Nations and negotiate a purchase treaty.[1] The goal was to expedite the designation and surveying of land for the redemption of depreciation certificates. While Pennsylvania was planning its action, the recently formed Second Continental Congress also appointed commissioners to meet with the Six Nations concerning territory to the west of Pennsylvania. Combining the meetings, both groups of commissioners met with the Indians at Fort Stanwix (Rome, New York) in October 1784 and reached an agreement whereby the Six Nations surrendered their rights to the remaining land within Pennsylvania for the purchase price of five thousand dollars.[2] The region is commonly called the Last Purchase, but for clarity this GUIDE refers to it as the Purchase of 1784.

Among other points the treaty of 1784 settled the controversy over the 1768 boundary. Learning that the Indians had meant Pine Creek to be the boundary rather than Lycoming Creek, the Land Office was able to mount a special preemption program to handle the claims of settlers who had moved into the disputed area between the two creeks.

As soon as the Pennsylvania commissioners had finalized the Purchase of 1784, they concluded another treaty with the Wyandot and Delaware Indians, who also claimed rights in the same area. Traveling to Fort McIntosh on the Ohio River at the site of the present town of Beaver, the commissioners met with the Indians in January 1785 and agreed to pay them two thousand dollars for their rights.

---

[1]PA (1) 10:111.
[2]Pat. Bk. P-3-110.

IV.C.2. County Formation, 1779–1792

During the period of the Revolutionary War, state government continued to function. Sufficient population growth in the western part of the Commonwealth justified the formation of two new counties: Washington (1781) and Fayette (1783). No new counties were immediately created out of the territory added by the Purchase of 1784, however. Comprising approximately five sixteenths of the total area of the state, the new land was divided and attached to existing counties. The land east of the Allegheny River and Conewango Creek became part of Northumberland County. The land to the west of the Allegheny River and Conewango Creek became part of Westmoreland County. However, within the following few years, eight additional counties were formed as indicated in Chart 8.

IV.C.3. Purchase of 1792

The triangular piece of land along Lake Erie was added to Pennsylvania in 1792. Although the area was not originally within the charter boundaries, certain political interests were anxious to add a western lake port to the state. The claimants Massachusetts, Connecticut, and New York ceded their rights in the Erie triangle to the federal government in 1781 and 1785. Anticipating its annexation to Pennsylvania, state officials paid the Six Nations $2,000 in 1789 to relinquish their rights.[1] The triangle was then sold to Pennsylvania via a deed dated March 3, 1792, citing George Washington, president of the United States, as grantor. The purchase price was $.75 per acre, or a total of $151,640.25 for 202,187 acres.[2] The Erie triangle became part of Allegheny County and was not formed into the county of Erie until 1800.

---

[1]Com. Bk. A-1-309.
[2]For a copy of the deed see Philadelphia County Deed Book E-F-31:107.

IV.C.4. County Formation, 1792–1878

By the time the territorial limits of Pennsylvania were completed in 1792, the state was composed of twenty-one counties; one may almost say the Commonwealth had come of age. Between 1792 and 1878 the remaining forty-six counties were created by subdividing the existing ones. All but one of these new counties were formed before the Civil War. Chart 9 recites the dates of county formation, 1792–1878.

IV.C.5. Melish-Whiteside County Maps

Pennsylvania's first official county maps were constructed in 1817 and 1818. Containing township lines, geographic features, roads and distances, post offices, mills, factories, furnaces, forges, houses, churches, and other important information, these maps are a valuable adjunct to land records research. Based upon actual county surveys, they were the most accurate maps to have been produced up to their time.

Chart 8. Areas of Settlement and County Formation, 1779–1792

Date	Indian Deed Number*	County
1781	—	**Washington** (12) formed from Westmoreland
1783	—	**Fayette** (13) formed from Westmoreland
1784	—	**Franklin** (14) formed from Cumberland; **Montgomery** (15) formed from Philadelphia
1784	29–31	Northumberland and Westmoreland enlarged
1785	—	**Dauphin** (16) formed from Lancaster
1786	—	**Luzerne** (17) formed from Northumberland
1787	—	**Huntingdon** (18) formed from Bedford
1788	—	**Allegheny** (19) formed from Westmoreland and Washington
1789	—	**Delaware** (20) formed from Chester; **Mifflin** (21) formed from Huntingdon, Cumberland, and Northumberland

*Deed numbers refer to the Genealogical Map of the Counties (front.).

The maps were one of the many results of the work of John Melish, geographer, traveler, and entrepreneur.[1] His approach involved contracting with deputy surveyors "for the formation of a Map of each of the counties." Since each county map would be drawn to the same scale, Melish proposed fitting the counties together like a giant jigsaw puzzle to form a state map. He convinced the Pennsylvania legislature of the advantages of his project, and the body passed enabling legislation on March 19, 1816.[2]

Within one and one-half years, Melish reported that nearly all of the newly constructed county maps were in his hands.[3] Contracts drawn in amounts between two and six hundred dollars depending upon the predicted difficulty of the task had been negotiated between the deputy surveyors and the surveyor general and the secretary of the Land Office. Attended by a host of unforeseen surveying problems, such rapid production of the county maps was truly remarkable.[4]

The deputy surveyors performing the work delivered the completed maps to the surveyor general. Before the surveyor general sent the original map to Melish for copying and engraving, a clerk made an office copy of the original. Hired expressly for copying maps, the first clerk, John Whiteside, signed each copy, and hence the copies of the county maps are known as the Whiteside maps. Several county maps also were copied by Dan Small but are not known by his name.

Melish completed his state map and exhibited a copy to the legislature in March 1822. A joint legislative committee appointed to examine the map wrote a glowing report. In their estimation the map was "an exquisite specimen of graphic skill" and worthy of the $29,276.75 expenditure. Published on August 26, 1822, copies were sent to county, state, and federal offices.[5]

Before the state had reimbursed him with the additional $9,833.23 that he claimed, Melish died. His heirs sold his Philadelphia "Geographical Establishment" to Andrew Goodrich, who carried some of the county maps off with him to New York City.[6] Anxious to settle Melish's estate, his engraver, Benjamin Tanner, made arrangements with the Pennsylvania legislature to correct and publish another edition of the state map. For this edition, Tanner claimed to have retrieved the original county maps from Goodrich and to have collected the remaining maps from Melish's estate. Tanner published his corrected and updated version of the state map in 1826. Apparently the original maps were never returned to the surveyor general, however, and their current location is unknown.[7] Copies of both the 1822 and the 1826 state maps are available in the state archives and in many libraries.

Chart 9. Areas of Settlement and County Formation, 1792–1878

Date	Indian Deed Number*	County
1792	32–33	Allegheny enlarged
1795	—	**Somerset** (22) formed from Bedford; **Lycoming** (23) formed from Northumberland
1796	—	**Greene** (24) formed from Washington
1798	—	**Wayne** (25) formed from Northampton
1800	—	**Armstrong** (26) formed from Allegheny, Westmoreland, and Lycoming; **Adams** (27) formed from York; **Butler** (28) formed from Allegheny; **Beaver** (29) formed from Allegheny; **Centre** (30) formed from Mifflin, Northumberland, Lycoming, and Huntingdon; **Crawford** (31) formed from Allegheny; **Erie** (32) formed from Allegheny; **Mercer** (33) formed from Allegheny; **Venango** (34) formed from Allegheny and Lycoming; **Warren** (35) formed from Allegheny and Lycoming
1803	—	**Indiana** (36) formed from Westmoreland and Lycoming
1804	—	**Jefferson** (37) formed from Lycoming; **McKean** (38) formed from Lycoming; **Potter** (39) formed from Lycoming; **Tioga** (40) formed from Lycoming; **Cambria** (41) formed from Huntingdon, Somerset, and Bedford; **Clearfield** (42) formed from Northumberland, Huntingdon, and Lycoming
1810	—	**Bradford** (43) formed from Luzerne and Lycoming; **Susquehanna** (44) formed from Luzerne
1811	—	**Schuylkill** (45) formed from Berks and Northampton
1812	—	**Lehigh** (46) formed from Northampton
1813	—	**Lebanon** (47) formed from Dauphin and Lancaster; **Columbia** (48) formed from Northumberland; **Union** (49) formed from Northumberland
1814	—	**Pike** (50) formed from Wayne
1820	—	**Perry** (51) formed from Cumberland
1831	—	**Juniata** (52) formed from Mifflin
1836	—	**Monroe** (53) formed from Northampton and Pike
1839	—	**Clarion** (54) formed from Venango and Armstrong; **Clinton** (55) formed from Lycoming and Centre
1842	—	**Wyoming** (56) formed from Luzerne
1843	—	**Carbon** (57) formed from Northampton and Monroe; **Elk** (58) formed from Jefferson, Clearfield, and McKean
1846	—	**Blair** (59) formed from Huntingdon and Bedford
1847	—	**Sullivan** (60) formed from Lycoming
1848	—	**Forest** (61) formed from Jefferson and Venango
1849	—	**Lawrence** (62) formed from Beaver and Mercer
1850	—	**Fulton** (63) formed from Bedford; **Montour** (64) formed from Columbia
1855	—	**Snyder** (65) formed from Union
1860	—	**Cameron** (66) formed from Clinton, Elk, McKean, and Potter
1878	—	**Lackawanna** (67) formed from Luzerne

*Deed numbers refer to the Genealogical Map of the Counties (front.).

Photostatic copies of the Whiteside county maps are available for sale from the Land Office.

Maps exist for those counties formed before 1816.

RECORDS: LOOSE PAPERS

MELISH MAPS   LO micro.: 21.1, 21.4.

A collection of sixteen folders of correspondence, contracts, and reports concerning the construction of the first state and county maps based upon actual surveys.

WHITESIDE MAPS.

Available for the counties in existence up to 1816, these maps were the first official county maps constructed from actual surveys. The copies in this collection were made by John Whiteside and other clerks in the surveyor general's office. County maps missing from this collection may be found in the state archives map collection. Photostatic copies are available for sale.

---

[1]Marvin E. Wolfgang, "John Melish, 'American Demographer,'" *PMHB* 82 (1958): 65–81.
[2]*SmL* 6:374.
[3]Melish Maps, Folder 1; LO micro.: 21.4.
[4]John Melish, "Observations on the State Map of Pennsylvania," Melish Maps, Folder 5; LO micro.: 21.4.
[5]*SmL* 7:441–43.
[6]Andrew Goodrich to Rees Hill, March 27, 1823, Melish Maps, Folder 12; LO micro.: 21.4.
[7]Benjamin Tanner to Gabriel Hiester, August 17, 1824, Melish Maps, Folder 16; January 30, 1826, ibid., Folder 12; LO micro.: 21.4.

IV.D. Categories of Purchasers

This subsection discusses the several categories of purchasers created by the land laws of the Commonwealth. In some respects these categories differed from those of the proprietary era and existed only as long as the particular policies that created them were in effect. During and immediately following the Revolutionary War, special consideration was given to Pennsylvania veterans of the continental service. Settlers in southwestern Pennsylvania holding land under Virginia warrants formed another group that was given favored treatment. Using the Virginia program as an example, the Pennsylvania legislature also provided for settlers in northeastern Pennsylvania who had settled under the auspices of the Connecticut-based Susquehanna Company. Squatters, or presumptive settlers, were also handled as a special category of purchaser. Making every effort to avoid conflict, the legislature developed special programs for squatters who had occupied and improved their tract without first

applying for a warrant. Speculators posed a different set of problems to the Commonwealth government. For a period of time speculators gained virtual control of the Land Office and bought up much of western Pennsylvania. Finally, regular purchasers, those who applied for land before they settled on it, composed a dwindling category and were ultimately eliminated by Commonwealth law.

IV.D.1. Revolutionary War Veterans

Revolutionary War veterans of the Pennsylvania Line were one of the first groups to be given special consideration under the land laws of the Commonwealth. Two different pay incentive programs, the Depreciation Land program and the Donation Land program, were designed especially for them. Both enacted in March 1780, the programs affected two particular groups of veterans.

Soldiers and officers who had received regular pay in depreciated currency were offered certificates that could be redeemed for the lost pay or applied toward the purchase of land anywhere in the state. Auditors from the comptroller general's office, among them John Nicholson, who later became comptroller general, visited army posts validating service records and distributing certificates. The accounts of veterans who received the certificates may be studied in the records of the comptroller general's office cited in IV.E.2.b(1), Depreciation Lands.

To provide a fund to redeem the certificates, a large tract immediately north of the Allegheny and Ohio rivers was surveyed and sold in lots of 200–350 acres after 1785. By then many veterans had sold their certificates to speculators such as Nicholson or applied the certificates to land purchases elsewhere.

Soldiers and officers who served to the end of the war were given outright grants of land. Based upon rank, veterans were eligible to receive between one and four tracts of 200–500 acres each. A group of auditors similar to those who distributed depreciation certificates certified veterans entitled to donation tracts. Lists of the entitled men appear in several Donation Land volumes cited in IV.E.2.b(2), Donation Lands.

The donation tracts, located in the area between the Allegheny River and the Ohio border, just north of the Depreciation Land, were surveyed before they were granted. As with depreciation certificates, many veterans sold their Donation Land claims. Speculators in advantageous positions, such as Comptroller General Nicholson, carried on an active trade in the purchase and sale of donation claims.

IV.D.2. Virginia Claimants

During the latter part of the colonial era, the southwestern corner of Pennsylvania was claimed also by Virginia. Pennsylvania's claim stemmed from William Penn's charter rights, which fixed the western boundary of the province at five degrees longitude west of the Delaware River. Unsurveyed until after the Revolutionary War began, the exact location of the western boundary was not known. The claim of Virginia began in conjunction with the French and Indian War and was reinforced by Virginia's efforts to build

a fort at the confluence of the Ohio and Monongahela rivers in 1754.

Settlers anxious to move into the area west of the Laurel Mountains and south of the Ohio River found it easier to settle under Virginia rights. Pennsylvania had prohibited legal settlement in the area until after the Purchase of 1768. With its only Land Office located in Philadelphia and closed between 1776 and 1781, Pennsylvania found it impossible to serve the settlers. In contrast, Virginia had treated the area as part of Augusta County since 1754 and partitioned the land into three counties in 1776: Monongalia, Yohogania, and Ohio. Encouraging settlement, Virginia established a surveyor and a Land Office in each county. To protect themselves, some settlers warranted the same tract of land first under Virginia rights and then under Pennsylvania rights. This created a dual set of land records for the region and in many cases a dual set of records for the same tract of land.

In 1779, Pennsylvania reached an agreement with Virginia to settle the jurisdictional dispute. The first order of business was to determine the boundary line between the two states. Before the boundary could be run, however, Virginia authorities offered certificates to persons who had settled under Virginia rights. Settlers holding Virginia certificates who lived north of the new boundary line were eligible for Pennsylvania warrants. As the records in the volume Virginia Entries indicate, over one thousand Virginia tracts covering an area of 633,000 acres came under undisputed Pennsylvania jurisdiction. Many of the tracts conflicted with prior Pennsylvania warrants.

The Commonwealth Land Office, not in operation until after the boundary agreement was reached, first addressed itself to settling the issue of Virginia certificates in 1784. Acquiring transcripts of the Virginia grants from the government of Virginia, the Board of Property ordered the surveyor general to furnish copies to his deputies.[1] However, few Virginia transcripts remain among the land records, perhaps indicating that the transcripts rather than copies were sent to the deputies. Settlers claiming land under a Virginia right applied directly to the Pennsylvania deputy surveyor for a resurvey. To give fair warning to conflicting claimants, the deputy surveyor posted public notice of the time when he would make a resurvey. After making the resurvey, the deputy surveyor sent a tract drawing

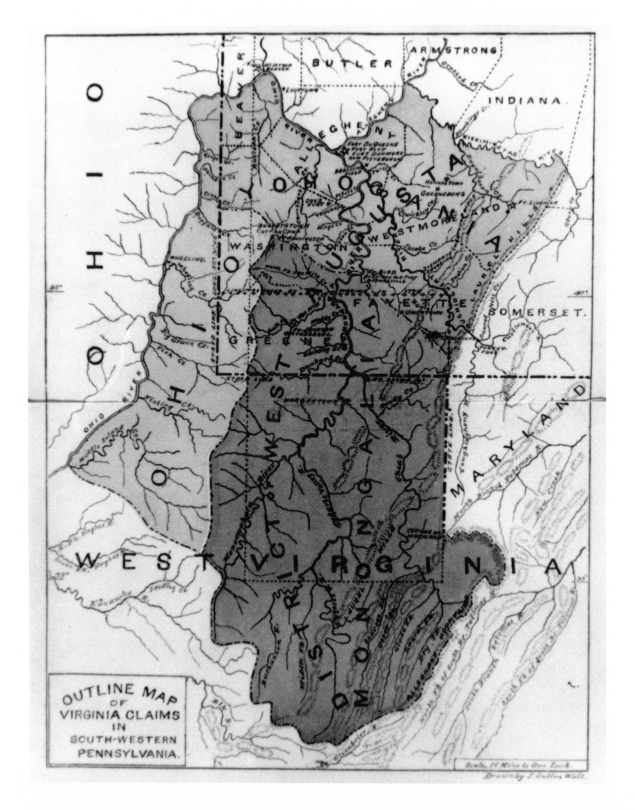

Map 2. The area of Pennsylvania where Virginia claims were accepted. (Pennsylvania Department of Internal Affairs *Annual Report of the Secretary of Internal Affairs,* 1895)

and supporting documentation such as depositions and notations of interference to the surveyor general. The deputy surveyor also noted

---

Table 21. Research Aids: Virginia Claimants

Crumrine, Boyd, ed. *History of Washington County*. 1882. Reprint. Evansville, IN, 1975. See pp. 182–222.

Fo[r]ster, Robert H. "The Disputed Territory between Pennsylvania and Virginia, and Land Titles Therein." Pennsylvania Department of Internal Affairs *Annual Report of the Secretary of Internal Affairs* (1895): A.197–A.214. In *PA* (3) 3:483–504.

---

whether a survey under a Pennsylvania warrant had ever been made. In cases of conflict, ownership was always awarded to the older or prior right regardless of the state under which it had been acquired.[2]

Records pertaining to Virginia Claimants may be accessed in the regular warrant registers of the proper Pennsylvania counties of jurisdiction: Westmoreland, Washington, Fayette, and Allegheny (south and west of the Ohio River). The survey will include reference to the Virginia certificate. The warrant will be a warrant to accept, prepared after the survey was returned to the surveyor general. A separate book, listing names of individuals who claimed land on Virginia rights, references the survey and in whose name the survey was made. These sources are cited below.

RECORDS: LOOSE PAPERS

RETURNS   VIRGINIA CLAIMANTS   LO micro.: 5.119.

One folder containing a few typed copies of Virginia deeds and handwritten depositions.

RECORDS: BOUND VOLUMES

VIRGINIA ENTRIES   1779–1780   (With index).

An alphabetically arranged volume containing lists of Virginia Claimants and giving for each individual the settling date, acres, and location. The lists are grouped by the returns of each deputy surveyor. If known, the survey is cited as well as the name of the person for whom the survey was returned.

VIRGINIA ENTRIES   *PA* (3) 3:507–73.

Gives a chronological listing of Virginia Claimants by date of settlement and cites acres and location. Penciled references give the survey volume, book, and page and make this a working volume for the Land Office. The *PA* transcript does not include survey references.

---

[1]See Boyd Crumrine, *Virginia Court Records in Southwestern Pennsylvania, 1775–1780* (Baltimore, 1974).
[2]Min. Bd. Prop. Bk. 3 (1782–1789): 53, 55, 59; *PA* (3) 1:456–60.

IV.D.3. Connecticut Claimants

Pennsylvania's northeastern quadrant, like its southwestern quadrant, was claimed by settlers from another colony. Along the Susquehanna River in the area later to become Luzerne, Lackawanna, Wyoming, and Bradford counties, a large number of families settled under the auspices of the Connecticut-based Susquehanna Company. The company had purchased the

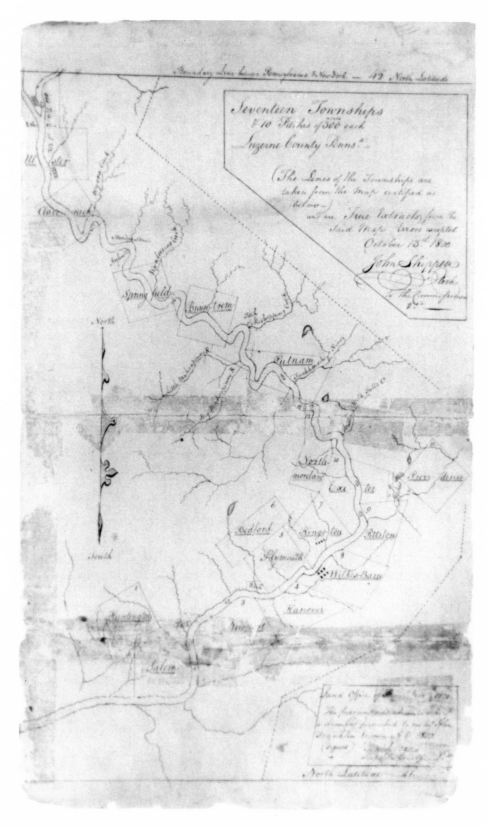

Map 3. The seventeen certified townships of the Susquehanna Company. (Names of Releasors—John and Richard Penn by Their Attorney Edmund Physick, Vol. A)

Table 22. Research Aids: Connecticut Claimants

Munger, Donna Bingham. *A Database of Purchasers Prepared from the Susquehanna Company Account Books.* In progress.

———. "Following Connecticut Ancestors to Pennsylvania: Susquehanna Company Settlers." *The New England Historical and Genealogical Register* 139 (April 1985): 112–25.

Susq. Co. Papers.

Susquehanna Company Account Books. 9 vols. Connecticut Historical Society. Microfilm in PSA.

Indian rights to the land several years before Pennsylvania had negotiated its ownership of the same land through the Purchase of 1768. A few hardy Connecticut frontiersmen had ventured to settle along the Susquehanna River in 1762 and 1763. Indian raids delayed significant settlement, however, until after the 1768 treaty at Fort Stanwix established a clear settlement line further west. Almost immediately thereafter hundreds of Connecticut settlers moved into northeastern Pennsylvania creating a land dispute of extraordinary proportions.

Although the area was legally opened to Pennsylvanians after the Purchase of 1768, settlers were slow to move over the Lehigh hills and into the area. The Land Office was prohibited from accepting applications for land until all squatters within the Purchase of 1768 were given the opportunity to apply for the land they had preempted.[1] The delay caused by this proprietary decision gave the Connecticut settlers in the Wyoming Valley at least a two-year lead on Pennsylvania settlers. Connecticut settlers established their own townships, subdivided them into lots, and built subsistence farms. Factional wars erupted, lasting until the British and Indians made the region unsafe for settlement during the Revolutionary War.

At the close of the war the Trenton Decree of 1782 nullified all Connecticut jurisdiction in Pennsylvania but left the issue of individual land ownership unsettled.[2] Connecticut settlers and Philadelphia speculators continued to vie for control of the area. Each group purchased land in its own way: Connecticut settlers through a radical faction of the Susquehanna Company, Pennsylvania speculators by warrant and patent. Many tracts overlapped.

Finally, in 1799 the legislature passed a compromise law.[3] The law created a board of commissioners whose job it was to examine Connecticut claims, determine their authenticity, and award title. The process of title certification allowed room for much controversy, and it was 1801 before commissioners were selected who could work together. Identifying Connecticut settlers in 17 of over 250 townships as qualified claimants, the commissioners awarded certificates to the claimants. The certificates permitted a resurvey and a patent provided the newly assessed valuation was paid as a purchase price. Records of the first board of commissioners were bound in one Land Office volume: Connecticut Claimants, volume 1. Records of the 1801 board were entered in three Land Office volumes: Connecticut Claimants, volume 2; Connecticut Claimants, volume 3; and Minutes of Evidence Respecting the Titles of Connecticut Claimants.

The names of the certified townships were Bedford, Braintrim, Claverack, Exeter, Hanover, Huntington, Kingston, Newport, Northmoreland, Pittstown, Plymouth, Providence, Putnam, Salem, Springfield, Ulster, and Wilkes-Barre. All seventeen townships were formed and settled by the Susquehanna Company prior to December 1782, the date of the decree of Trenton. Few of the certified townships relate geographically to Pennsylvania townships of the same name later formed in the same area.

The 1799 legislation also dealt with Pennsylvania claimants. The law permitted pre-1782 warrantees and patentees to release their land to the Commonwealth and receive just reimbursement. For records of Pennsylvania landholders taking advantage of this provision, see the Release volumes cited below.

In places where claims of qualified Connecticut settlers and Pennsylvania landholders overlapped, further legislation was needed. In 1807 an amendment to the 1799 law allowed Pennsylvania landholders to receive compensation for releases of land that they had warranted and patented after the Trenton Decree of 1782.[4] These releases are also entered in volumes cited below. The claims of Connecticut settlers are entered in the Book of the Fifteen Townships.

The settlement of individual land titles was finally completed in 1810 with the recertification of two temporarily disqualified Connecticut townships: Bedford and Ulster. Connecticut settlers in Bedford and in the original 1775 grant of Ulster were required to prove acquisition and occupancy back to March 1787 in any one of the seventeen townships.[5] Copies of deeds and documents gathered under this law are bound in the Journal of the Commissioners 1810.

Patents granted to Connecticut Claimants supplanted any Pennsylvania warrants and patents for the same tract. Pennsylvania warrantees and patentees released their titles and deeded them back to the Commonwealth. Connecticut Claimants who met the time and chain of title qualifications received a certificate permitting a resurvey and a patent after paying the assessed purchase price. Certificates and resurveys granted to Connecticut Claimants are hand copied in twelve volumes, Seventeen Certified Townships, Surveys and Certification. Another volume, Certified Townships Luzerne, serves as an index to the survey volumes and to the patents granted. Two other volumes, Classification 17 Townships—Luzerne and Classification and Valuation Bedford and Ulster, contain the rates and valuations for the lots. Original loose records including applications, claims, deeds, and oaths of single title, all cited below, are the raw material from which these volumes were prepared.

Warrant tract maps of the seventeen certified townships were constructed in the early 1820s. Mapmaker and historian Isaac Chapman might have been the cartographer of these early warrant tract maps. They are similar to those of Luzerne and Susquehanna counties that he produced for the state map program.[6] The maps can be located by consulting the Land Office Map Inventory.

Land records for Connecticut Claimants in the seventeen certified townships are not included in the warrant registers but can be found by consulting the records cited in this section. The index volume Certified Townships Luzerne is the place to begin. The specific location of each Connecticut Claimant's lot can be determined by consulting two Land Office sources: 1) the original tract maps of each certified township and 2) the current warrantee township maps.

RECORDS: LOOSE PAPERS

SEVENTEEN (17) TOWNSHIPS LO micro.: 9.1–20; partial transcript in *PA* (2) 18:611–780.

Consists of 450 folders of loose papers. The first portion is filed by Connecticut township and then by topic: applications, claims, deeds, oaths of single title, and miscellaneous papers. The remaining folders are manuscript sources for the bound volumes including Board of Property certificates, surveys, Pennsylvania releases, lists of qualified settlers for each township, and deeds to the Commonwealth.

RECORDS: BOUND VOLUMES

CERTIFIED TOWNSHIPS LUZERNE LO micro.: 1.22.

Serves as an index to the surveys and patents granted to Connecticut settlers. All individuals who received certificates and to whom the tracts were patented are listed by township.

SEVENTEEN CERTIFIED TOWNSHIPS, SURVEYS AND CERTIFICATION.

Volumes numbered 1 through 12 containing hand copies of the resurveys of all lots granted to qualified Connecticut Claimants. The index to these volumes is Certified Townships Luzerne.

CONNECTICUT CLAIMANTS, VOL. 1   (Binding No. 71)   LO micro.: 25.32.

Contains the records of the first board of commissioners selected to settle conflicts over individual landownership. Including abstracts of conveyances between Connecticut settlers, it references the Luzerne County deed books in which the conveyances are recorded.

CONNECTICUT CLAIMANTS—VOL. 2   (Binding No. 72)   LO micro.: 25.32.

Contains Minutes of Evidence for Claverack, Northmoreland, Bedford, Huntington, Exeter, Braintrim, Springfield, and Salem. For each township a list of claimants is followed by each claimant's chain of title.

CONNECTICUT CLAIMANTS—VOL. 3   (Binding No. 73)   LO micro.: 25.32.

Contains Minutes of Evidence for Plymouth, Pittstown, Providence, and Putnam. For each township a list of claimants is followed by each claimant's chain of title.

LETTERS OF EVIDENCE—HANOVER, NEWPORT, WILKES-BARRE, KINGSTON   (Binding No. 57)   LO micro.: 25.30.

Similar to the two volumes above, containing chains of title for Connecticut settlers in the townships listed in the title.

BOOK OF THE FIFTEEN TOWNSHIPS   (Binding No. 61)   LO micro.: 25.30; *PA (2)* 18:515–72.

Contains the chains of title of Connecticut settlers claiming under the Supplement of 1807 to the Compensating Act of 1799.

JOURNAL OF THE COMMISSIONERS   1810   (Binding No. 23)   LO micro.: 25.21; *PA (2)* 18:573–609.

Contains the minutes of hearings at which claims were submitted for settling titles in Bedford and Ulster under the act of March 19, 1810.

CLASSIFICATION 17 TOWNSHIPS—LUZERNE   (Binding No. 70)   LO micro.: 25.31–32.

Arranged by township and then by division, showing the owner and particular valuation of each lot. Only fifteen of the seventeen certified townships are included; Bedford and Ulster compose their own volume.

CLASSIFICATION AND VALUATION   BEDFORD AND ULSTER   (Binding No. 60)   LO micro.: 25.30.

Shows the owner and particular valuation for each lot in the townships of Bedford and Ulster.

NAMES OF RELEASORS—JOHN AND RICHARD PENN BY THEIR ATTORNEY EDMUND PHYSICK   VOL. A.

A listing of Pennsylvania landholders within the seventeen certified townships who released their land to the Commonwealth. The following information is given: the releasor's name, warrantee's name, tract's name, acreage, water it is on or near, warrant or patent date, and Connecticut township, with remarks.

NAMES OF RELEASORS—JOHN AND RICHARD PENN BY THEIR ATTORNEY EDMUND PHYSICK   VOL. B.

Contains two alphabetical lists of Pennsylvania releasors, giving the following information: warrantee; acreage; warrant date; survey date; general description; adjoining owners; whether claimed by warrant, survey, or patent; township; by whom released; and whether defective.

LUZERNE RELEASE BOOK NO. 1.

Contains copies of the deeds between the Pennsylvania releasors and the Commonwealth made possible by the Compromise Law of 1799.

LUZERNE RELEASE BOOK NO. 3.

A continuation of the deeds between the Pennsylvania releasors and the Commonwealth. It also contains the master index to Luzerne Release Books 1 and 3.

LETTERS—PENNSYLVANIA CLAIMANTS 1800 (Binding No. 62) LO micro.: 25.30; *PA* (2) 18:323–88.

Contains copies of letters between the commissioners and Pennsylvania landholders concerning the releasing of land.

LETTERS FROM THE SECRETARY OF THE [Land Office to the] COMMISSIONERS 1801–1804   (Binding No. 59)   LO micro.: 25.30; *PA* (2) 18:431–513.

Contains two sections, letters from the secretary of the Land Office to the commissioners appointed to settle the Connecticut land claims, and those from the commissioners to various individual Pennsylvania landholders.

---

[1]See III.E.2, Land within the Purchase of 1768.
[2]Pat. Bk. P-2-292–325.
[3]*SmL* 3:352–69.
[4]Ibid. 4:411–12.
[5]Ibid. 5:127–31.
[6]See IV.C.5, Melish-Whiteside County Maps.

IV.D.4. Squatters

In the early decades of the Commonwealth the most numerous group of purchasers consisted of squatters. Frequently referred to as actual settlers in the early literature, squatters were the same persons categorized as presumptive settlers in the proprietary era. Although usually thought of as a derogatory term, the word "squatter" best identifies the person who settled upon vacant land without first obtaining a warrant and a survey. After improving the land, squatters often sold their improvements to others who obtained a warrant, survey, and patent.

A series of laws dealing with the distribution of land within the Purchase of 1784 gave squatters increasing preference in landownership. The first indication of preferred treatment was the offer of preemption certificates to actual settlers who had occupied and improved tracts of land along the West Branch of the Susquehanna River between Lycoming Creek and Pine Creek.[1] The Northumberland Lottery came immediately thereafter. The lottery offered squatters who had settled within the eastern portion of the Purchase of 1784 the option of warranting the land they had improved before the area was opened for general sale.[2]

Similar treatment was later extended to squatters who had settled west of the Allegheny River and Conewango Creek. The 1792 law to encourage settlement in northwestern Pennsylvania condoned squatting. Applicants were required to submit a proof of settlement statement, which documented the construction of a dwelling, residency therein for a minimum of five years, and cultivation of at least two of every one hundred acres. Applicants were limited to four hundred acres and required to apply within ten years after beginning an improvement.[3]

By 1794 the Commonwealth had placed the burden of determining vacancy upon the squatter. Realizing that settling upon the land without a warrant had become the preferred procedure, the legislature made prewarrant settlement mandatory by extending the land law of 1792 to the east side of the Allegheny River. Since surveys were found to be more accurate if the actual settler was inhabiting the land prior to the survey, a 1794 law made occupancy and improvement mandatory before submission of an application.[4] This statewide policy was in effect until 1817.

Squatters frequently came into conflict with speculators. The most common problem squatters faced was occupying and improving a portion of a larger tract previously warranted to an absent speculator. Although deputy surveyors in the northwestern portion of the state were to keep plat maps available for public use, connected warrantee tract maps did not exist. The Land Office occasionally issued warrants for improved land to squatters although the same tract had been warranted to someone else previously. During the early 1800s the Board of Property heard many caveats against granting warrants, and the courts of law heard many ejection suits.

---

[1] See IV.E.2.a(1), Preemption Applications.
[2] See IV.E.2.a(2), Northumberland Lottery.
[3] See IV.E.2.b(4), Vacant Unwarranted Land.
[4] September 22, 1794, *SmL* 3:193–94.

IV.D.5. Speculators

Land speculators, persons who made advance purchases of multiple tracts of land for resale later at a higher price, played a very important role in the distribution of Commonwealth-owned land. The leading speculators were men prominent in public life and the business community. Some held important government posts and used their position to promote their own interests in land. For the most active speculators, acquiring land became an obsession beyond reality and culminated in their eventual ruin.

In particular, speculators were active after 1792 when the price of vacant land in the Purchase of 1784 was reduced to £5 ($13.33) per one hundred acres. Land could be bought on credit or with depreciation certificates.[1] Settlement and improvement requirements were generally overlooked. Land Office representatives, if not directly involved, were often very cooperative.

Speculators relied upon surveyors to act as their agents. Surveyors associated with the exploration and mapping of northern Pennsylvania between 1789 and 1793 were particularly involved. Assigned to the various commissions formed to report on the navigability of streams and to plan roads, the surveyors became experts in locating the best land.[2] Their usual procedure was to survey several tracts and then take out the required warrants.

WE do hereby certify, that *Michael Groves* the Grantee, hath been prevented from making a settlement on a tract of land, containing *four hundred & one acres One hundred & fifty perches* with the allowance of six per centum for roads and highways, lying north and west of the rivers Ohio and Allegany, and Conewango creek, situated in district number 2 — surveyed upon a warrant dated the *30th day of May 1792* and adjoining lands of *John Groves* in the county of Allegany, conformable to the proviso contained in the ninth section, of the Act entitled an " Act for the sale of vacant lands within this commonwealth, passed the third day of April 1792," by force of arms of the enemies of the United States, and that he the said *Michl Groves* by his assigns, Theophilus Cazenove, William Irvine, George Meade, Daniel Leet, John Hoge and Walter Stewart, have persisted in their endeavours to make such settlement.

Meadville 29 Octr 1798 —

John Gower Jr

John Roe

John Barron

Prevention certificate for the Pennsylvania Population Company, 1798.

The relationship between speculator William Bingham and surveyor John Adlum is a good example of how business worked. Bingham contracted with Adlum to acquire 1 to 2 million acres of land. As pay, Adlum was given an annual expense allowance, one third of the profits from sales, and a portion of the unsold land remaining at the end of five years. Working from his home near the mouth of Lycoming Creek, he surveyed over 340,000 acres for Bingham. He also prepared elaborate descriptions of the land, trees, soil, mineral and water resources, and navigable streams.

Examination of the warrant register for the Purchase of 1784 reveals thousands of acres east of the Allegheny River warranted to the same few speculators. A maximum of 1,000 acres could be taken on a single warrant, but many speculators secured multiple warrants into the hundreds. The pretext of using false names was not necessary. The Land Office permitted as many warrants per individual as anyone wished to request and paid little attention to collecting the purchase price.

John Nicholson, comptroller general of Pennsylvania from 1782 to 1794, was also an important land speculator. He entered the service of the Commonwealth as one of the auditors for settling the depreciation accounts of Pennsylvania's Continental troops of the Revolutionary War. Soon becoming the fiscal director of Pennsylvania, Nicholson used his position and connections, especially with Daniel Brodhead, the surveyor general, to amass a paper fortune in land.

With other investors, Nicholson formed the Pennsylvania Population Company as a cover for their monopoly of land in the Erie triangle. As the state's chief financial officer, Nicholson had negotiated the purchase of the 202,000-acre tract from the national government in 1792. At the same time, he applied for 390 warrants from the Land Office, enough to blanket the entire Erie triangle. Adding these to other warrants, Nicholson controlled approximately 500,000 acres. He and his associates capitalized these warrants into the Pennsylvania Population Company, whose managers were Theophile Cazenove, principal agent of the Holland Land Company; William Irvine, commander at Fort Pitt; George Mead, Philadelphia merchant; Daniel Leet and John Hoge, deputy surveyors; and Walter Stewart, federal revenue inspector for the port of Philadelphia. The major investors were Aaron Burr, Robert Morris, James Wilson, and Nicholson.

Land values fell, however, before the company could mount a program to sell its tracts. To preserve the investment, the managers tried to hold the land and sell as few tracts as possible. This policy brought the company into direct conflict with the law of 1792, which required that, for every 400-acre tract, the warrantee occupy, clear, and cultivate 10 acres within two years. Resorting to a loophole in the law, the Population Company, supported by friendly justices of the peace, secured prevention certificates in the names of grantees, both real and imaginary. The prevention certificates excused the settlement, cultivation, and improvement requirements if the warrantee had been "prevented or driven off by force of arms of enemies of the United States."[3] The phrase, of course, referred

Table 23. Research Aids: Land Speculators

Arbuckle, Robert D. *Pennsylvania Speculator and Patriot, the Entrepreneurial John Nicholson, 1757–1800.* University Park, PA, 1975.

Doerflinger, Thomas M. *A Vigorous Spirit of Enterprise: Merchants and Economic Development in Revolutionary Philadelphia.* Chapel Hill, NC, 1986. See pp. 314–29.

Evans, Paul. *The Holland Land Company.* Buffalo, NY, 1924.

Guide to the Microfilm of the John Nicholson Papers in the Pennsylvania State Archives. Harrisburg, 1967.

Hale, R. Nelson. "The Pennsylvania Population Company." *Pa. Hist.* 16 (1949): 122–30.

Records of the Pennsylvania Population Company. Harrisburg, 1939. WPA transcripts of originals in the Allegheny College Library, Meadville, PA.

Satran, Franciska. "The Preservation of the Holland Land Company Records." *New York History* 69 (April 1988): 103–83.

Wilkinson, Norman B. *Land Policy and Speculation in Pennsylvania, 1779–1800.* New York, 1979.

———. "The 'Philadelphia Fever' in Northern Pennsylvania." *Pa. Hist.* 20 (1953): 41–56.

to the Indian problems in northwestern Pennsylvania into the mid-1790s. A warrantee's proof that he had been driven off consisted of a sworn statement notarized by a justice of the peace. The Population Company's prevention certificates are filed in forty-two folders in the Land Office and are cited below.

Nicholson was impeached in 1794 for diversion of state funds and resigned his position as comptroller general. Instead of mending his ways, he became an even more active speculator in several land companies. He and his partners greatly overextended themselves, and the state ultimately placed a lien on some of their land. Morris, Nicholson's major partner, went to debtor's prison in 1798. Nicholson joined him in prison late in the summer of 1799 and died not long thereafter. In conjunction with the case the Commonwealth seized Nicholson's papers and titles to property.

Between 1806 and 1843 the state attempted to discharge its lien on the Nicholson properties and convey the land to private ownership. The Nicholson papers were placed in the Land Office to be available for the study of each individual situation. Records of the proceedings and of the deeds of conveyance to individuals are in two bound volumes in the Land Office and cited below. Releasing its lien to the remaining Nicholson land in 1843, the state closed its books on the case.

Nicholson's papers remained in the Land Office until their transfer to the Pennsylvania State Archives in 1957. The archives prepared a finding aid and microfilmed some of the papers (see Table 23). The bound volume of the Nicholson court of pleas was transferred to the archives at a later date and is cited below.

The Holland Land Company, formed in 1796 by investors from the Netherlands, was another organization engaged in active speculation in Pennsylvania land. Many titles in both the eastern and the western portions of the Purchase of 1784 trace their origin to warrants obtained by Wilhelm Willinck, chief agent for the Holland Land Company. The Last Purchase 1784 warrant register indicates that, after the purchase price of land was reduced in 1792, Willinck bought over 1,100 warrants in his own name and later purchased almost as many warrants from other speculators.

Unable to meet the settlement, cultivation, and improvement requirements in the western portion of the Purchase of 1784, the Holland Land Company, like the Pennsylvania Population Company, resorted to the prevention clause of the law of 1792 as a means of patenting its tracts. The Holland Land Company's prevention certificates are filed in thirty-nine folders in the Land Office and are cited below.

The company's land holdings in the eastern portion of the Purchase of 1784 fared even less well. Devastated by the drop in land values, the Holland Company at first withheld its land from sale but later entered into a variety of sales agreements simply for the sake of divesting itself of its holdings. Local taxation and untillable land created much of the problem. Ultimately the Holland Land Company absorbed heavy losses on its investment.

Speculators can usually be identified in the warrant registers by the repetitive entry of their names. Large and small speculators alike abounded in Pennsylvania land dealings. Across the northern part of the state and in the northwest, the original warrantee of a tract of land is more often a speculator than an actual settler.

RECORDS: LOOSE PAPERS

HOLLAND LAND COMPANY   LO micro.: 10.1–2.

Thirty-nine folders containing prevention certificates. Filed under the law of April 3, 1792, they explain why certain Holland Land Company purchasers could not settle on their tracts. Alphabetically arranged, they gave the grantee's name, acres, warrant date, surveying district, and adjoining owners. Grantees' names may be fictitious.

POPULATION LAND COMPANY   LO micro.: 10.2–3.

Forty-two folders containing prevention certificates. Filed under the law of April 3, 1792, they explain why certain Population Land Company purchasers could not settle on their tracts. Alphabetically arranged, they give the grantee's name, acres, warrant date, surveying district, and adjoining owners. Many of the names are fictitious.

RECORDS: BOUND VOLUMES

NICHOLSON LANDS—COMMISSIONERS RETURN OF SALE   (With index)   LO micro.: 25.118–19.

Contains miscellaneous records pertaining to the settlement of Nicholson-owned lands in several different land companies of the 1795–1797 era. Especially valuable is a list by county of tract owners and acreages. The bulk of the volume contains extracts of the 1840s proceedings to settle the Commonwealth's case against Nicholson.

DEED BOOK—NICHOLSON LANDS   LO micro.: 25.119.

Deeds of conveyance between the Commonwealth and individuals under the act of 1840 to settle the estates of Nicholson and merchant Peter Baynton, who was a state treasurer (1797) and adjutant general (1799).

BOARD OF COMMISSIONERS CONSTITUTED UNDER ACT OF APRIL 16, 1840   LO micro.: 25.119.

A book of minutes of the meetings of the commissioners appointed to settle the ownership of Nicholson lands.

MINUTE BOOK OF NICHOLSON'S COURT   LO micro.: 25.118.

Contains minutes of the 1841 court proceedings in the Nicholson land case.

---

[1]See IV.E.2.b(1), Depreciation Lands.

[2]"The Report of the Commissioners appointed to view and explore the rivers Susquehanna and Juniata," in *Journal of the 26th House of Representatives* (Harrisburg, 1815); Appendix, 1–84.

[3]*SmL* 3:70.

IV.E. Categories of Land

Under the early Commonwealth, land was distributed according to one of two geographic regions: 1) the purchases of 1768 and earlier or 2) the Purchase of 1784. This policy created two distinct categories of land and several subcategories.

Land within the purchases of 1768 and earlier can be divided into three subcategories: 1) land that had been granted by the proprietors and improved but not titled, 2) vacant unwarranted land, and 3) unimproved Philadelphia and proprietary town lots.

Land within the Purchase of 1784 was divided into two geographic sections: 1) land east of the Allegheny River and Conewango Creek and 2) land west of the Allegheny River and Conewango Creek and north of the Ohio River.

Much of the land east of the Allegheny River had been settled and improved by squatters prior to the Purchase of 1784. These settlers were given preference in warranting their land through two newly created programs: the preemption program and the Northumberland Lottery program. Unsettled land to the east of the Allegheny River was classed as vacant and unappropriated. To encourage the purchase of vacant land, tracts as large as one thousand acres were sold.

Land west of the Allegheny River was initially reserved for two special programs: 1) the Depreciation Land program and 2) the Donation Land program. Small portions of land were also reserved for the Commonwealth's military purposes and for county towns. The residue of unsettled land was classed as vacant and unappropriated and was distributed under the land law of 1792.

Islands and riverbeds were the exceptions to the geographic categorization of land. Traditionally constituting a third, nongeographic category, islands and riverbeds were governed by different laws and procedures.

Separate categories of land were eliminated between 1814 and 1817. Legislation placed all remaining unwarranted land in the Commonwealth into one of two classes: improved or unimproved. A uniform price of $26.66 per one hundred acres was set. The law also required applicants to register the date of original settlement or first improvement, whether their own or a previous squatter's.

IV.E.1. Land within the Purchases of 1768 and Earlier

When the Commonwealth government was formed in 1776, the only land that could be legally titled was encompassed within the purchases of 1768 and earlier. Although a significant portion of that region had been transferred to private ownership, the proprietary government had by no means granted warrants or patents on the entirety. Many individuals had settled on warrant rights but had completed neither a survey nor a patent. Others had settled without a warrant. Lots within proprietary towns and certain Philadelphia city lots also remained unsold. This subsection discusses how the Commonwealth government handled these situations.

IV.E.1.a. Land Granted by the Proprietary Government

Completion of land titles begun under the proprietary government was the first concern of the new Commonwealth Land Office. Opening in 1781 to address only this issue, the Land Office sought to use the outstanding purchase price and interest as sources of income. Among the few potential sources of revenue in the years immediately following the Revolutionary War, they would provide the money needed to redeem bills of credit granted earlier for the support of the army.

All persons who had commenced the process of patenting land before December 10, 1776, were given an opportunity to complete their titles by complying with certain procedures outlined in the Commonwealth's first land law.[1] If a survey had not been made or returned, the payment of one third of the purchase money by April 9, 1782, entitled the settler to a survey. If a survey had been made and returned, the payment of the remaining purchase price and fees entitled the settler to a patent. The purchase price remained the same as in 1765: five pounds sterling per one hundred acres. If the land was unimproved, interest accrued from six months after the date of the warrant; if the land was improved, interest accrued from the date of the improvement.

For those who could not afford to pay the purchase price, the Land Office devised a mortgage plan. The plan called for the payment of one quarter of the purchase money each year for four years. A lapse of six months without a payment meant possible land seizure and a tax sale at the county level. For those who met their payments, a patent was granted upon payment of the last installment.

When one considers the general shortage of money, the opportunity to establish clear title to land seems to have attracted quite a few settlers. The new patent series started by the Commonwealth government, the P series, shows that approximately one thousand patents were completed on proprietary warrants between 1781 and 1784.

Many settlers, however, could not afford to make payments toward the purchase price of their land. Taking advantage of another mortgage plan devised in early 1785, some of the poorer settlers borrowed from the new Loan Office and used their land and improvements as collateral.[2] Original mortgage certificates taken out under this law are on file in the Land Office and cited below. Duplicate mortgage certificates, authorizations for sheriffs' sales, correspondence, and account books, all pertaining to the mortgage program, are filed with the records of the General Loan Office and state treasurer and cited in the records below.

Despite these revenue-generating land programs, insufficient money was collected to redeem the bills of credit. Desperate for income by the middle of 1785, the legislature enacted another law to "compel" the completion of titles

Pennsylvania ss.

On the sixth day of December 1785. Before me the Subscriber one of the Members of the Supreme Executive Council of the Commonwealth aforesaid; Personally appeared Adam Breining of Hempfield Township in the County of Westmoreland Miller, who upon his solemn Affirmation doth declare and say, That he this Affirmant was well acquainted with Abraham Bowers of Westmoreland County aforesaid Millewright, that he the said Abraham Bowers about twelve Years ago (as near as he this Affirmant can recollect) took up a Tract of Land in said County and Improved the same with a small log Tenement; that he the said Abraham Bowers lived on the said Land for the Space of about six Years (as near as he this Affirmant can recollect) when the Indians committing Depredations in in the Neighbourhood of the said Abraham Bowers and took his next Neighbour's Children Prisoners, Whereupon the said Abraham Bowers with his Family abandoned his said Land and Improvement and fled to for safety — And further this Affirmant says not

Affirmed before me the Day
and Year aforesaid

John Woods.

Exoneration certificate, Westmoreland County, 1785.

begun under the proprietary government.[3] The Commonwealth argued that, because the war was over and the Land Office was better organized, settlers would be more willing to go into debt. The law permitted the seizure of all land claimed by persons who neglected to take advantage of this final opportunity to mortgage their land. Practicing leniency, however, the state periodically extended the mortgage program until 1811. Records of seized land can be found among the records of the General Loan Office cited below.[4] Mortgage certificates taken out under this law are on file in the Land Office and cited below.

A loophole in the 1785 law impeded the collection of revenue but provided records documenting actual settlement dates. Settlers who resided on the northern and western frontiers and were driven from their homes by the Indians during the Revolutionary War were exonerated from paying interest for the years 1776–1784 on the purchase money due. Exoneration certificates attested by a credible witness, taken before the justice of the peace of the county of jurisdiction, and submitted to the Land Office compose part of the Land Office collection and are cited below.

The state made one final effort in 1820 to recover money due the Commonwealth from persons holding land granted by the proprietary government. An act somewhat more stringent in character than previous laws called for the surveyor general to construct county lists of all unpatented land granted by the proprietary government. These unpatented land lists and tickets for calculating interest are cited in the records below. Delinquent owners could avoid suit and receive patents by paying the purchase price or by executing a ten-year mortgage in the name of the governor.[5] Mortgages executed in pursuance of this act were filed in the Land Office and are still part of its collection today. Two bound volumes cited below serve as a compilation of the liens and mortgages under this law.

RECORDS: LOOSE PAPERS

RECOVERY OF UNPAID MONEY   LO micro.: 20.3.

Four folders containing written contracts between individuals and the governor for the payment of liens against unpatented land under the acts of March 22, 1820, and April 11, 1825.

MORTGAGES   LO micro.: 15.1–4.

Sixty-five folders filed by county, containing mortgage certificates under several different plans. Each mortgage gives the mortgagee's name, date and amount of the mortgage, full description of the land, terms of payment, and sheriff's certification of the last payment received.

MORTGAGES AND RELATED PAPERS, 1773–1793   (RG-8).

Five boxes of papers filed by county and then alphabetically. Contents include an index to the loans of 1774 and 1784, mortgage certificates, correspondence with county commissioners who let the loans, certificates declaring the amount of an individual's land that was unpatented, and precepts (orders to sheriffs) of sale.

CERTIFICATES OF EXONERATION   LO micro.: 20.1–3.

Fifty folders filed chronologically, containing statements giving the name of each settler driven from his land, the location of his land, an adjoining owner's name, and sometimes the date of the warrant and other pertinent information. Each certificate bears the date of the statement, includes the name of a witness under oath, and is signed by the justice of the peace.

UNPATENTED LAND LISTS   1820–1887.

Master lists of unpatented land prepared in the surveyor general's office under the law of March 22, 1820.

UNPATENTED LAND TICKETS   1822–1827.

Tickets prepared in the surveyor general's office under authority of the act of March 22, 1820, and addressed to the secretary of the Land Office. The collection contains a volume of tickets for each county. Each ticket gives the date, acres, township, warrant date, occupier or owner, outstanding purchase price, and interest.

RECORDS: BOUND VOLUMES

MORTGAGE BOOK NO. 1   (With index)   LO micro.: 25.34–35.

A ledger-style volume containing a "List of Liens" and a "List of Mortgages" apparently drawn up following the act of March 22, 1820. The liens are listed by county and give the following information: name, ledger and folio pages, quantity of land, county, amount of lien, date of lien, amount paid in principal and interest, when paid, amount due, and remarks. There are 279 entries, the majority for Luzerne County. The mortgage list gives the same information. There are 538 entries in this volume, and they continue into Mortgage Book No. 2, below.

MORTGAGE BOOK NO. 2   LO micro.: 25.35.

A continuation of Mortgage Book No. 1, above. The entries are numbered 539 through 709; dates of entry run through August 1834.

MORTGAGE BOOKS   [1774–1788]   (RG-8; with index).

Four volumes containing duplicate copies of mortgage certificates. Each certificate indicates the yearly payment and the date the loan was satisfied. Bound in chronological order, the volumes are indexed by name.

RECORD OF MORTGAGORS, LAND MORTGAGES AND CASH RECEIVED 1786–1787 (RG-8).

The first section of this single volume is organized by county and gives the mortgage date, mortgagor's name, lands mortgaged, and sum lent. A second section lists payments received by date.

NEW LOAN   DAVID RITTENHOUSE   1787   (Binding Volume 130).

Shows the interest paid on New Loan Certificates purchased by investors between April 2 and May 19, 1787. Listings cite the purchase date, certificate numbers, amount, purchaser's name, and interest paid.

[1]April 9, 1781, *SmL* 1:529–33.
[2]April 4, 1785, ibid. 2:313–16.
[3]September 16, 1785, ibid., 339–43.
[4]*Purdon* 64 § 33.
[5]March 22, 1820, *SmL* 7:280–85.

IV.E.1.b. Vacant Unwarranted Land

Before opening the newly purchased northwestern quadrant of the state to legal settlement, the Land Office sought to transfer the remaining land within the purchases of 1768 and earlier to private ownership. Some of this older land was unoccupied, some was occupied and improved by squatters, but all was considered vacant if no proprietary warrant was on file. Under a new law initiating the sale of vacant land within the purchases of 1768 and earlier, the Land Office began to accept applications on July 1, 1784.[1] The law set the price per one hundred acres at £10 ($26.66) for land east of the Allegheny Mountains but only £3 10s ($9.33) for land west of the Allegheny Mountains. Allowing a maximum of four hundred acres on each application, the state set no limit on the number of applications per person. The burden of proving the vacancy was placed upon the applicant by requiring three items: 1) a particular description of the land; 2) a statement specifying whether the land was improved or unimproved and, if improved, when the improvement was made; and 3) the signatures of two justices of the peace of the proper county. Lacking a preemption right clause, the law was amended in 1786 to permit squatters two years to complete their titles before the land was opened to general settlement.[2] After April 10, 1788, unwarranted land was available to anyone who applied. Although warrants granted on applications submitted between July 1, 1784, and the end of 1786 for land within the Purchase of 1784 may be found in the regular warrant register, researchers wishing to pursue statistical or demographic studies may prefer to consult the chronological application registers cited in the records below.

Other measures at later dates specifically affected land within the purchases of 1768 and earlier. To hasten the sale of all vacant land within the Commonwealth, the land law of 1792 reduced the price of unappropriated land within the purchases of 1768 and earlier to fifty shillings per one hundred acres.[3] The burden of proving the vacancy was placed even more upon the applicant in 1807 by requiring him to submit a deposition to the effect that no prior warrant for the same land in the same name or chain of title had been issued.[4]

By 1814 most of the land within the purchases of 1768 and earlier had been transferred to private ownership. The price of land was restored to the old rate of £10 ($26.66) per one hundred acres, and specific dates were set from which interest was charged if new applicants could not obtain proof of the time the tract was first improved.[5] Actual settlers were given preference over new applicants, however, and deputy surveyors were admonished to be particularly careful that new surveys not interfere with the tracts of bona fide settlers.[6]

Warrantees of vacant unappropriated land within the purchases of 1768 and earlier are listed in the warrant register of the county of jurisdiction at the date of the warrant. If the land was improved before it was warranted, the warrant will be a warrant to accept; if the land was not improved before it was warranted, the warrant will be a warrant to survey.

RECORDS: BOUND VOLUMES

APPLICANTS   1784–1785   (Binding No. 99)   LO micro.: 25.116.

Organized by pre-1784 counties, giving the following information: application date, applicant's name, number of applications, and situation.

RECORD OF LAND APPLICANTS   JULY 5, 1784–FEBRUARY 28, 1785   (Binding No. 100)   LO micro.: 25.116.
RECORD OF LAND APPLICANTS   MARCH 9, 1785–DECEMBER 31, 1785   (Binding No. 101)   LO micro.: 25.116.
RECORD OF LAND APPLICANTS   FEBRUARY 1, 1786–DECEMBER 29, 1786   (Binding No. 102)   LO micro.: 25.116–17.

Organized in chronological order, giving the date, name of applicant, number of applications, and situation.

---

[1]April 1, 1784, *SmL* 2:102.
[2]December 30, 1786, *Statutes* 12:350–51.
[3]April 3, 1792, *SmL* 3:70–71.
[4]April 13, 1807, *PaL*, 284. Also in *SmL* 4:471.
[5]March 28, 1814, *PaL*, 239.
[6]Surveyor General Letter Book, 1810–1821, 43; reel 467; LO micro.: 25.31.

IV.E.1.c. Philadelphia City Lots and Proprietary Towns

The first and last chapters in state ownership of Philadelphia lots and proprietary towns were written in the early days of the new Commonwealth. A surprising number of Philadelphia lots had never sold. Obtainable only under the rights of an Original Purchaser, they had remained in the hands of the proprietors until the Divesting Law of 1779. The Commonwealth considered the lots to be of particular value and assumed ownership of them as well as the unsold lots in proprietary towns.

The earliest efforts to sell the Philadelphia lots came in 1781 and 1782. In order to back a special £100,000 issue of bills of credit, the vacant lots were offered for sale at auctions held between July 1781 and May 1782.[1] Sale results were recorded in a volume titled "[Philadelphia] City Lots" cited in the records below under Loose Papers.

Unsold Philadelphia lots were again offered at auction in 1786 and 1797.[2] Sales in 1786 amounted to approximately £80,000. Lots sold in 1797 included the barracks lots in the northern liberties where the British troops had been quartered during the Revolutionary War. A plan of the lots sold is filed in the Land Office and can be located through the Land Office Map Inventory.

Warrants were not generated through the sales of the Philadelphia lots. Thus the Philadelphia County warrant register carries no reference to individuals who purchased city lots from the Commonwealth. But, after the owner paid the purchase price, a patent was executed, and purchasers are indexed in the patent registers. The warrantee appears as the lot number, and the warrant date is the date of the act authorizing the sale of the lots. The patent itself was granted by the Supreme Executive Council of the Commonwealth of Pennsylvania.

Philadelphia lots sold by the Commonwealth after 1797 were passed by deed poll, and clear title was guaranteed by the Commonwealth. As with proprietary town lots these Philadelphia lots were recorded in the county records with the Commonwealth as grantor.

The state also established definite procedures for patenting lots that had already been warranted. Untitled Philadelphia lots and lots adjoining Reading, York, Carlisle, Easton, Bedford, Sunbury, and Hannah's Town were placed in the care of town wardens or justices of the peace.[3] Occupants of unpatented lots were given seven years to complete pre-1733 warrants and ten years to complete post-1733 warrants. Under these procedures several Philadelphia lots were patented to individuals claiming old rights.[4] The records are entered in the volume Claims to Philadelphia Lots in Rights of Original Purchasers cited below under Loose Papers. Occupants of proprietary town lots completed their titles by purchasing their lots outright from the wardens or the justices of the peace. Records of these transactions will appear in the county of jurisdiction with the wardens or justices as grantors.

RECORDS: LOOSE PAPERS

[Philadelphia] CITY LOTS   1781 TO 1786   LO micro.: 21.4.

Folders 3 and 4 of the Philadelphia city lot collection contain manuscript volumes relating to the sales of city lots. The volume City Lots 1781 to 1786, compiled in 1798 by a Land Office clerk named James Parsons, contains an account of sales of the State (or Province) Island, May 18, 1781, and Philadelphia lots, July 5, 1781, through May 30, 1782, and June 11, 1786, through December 26, 1787. Columns are headed date, number, names, to whom patented, amount, and total. The volume Claims to Philadelphia Lots in Rights of Original Purchasers, 1781–1788, contains the claimant's name and Original Purchaser's name. Many chains of title are cited.

RECORDS: BOUND VOLUMES

LIST OF SALES PHILADELPHIA LOTS   1781–1788   (Binding No. 92).

Divided into two sections: The first section lists lots by ward, giving the lot number, purchaser, and amount paid; the second section lists lots numerically, giving the purchaser, date when sold, and amount paid.

JOURNAL—DEPRECIATION LANDS, PHILADELPHIA AND BEAVER TOWN LOTS   [November 21, 1785–March 3, 1896]   LO micro.: 25.78.

Contains accounting of sales usually in monthly entries but becoming less frequent after 1800. The volume gives the purchaser's name, lots purchased, amount and date when paid, and type of money used (Pennsylvania certificates, depreciation certificates, or specie).

LEDGER DEPRECIATION LANDS, PHILADELPHIA AND BEAVER TOWN LOTS
LO micro.: 25.36.

An account book containing some information concerning Philadelphia lots. It gives the name of the purchaser, the amount of land purchased, how many tracts, and how they were paid for (such as cash, specie, depreciation certificates, or Pennsylvania certificates). The ledger includes accounts for Depreciation Lands and Beaver town lots as well.

[1]February 28, 1780, *SmL* 1:484; April 10, 1781, ibid., 533.
[2]Ibid. 2:380, 3:330.
[3]Hannah's Town functioned as a county seat but was never officially designated as such. *SmL* 1:533–39.
[4]See II.D.1.b, Original Purchasers.

IV.E.2.   Land within the Purchase of 1784

The disposal of land within the Purchase of 1784 was handled differently from the disposal of land within the older portions of the state. Not tied to procedures established under the proprietary government, the General Assembly used the Purchase of 1784 as its first opportunity to develop new land laws and procedures. In effect the assembly divided the area into two sections by setting aside the land to the west of the Allegheny River and Conewango Creek, still dominated by Indian troubles in 1784, for the Depreciation and Donation lands. Land to the east of the Allegheny River and Conewango Creek was opened to settlement as soon as obligations to certain actual settlers were met.

Covering the largest portion of land yet to be opened for settlement at one time, the Purchase of 1784 was known as the Last Purchase. Thus the major register for the sale of these lands is called the Last Purchase 1784 register.

In surveying the region the Land Office adopted the federal system of surveying tracts before they were sold. This procedure marked a significant change in policy. Warrantee tract maps of the land north and west of the Susquehanna and Allegheny rivers show nearly all rectangular or square warrantee tracts as compared to the jigsaw-puzzle appearance of the older portions of the state.

IV.E.2.a.   East of the Allegheny River and Conewango Creek

Land east of the Allegheny River and Conewango Creek was first offered for sale on May 1, 1785.[1] Tracts of up to one thousand acres could be purchased at the price of thirty pounds per one hundred acres. In Pennsylvania currency this amounted to eighty cents per acre. The full purchase price was to be paid before the warrant was issued. However, the land was not available for general settlement until the assembly pro- vided for two special programs.[2] The first program involved the granting of preemption applications to squatters who had settled in the area between Lycoming Creek and Pine Creek before 1780. The second program, designed to handle the large number of applications expected, was called the Northumberland Lottery.

[1]*SmL* 2:272–75.
[2]Ibid., 317–25.

IV.E.2.a(1)   Preemption Applications

Shortly after finalizing the Purchase of 1784 but before the area was opened to general settlement, the state offered preemption applications to certain people who had earlier settled along the West Branch of the Susquehanna River.[1] The situation of these squatters was peculiar. The proprietors had refused to accept applications for land located between Lycoming Creek and Pine Creek not knowing which was the actual boundary line in the Purchase of 1768. In defiance of warnings and proclamations, many self-reliant families persisted in occupying the forbidden area. They served as a buffer between legal Pennsylvania settlers and Indians and discouraged Connecticut settlers in northeastern Pennsylvania from moving further westward. Without law or government they banded together for protection and mutual support and called themselves the Fair Play Settlers.

Service to their country was one reason adopted for granting the Fair Play Settlers preemption applications to their tracts. Many settlers had served in the army during the Revolutionary War. The others were simply granted preemption if they could prove settlement prior to 1780.[2] Applications were limited to three hundred acres, and the purchase price was to be paid by May 1, 1785, the date the Land Office began to accept regular applications for land in the eastern portion of the Purchase of 1784.

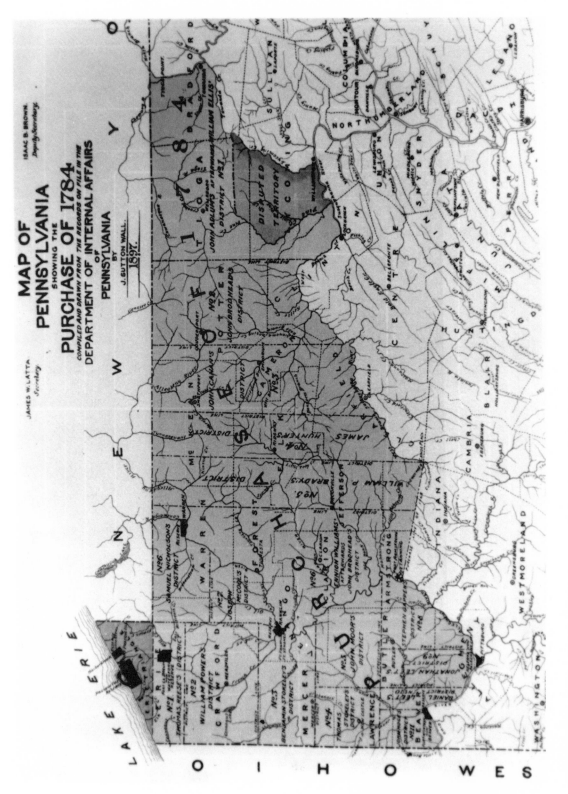

Map 4. The Purchase of 1784 (darkened area), with new surveying districts superimposed over current counties. (Pennsylvania Department of Internal Affairs *Annual Report of the Secretary of Internal Affairs*, 1896)

Preemption applications contained information similar to exoneration certificates.[3] Of particular significance was the date of initial settlement. The Land Office charged interest on the purchase price from that year. Filed with the applications but separately, preemption applications can be accessed through the Northumberland County warrant register under the warrantee's name. The warrant will be dated between May and October 1785, immediately after the Land Office began to grant warrants for land in the Purchase of 1784. The application, although not listed in the warrant register, is usually dated the same as the warrant.

Table 24. Research Aids: Fair Play Settlers

Linn, John Blair. "Indian Land and Its Fair-Play Settlers." *PMHB* 7 (1883): 420–25.

Meginness, John F. *History of Lycoming County, Pennsylvania.* 1892. Reprint. Evansville, IN, 1974. See pp. 193–203.

Wolf, George D. *The Fair Play Settlers of the West Branch Valley 1769–1784.* Harrisburg, 1969.

RECORDS: LOOSE PAPERS

PRE-EMPTION APPLICATIONS   1785   LO micro.: 7.5.

Six folders of applications dated May 4–October 24, 1785. Each document carries the name of the applicant, chain of title from the original squatter, location and adjoining owners, statement by at least one deponent, and certification by a justice of the peace.

[1]December 21, 1784, *SmL* 2:273–74.
[2]Min. Bd. Prop., May 2, 1785; *PA* (3) 1:461.
[3]See IV.E.1.a, Land Granted by the Proprietary Government.

IV.E.2.a(2) Northumberland Lottery

The initial sale of land in the eastern portion of the Purchase of 1784 was done by lottery. This method was selected to avoid giving preference to certain speculators and to enable the state to handle the large number of applications expected on the first day. At the time, all the land for sale lay within Northumberland County, hence the name Northumberland Lottery.

All applications received during the first ten days of May 1785 were actually placed in a lottery wheel. Numbered tickets were placed in a second wheel. The two wheels were spun the same number of times, and then one ticket and one application were simultaneously drawn from each wheel. The number of the numbered ticket was given to the application, and to the ensuing warrant. As soon as the purchase price was paid, the warrant was good for a survey that could be located anywhere east of the Allegheny River within the Purchase of 1784. The survey could be made on a tract improved by the applicant or by someone else or on an unimproved tract. The only exception was a tract of one thousand acres at the forks of Sinnemahoning Creek, held by General James Potter under a preemption application.[1]

The lottery apparently did not attract as many purchasers as anticipated. During the ten-day period allotted, the Land Office received approximately six hundred applications. Applicants were permitted to apply for as many as one thousand acres, but generally they applied for much less. Many purchasers submitted several applications, however.

The Northumberland Lottery warrants are filed with the warrants but separately. The register, or index, to the warrants may be found at the end of Warrant Register 14: Franklin, Fulton, Juniata, Mifflin, Perry, Snyder, Union [Counties]. All warrants were dated May 17, 1785.

Preemption application for a tract between Pine and Lycoming creeks, 1784.

RECORDS: LOOSE PAPERS

ORIGINAL WARRANTS   NORTHUMBERLAND LOTTERY   LO micro.: 3.7–8.

Thirty-three folders filed alphabetically, containing Northumberland Lottery warrants all dated May 17, 1785. Each warrant carries two numbers: 1) the order in which it was drawn and 2) the number it represents under its letter of the alphabet. The warrant gives the name of the warrantee, acres, and date of the return of survey.

RECORDS: BOUND VOLUME

WARRANT REGISTER 14   FRANKLIN FULTON JUNIATA MIFFLIN PERRY SNYDER UNION   LO micro.: 1.3; partial transcript in *PA* (3) 25:359–74.

Pages 321–45 provide reference to warrant, survey, and patent volumes for the Northumberland Lottery. The *PA* version published 1898–99 is incomplete and omits the reference information.

---

[1]April 8, 1785, *SmL* 2:317–25.

Table 25. Research Aid: Purchase of 1784

Forster, R[obert] H. "The Purchase of 1784." Pennsylvania Department of Internal Affairs *Annual Report of the Secretary of Internal Affairs* (1896): A.15–A.32.

IV.E.2.a(3) Vacant Unwarranted Land

After the ten days allotted to the Northumberland Lottery, the Land Office began to accept applications for vacant unwarranted land in the eastern portion of the Purchase of 1784. Nondescriptive applications were encouraged for as many as one thousand acres. The Land Office originally divided the area into eighteen surveying districts and assigned a deputy surveyor to each district. The deputy surveyor was responsible for surveying tracts before they were sold. The districts were numbered consecutively beginning with number one on the Allegheny River and running eastward to number eighteen on the North Branch of the Susquehanna River.[1]

Desire to obtain land had waned, however, probably due to the high price of £30 per one hundred acres. The Last Purchase 1784 warrant register shows that, between the end of the drawing of the Northumberland Lottery in 1785 and 1792, not more than 400 warrants were granted. Of those granted, 112 warrants, amounting to fifty-two thousand acres, went to religious and educational institutions to enhance their endowments. Despite a reduction in price in 1789 to $.53$\frac{1}{2}$ per acre, or £20 per one hundred acres, land simply did not sell.[2]

A marked change came about in 1792 under the new surveyor general, Daniel Brodhead. He consolidated the original eighteen districts into six and numbered them from east to west. Then he appointed six new deputy surveyors (see Map 4, The Purchase of 1784). The new surveying districts permitted a three-way conspiracy of interests among Brodhead, the new deputy surveyors, and several large speculators, including John Nicholson, the comptroller general.

Through their political contacts, Brodhead and Nicholson succeeded in having the legislature reduce the price of land to $13.33 (£5) per one hundred acres in 1792.[3] Sales that were almost astonishing in extent resulted as Pennsylvania entered the age of land speculation. In the years 1792, 1793, and 1794 more than 5,000 warrants of nine hundred and one thousand acres each covering almost five million acres were granted. The warrants were nondescriptive, and theoretically the tracts could be located anywhere east of the Allegheny River and Conewango Creek and north of the Susquehanna River. In actuality deputy surveyors had already surveyed the tracts and told their patron speculators how many warrants and which tract numbers to request. For example, the Holland Land Company, through several different agents, bought 1,105 warrants of nine hundred acres each. Other speculators were wealthy Philadelphia landholders. Among them were James Wilson, buying 510 warrants of nine hundred acres each; Thomas M. Willing, 311 warrants of one thousand acres each; Robert Morris, 185 warrants of one thousand acres each and 44 warrants of five hundred acres each; John Nicholson, 300 warrants of one thousand acres each; and William Bingham, 125 warrants of one thousand acres each.

To stem this widespread speculation, the cultivation, improvement, and settlement provision of the infamous land law of 1792 was extended to the east side of the Allegheny River.[4] This law also declared that all applications made after April 1, 1784, on which the purchase money had not been paid by September 22, 1794, would be null and void. Speculators scrambled to meet their obligations on time. Some, like John Nicholson, were not able to do so.[5]

The warrants granted for vacant unappropriated land east of the Allegheny River and Conewango Creek, except the Northumberland Lottery warrants, are entered in a separate warrant register titled "Last Purchase 1784." These warrants, with a few exceptions, cover the period 1785–1817. In any search for names of warrantees in the counties that were formed before 1817–1820 out of the eastern portion of the Purchase of 1784, the Last Purchase warrant register must be consulted.

In 1817, when the sale of land in the entire state was placed on a uniform basis, the price of land in the eastern portion of the Purchase of 1784 was raised to $26.66 per one hundred acres to correspond to the price of land in the older purchases.[6] The burden of proving the vacancy also was placed squarely on the applicant. Each applicant was required to submit a description of the land with his application. The Last Purchase warrant register was closed, and from 1817 until the present warrants have been entered in the warrant registers of the proper county.

RECORDS: LOOSE PAPERS

ORIGINAL WARRANTS   LAST PURCHASE   LO micro.: 3.1–7.

All warrants granted between 1786 and 1817 for land in the eastern portion of the Purchase of 1784 (east of the Allegheny River and Conewango Creek) are grouped under the title "Last Purchase Warrants" and filed alphabetically by the first letter of the last name and then numbered chronologically.

RECORDS: BOUND VOLUMES

LAST PURCHASE 1784   LO micro.: 1.9; partial transcript in *PA* (3) 26:701–905.

The warrant register that indexes all warrants granted between 1786 and 1817 (with a few into the 1820s) for land in the Purchase of 1784 east of the Allegheny River and Conewango Creek. The register gives the warrant number, tract number, quantity, warrant date, return date, acres returned, patentee, patent volume, and survey volume. The transcript in *PA* omits the warrant number and survey and patent volumes.

LAST PURCHASE [Warrant] REGISTER   1785–1821.

A second copy of the Last Purchase 1784 warrant register.

LAST PURCHASE   (Binding Volume 164).

An earlier warrant register giving the date, warrantee name, place of residence, warrant number, quantity, warrant sent to which deputy surveyor, warrant date, number of warrants, and purchase price.

---

[1]See Reading Howell, *A Map of the State of Pennsylvania*, 1792. In *PA* (3) Appendix 1-10.
[2]*SmL* 2:453–54.
[3]Ibid. 3:70–75.

4September 22, 1794, ibid., 193–94. See IV.E.2.b(4), Vacant Unwarranted Land.
5See IV.D.5, Speculators.
6March 10, 1817, *SmL* 6:420.

IV.E.2.b. West of the Allegheny River and Conewango Creek

Land west of the Allegheny River and Conewango Creek and north of the Ohio River lay within the western portion of the Purchase of 1784. Reserved for the Depreciation and Donation land programs, the area was open for general settlement after 1792. Partly because the northwestern land was plagued with minor Indian hostilities, the legislature established programs that took some time to be placed in operation. The southern portion of this northwestern land was designated for the Depreciation Land program and offered for sale near the end of 1785. Land in the northern portion was set aside for the Donation Land program and distributed near the end of 1786. A very small portion of land within the area was reserved for the use of the Commonwealth. Only after the Depreciation and Donation land programs had run their course was the unsold land opened for sale as vacant unwarranted land.

IV.E.2.b(1) Depreciation Lands

Located in the southwestern portion of the Purchase of 1784, the area designated for the Depreciation Lands was within the V formed by the Allegheny and Ohio rivers, immediately north of the town of Pittsburgh. Tracts in this area, chosen for its excellent location, were to be sold to raise money to underwrite depreciation certificates. These certificates were given to Pennsylvania's Revolutionary War troops who had received depreciated currency for pay. Men who had served in the Continental forces as part of the Pennsylvania Line or Pennsylvania Navy or who had been prisoners of war qualified for the certificates.

The depreciation certificates represented the difference in pay between the amount the troops should have been paid and the amount they were actually paid. Between January 1777, when enlistments began, and July 1780, when the issue came to a head, Continental money had depreciated in relation to gold from a ratio of 1.5 to 1 to a ratio of 64.5 to 1. The Continental Congress, having no authority to raise funds, asked each state to make up the losses to its own troops. Pennsylvania responded by issuing depreciation certificates and made the certificates equal to gold and silver toward the purchase of confiscated estates or unappropriated land. Recipients could also sell validated certificates.[1]

Auditors established a scale for the amount of lost pay and determined how much each soldier, sailor, and officer was eligible to receive in depreciation certificates. Visiting army posts to validate service records and distribute certificates, the auditors also established regional offices in Carlisle, Yellow Springs, York, and Lancaster for the convenience of veterans, widows, and heirs. In the advantageous position of administering the distribution of certificates, the auditors, including the infamous speculator John Nicholson, yielded to temptation and bought up certificates cheaply. Depreciation certificates thus fell prey to the speculator's art.

In an effort to create sufficient funds to redeem the certificates, the General Assembly enacted several different programs. The first program was designed to placate certificate holders by providing them with partial reimbursement before the war was over. Authorizing one-third repayment to troops who applied, the state raised the money by offering for sale unappropriated lots in the city of Philadelphia and on Province (or State) Island.[2] Unredeemed certificates or portions of certificates began to accrue interest at this time. Certificate interest accounts of individual veterans can be studied in the volume Depreciation Certificate Interest Accounts, 1781–1792, cited below.

The redemption of all the depreciation certificates necessitated more money than the Philadelphia lot sales generated. Consequently the legislature designated the sale of a specific segment of land within the Purchase of 1784. Called Depreciation Lands, the area was located west of the Allegheny River and north of the Ohio River. The Depreciation Lands' northern

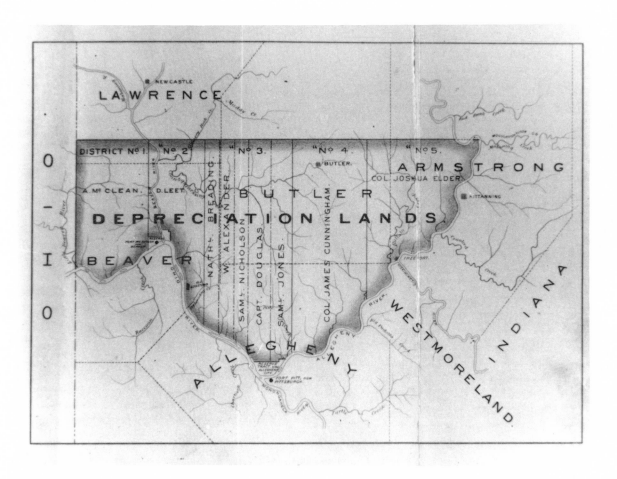

Map 5. The five surveying districts of the Depreciation Lands superimposed over current counties. (Pennsylvania Department of Internal Affairs *Annual Report of the Secretary of Internal Affairs*, 1892)

boundary was an east-west line between the mouth of Mogulbughtiton (now Mahoning) Creek and the western border of the state. Approximately 720,000 acres were involved.

In a break with past surveying procedures, the Depreciation Lands were divided into five surveying districts. Each of the five districts had its own deputy surveyor (see Map 5, The five surveying districts of the Depreciation Lands). Surveyors were to lay out adjoining rectangular tracts of 200 to 350 acres, number the lots in order, and construct a connected draft. Only after the first one hundred tracts had been surveyed and plotted could the land be sold. The

connected draft, with notable geographic features marked, was to form an accurate map of the area.[3] Surveying began in the summer of 1785.

Tracts in Daniel Leet's depreciation district number 2 had the distinction of being the first on the auction block. Others soon followed. Several auctions were held in Philadelphia and Lancaster between November 1785 and March 1787. No auctions were held farther west. Depreciation certificates as well as specie could be used to buy tracts. The auctions, however, failed so miserably that sales ceased. Surveyors completed their work in July 1789, and in the spring

Table 26. Research Aids: Depreciation Lands

Fo[r]ster, Robert H. "Depreciation Lands."
Pennsylvania Department of Internal Affairs
Annual Report of the Secretary of Internal Affairs
(1892): A.22–A.31. In *PA* (3) 3:761–71.

"Pennsylvania Soldiers of the Revolution
Entitled to Depreciation Pay." *PMHB* 27
(1903): 449–71; 28 (1904): 45–59, 201–3.

Winner, John E. "The Depreciation and
Donation Lands." *WPHM* 8 (1925): 2–11.

of 1790 the Land Office attempted one last auction. Only because John Nicholson, the state's comptroller general, bid up the prices, was success even marginal.[4] The surveyors' connected drafts are part of the Land Office collection and can be located by consulting the Land Office Map Inventory.

Depreciation Land auction sales had not gone well. Only half of the designated land, 1,315 tracts totalling 316,935 acres, was sold. If all individuals who had purchased tracts had completed their transactions, the average price per acre would have been thirty-four cents. The

accounts of the auction sales and the persons who bought the tracts can be studied in two volumes of the records of the comptroller general's office cited below.

Several excuses were advanced for the poor sales. Receiver General Francis Johnston believed the land was too far from the eastern seaboard to attract purchasers. He also blamed the lower prices and private sales of the neighboring Donation Lands. Whatever the reason, unsold tracts within the Depreciation Land district were opened to sale by the regular method in 1792.[5]

Individuals who received depreciation certificates and those who bought Depreciation Land tracts are not necessarily one and the same. Many servicemen wanted ready cash, not land in the wilderness. They sold their certificates to land speculators who used the documents to buy depreciation tracts as well as land elsewhere. Furthermore, the depreciation tracts could be purchased for gold or silver by people who did not hold certificates.

Records for Depreciation Land purchasers consist of warrants, surveys, returns of survey, and patents. Since the land was bought at auction, there was no application form. The records must be accessed through the Depreciation Land register.

RECORDS: LOOSE PAPERS

ORIGINAL WARRANTS   DEPRECIATION LANDS   LO micro. 3.8–9.

Original warrants for depreciation lot purchasers are filed with the warrants but separately. The warrants are arranged alphabetically by last name and accessed through the bound register titled "Depreciation Land."

DEPRECIATION TRACT MAPS.

Original surveyors' tract maps returned to the Land Office. They may be located through the Land Office Map Inventory.

RECORDS: BOUND VOLUMES

DEPRECIATION LAND [Register]   LO micro.: 79; Reel 3428.

The master index for Depreciation Land purchasers, equivalent to a warrant register. It is arranged in three sections. The first section lists purchasers by surveyor district and gives the following information: lot number; acres; patent date; patentee; patent volume, book, and page; and survey volume, book, and page. The second section is an alphabetical list of patentees and gives the district number and lot number, patentee, and page where entered in the first section. The third section is an alphabetical list of purchasers of depreciation tickets and gives the ticket number, lot number, district number, warrant date, and patent date.

DEPRECIATION LANDS   LO micro.: 25.35–36.

A register of Depreciation Land sales, arranged in two sections. The first section is organized by district and gives the ticket number, name, acres, price, date the survey was returned for patenting, and individual to whom it was patented. The second section is an alphabetical listing of ticket holders and gives the lot number, district number, and date of the order to prepare a warrant to accept.

LEDGER   DEPRECIATION LANDS, PHILADELPHIA AND BEAVER TOWN LOTS   LO micro.: 25.36.

An account book containing some information concerning Depreciation Lands. It gives the name of the purchaser, the amount of land purchased, how many tracts, and how they were paid for (such as cash, specie, depreciation certificates, or Pennsylvania certificates). The ledger includes accounts for Philadelphia and Beaver town lots as well.

DEPRECIATION CERTIFICATES CANCELLED   (Binding Volume 137).

Contains a listing, in no particular order, of the original depreciation certificate holders, the ticket numbers, and their values. The inside title seems to indicate that "Cancelled" refers to the fact that the ticket had been delivered to the register general as partial payment for land.

DEPRECIATION CERTIFICATE INTEREST ACCOUNTS   1781–1792   (RG-4).

A collection of eleven boxes and nine volumes of loose redeemed depreciation certificates and bound ledgers. Each certificate gives the veteran's name, regiment, and amount of interest. See also "Soldiers Who Received Depreciation Pay As Per Cancelled Certificates . . .," in PA (5) 4:105–83.

WASTE BOOK CONTAINING SALES BY AUCTION OF DEPRECIATION LANDS, CITY LOTS, RESERVED TRACTS, ISLANDS   1785–1809   1 VOL.

Contains the name of the purchaser, depreciation lot number, acres, amount paid, and type of money paid, including a separate listing for depreciation certificates.

JOURNAL—DEPRECIATION LANDS, PHILADELPHIA AND BEAVER TOWN LOTS   [November 21, 1785–March 3, 1896]   LO micro.: 25.78.

The first part of this volume contains a copy of the volume Auction of Depreciation Lands. The remainder of the book covers the period 1809–1896.

---

[1]December 18, 1780, *Statutes* 10:233–38.
[2]April 10, 1781, ibid., 314–17. See IV.E.1.c, Philadelphia City Lots and Proprietary Towns.
[3]PA (1) 10:53–54.
[4]Ibid. 11:702.
[5]See IV.E.2.b(4), Vacant Unwarranted Land.

IV.E.2.b(2) Donation Lands

Pennsylvania's experience in keeping men in the fighting ranks during the Revolutionary War had been like that of other states—increasingly difficult as hostilities dragged on. Early in 1780 the state had found it necessary to offer two pay incentive programs to induce men to stay in service: the Depreciation Land program discussed in subsection IV.E.2.b(1) and the Donation Land program.[1] Each Pennsylvania Line soldier and officer who served in the Continental forces to the end of the war was to receive a bounty, or donation, of a tract of land; the size was to be based upon his rank.

The Donation Lands were located west of the Allegheny River within the Purchase of 1784.[2] Lying immediately north of the Depreciation Lands, the Donation Lands were bounded on the east by the Allegheny River, on the west by the Ohio border, and on the north by the New York border.

Comptroller-General John Nicholson and his staff assumed the task of certifying the service of men entitled to Donation Land tracts and of fixing the quantity for each claimant. Allotments were made according to rank, and heirs could claim the land of a deceased soldier or officer. Nicholson's position gave him the perfect opportunity to purchase donation claims. He became an active speculator in Donation Land tracts, keeping some tracts for himself and selling the rest to Philadelphia investors and others. Later, Nicholson was caught at his speculator's folly and tried for high misdemeanors.[3]

The total number of donation tracts surveyed matched the total number of claimants. Dividing the entire Donation Land area into ten surveying districts, each with a different deputy surveyor, the Land Office alloted an equal number of tracts to each district. The tracts varied in size from 200 to 500 acres. By tallying the number of eligible claimants and their amounts of land, the Land Office calculated that 2,570 lots amounting to a total of 585,200 acres needed to be surveyed. Large portions of each district remained unsurveyed.

Distribution of the donation tracts was by lottery. After connected drafts of the finished surveys had been received at the Land Office, each lot was numbered, and slips bearing corresponding numbers were placed in one of four lottery wheels, one for each size of tract. On designated days the numbered tickets were drawn from the wheels. Land was distributed according to the scale in Chart 10. The drawing began on October 1, 1786, but persons entitled to lands were very slow in filing claims. Usually Land Office officials drew the lots and set aside the patents until claimants applied. Those eligible had a one-year limit, but extensions were periodically granted so that applicants were accepted through April 1, 1810.[4]

Since donation tracts were not purchased, patents for Donation Lands were handled differently from patents for other land. A master survey map showing each claimant's name, rank, and lot was filed with the master of the rolls and served as a permanent record of title. Part of the Land Office map collection, these Donation Land maps are available to researchers. Patents signed by the governor were given to each claimant after the surveying fees were paid. Transmittal forms accompanying the patent on its trip to the governor for his signature are also part of the Land Office collection. Some Donation Land patents were recorded in the regular patent books, mainly Pat. Bks. P-9 and P-17.

The Donation Land program ran into three major problems. The most glaring problem was the large encroachment of district number 10 into New York State. The oversight was detected when the Pennsylvania-New York boundary was run in 1787, but not until 1793 were district 10 claimants permitted to choose tracts in any of the other surveyed districts. Patents returned to the Land Office in exchange for tracts located elsewhere are filed as loose papers and cited below. Another problem involved a large amount of land in district number 2 unfit for cultivation. Removed from the offering, the untillable area became known as the Struck District. Officials were ambivalent about this decision, however, and many legal battles were fought over the district. Finally the Struck District tracts were added to the unappropriated lands and opened to sale and settlement. The third problem involved the list of eligible claimants. In making the final drawing on behalf of those eligible, the Land Office realized that the names of many qualified officers and soldiers had not appeared on the original list. Some historians have attributed this to an oversight of Comptroller General Nicholson. A corrected list of eligibles was prepared, and the veterans were awarded their land.

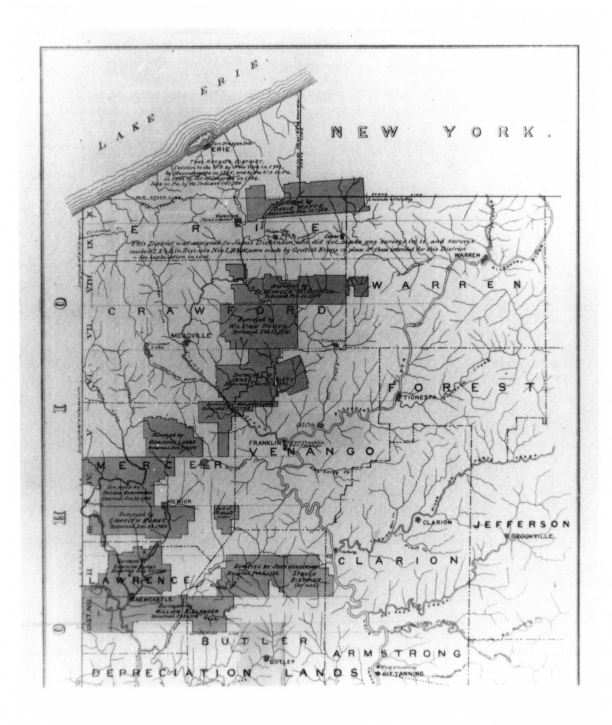

Map 6. Tracts actually surveyed within the Donation Lands superimposed over current counties. (Pennsylvania Department of Internal Affairs *Annual Report of the Secretary of Internal Affairs, 1893*)

Chart 10. Donation Land Rank and Allotment

Rank	Allotment
Major general	Four 500-acre tracts
Brigadier general	Three 500-acre tracts
Colonel	Two 500-acre tracts
Lieutenant colonel	One 500-acre tract and one 250-acre tract
Surgeon, chaplain, major	Two 350-acre tracts
Captain	One 500-acre tract
Lieutenant	Two 200-acre tracts
Ensign, surgeon's mate, sergeant, sergeant major, quartermaster sergeant	One 250-acre tract
Drum major, fife major, drummer, fifer, corporal, private	One 200-acre tract

A list of the names of those affected appears at the end of the Donation Land register.

The amount of land given away in 1786 and 1787 through the Donation Land program totaled 460,450 acres. Valued at the prevailing price for land in other parts of the Purchase of

Table 27. Research Aid: Donation Lands

Fo[r]ster, Robert H. "The Donation Lands of Pennsylvania." Pennsylvania Department of Internal Affairs *Annual Report of the Secretary of Internal Affairs* (1894): A.19–A.41. In *PA* (3) 3:575–603.

1784, $.80 per acre, Pennsylvania's giveaway in bounty land amounted to $368,360. Nicholson billed the federal government this amount plus 6 percent interest for two years, or a total of $412,563. Having already paid for the Depreciation Land program, Pennsylvania was not willing to underwrite the total cost of its participation in the Revolutionary War by also funding the Donation Land program.

Aside from the Donation Land district maps, records for Donation Land claimants consist of claim papers, surveys, and patents. The surveys and patents must be accessed through the Donation Land register. Claim papers are filed separately. All are cited below.

Undrawn Donation Land tracts became available to the general public in 1813. Actual settlers who had resided on a donation tract for three years and cleared, fenced, and cultivated at least ten acres received preference. The purchase price was $1.50 per acre with interest from three years after settlement. Applicants were to submit a deputy surveyor's statement certifying the original survey and the number and acreage of the tract.[5]

RECORDS: LOOSE PAPERS

DONATION CLAIMANTS   LO micro.: 8.1–4.

Eighty-nine folders containing miscellaneous records pertaining to Donation Land claimants. Filed alphabetically, the records include deeds of conveyance, discharge certificates, power of attorney certificates, and application forms.

TRANSMITTAL OF PATENTS   1803–1809.

Contains forms or certificates to accompany Donation Land patents sent to the governor for his signature. The forms are dated and cite the patentee, lot and district numbers, current county, and acres.

DONATION PATENTS   LO micro.: 8.4.

Twenty-three folders containing patents for district number 10 surrendered to the Commonwealth in return for patents to land in other districts and some patents in the name of John Nicholson.

RECORDS: BOUND VOLUMES

DONATION LAND [Register]   LO micro.: 79; Reel 3428.

The current register in use for Donation Lands, arranged as follows: pages 2–84, a list of tracts arranged by district, individual to whom patented, reference to survey and patent volumes, and date recorded in surveyor general's office; pages 85–128, an index to the preceding; pages 129–73, the claimant's regiment, rank, and acres and if drawn; pages 174–77, the names, ranks, and regiments of claimants in district number 10 found to be in New York; page 178, lots partly in Pennsylvania and partly in New York, with lots afterward drawn in their place; page 179, lots drawn for widows and children; pages 180–85, a list of officers and men entitled to Donation Lands for whom there was no number in the wheel; pages 186–88, an account of fees received by James Trimble, clerk of the Donation Land program, in 1792.

DONATION LANDS   (Binding Volume 34).

A collection of five different lists bound together, plus the report of the drawing of the Donation Land lottery on December 20, 1794.

DONATION LAND LOTS LYING IN NEW YORK   (Binding Volume 135).

Contains various lists, lot numbers, and amounts of land in district number 10 lots.

DONATION LAND CLAIMANTS   (Binding Volume 136).

Contains several different lists, each giving the name, rank, and regiment and whether a lot was drawn.

DONATION LANDS GRANTED PENNSYLVANIA LINE   LO micro.: 25.35.

In this volume names are grouped by the first letter of the last name, and information for each person includes the rank, regiment, number of his lot, and district.

DONATION LANDS   PENNSYLVANIA LINE   (With index)   LO micro.: 25.29; PA (3) 7:659–795.

Contains a list of the donation tracts granted to the officers and soldiers of the Pennsylvania Line in the Continental army. The list gives the district, number, quantity of acres, name of the patentee, and date the tract was returned for patenting. It is inscribed as follows: "Surveyor General's Office, Harrisburg 26 April 1813."

REGISTER OF DONATION   [Patenting Fees].

An account book belonging to James Trimble giving the names, amounts, and dates of individuals who submitted payment for patenting fees.

PENNSYLVANIA LINE ENTITLED TO DONATION LAND   LO micro.: 25.35; PA (3) 3:607–757.

Gives the name, rank, regiment, and acres and whether a lot was drawn, with comments.

DONATION LAND BOOK   LO micro.: 25.35.

A compilation of material relating to the Donation Lands, including copies of laws, a list of patentees, and an extensive collection of lists and papers.

CLAIMANTS FOR DONATION LANDS   LO micro.: 25.35.

A collection of five lists dealing with claimants, including such information as war casualties and second, third, and fourth conveyance.

---

[1]March 7, 1780, SmL 2:63.
[2]March 12, 1783, ibid., 62–65.
[3]See IV.D.5, Speculators.
[4]March 24, 1785, SmL 2:290–99.
[5]March 26, 1813, ibid. 6:64.

IV.E.2.b(3) Reserved Land

Just as William Penn and his heirs had set aside land for themselves, the Commonwealth reserved particular tracts for its own use. These reserved tracts were all located within the Purchase of 1784 and frequently offered something of strategic importance to the state.

IV.E.2.b(3)(a) Military Tracts

The state at first reserved land only for military purposes. In the same legislation that designated Depreciation Lands, the assembly created two military reservations of three thousand acres each. One reservation included Fort Pitt at the confluence of the Allegheny and Ohio rivers, and the other included Fort McIntosh at the confluence of the Ohio River and Beaver Creek.[1]

Later, in 1792, the state reserved several tracts within the Erie triangle for military purposes. The largest, the entire peninsula of Presque Isle, the state retained for strategic use.

Three smaller tracts in the town of Erie were also designated for the erection and maintenance of forts, magazines, and dockyards.[2] Another reservation, a tract of two thousand acres at the mouth of Harbor Creek, was granted to General William Irvine in return for his loss of Montour's Island (Neville Island) in the Ohio River below Pittsburgh to a person holding the same island under a prior Virginia right.

Reserved tracts at the mouth of French Creek, at Fort Le Boeuf, and at the mouth of Conewango Creek, originally designated for military purposes, were not needed and quickly developed into two sites as discussed below.

---

[1]March 12, 1783, SmL 2:62.
[2]April 3, 1792, ibid. 3:70–75; April 18, 1795, ibid., 233–39.

IV.E.2.b(3)(b) Town Lots

The Commonwealth continued the proprietary policy of laying out towns in strategic locations and overseeing the sale of the lots. Five of the six town sites chosen eventually became county seats. As with the proprietary towns, a rectilinear plan was followed. Streets emanating from a center public square permitted towns to be surveyed into town lots, out lots, and reserved lots. Town lots varied in size depending upon the lay of the town land but were consistent for each town. Out lots contained either five or ten acres depending upon the town. Erie, being unusually large, was divided into three equal parts with three town squares. Original surveys of each of these towns are in the Land Office and can be found through the Land Office Map Inventory.

Town lots were usually sold at auction to the highest bidder. Although a commissioner or town warden responsible for the sale of the tracts resided in each town, the auctions were usually held in other towns. The tracts were graded in quality and priced accordingly. A certificate of sale was completed, but no warrants were issued for town lots. Therefore, lot purchasers will not be found in the warrant registers. Patents were issued, however, after the entire purchase price was paid. Two years were usually allowed between original purchase and final payment in order to give purchasers time to build the required dwelling. Patentees of lots are entered in the patent registers.

Allegheny

In 1787 the town of Allegheny was laid out on the reserved land opposite Fort Pitt. Often referred to as the reserved tract opposite Pittsburgh, Allegheny eventually became part of Pittsburgh. Founded to raise money to help pay off the state Revolutionary War debt through the sale of lots, the tract was surveyed into town and out lots and sold at public auction.[1] Town lots measured 60 by 240 feet; out lots contained 5 to 10 acres. One 312-acre tract was patented to James O'Harra, May 5, 1789. Two bound volumes cited below contain survey and purchaser information.

Beaver

Within the Depreciation Lands, 3,000 acres were reserved for a town site. Following enabling legislation in 1791, 200 acres were surveyed into town lots and 1,000 acres into out lots.[2] The town was named Beaver in 1791, and Beaver County was formed in 1800. The town became the county seat. The original survey of Beaver and purchaser information is given in a bound volume cited below.

Erie, Franklin, Waterford, Warren

The towns of Erie, Franklin, Waterford, and Warren were established by an act passed April 18, 1795.[3] Similar regulations for the sizes of lots and provisions for streets, lanes, alleys, and land for public use applied to each town. Public auction was the uniform method for the sale of lots.

Erie was laid out on part of the large reservation at Presque Isle. A total of 5,000 acres was allocated: 1,600 acres for town lots and 3,400 acres for out lots. One third of the lots were sold at auction during the first round of sales. If within two years a purchaser built a house containing a minimum of 256 square feet and at least one brick or stone chimney, he could receive a patent.

Franklin, surveyed out of the reserved land at the mouth of French Creek, and Warren, laid out at the mouth of Conewango Creek, were originally the same size. In each town, 300 acres were allocated for town lots and 700 acres for out lots.

Waterford, the only town of the four not to become a county seat, developed from a settlement previously surveyed by Andrew Ellicott at Fort Le Boeuf. The legislature approved Ellicott's plan but appropriated an additional 500 acres for out lots. Settlers who had built houses while Waterford was still Fort Le Boeuf were given a right of preemption to the lots on which they had settled. Descriptions of the town lots, purchasers, and patentees were recorded in a bound volume cited below.

Daybooks recording sales of town lots by auction and journals and ledgers containing information about the sale of town lots are all cited below. Maps of the original layouts of the towns are also available and may be located by consulting the Land Office Map Inventory.

RECORDS: LOOSE PAPERS

TOWN LOTS   LO micro.: 11.1–4, 11.6.

Ninety-one folders arranged in the following order: town and out lots, reserved lots, bonds, and miscellaneous. The contents of each folder consist of statements of sales and receipts giving the purchaser's name, lot number, and terms of sale. The miscellaneous folders contain lists of purchasers at each sale, manuscripts of historical information, and plans of the towns.

RECORDS: BOUND VOLUMES

ALLEGHENY TOWN AND OUT LOTS   LO micro.: 25.36.

Contains certificates and records of sales of lots in the reserved tract opposite Pittsburgh, 1788–1797, including purchasers' names and terms of sale.

IN AND OUT LOTS RESERVED TRACT OPPOSITE PITTSBURGH   1791.

Compiled by William Clark, a clerk in the receiver general's office, this volume contains descriptions of boundaries or particular situations of town and out lots in the town of Allegheny. Only a few purchasers' names are given.

ERIE, FRANKLIN, WARREN AND WATERFORD TOWN OUT LOTS   (With index).

Appears to be two books bound as one. Pages 1–32 contain a lot-by-lot survey of the town of Franklin but no purchasers' names. Pages 33–265, indexed, give a mixed account of sales of lots in all the towns for the period 1797–1809. Each entry gives a description of the lot, lot number, purchaser, and patentee. The last several pages, not numbered, are lists of lots by town, rate, and valuation.

ERIE LOTS   LO micro.: 25.36.

Contains accounts of the sales of Erie lots for August 3, 1801–September 19, 1810. Each entry gives the purchaser's name, lot number, and amount paid.

ERIE LOTS—RESERVE TRACTS—WATER LOTS.

Similar to a warrant register, this volume indexes purchasers and references lot number, price, date of sale, patentee, date of return, and patent record.

SUNBURY, FRANKLIN, WARREN AND BEAVER TOWN LOTS.   FRANKLIN, WAR-REN, WATERFORD RESERVE TRACTS.

Similar to a warrant register, this volume indexes purchasers and references lot number, price, date of sale, patentee, date of return, and patent and survey record.

BEAVER TOWN LOTS   (With index)   LO micro.: 25.36.

Contains copies of all laws and commissions pertaining to the sale of Beaver lots, pages 1–15. Daniel Leet's original survey of Beaver is an insert on page 19. The rest of the volume contains certificates of sales, giving the lot number, purchaser's name, amount paid, patentee, and date.

DAY BOOK OF SALES BY AUCTION   1785–1809   LO micro.: 25.50.

Entries in this volume are a chronological account of sales of Depreciation Lands, city lots, reserved tracts (towns), and islands. Information includes the purchaser's name and amount paid.

BOOK OF ENTRIES OF PATENTS ISSUED FOR IN AND OUT LOTS IN AND NEAR THE TOWNS: ERIE, WARREN, WATERFORD, FRANKLIN   LO micro.: 25.37.

Lot descriptions listed in random order, giving the patentee and lot numbers.

IRREGULAR LOTS   WARREN, FRANKLIN, AND ERIE   LO micro.: 25.37.

Contains connected surveys and street bearings of the irregular lots.

JOURNAL—DEPRECIATION LANDS, PHILADELPHIA AND BEAVER TOWN LOTS   [November 21, 1785–March 3, 1896]   LO micro.: 25.78.

A journal started by the receiver general. It contains a chronological account of sales, giving the purchaser's name and amount paid.

JOURNAL FOR ERIE LOTS   1801–1920   LO micro.: 25.79.
JOURNAL FOR FRANKLIN LOTS   1801–1907   [2 volumes]   LO micro.: 25.79.
JOURNAL FOR WARREN LOTS   1801–1909   [2 volumes]   LO micro.: 25.79.
JOURNAL FOR WATERFORD LOTS   1801–1902   [2 volumes]   LO micro.: 25.79.

Journals started by the receiver general and added to by his successors. They contain chronological accounts of sales of lots in the respective towns, giving the purchaser's name and amount paid.

LEDGER   DEPRECIATION LANDS, PHILADELPHIA AND BEAVER TOWN LOTS   LO micro.: 25.36.
LEDGER FOR ERIE LOTS   1801–1923   (With index)   LO micro.: 25.104.
LEDGER FOR FRANKLIN LOTS   1801–1907   (With index)   LO micro.: 25.105.
LEDGER FOR WARREN LOTS   1801–1909   (With index)   LO micro.: 25.105.
LEDGER FOR WATERFORD LOTS   1801–1902   (With index)   LO micro.: 25.105.

Master account books prepared from journal entries, listing each purchaser's credits and debits.

---

[1]September 11, 1787, *SmL* 2:414–16.
[2]September 28, 1791, ibid. 3:56–57.
[3]Ibid., 233–40.

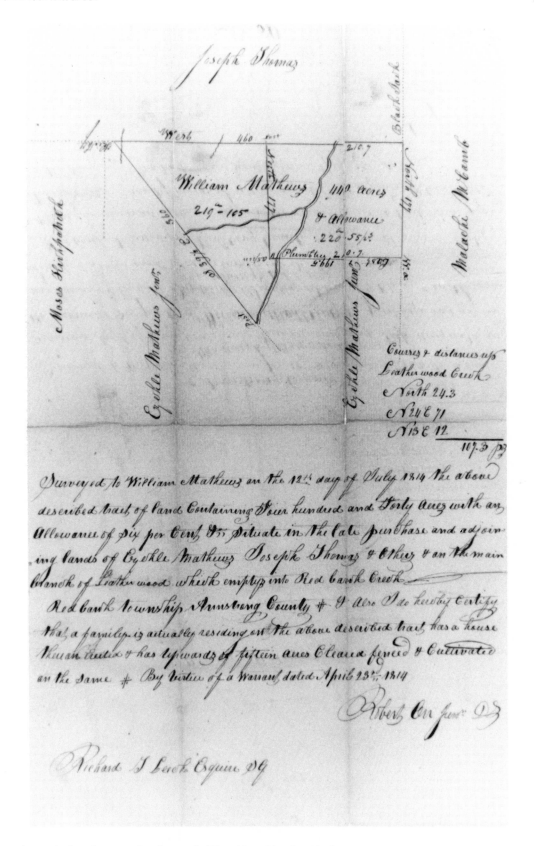

Survey and proof of settlement, Purchase of 1784. (Sur. Bk. C-168-5)

Table 28. Research Aid: Pennsylvania's Northwestern Land

Henderson, Elizabeth K. "The Northwestern Lands of Pennsylvania." *PMHB* 60 (1936): 131–60.

IV.E.2.b(4) Vacant Unwarranted Land

After the individual depreciation and donation tracts had been surveyed, a large amount of vacant unwarranted land remained in the region north and west of the Ohio and Allegheny rivers. Including the Erie triangle, this land was opened to the general public for legal settlement in 1792. The law governing its distribution was probably the most controversial of all state land laws.[1] Differing from previous laws, the 1792 act required that purchasers or their representatives settle, improve, and cultivate the vacant land before a patent could be granted. Designed to put an end to rampant land speculation, the law instead opened the doors to greater conflict.

Ostensibly written to reduce the price of vacant land, the terms of the law provided for the sale of tracts of not more than four hundred acres at the reduced price of seven pounds ten shillings in Pennsylvania currency for every one hundred acres. This was equivalent to twenty cents per acre. Dividing the area into eleven surveying districts, the Land Office assigned a deputy surveyor to each district (see Map 4, The Purchase of 1784). Squatters who were already on the land and had made actual settlements and improvements were to apply directly to the deputy surveyor rather than to the Land Office. Deputies were to complete surveys within six months of receiving a squatter's application. They also were to keep a book of completed surveys available for the public to study, although they could charge a slight fee. Every February, all survey plats, connected together in one general draft where possible, were to be returned to the Land Office. Warrants to accept were then issued to the applicants.

The law, however, did not permit the Land Office to issue a patent until the warrantee had met the terms of the cultivation, improvement, and settlement clauses. Warrantees submitted proof of settlement certificates demonstrating five years of residency following their first date of settlement. Sworn before two justices of the peace by an impartial witness, the statement included the nature of the improvement and the adjoining settlers. Proof of settlement certificates submitted by applicants for patents are part of the Land Office collection and are cited below.

An escape provision in the 1792 law permitted the waiver of settlement and improvement requirements if warrantees were prevented from complying "by force of arms of the enemies of the United States."[2] This policy was an adaptation of the 1785 law that permitted the exoneration of interest payments for all actual settlers driven from their homes by Indians in the course of the Revolutionary War. As there was chronic Indian warfare in northwestern Pennsylvania into 1794 and 1795, this superficially innocuous provision proved a bonanza for speculators. On behalf of their companies, particularly the Pennsylvania Population Company and the Holland Land Company, the speculators promptly proceeded to take out immense numbers of warrants directly through the Land Office using fictitious names. Although the warrants contained the clause requiring actual settlement, most of the speculators made no pretense of complying. The Holland Land Company, as an example, took out eleven hundred warrants in the names of individual directors. John Nicholson, comptroller general of the Commonwealth, was another purchaser who held large numbers of warrants. Most of his warrants, on behalf of the Pennsylvania Population Company, lay within the Erie triangle.

It seemed as if the speculators would gobble up all the land. In 1797 the Board of Property ruled that patents might be granted without settlement if a valid prevention certificate could be produced. Attested before two justices of the peace and signed by the deputy surveyor, the vast majority of prevention certificates were submitted by land companies on behalf of settlers. These certificates are filed with the particular company's papers in the Land Office collection.[3] Until 1800 many patents were granted on the basis of prevention certificates.

A change of policy favoring actual settlers came with the new state government administration in October 1799. To eliminate the connection between speculator and deputy surveyor, surveying districts were redrawn by county, and new deputy surveyors were appointed. The Commonwealth Supreme Court also reversed the

Board of Property decision and ruled that a warrantee must show proof of actual settlement within two years of the date when prevention ceased. Prevention certificates alone were no longer sufficient to receive a patent.

At the same time, stimulated by reports that settlement was sufficient title in itself, new settlers deliberately squatted on tracts warranted by speculators. Some of the problems were solved when the speculator's right to settlement by improvement ran out. This right was forfeited if the speculator had not met settlement requirements and applied for a patent within ten years after 1792, the date of the original law. Thus, as early as 1802, squatters on speculators' land were eligible to apply for new warrants. However, the Commonwealth Supreme Court ruled that new warrants were not to be issued. Instead, a speculator's original application was to stand, and a squatter was to pay for a vacating warrant, submit his proof of settlement, and pay the purchase price before securing a patent.

Because so many actual settlers were too poor for this complicated patenting process, another solution developed in 1804. Squatters' applications were given the force of vacating warrants, and no fees were required. Court battles over the new procedure brought stringent conditions. To be eligible, the filing date of the application had to be prior to any ejectment suit a speculator had initiated.

It was not until 1811 that compromise legislation provided for the needs of both squatters and speculators who claimed the same land.[4] In a case where the actual settler was on a 400-acre tract warranted to a speculator, the Land Office would grant patents to both squatter and speculator if the speculator would release to the actual settler 150 acres including the improvement. If the speculator had assisted the squatter in making a settlement, then the speculator needed to release only 50 acres to the squatter. Proof of settlement was needed in the usual way, and a deed poll as evidence of agreement was to be filed in the county recorder of deeds office, with a certified copy sent to the secretary of the Land Office. Filed under the category Title Papers, these deed polls are part of the Land Office collection and are cited below. To assist actual settlers the Commonwealth offered ten-year mortgages. The patent was not contingent upon paying off the mortgage but was issued in the usual way. These mortgage papers are filed with those of all other mortgage programs in the Land Office collection.

Finally, in 1814 actual settlers were given legal priority over speculators.[5] For the first time, speculators were required to prove that they or their representatives were individually prevented from settling by enemies of the United States during the two years after the date of the warrant. This requirement placed the speculator on very different ground. Previously the speculator had not needed to prove that he was individually prevented but only that there was sufficient danger to deter any prudent man from attempting a settlement before the 1795 Treaty of Greenville. Despite this success for actual settlers, disputed tracts continued to be such a problem that land laws applying to the area north and west of the Allegheny and Ohio rivers were periodically extended until April 1, 1836.

In addition to the special records cited below, regular records for purchasers of vacant land north and west of the Ohio and Allegheny rivers and Conewango Creek consist of applications, warrants, surveys, returns of survey, and patents. Many of the applications are entered on long lists filed separately from other loose applications. These records may be accessed through the regular warrant registers for the county of jurisdiction at the time.

RECORDS: LOOSE PAPERS

PROOF OF SETTLEMENT CERTIFICATES   LO micro.: 14.1–5.

One hundred and twenty-seven folders containing proof of settlement certificates required for patenting land under the vacant land law of 1792. Filed by current county within the area north and west of the Ohio and Allegheny rivers and Conewango Creek, the individual documents are arranged alphabetically. They document the patentee's original date of settlement, which may differ from the warrant date and may be in a different location. Adjoining owners and descriptions of tracts are included.

TITLE PAPERS   LO micro.: 12.1–8.

One hundred forty-eight folders containing prepatent deed polls from original warrantee to second owner. The documents were submitted in compliance with the 1811 law permitting both speculator and squatter to patent portions of the same warrant tract.

----

[1]April 3, 1792, *SmL* 3:70.
[2]Ibid., 73.
[3]See records under IV.D.5, Speculators.
[4]March 1, 1811, *PaL*, 54; *SmL* 5:198.
[5]*SmL* 6:130.

IV.E.3. Islands and Riverbeds

IV.E.3.a. Islands

During the period of the Commonwealth, as during the colonial era, islands were treated as a separate category of land. Although islands could be transferred to private ownership, they were subject to view and appraisal and were usually sold at auction to the highest bidder. Consequently the records documenting the transfer of islands to private ownership are filed separately in the Land Office.

As far as islands were concerned, the first order of business after the Revolutionary War was to settle their jurisdiction within the Delaware River. Although most of the islands in the Delaware had been titled to individuals, the county and state of jurisdiction was not absolutely clear. Following the practice of the proprietors, a special commission composed of Pennsylvania and New Jersey delegates assigned islands to the jurisdiction of the nearest state. To avoid possible confusion the more important islands were specifically named in the resulting legislation.[1] Further legislation in 1786 individually named each Pennsylvania island in the Delaware River and annexed the island to the adjacent county.[2]

The Commonwealth handled all untitled islands just as the proprietors had. Withheld from the vacant lands, islands were appraised on behalf of the Board of Property and disposed of by public or private sale.[3] Islands in the Susquehanna River suitable for cultivation were the first to be offered for sale. The price was set at not less than eight dollars per acre.[4] Islands in the rivers of the Purchase of 1784 were available for preemption and private purchase after 1795.[5] Unsold islands were offered at public sale in Pittsburgh on July 16, 1798.[6]

Warrant, survey, and patent information for islands can be located through the warrant registers. Applications for islands and the Board of Property appraisal reports, called Islands View and Appraisal, are filed separately under islands in the Land Office collection and cited below. Separate application and warrant registers for islands also exist. These references are cited below.

RECORDS: LOOSE PAPERS

ISLANDS   APPLICATIONS   LO micro.: 16.2–7.

Ninety-five folders containing applications dating mainly from 1757, with a few between 1757 and 1793. The last eight folders all contain applications from George R. Harlow dating from 1912 and relate to islands in the lower Susquehanna transferred to Pennsylvania Power and Light.

ISLANDS   VIEW AND APPRAISAL   LO micro.: 16.7–11.

Folders 96–165 containing appraisers' reports returned to the Board of Property. The reports give the location and description of the island, a report on any prior warrant or survey, and the appraised valuation. The early reports are written in longhand, the later ones on a form for that purpose.

RECORDS: BOUND VOLUMES

APPLICATIONS FOR ISLANDS   (Binding Volume 163; with index)   *PA* (3) 3:461–82.

An applications register covering the period 1791–1811, and giving the date, applicant's name, and location of the island.

ISLANDS IN THE SUSQUEHANNA   1793–1812   (Binding Volume 1; with indexes)   LO micro.: 25.36; *PA* 3:403–60.

A register of applications under the 1793 law, including a few dated earlier. Columns are headed date, applicant, acres, and situation. The volume includes an index by island and an index by name of applicant.

ISLANDS IN THE SUSQUEHANNA RIVER   DEC 14, 1797–APR 16, 1857   (With riverbed information and indexes)   LO micro.: 25.37.

The first 130 pages of this volume contain a warrant register for islands, giving the warrant date, warrant number, warrantee's name, quantity, and situation, with remarks. The dates included are actually 1802 through 1906. There is an index by owner and an index by island. The last section of this volume, pages 162–97, is a warrant register for riverbeds covering the period 1848–1857 and giving the warrant date, warrantee, acres, location, and river.

ISLANDS IN THE RIVERS DELAWARE, OHIO, ALLEGHENY, SCHUYLKILL, ETC.   (With riverbed information and index)   LO micro.: 25.37.

The first 113 pages of this volume contain a warrant register for islands for the period 1798–1899, giving the warrant date, warrant number, warrantee, acres, situation, and terms, with remarks. The index is by owner. The last section of this volume, pages 124–98, is a warrant register for riverbeds for the period 1848–1903, giving the warrant date, warrantee, acres, location, and river.

---

[1]September 20, 1783, *SmL* 2:77–79.
[2]September 25, 1786, ibid., 388–91.
[3]April 8, 1785, ibid., 322
[4]March 6, 1793, ibid. 3:93–95.
[5]T. Mifflin to the secretary, surveyor general, and receiver general of the Land Office, March 7, 1795, Applications for Islands (Binding Volume 163).
[6]"Meeting of Land Officers," April 9, 1798, ibid.

IV.E.3.b. Riverbeds

Riverbeds constitute another minor but separate category of land. Since riverbeds were valuable for their mineral deposits, the Commonwealth enacted a law in 1848 to sell tracts of land in the beds of its navigable rivers.[1] As long as navigation was not deterred and the bed of the river was not undermined, an applicant could warrant one hundred acres of riverbed. Retaining the option to revoke the warrant in twenty years, the Commonwealth required the applicant to pay only $4.50 in fees. If, after the survey was completed, the warrantee obtained a patent, then the purchase price was the same as for any other land. Few patents were granted, however, as the law was in effect for only one year. Repealed in 1849, it was revived for Allegheny County in 1856 and Fayette County in 1864.[2] Most of the patents that were issued were granted for the Northeast Branch of the Susquehanna River in Luzerne County where coal deposits were of interest.

Surveys in riverbeds meshed with the policies concerning riverbanks (or riparian rights) established under William Penn. Ownership of tracts adjoining navigable rivers extended to the low-water mark. Thus tracts in beds of rivers started at the low-water mark and ran across to the opposite bank at the low-water mark. Where streams were narrow, thin slivers of riverbed one mile or more in length were required to make up one hundred acres.

Warrant, survey, and patent information for riverbeds can be located through the warrant registers. Applicants, however, are filed separately and by the name of the river as cited below. Separate warrant registers for riverbeds may be found in the bound volumes for islands cited above.

RECORDS: LOOSE PAPERS

RIVER BEDS   APPLICATIONS   LO micro.: 16.11.

Twenty folders filed by river and containing applications for riverbed land. Each application gives the applicant's name, name of the river, and description of the desired location. The following rivers are involved: Allegheny, Bald Eagle, Beaver, Cheat, Juniata, Kiskiminetas, Monongahela, Ohio, Schuylkill, Susquehanna, Swatara, and Youghiogheny.

APPLICATIONS FOR RIVER BEDS   1864.

A group of applications for warrants issued and not issued under the law of 1864 for tracts in the beds of several major rivers in the western part of the state. The papers may be located through the Land Office Map Inventory.

---

[1]April 11, 1848, *PaL*, 533.
[2]March 29, 1849, ibid., 255; April 16, 1856, ibid., 365; April 18, 1864, ibid., 437.

IV.E.4. Unpatented Land and Land Lien Dockets

Well into the mid-1800s the records of the Land Office carried a significant amount of unpatented land. Understanding that the system interpreted ownership as dating from the warrant, many occupants simply failed to complete titles. They secured their land with neither a survey nor a patent. In most instances the unpaid balance on the purchase price due the Commonwealth was small, but in others it amounted to a considerable sum of money. Beginning in 1805 and finishing with the land lien law of 1899, the Commonwealth government made efforts to collect the amounts due and settle the titles.

At first the Commonwealth pursued a very liberal policy in its dealings with owners of warranted but unpatented land. In 1805 the Land Office provided an easy-term mortgage program for settlers who could not afford to pay the remaining amount of the purchase price in one

Table 29. Research Aids: Land Lien Laws

"Liens of the Commonwealth against Unpatented Lands." Pennsylvania Department of Internal Affairs *Annual Report of the Secretary of Internal Affairs* (1898, 1899): 16.A–A.41, 22.A–A.25.

Stephenson, John G. "Land Office Business in Pennsylvania." *Villanova Law Review* 4 (1959): 175–97. See especially pp. 181–83.

lump sum. Patents were issued to all who applied within three years, paid the usual office fees, and executed a ten-year mortgage to the Commonwealth in the name of the governor. The mortgage program was extended to settlers in the northwestern part of the state in 1811. Patents were issued to settlers who applied within two years and who had met the cultivation, settlement, and improvement requirements of the law of 1792 or 1794, provided they executed a ten-year mortgage. Over the ensuing several years the Land Office issued 988 patents on this law. All but 72 mortgages had been paid off when the legislature canceled the liens in 1899.[1]

In 1816 the Commonwealth attempted another approach to encourage the patenting of land on which purchase money was due. If the owner made a partial payment, the Commonwealth granted the patent and placed a lien on the land for the remainder. The recording of the patent at the county level along with the lien served as a notice to all subsequent purchasers that title was incomplete.[2] This law was no more successful than the mortgage program. The surveyor general, in his annual report of 1818, estimated that more than 1,750,000 acres of warranted land were unpatented.[3]

A still different approach to encourage patenting was attempted in 1835. The Land Office introduced a system of graduated land values and interest rates on land on which money was due the Commonwealth. Serving as a board of appraisers, the county commissioners valued each tract at the option and expense of the occupant. The commissioners' oaths of office are filed in five folders in the Land Office collection and cited below. Land valuations were limited to four rates. The commissioners' appraisal certificates for each tract of land involved are also on file in the Land Office and cited below.

Although the law was in effect until 1864, with adjustments to interest rates in 1858, official reports claim that it was loosely followed and ineffective.

Despite these several programs, many landholders still owed the Commonwealth a large amount of money. Faced with heavy Civil War expenses, the state turned to these landholders as it had during the Revolutionary War. The Land Office searched four different classes of unpatented land for purchase money due: 1) land granted by the proprietaries beginning in 1733 for which no purchase credit could be found on the books; 2) land granted under the application system of 1765–1769 for which no payment of the purchase price following the return of survey could be found; 3) land granted under the settlement, improvement, and cultivation provision of the law of 1792; and 4) land making up the difference between the quantity for which the warrant had been granted and for which the Commonwealth had received payment and the quantity returned in the survey. Governor Andrew G. Curtin, in his annual message of 1863, recommended the adoption of effective legislation to collect as much unpaid purchase money as possible.

The resulting land lien law of 1864, as amended in 1868, directed the surveyor general to compile and transmit lien dockets to the prothonotary of each county. The lien dockets list the warrantee's name, purchase money due, and interest and fees. Reporting in 1865, the surveyor general calculated that at least $1 million could be added to the state treasury if the liens could be collected. Simply the threat of being included in the lien dockets provoked settlers into paying over $90,000 to the Land Office in 1864 alone. This amount was almost as much as had been received during the previous seven years.

The lien dockets remained in each county prothonotary's office from 1868 until 1899 and still may be available. Many officials assumed that these lists were complete and accurate. However, many occupants could show that they had made payment in full and applied for and received releases. The main problem in such cases was usually caused by overlapping surveys. Applications for releases contain connected drafts and are on file in the Land Office collection. Applications are also listed in two bound volumes cited below.

The year after the lien dockets were sent to the counties, receipts of outstanding debts skyrocketed. The $140,000 collected was more than the combined amount brought in during the previous five years on all applications for patents. To ensure that collections would continue, the Board of Property in 1871 assumed discretionary power to bring suit against a current occupant. However, this threat meant little to most occupants, since the liens were entered in the name of the original warrantee or patentee. Few suits were filed, due to the Commonwealth's lenient policy and the pending economic depression.[4] A ten-year report of the effects of the lien law showed that nearly $537,000 had been collected, but $758,000 remained outstanding on 13,531 tracts of land representing 2,400,000 acres.[5]

Ironically, the final effort to collect outstanding purchase money and interest resulted in the closing of the lien dockets. In 1897 the legislature passed a strong law providing for the collection of all lien money. Public clamor from persons who had purchased land without carrying their title search back to the patent or warrant was so tremendous that the legislature recalled its law in 1899 and closed the lien dockets. From then until the present, the owner of warranted but unpatented land has been able to secure a patent from the Commonwealth upon the payment of a flat patent fee.

Transcripts of the 1860 land lien dockets are entered in four oversized bound volumes and are cited below. As the liens were paid and patents issued, a record was sent to the counties and entered in the Land Office warrant and patent registers. But some land still remains unpatented. Researchers who can find a warrant record but no patent may wish to consult the lien dockets.

RECORDS: LOOSE PAPERS

COMMISSIONERS CERTIFICATES   LO micro.: 27.1–12.

Filed by county and chronologically within county, these 325 folders contain certificates of appraisal under the act of April 10, 1835, to graduate the land on which money was due and unpaid to the Commonwealth. Each certificate gives the township, acres, warrant date, warrantee's name, classification of the land, and rate of appraisal; they are dated and signed by the commissioners.

OATHS OF COMMISSIONERS   LO micro.: 27.12.

Five folders containing county commissioners' oaths to act as appraisers of unpatented land under the 1835 law to graduate land.

UNPATENTED LAND LISTS.

Prepared by county and containing an alphabetical list of unpatented land as of 1864, the date of the first land lien law. The lists give the warrantee, warrant date, and township.

APPLICATIONS FOR AND RELEASE OF LIENS   LO micro.: 16.15–16.

Forty-four folders of applications filed by county and containing connected drafts of overlapping surveys.

APPLICATIONS FOR PATENTS   [1870–1953]   LO micro.: 4.1–11.

Applications to patent land on which a great deal of time had elapsed since the warrant and the chain of title was not known. Usually the land had been purchased at a sheriff's sale. The last few folders contain lists of money and fees sent to the Commonwealth treasurer.

RECORDS: BOUND VOLUMES

LIEN DOCKETS   LO micro.: 1.5–8.

Four volumes constructed between 1864 and 1868, arranged regionally and containing lists of land by county on which titles were not completed by 1864. The following information is given: warrant number, warrantee, warrant date, warrant quantity, township or location, quantity returned, quantity unpatented, rate percent of land, rate percent of interest, where the account was found, amount paid on the account, when paid, amount due, fees, aggregate amount due June 1, 1868, and remarks. Volume 1 contains Philadelphia, Montgomery, Berks, Schuylkill, Chester, Delaware, Lancaster, Dauphin, Lebanon, Bucks, Northampton, Lehigh, Carbon, Monroe, Pike, and Wayne counties. Volume 2 contains Northumberland, Luzerne, Columbia, Montour, Lycoming, Sullivan, Wyoming, Susquehanna, Bradford, Tioga, Potter, Clinton, Union, Centre, and Snyder counties. Volume 3 contains York, Adams, Cumberland, Franklin, Perry, Juniata, Huntingdon, Mifflin, Blair, Cambria, Clearfield, Cameron, Elk, McKean, and Forest counties. Volume 4 contains Bedford, Fulton, Somerset, Fayette, Westmoreland, Washington, Greene, Allegheny, Armstrong, Indiana, Jefferson, Clarion, Venango, Warren, Beaver, Butler, Mercer, Lawrence, Crawford, and Erie counties.

RELEASES—ACT OF 15 APRIL 1869–1875   NO. 1   (Binding No. 82; with index).

Contains copies of the surveyor general's orders, chronologically entered, granting release from the lien against the purchase price as entered in the official lien docket.

RELEASES—ACT OF 15 APRIL 1869–1875   NO. 2   (Binding No. 83).

A continuation of the above volume. The last entry is dated 1929.

---

[1]"Cancellation of Land Office Liens and Mortgages," Pennsylvania Department of Internal Affairs *Annual Report of the Secretary of Internal Affairs* (1913): 34.A–35.A.

[2]*SmL* 7:309.

[3]Surveyor General Letter Book, 1810–1821, 111; reel 467; LO micro.: 25.31.

[4]"Liens of the Commonwealth against Unpatented Lands," Pennsylvania Department of Internal Affairs *Annual Report of the Secretary of Internal Affairs* (1898): 24.A.

[5]*Annual Report of the Surveyor General* (1874): 6–7.

IV.F. Land Office

Resembling the proprietary model of four independent yet intertwined offices, the Land Office of the Commonwealth of Pennsylvania was formally constituted by the General Assembly on April 19, 1781.[1] Consisting of the secretary of the Land Office, surveyor general, receiver general, and master of the rolls, the Land Office interlinked four of the most powerful state officials. Each officer was appointed by the assembly for a five-year term and given the power to select his own deputies and clerks. Receiving the records and papers of his proprietary predecessor, each of the first officers under the Commonwealth adopted the established procedures, and consequently no noticeable change occurred in the records.

The significant difference between the Land Office of the Commonwealth and that of the proprietors was the base of authority. Whereas the proprietary Land Office was responsible only to the proprietors as sole owners of the land, the Commonwealth Land Office was responsible to the legislature. Commonwealth land officers were bound to act in accordance with all laws and to execute all legislative acts.

For assistance in the execution of their duties, the land officers had recourse to a Board of Property. The board, following the proprietary model, had authority to hear cases involving land disputes over warrants, surveys, and patents.

---

[1]*SmL* 1:529.

IV.F.1. The Office

During the early years of statehood the secretary's and surveyor general's offices were located at 23 High (now Market) Street in Philadelphia. Each officer maintained his own rooms and charged his own fees. The inadequate quarters and insufficient help soon gave the offices a reputation for disorganization and corruption. Faced with bags and trunks in which the proprietary warrants, surveys, and patents had been stuffed for the hurried wartime moves between Philadelphia and Lancaster, the Commonwealth land officers began their tenure with stacks of documents to sort and file.[1] Thousands of new warrants granted after 1784 also needed to be processed. The Land Office quickly became prey to political largess due to lack of direction, management, and leadership. Several years elapsed before the Pennsylvania government gained true control of the Land Office.

During its first three years, 1781–1784, the Land Office conducted unfinished business initiated under the proprietary government. Selecting December 10, 1776, as the cutoff date for proprietary warrants on which titles would be completed, the Commonwealth gave warrantees until 1784 to complete the patenting process. The time was later extended, but the Land Office threatened to rewarrant unpatented tracts to other applicants if original warrantees failed to comply.[2] A survey of the patent volumes reveals that approximately one thousand patents on pro-

prietary warrants were completed during these three years.

Beginning in 1784, the Land Office tackled the task of distributing the remaining lands of the Commonwealth. Since the Penns had disposed of only 6.33 million of the nearly 28 million acres, the vast majority of Commonwealth land remained to be sold.[3] Devising special programs such as the Depreciation Land and Donation Land offerings, the Northumberland Lottery, and preemption applications, the legislature planned to hasten the distribution of land among the rapidly growing population. These programs, all involving the Purchase of 1784, are discussed in detail in section IV.E.2, Land within the Purchase of 1784.

The reported disorder in the secretary's office continued, however. Finally, in 1794, alarmed by the dangerous situation of the public records, the surveyor general requested safer quarters and more clerks. The governor authorized a move into larger quarters located at 236 High Street in Philadelphia, only to expose the records to a new danger—rats![4] Repeated pleas to the legislature for increased Land Office funding brought no results.

The secretary's report prior to his resignation in 1799 indicated little improvement. He claimed that the application books had not been posted since June 1, 1791; the patent books had not been posted for more than eleven years; and the minutes of the Board of Property had not been recorded since September 1, 1795. This backlog is, indeed, believable in light of the secretary's calculation of the number of warrants granted. He reported that between June 1791 and September 1793 more than sixteen thousand warrants had been issued for approximately seven million acres of land.[5]

The incoming secretary's report in 1800 corroborated the previous assessment of the magnitude of the problem. He reported that the indexes to the warrant books were in arrears from 1786, and the indexes to the patent books were in arrears from 1789. He had also found the prerevolutionary loose proprietary records stuffed in three large chests, one trunk, and five bags. Many records had been defaced and torn as a result of being hauled to different offices in Philadelphia and Lancaster. The bound proprietary records of applications, warrants, patents, and other documents were generally in good condition, however, but needed to be indexed.

Table 30. Research Aids: Pennsylvania's Land Offices

Blatt, Genevieve. "Sources for Pennsylvania History in the Department of Internal Affairs." *Pa. Hist.* 24 (1957): 1–33.

Colson, William W., ed. *The State Capitol of Pennsylvania.* Harrisburg, 1906.

Cummings, Hubertis. "Pennsylvania's State Houses and Capitols." *Pa. Hist.* 20 (1952): 409–15.

Heiges, George L. "When Lancaster Was Pennsylvania's Capital." *Lancaster County Historical Society Papers* 55, 56, 58 (1951, 1952, 1954): 3–48, 45–84, 118–41.

Heritage, Inc. *The Pennsylvania Capitol: A Documentary History.* 4 vols. Harrisburg, 1987.

Optimistically the secretary anticipated that his office would be able to straighten out affairs if one more clerk was added to the five already in the office.[6]

In June 1799 the Land Office, along with all other offices of state government, moved to Lancaster. Various departments were housed in private homes while the legislature met in the second brick court house. The secretary of the Land Office rented a wooden house. However, within a year the new secretary, Tench Coxe, moved to a brick dwelling with safe chimneys and fireplaces and used three of the rooms for the Land Office.[7] Beginning a new set of books and files as of January 1, 1800, Coxe planned to keep the current records up-to-date. He also attempted to clean up the backlog. Although giving priority to the ten years prior to 1777, he made a special point of placing the original records signed by William Penn in a single case.[8] The surveyor general rented space for his office in a building situated between two smithies. After spending three years in these potentially dangerous surroundings, he moved to the Masonic hall next door to the old city hall.[9]

The first major revision in the Land Office occurred in 1809. The governor abolished the offices of receiver general and master of the rolls and transferred their duties to other offices. The state treasurer was to collect patent fees, and the secretary of the Land Office, to enroll the patents. The governor, transferring his authority to grant patents to the secretary of the Land Office, also authorized the secretary to purchase a Land Office seal to be applied to all warrants, patents, and other papers authenticated in the secretary's office. Finally, having received appointive powers under the 1790 constitution, the governor reduced the terms of office of the secretary and the surveyor general from five to three years to coincide with his own term of office.

The seat of government moved to Harrisburg in 1812, and with it moved the secretary of the Land Office and the surveyor general. Conditions were better than they had been in Lancaster. The books and records of state officers were deposited in new, so-called fireproof buildings constructed specifically for them. The buildings, with great stone porticoes on their façades, sat on either side of the lot on which the capitol building was erected in 1821.

Within several years the Land Office began the ambitious task of preserving the original records. Worn and defaced by daily handling, the flimsy paper on which some of the records were prepared was falling to pieces, and it was becoming impossible to decipher the courses and distances on many surveys. Legislation in 1833 authorized the copying of old surveys onto sheets of paper for binding into books, but it was not until the 1850s that the long-term project got under way.[10]

The second major revision in the Land Office occurred in 1843. In an effort to streamline the operation of state government, the position of secretary of the Land Office was abolished, and its duties were concentrated in the office of the surveyor general. Consolidating the records in one office created space problems but facilitated a more workable arrangement.[11] Only one brief sojourn in another location during the Civil War caused significant problems in this period. The records, hastily packed in barrels, boxes, hogsheads, and other containers, were run by railroad to a safe location. Some bundles accidently broke open, and a few records were lost, but the vast majority was returned to its own building when Harrisburg was again considered safe.[12]

The third major revision in the Land Office occurred in 1875 as a result of the new state constitution of 1873. The constitution abolished the office of surveyor general and transferred all

Land Office duties to the newly created Department of Internal Affairs. The secretary of the department, an elected official, depended upon support from the political party in power. When the governor was from the same party, rapid strides were made in copying and indexing the original records. At other times little was accomplished.[13] However, an addition to the old building was completed for what was then known as the Land Department, and the warrants and surveys were transferred to iron cases built into the thick brick walls of the building.

Fortunately for posterity, the records were in their own building and not consumed by the fire that destroyed the main capitol building on February 2, 1897. While planning a new and safer Capitol Park, the legislature met in the Grace Methodist Church, resplendent with new electric lights and carpeting, and the Land Office moved to the old Bay Shoe Factory. This dilapidated building was located between a lumberyard and the railroad tracks. Concern over the safety of the land records caused officials to build a new brick building just large enough to house a steel vault for the temporary storage of the records.[14]

When the new Capitol building was completed in 1906, the Land Office and drafting room moved into quarters on the entresol level of the north wing. Instead of occupying the fireproof vault shown in the plans, however, the land records had a new home "no more fireproof than any other portion of the Capitol building."[15] Routine office work and the hand copying of original warrants and surveys continued.

The Land Office received a significant boost in 1907 when the legislature authorized the construction of warrantee tract maps. Office draftsmen were assigned different counties, and the difficult work of piecing survey tracts together commenced. By 1910 three counties were in various stages of completion, and the warrantee township map project was well on its way to becoming the most complex and time-consuming ever undertaken by the Land Office.[16]

Fifty years passed before renewed interest in the Land Office resulted in a complete reorganization. In 1957 the new secretary of the Department of Internal Affairs, Genevieve Blatt, found the land records "filthy, in disorder, and in varying stages of disintegration."[17] To solve the problem she pursued a cleanup and preservation program accompanied by an overall records management program. The original loose records and bound volumes were laminated and microfilmed. As part of this project, many records of a historical nature were transferred to the Pennsylvania State Archives. The remaining records were inventoried and rearranged so that original copies, book copies, and microfilm followed the same shelf listings.

The final step in the reorganization of the Land Office was not accomplished at this time, however. The department had planned on the publication of a "catalog or guide to the records holdings" to make "readily available the wealth of historical information" in the Land Office.[18] Now, with the publication of this GUIDE, that need is fulfilled.

The Land Office has seen several other changes since its 1957 reorganization. In 1966 the Department of Internal Affairs was abolished, and the Land Office moved to the south office building, becoming a bureau within the newly created Department of Community Affairs. To further streamline state government, another reorganization in 1981 moved the Land Office to the Pennsylvania Historical and Museum Commission, where it is currently part of the state archives.

---

[1]Tench Coxe to the house of representatives, February 27, 1800, Reports of the Secretary of the Land Office, LO micro.: 20.5.

[2]See IV.E.1.a, Land Granted by the Proprietary Government.

[3]Affidavit, Penn Property in the Province, Accounts 4:91–95, Penn-Physick Mss. The figures were calculated minus the Erie triangle purchased in 1792.

[4]Daniel Brodhead to Thomas Mifflin, December 3, 1794, Surveyor General Letter Book, 1790–1808, Proprietary Papers, folder 11, 57; LO micro.: 23.1.

[5]John Hall to Thomas Mifflin, November 6, 1799. Quoted in Norman B. Wilkinson, *Land Policy and Speculation in Pennsylvania, 1779–1800* (New York, 1979), 140. The original is missing.

[6]Tench Coxe to the house of representatives, February 27, 1800, Reports of the Secretary of the Land Office, LO micro.: 20.5.

[7]Tench Coxe to Thomas McKean, July 17, 1800, Secretary of the Land Office Letter Book, 1800–1811, 98; LO micro.: 25.31.

[8]Secretary's report, January 4, 1801, ibid., 222–25. See also "Report of Secretary to Governor," November 4, 1800, *PA* (2) 18:741–48.

[9]Surveyor General Letter Book, 1790–1808, p. 148, Proprietary Papers, folder 11; LO micro.: 23.1.

[10]"Bureau of Land Office Records," Pennsylvania Department of Internal Affairs *Annual Report of the Secretary of Internal Affairs* (1906): A.29.

[11]April 7, 1843, *PaL*, 324–25.

[12]"The Preservation of Decaying Records," Pennsylvania Department of Internal Affairs *Annual Report of the Secretary of Internal Affairs* (1885): 10.A.

[13]Ibid. (1924): 4.A.

[14]Ibid. (1902, 1903): 17.A–22.A, 17.A–29.A

[15]Ibid. (1906): 27.A–28.A.

[16]Ibid. (1910): 10.A. See also V.C, Warrant Tract Maps.

[17]Blatt, "Sources for Pennsylvania History" (cited in Table 30), 4.

[18]Ibid., 9–10.

IV.F.2. Board of Property

In 1782, one year after its Land Office opened, the Commonwealth established a Board of Property. The board had power to settle disputes over land. Similar to the Board of Property of the proprietary era, the new board served as a higher authority whose purpose was to mediate in disputes.[1] The board consisted of the president or vice-president of the Supreme Executive Council, a second council member appointed by the council, the secretary of the Land Office, the surveyor general, and the receiver general.

The board had authority to hear difficulties or irregularities in the issuing of warrants and patents and to resolve controversies over land in which caveats had been filed. The secretary of the Land Office served as secretary of the board, receiving caveats against the granting of warrants or patents and setting the meeting times and agenda. While the board had broad powers, its decisions were not final. Appeal in the courts of law was always available.

Among the board's more frequent hearings in the early 1800s were those involving surveys made in unusual ways and resurveys to correct mistakes. Sometimes, when the regular surveyor failed to discharge his duty, the board ordered a survey by a disinterested surveyor. Usually the board made every effort to decide hearings on the side of occupants who claimed ownership by settlement and improvement.

With time the composition of the Board of Property changed. When the constitution of 1790 eliminated the Supreme Executive Council, the secretary of the Land Office, the receiver general, and the surveyor general were joined on the board by the master of the rolls. In 1809, when the positions of receiver general and master of the rolls were abolished, the secretary of the Commonwealth joined the board. With the adoption of the constitution of 1873, the board again changed to consist of the secretary of the Commonwealth, the attorney general, and the secretary of internal affairs. The board has retained that composition, with the exception of the 1966 change of the name of the Department of Internal Affairs to that of Community Affairs.

Restricted by the enabling legislation, the board's duties are more advisory than legal. As public agents, the members have limited authority. After the board makes its decision, the caveator has a right to file his protest. The decisions of the board on caveats against granting a patent have always been much more important than the decisions against the granting of a warrant or acceptance of a survey. Since 1874 the patent has been stayed for six months while the caveator has the opportunity to enter a suit at common law.

The cases presented to the Board of Property; the original papers, caveats, and petitions; and the board's decisions are part of the Land Office collection and cited below. Clues about chains of title and actual dates of settlement are frequently found in the records. The records are retained in original, bound, and microfilm forms as indicated below.

RECORDS: LOOSE PAPERS

BOARD OF PROPERTY   PETITIONS   LO micro.: 22.1–6.

Dated between 1682 and 1900, these folders contain the original petitions or requests submitted to the Board of Property. The documents give the petitioner's name, specifics of the request, and, often, deputy surveyor's testimony, with the board's decision. Most are entered in the bound minute books cited below.

BOARD OF PROPERTY   PAPERS   LO micro.: 22.6–34.

A collection of 607 folders dating from 1682 to 1957 and containing petitions, depositions, certificates of payment, and many other sorts of papers used in Board of Property cases.

CAVEATS   LO micro.: 13.1–11.

Folders containing requests to refrain from granting warrants and patents and to give the caveator an opportunity to present his case. Most are copied in the caveat books cited below.

DEPOSITIONS   LO micro.: 18.1–7.

Sworn statements taken at Board of Property hearings. One portion is filed chronologically, and another portion is filed alphabetically.

RECORDS: BOUND VOLUMES

MINUTE BOOK NUMBER 3   1782–1789   (Binding Volume 3)   LO micro.: 24.21–22.

MINUTE BOOK NUMBER 4   1789–1795   (Binding Volume 4)   LO micro.: 25.22.

MINUTE BOOK NUMBER 5   1795–1801   (Binding Volume 5)   LO micro.: 25.22–23.

MINUTE BOOK NUMBER 6   1801–1806   (Binding Volume 6)   LO micro.: 25.23.

MINUTE BOOK NUMBER 7   1806–1811   (Binding Volume 7)   LO micro.: 25.23.

MINUTE BOOK NUMBER 8   1811–1824   (Binding Volume 8)   LO micro.: 25.23.

MINUTE BOOK NUMBER 9   1824–1839   (Binding Volume 9)   LO micro.: 25.24–25.

MINUTE BOOK NUMBER 10   1840–1858   (Binding Volume 10)   LO micro.: 25.25.

BOARD OF PROPERTY MINUTE BOOK NO 11   1859–1900   LO micro.: 25.25–26.

BOARD OF PROPERTY MINUTE BOOK NO 12   1900–1955.

BOARD OF PROPERTY MINUTE BOOK NO 13   1969–1977.

BOARD OF PROPERTY MINUTE BOOK NO 14   1977–1980.

BOARD OF PROPERTY   1809–1821   (Binding Volume 145).

An index or register giving the names of parties, under whom the claim was made, the ground of the claim and date, and the situation.

DOCKET   BOARD OF PROPERTY   (With index).

Covers the period 1860–1952 and gives the names of parties, date of the caveat, date of the citation, and the date when returnable.

INDEX   CAVEAT BOOK 1 TO 7   1748–1792   (Binding No. 1)   LO micro.: 25.14.

CAVEAT BOOK   JULY 19, 1771 TO DEC. 27, 1784   (Binding No. 4; with index)   LO micro.: 25.14–15; PA (3) 2:472–660.

Has no entries for the period December 2, 1776–July 30, 1781.

CAVEAT BOOK NO. 5   (Binding No. 5; with index)   LO micro.: 25.14.

Covers the period October 23, 1769–December 31, 1785.

CAVEAT BOOK NO. 6   (Binding No. 6; with index)   LO micro.: 25.15.

Covers the period December 29, 1784–May 30, 1787.

CAVEAT BOOK NO. 7   (Binding No. 7; with index)   LO micro.: 25.15.

Includes entries for March 7, 1787–May 19, 1792.

INDEX   CAVEAT BOOK NOS. 8 & 9   (Binding No. 8)   LO micro.: 25.16.

CAVEAT BOOK NO. 8   (Binding No. 9; with index)   LO micro.: 25.16.

Covers the period May 21, 1792–December 9, 1794.

CAVEAT BOOK NO. 9   (Binding No. 10; with index)   LO micro.: 25.16.

Covers the period December 10, 1794–March 16, 1798.

CAVEAT BOOK NO. 10   (Binding No. 11; with index)   LO micro.: 25.17.

Covers the period March 17, 1798–February 13, 1804.

CAVEAT BOOK NO. 11   (Binding No. 12; with index)   LO micro.: 25.17.

Covers the period February 15, 1804–September 28, 1814.

CAVEAT BOOK NO. 12   (Binding No. 13; with index)   LO micro.: 25.17–18.

Covers the period October 4, 1814–June 30, 1840.

CAVEAT BOOK NO. 13   (Binding No. 14; with index)   LO micro.: 25.18–19.

Includes entries for the period June 29, 1840–June 19, 1865.

CAVEAT BOOK NO. 14   (Binding No. 15; with index)   LO micro.: 25.19.

Covers the period June 21, 1865–November 30, 1878.

CAVEAT BOOK NO. 15   (Binding No. 16; with index)   LO micro.: 25.19.

Covers the period December 11, 1878–June 29, 1884.

CAVEAT BOOK NO. 16   (Binding No. 17; with index)   LO micro.: 25.19–20.

Includes entries for July 31, 1884–December 23, 1897.

CAVEAT BOOK NO. 17   (Binding No. 18; with index).

Covers the period December 31, 1897–February 4, 1920.

CAVEAT BOOK NO. 18   (Binding No. 19; with index).

Covers the period August 9, 1921–June 6, 1940.

----

[1]PA (1) 9:409–10.

IV.F.3. Secretary of the Land Office

The secretary of the Land Office played a much less important role under the Commonwealth than under the proprietors. Directly answerable either to the assembly, if he was elected, or to the governor, if he was appointed, the secretary was no longer directly responsible for encouraging the sale of land. Instead, he was to enforce the land laws and keep accurate records of all land transactions. Although during the early period of the Commonwealth the secretaries still managed to manipulate the granting of warrants, they gradually lost control to the surveyor general.

The first secretary of the Commonwealth Land Office was elected by the General Assembly for a five-year term. Bonded for ten thousand pounds, the secretary received a salary, appointed his own clerks, and collected fees for office services as set by law. The secretary, however, no longer signed warrants. The president or vice-president of the Supreme Executive Council had that honor and duty until the state constitution was changed in 1790.

Under the constitution of 1790 the Supreme Executive Council was replaced by a governor with broad appointive powers. The secretary of the Land Office became a governor's appointed position. The secretary's term was reduced to three years to coincide with the governor's term of office. The governor assumed the duty of signing warrants and patents, and the secretary's report of 1800 indicates that the Land Office employed one clerk, whose sole duty was passing papers from one office to another and to the governor for his signature.

Several duties changed hands in 1809 when the offices of receiver general and master of the rolls were abolished. The burden of signing so many papers had become more than the governor wanted to handle, and he gave the secretary of the Land Office authority to sign warrants and patents and to purchase a seal for the Land Office. Henceforth the seal has been applied to all warrants, patents, and other papers authenticated in the Land Office.

The secretary held the responsibility of signing and certifying warrants and patents until 1843. In that year, in an effort to reduce the expenses of government, the position of secretary was abolished. The powers and duties of the secretary and the secretary's records were transferred to the surveyor general.

Between 1781 and 1843, while the Land Office was considered an independent government

Table 31. Research Aids: Secretaries of the Land Office

Cooke, Jacob E. *Tench Coxe and the Early Republic.* Chapel Hill, 1978.

Mathews, Catherine V. *Andrew Ellicott, His Life and Letters.* New York, 1908.

Chart 11. Secretaries of the Land Office, 1781–1843

Name	Commission Date
David Kennedy	April 10, 1781
John Hall	August 1, 1796
Nathaniel Luffborough	December 9, 1799
Tench Coxe	January 3, 1800
Andrew Ellicott	October 1, 1801
John Cochran	April 4, 1809
William Clark	May 11, 1818
James Brady	May 11, 1821
Joshua Dickinson	May 11, 1824
Samuel Workman	May 11, 1830
John Gebhart	May 10, 1836
John Klingensmith	May 10, 1839
William Hopkins	May 10, 1842

agency, few illustrious men served as secretary. Certainly, Tench Coxe, who held the position for less than two years in 1800 and 1801, and Andrew Ellicott, who was in the position from 1801 to 1809, stand out from the rest.

The first secretary of the Land Office, David Kennedy, perhaps had the most difficult job. He took over in 1782, notwithstanding certain lists in print to the effect that James Tilghman, the last proprietary secretary, was in office. All Board of Property records indicate that Kennedy attended every meeting in 1782 as secretary, and Tilghman's name is nowhere to be found. Not only was Kennedy responsible for a smooth transition from proprietary to Commonwealth operation, but he also held the position when the Purchase of 1784, the single largest purchase of land ever made from the Indians, became available for settlement. It is obvious from reports written by his successors that Kennedy did not have the staff to keep up with the job, but he held the position until his death in 1796. Upon Kennedy's death, John Hall was appointed secretary. According to one recent historical study, Hall doubled as John Nicholson's informant and land broker.[1] Hall resigned in 1799, and Nathaniel Luffborough was appointed. Luffborough held the job for only one year.

The newly elected governor, Thomas McKean, was determined to run a responsible Land Office. He removed all incumbents and appointed Coxe to be secretary. Coxe was a merchant and land speculator who had played an active role in the McKean campaign. He hired new clerks, including his own son, Tench, Jr., and set out to organize the land records. To Coxe probably goes the credit for initiating some of the major indexes still in use today, such as the Original Purchases register and the Proprietary Rights register. With the help of his chief clerk, George Worrall, Coxe claimed to have made rapid strides in cataloging and recording records that had been neglected for decades. He

also drew up and publicized procedures governing land purchases. He intended to attract poorer settlers and immigrants, advertising in newspapers and seaports the law enabling aliens to purchase land in Pennsylvania.[2] Just when he seemed to have the secretary's office under control, Coxe rashly resigned, expecting a more important position in the newly forming federal administration of Thomas Jefferson.

Andrew Ellicott replaced Coxe on October 1, 1801. Ellicott was a surveyor and astronomer who brought an entirely new dimension to the secretary's office. Adding a degree of scientific professionalism that the position had never had, Ellicott took an active role in all the major surveys conducted while he was in office. A member of the American Philosophical Society and a correspondent with Jefferson, Ellicott indicates in his letters that the office was very busy when the legislature was in session. Apparently, as today, constituents wrote to their legislators for assistance in transacting business, in this case securing warrants and patents. Unhappy about the decision to move the capitol to Harrisburg and disliked by incoming Governor Simon Snyder, Ellicott left office in 1809.

From 1809 until the office was abolished in 1843, the position of secretary was filled by political appointees whose terms lasted as long as those of the governors who appointed them. In 1843 the records, papers, and duties of the secretary of the Land Office were transferred to the surveyor general.

RECORDS: LOOSE PAPERS

REPORTS OF THE SECRETARY OF THE LAND OFFICE   LO micro.: 20.5.

One folder of the secretary's reports to the governor and state house of representatives for the period 1792–1804.

GENERAL CORRESPONDENCE   1687–1853   (RG-17).

Secretary's correspondence interfiled with that of the surveyor general. Correspondence for 1776–1853 has not been microfilmed.

SECRETARY OF THE LAND OFFICE LETTER BOOKS, 1800–1811, 1838–1839 2 VOLS.   LO micro.: 25.31.

Contain copies of official correspondence.

FEE BOOKS OF THE SECRETARY OF THE LAND OFFICE   1785–1838   LO micro.: 25.27, 25.53–54.

Contain accounts of the fees received by the secretary of the Land Office including accounts of the expenditures of the Land Office and balances paid to the state treasurer.

---

[1]Robert D. Arbuckle, *Pennsylvania Speculator and Patriot, the Entrepreneurial John Nicholson, 1757–1800* (University Park, PA, 1975), 36.

[2]Tench Coxe to the governor (Thomas McKean), May 4, 1800, Secretary of the Land Office Letter Book, 1800–1811, 69–74; LO micro.: 25.31; *Intelligencer & Weekly Advertiser* (Lancaster), August 26, 1801.

IV.F.4. Surveyor General and Deputies

IV.F.4.a. Surveyor General

During the first one hundred years of the Commonwealth, the most important member of the Land Office team was undoubtedly the surveyor general. His power to appoint and supervise the deputy surveyors gave him virtual control over who settled where. The system bred corruption and permitted profitable collusion with speculators. The greatest proof of the strength of the surveyor general's position, however, was the vesting of the entire Land Office operation in his jurisdiction in 1843 when the position of secretary was abolished.

The surveyor general's position, like that of the secretary, underwent several changes between 1776 and 1874. At first the surveyor general was an officer elected by the General Assembly for a term of five years and bonded for ten thousand pounds. Under the constitution of 1790, however, the surveyor general became a governor's appointee. His term was reduced to three years to coincide with the governor's, and from then until 1850 most surveyors general held office as long as the governor who appointed them. The first weakening of the position of surveyor general came in 1850 when his and all county surveyor positions became elective.[1] Unable to survive the reorganization of 1874, the position of surveyor general was abolished when the Land Office became part of the newly formed Department of Internal Affairs.

In addition to supervising the deputy surveyors, the surveyor general performed important office duties. When a purchaser applied for a patent, the surveyor general took the original survey from his file and prepared a voucher, or ticket, containing the date of the warrant, date of the survey, number of acres, and location. He sent the voucher to the receiver general's office. The receiver general (later the treasurer) settled

Chart 12. Surveyors General, 1781–1875

Name	Commission Date
(Elected by General Assembly under Constitution of 1776)	
John Lukens	April 10, 1781
(Appointed by governor under constitutions of 1790 and 1838)	
Daniel Brodhead	November 3, 1789
Samuel Cochran	April 23, 1800
Andrew Porter	April 4, 1809
Richard T. Leach	December 6, 1813
Jacob Spangler	February 13, 1818
Samuel Cochran	May 11, 1821
Gabriel Hiester	May 11, 1824
Jacob Spangler	May 11, 1830
John Taylor	May 10, 1836
Jacob Sallade	May 10, 1839
John Laporte	May 10, 1845
(Elected by Voters under act of April 9, 1850)	
J. Porter Brawley	1851–1857
John Rowe	1857–1860
William H. Keim	1860–61
Henry Souther	1861–1863
James P. Barr	1863–1866
Jacob M. Campbell	1866–1872
Robert B. Beath	1872–1875

the account, receipted the balance paid, and sent the receipt to the secretary's office. The secretary certified this information to the surveyor general and requested that a return of survey be made.[2] Tickets and purchase vouchers dating from 1784 are part of the Land Office collection and are cited below. The surveyor general composed the return of survey in words at length from the details in the warrant and survey and sent it as requested to the secretary. At the same time, the surveyor general made a copy of the survey plot to accompany the patent and filed the original drafts with the patent files.[3]

The original strength of the surveyor general's position may have come from the continuity implicit in the appointment of John Lukens, the last proprietary surveyor general, to be the first surveyor general of the Commonwealth. Lukens served during the first eight years of the new government, helping to complete the surveying and patenting of land warranted under the proprietaries. Also under Lukens's direction the surveying of the state boundaries was completed. Lukens himself participated in the extention of the Mason-Dixon Line west of Dunkard Creek until it reached five degrees longitude west of the Delaware River, the charter limits of the original grant to William Penn. The completion of the western boundary of the state and the entire northern boundary survey by Andrew Ellicott and others was carried out under Lukens's direction. Lukens was also responsible for assigning the original surveying districts within the Purchase of 1784 and within the Depreciation and Donation lands. The extent of Lukens's accomplishments can best be grasped by studying Reading Howell's 1792 *Map of the State of Pennsylvania.*[4]

Upon Lukens's death in 1789 his honest effort to assist in the settlement of the Commonwealth gave way to the most corrupt era in the history of the Land Office. As Norman Wilkinson's study of Pennsylvania land policy from 1780 to 1800 has demonstrated, the next surveyor general, General Daniel Brodhead, amassed a fortune through his close collaboration with some of the most active speculators of the day.[5] Brodhead's cleverness in complicity with John Nicholson, the state's comptroller general, and others was matched by his extraordinary ineptness as an administrator. Serving as a deputy surveyor under Lukens and as commandant at Fort Pitt from 1779 to 1781, Brodhead became versed in Indian relations. However, it was probably his marriage to the widow of Samuel Mifflin, the governor's brother, that brought Brodhead the strongest recommendation for the job of surveyor general. From 1789 to 1800, Brodhead ran the surveyor general's office. A letter book spanning his administration has survived and is in the collection titled "Proprietary Papers" in the Land Office. Many complaints were received about Brodheads's operation, and these complaints undoubtedly contributed to his removal from office when Thomas McKean became governor.

The surveyors general following Brodhead were not nearly so colorful. Samuel Cochran served for nine years while the Land Office was in Lancaster. A partial record of his administration is contained in the same letter book that covers Brodhead's. At least the backlog of un-recorded records that Brodhead and perhaps Lukens had left was apparently cleaned up by the time the office moved into its new quarters in Harrisburg. Surveyor General Andrew Porter's report for 1812, contained in the Surveyor General Letter Book, 1810–1821, claims that his seven clerks had lately made a methodical arrangement of the records in their new commodious apartment. In the following year, Surveyor General Richard T. Leach reported that all of the nine hundred returns of survey prepared during the year had been compared with the warrant register, examined as to their correctness, entered in the respective deputy surveyor lists, endorsed with the time of acceptance, numbered, and filed. Perhaps it was only the fewer number of warrants and the larger staff that permitted such a difference in a period of less than twenty years.

As a result of the consolidation of state offices in 1843, the surveyor general took over the duties of the secretary of the Land Office. Issuing warrants to survey land, the surveyor general now filed the original warrant in his office. This arrangement continued until May 1875 when the duties of the Land Office were transferred to the new Department of Internal Affairs, and the position of surveyor general was abolished.

RECORDS: LOOSE PAPERS

SURVEYOR GENERAL   GENERAL CORRESPONDENCE   1783–1839   LO micro.: 21.3; SURVEYOR GENERAL   GENERAL CORRESPONDENCE   1840–1873   LO micro.: 20.5.

Consist mainly of letters expressing concern over surveys.

SURVEYOR GENERAL LETTER BOOK, 1790–1808   (Proprietary Papers, folder 11)   LO micro.: 23.1.

Contains copies of several official reports.

SURVEYOR GENERAL CERTIFICATES   LO micro.: 20.4.

Twenty-seven folders of papers dating from 1734 to 1872 and mainly consisting of tickets sent by the secretary of the Land Office to the surveyor general requesting the return of survey. The tickets give the warrantee's name, date, name of the person for whom the land was surveyed, acres, location, and amount paid.

PURCHASE VOUCHERS   1784–1949.

Numbered forms stating the amount remaining to be paid after the survey was completed. The top portion, completed in the surveyor general's office, gives the date prepared, acres surveyed, township, county, person for whom the land was surveyed, warrant date, and signature of a clerk. The bottom portion was completed in the secretary's office where amounts paid and outstanding were calculated and noted on the voucher. The vouchers are listed by number in the fee books of the receiver general according to when payment was made. Purchase vouchers were filed separately under purchases of 1768 and earlier (Old Purchase) and Purchase of 1784 (New Purchase).

RECORDS: BOUND VOLUMES

SURVEYOR GENERAL LETTER BOOK, 1810–1821   Reel 467; LO micro.: 25.31.

Contains copies of official incoming and outgoing correspondence.

SURVEYOR GENERAL   LETTER PRESS BOOKS   1870–1875.

Six volumes containing copies of official correspondence.

SURVEYOR GENERAL FEE BOOKS   LO micro.: 25.54–57, 25.63.

Nine volumes covering 1789–1855 and 1860–1870. They give a daily chronological account of fees collected in the surveyor general's office citing the date and amount, with a description.

---

[1]April 9, 1850, *PaL*, 434–35.
[2]See IV.G.4, Returns of Survey.
[3]Daniel Brodhead, Surveyor General Letter Book, 1790–1808, pp. 58–59, Proprietary Papers, folder 11, LO micro.: 23.1.
[4]In *PA* (3) Appendix 1-10.
[5]Norman B. Wilkinson, *Land Policy and Speculation in Pennsylvania, 1779–1800* (New York, 1979).

IV.F.4.b. Deputy and County Surveyors

Deputy surveyors played a key role in the distribution of Commonwealth-owned land. They functioned as the middlemen between the purchaser and the Land Office and in most instances were probably the only land officers purchasers ever met. Usually nominated at the county level, until 1850 deputies were officially appointed by the surveyor general. A small collection of nominating letters filed by county is part of the larger collection titled "Deputy Surveyors Duplicate Commissions and Instructions" dating from before 1850 and cited in the records below.

Specific geographic areas were assigned to deputy surveyors. The more established counties had only one deputy, but the less settled counties were divided among two or more deputies. Extremely large counties were divided into many surveying sections. Northumberland County serves as a good example. The western portion of the county lay entirely within the Purchase of 1784 and was originally laid out in eighteen surveying districts. Surveying districts changed, however, as politics changed, and so researchers interested in studying deputy surveyors must pay particular attention to dates. Reference to two volumes cited below will give a deputy surveyor's name, commission date, and original district.

Deputy surveyors' duties were carefully outlined in a set of instructions that each received along with his commission. For the most part, procedures remained the same as those followed under the proprietary government: The deputy surveyor had six months to conduct the survey, his chain carriers worked under oath sworn before a magistrate, and he was required to keep a field book of survey plots. One procedure in particular differed, however. In addition to returning a copy of the survey to the surveyor general's office, the deputy surveyor was permitted to give the owner a draft of the survey after the surveying fees were paid. This change probably came about because most surveys were conducted on tracts that had already been settled. A record of the surveys that the deputy surveyors sent to the surveyor general appears in nine volumes cited below.

After the land law of 1792 was passed, deputy surveyors assumed a great deal more responsibility. Most importantly they began to perform functions that could not be conducted in the Land Office. The deputy surveyor determined whether a newly ordered survey interfered with an earlier survey, whether the land had been improved, and for how long. He also provided the earliest warrantee tract maps by constructing connected drafts of survey tracts and sending them to the Land Office once every year in February.

When the surveyor general's position became elective in 1850, the deputy surveyor's followed suit. With his title changed from deputy surveyor to county surveyor, the holder of the office was no longer responsible to the surveyor general but to the county commissioners. However, certified duplicate election returns and oaths of county surveyors, as required by law, were filed in the surveyor general's office and are currently part of the Land Office collection.

County surveyors assumed the deputy surveyors' major duties, but because the surveyors were now ethically and fiscally responsible to the county commissioners, county surveyors also were charged with supplying the county with certain information. Of particular need was information

that would assist in levying taxes. During the years of lien docket preparation, beginning in 1864, county surveyors supplied the surveyor general with the names and addresses of owners of unpatented tracts. If the tracts were later patented, the county surveyor performed a new survey at the request of the surveyor general. A record of the surveys that county surveyors sent to the surveyor general is contained in two of the nine volumes of lists of returns cited below.

Although no laws required the county surveyor to maintain and preserve records, some counties developed quite a full set of records. Among them, researchers may find copies of applications, warrants, surveys, field books, reports, and warrantee maps.

The law requiring the election of county surveyors continued in effect until the state constitution of 1968 provided for home rule. A gradual process of attrition followed. By 1978 no county could claim a county surveyor.

RECORDS: LOOSE PAPERS

DEPUTY SURVEYORS   DUPLICATE COMMISSIONS AND INSTRUCTIONS   LO micro.: 19.1–4.

Ninety-six folders containing nominating letters and copies of commissions and instructions sent to deputy surveyors, 1713–1848.

COUNTY SURVEYORS   ELECTION RETURNS AND OATHS   LO micro.: 19.6–9.

A set of 124 folders filed by county and containing forms certifying election results and oaths of office.

FIELD NOTES   LO micro.: 20.5.

A very small collection (three folders) of deputy surveyors' field notes and calculations.

RECORDS: BOUND VOLUMES

LIST OF DEP[UTY] SURVEYORS   [1713–1850]   LO micro.: 25.29.

Contains a complete listing of appointed deputy surveyors giving the commission date and original district. An alphabetized card file prepared from the information in this volume is available in the Land Office.

DEPUTY SURVEYOR'S DISTRICTS   1791–1799   (Binding Volume 167).

Contains 1) a list of deputies appointed in 1791 and 1792 to work in the region of the purchases of 1768 and earlier and 2) a list of the deputies and a description of the eleven original districts in the western part of the Purchase of 1784 after the Depreciation and Donation lands were surveyed.

DEPUTY [and County] SURVEYORS' LISTS OF RETURNS   [1762–1887; 9 volumes]   LO micro.: 25.27–29.

List the surveys that each deputy and/or county surveyor returned to the surveyor general giving the date, warrant number, warrantee's name, and acres.

DEPUTIES LIST [of Returns   Purchase of 1784].

Lists the surveys that each deputy surveyor returned to the surveyor general in the Purchase of 1784 giving the date, warrant number, warrantee's name, and acres.

DEPUTY SURVEYORS ACCOUNT BOOK   1799–1827   (With index)   LO micro.: 25.27.

Record of deputy surveyors' remittances of fees to the surveyor general's office and payments on account.

COUNTY SURVEYORS   [1850–1954; 2 volumes]   LO micro.: 25.26–27.

County surveyors are listed by county, with the dates of election, when their oaths were filed, and their post office addresses.

LISTS OF COUNTY SURVEYORS   [1850–1957; 2 volumes]   (RG-17).

County surveyors are listed by county, with the dates of election.

COUNTY SURVEYORS   LIST OF RETURNS.

Lists by county the surveys returned to the Land Office, 1887–1940s.

IV.F.5. Receiver General

Until 1809, when the position was abolished, the receiver general was the third member of the Commonwealth Land Office. His role was similar to that of the proprietary receiver general, and he continued to maintain the same records in the same way. His position constituted a check on the offices of secretary and surveyor general, since he collected the purchase money due on all land sales. When land sales were booming during the early days of the Commonwealth, the receiver general provided needed assistance. When land sales slowed, the office was abolished.

Acting as the accounting branch of the Land Office, the receiver general collected the purchase money and interest due on tracts of land. Several different forms of money could be used. Gold, silver, and paper money of the state were preferred, but certificates issued under various state monetary programs were also allowed. Certificates of depreciation given to the officers and soldiers of the Pennsylvania Line and certificates for money lent to the United States were commonly used to pay for land. Not so common were the certificates given by the commissaries, quartermasters, and forage masters who supplied the revolutionary army.[1] Among the receiver general's loose papers in the Land Office are certificates issued in 1780 by the commissioners to furnish the federal army with a supply of meat and which in turn were submitted to pay for land.[2]

The receiver general used four sets of account books to record transactions: fee books, daybooks, journals, and ledgers. The daybooks, journals, and ledgers were divided into three sections: one section for land within the purchases of 1768 and earlier (Old Purchase), one section for land within the Purchase of 1784 (New Purchase), and one section for town lots.

One can reconstruct the receiver general's procedures by analyzing his books and a brief explanation left by Tench Coxe, secretary of the Land Office.[3] The receiver general received a purchase voucher from the surveyor general stating the amount the purchaser owed accompanied by the payment. He receipted the payment and entered the amount paid in two different sets of records. One entry was made in the appropriate daybook as a daily accounting of office activity. Another entry, along with the voucher number, was made in the appropriate fee book. The receiver general then sent the receipt to the secretary of the Land Office.

Clerks in the receiver general's office later recorded the transaction in two other sets of records: journals and ledgers. They entered a condensed version of the daybook entry into a journal. The journal, organized chronologically, recorded the page number of the daybook entry

and also the page number of the ledger entry. The ledger entry contained a block for each payer in which all payments were credited. The ledger also recorded the daybook page of the entry and the page in the ledger where the entry was tabulated. All of these records—daybooks, fee books, journals, and ledgers—are cited below. To locate an individual in the receiver general's records, researchers may find it best to begin with the ledgers and work backward. Some ledgers are indexed.

After 1809 the Treasury Department kept the records of land purchases. Ledger books and duplicate receipts are cited in the records.

During much of the Revolutionary War, Edmund Physick, the proprietors' receiver general, continued to maintain and care for the daybooks, journals, and ledgers. Physick transferred the volumes to the Supreme Executive Council, the executive branch of the new state government, in February 1780.

Francis Johnston, the first receiver general of the Commonwealth, assumed office in June 1781. On the occasion of the transfer of the receiver general's records to him, the Supreme Executive Council listed the existing records in its minutes.[4] Johnston, a resident of Chester County, had been active in state politics and had risen to the rank of colonel in the Pennsylvania Continental Line before assuming office.[5] He held the office until 1800.

In Governor Thomas McKean's clean sweep of appointive offices, Johnston was replaced by Frederick A. C. Muhlenberg. Defeated in his bid for reelection to Congress in 1796, Muhlenberg had settled into the role of businessman. However, the call to public service struck a responsive note, and Muhlenberg moved to Lancaster in 1800 to assume office. He hired his son, David, and his nephews Peter and John Philip as his only clerks. The public accused Muhlenberg of nepotism, but his son and nephews did their jobs well. After the elder Muhlenberg's death in 1801, his successor John McKissick retained the three young Muhlenbergs in office.

A Lancaster resident, McKissick served as receiver general for eight years. By 1809 land sales had so diminished that the office was abolished, and the duties were assumed by the secretary's office and the state treasurer.

RECORDS: LOOSE PAPERS

RECEIVER GENERAL CERTIFICATES   [1785–1852]   LO micro.: 20.3–4.

Seventeen folders containing dated receipts giving the name of the payer, amount paid, acreage, and location.

CERTIFICATES OF INDEBTEDNESS   LO micro.: 20.3.

Certificates of indebtedness were granted to farmers who provided the federal army with cattle, sheep, or salted provisions during the Revolutionary War. By law the certificates could be used to pay for land. The certificates in this collection were paid to the receiver general.

LAND WARRANT AND PATENT RECEIPTS   1781–1809.

Consists of two parts. One part is a group of receipts certifying the full payment of the purchase money and interest on tracts of land granted by application by the proprietary government but not patented until the era of the Commonwealth. Receipts for Philadelphia City and barracks lots are also included. The certificate gives the payer's name (usually the patentee), amount paid, acres, county, township, person for whom the land was surveyed, application number, and date. The other part consists of daily reports listing persons who paid the receiver general for land granted to them on warrants initiated under the Commonwealth. The list gives the warrantee's name, amount paid, acres, county, and warrant date and accompanied the warrants being sent to the president of the Supreme Executive Council for signing.

LAND WARRANT AND PATENT RECEIPTS, 1809–1885   (RG-28).

Thirty-four boxes filed chronologically, containing office copies of receipts for warrant and patent fees.

CERTIFICATES OF PAYMENT OF PURCHASE MONEY   1786–1809   (RG-17).

A collection of receipts certifying the full payment of purchase money and interest in arrears on land granted by warrant under the proprietary government but not patented until the era of the Commonwealth. The certificate gives the payer's name, amount paid, acres, county, township, person for whom the land was surveyed, warrant date, and patentee's name.

RECORDS: BOUND VOLUMES

DAY BOOKS [of the Receiver General   1781–1809]   LO micro.: 25.37–51, 25.63.

Give a daily chronological account of money received by the receiver general. They give the name of the payer, the individual or account to which payment was directed, and miscellaneous information such as the township, acres, application number, and interest. Entries were made in these books before being made in the journals or ledgers. There is one set of daybooks for the purchases of 1768 and earlier (Old Purchase), one set for the Purchase of 1784 (New Purchase), and one set for town lots.

JOURNALS [of the Receiver General   1781–1955]   Reels 469–70; LO micro.: 25.57–78.

Contain a daily chronological account of money received by the receiver general. They give for each payer the page number of the same entry in the daybook (see above) and the page number in the ledger (see below) where the amount paid is tabulated. Apparently prepared at the same time that the ledger was prepared, the journal is a condensed version of the daybook entry. There is one set of journals for land in the purchases of 1768 and earlier (Old Purchase), one set for the Purchase of 1784 (New Purchase), and one set for town lots.

LEDGERS [of the Receiver General   1781–1955]   (With index)   LO micro.: 25.80–104.

Master account books for tracking multiple payments made by purchasers. A block of space for each person contains a list of all payments made during the period of the ledger. Prepared at the same time as the journals, the information in the ledgers includes the payer's name, date paid, page in the daybook, account to which payment was credited (such as interest on acreage, purchase price of land, or sundries), page in the ledger where the amount paid was tabulated, and amount paid, how it was paid, or by whom. There is one set of ledgers for land in the purchases of 1768 and earlier (Old Purchase) and one set for land in the Purchase of 1784 (New Purchase). To find an individual in the receiver general's records, begin with the index located in these volumes.

FEE BOOKS   [Blotters of the Receiver General   1784–1955]   LO micro.: 25.52–57, 25.63.

Comprise a daily chronological account of fees collected by the receiver general until 1809 and by the various succeeding offices. The books are organized in three sections: one for the purchases of 1768 and earlier (Old Purchase), one for the Purchase of 1784 (New Purchase), and one for town lots. Entries cite the surveyor general's voucher number, date, description, purchase containing the land, and fees. The term blotter was used until 1800.

LIST OF MONIES RECEIVED BY FRANCIS JOHNSTON, ESQ., LATE RECEIVER GENERAL   1790–1794   (RG-17).

Consists of two volumes: a warrant payment book and a patent payment book. The books are arranged chronologically and give the date, payer's name, acres, and amount received.

CASH RECEIVED FOR LAND AND LAND OFFICE FEES   1809–1815, 1829–1916   (RG-28).

Five volumes organized in chronological order with columns for the purchaser's name, purchase money, and fees. Sums were calculated monthly.

---

[1]April 1, 1784, *SmL* 2:102.
[2]*Statutes* 10:214–18.
[3]Secretary of the Land Office, Letter Book, 1800–1811, 368–76; LO micro.: 25.31.
[4]CR 12:755–57.
[5]"Notes and Queries," *PMHB* 29 (1905): 361.

IV.F.6. Master of the Rolls

The master of the rolls of the Commonwealth was another position held over from proprietary times. A member of the Land Office by virtue of his duty to record patents and affix the seal of the Commonwealth, the master of the rolls did not play as active a part in land affairs as the other three members of the Land Office.

Although the Land Office was closed during the peak years of the Revolutionary War, 1777–1781, the position of master of the rolls continued to function. The need to affix the great seal and record all official documents transcended the events of the war. Accordingly the Council of Safety, the first governing body of the newly formed state, appointed John Morris to be master of the rolls. Morris held the position from March 1777 until his death in 1785.[1]

Two other men served as masters of the rolls before the position was abolished in 1809. Matthew Irwin was appointed in 1785 after Mor-

ris's death. Irwin served as master of the rolls for fifteen years. During Irwin's tenure the state constitution of 1790 placed the master of the rolls on the Board of Property. The minutes of the board indicate that Irwin attended meetings irregularly, while Timothy Matlack, his successor, took the assignment quite seriously and attended regularly. Matlack had been the first secretary of state under the Commonwealth. He served as master of the rolls from 1800 to 1809.

In 1809, when the position of master of the rolls was abolished, the patent books were placed in the care of the secretary of the Land Office. Other official state documents were transferred to the secretary of the Commonwealth. Years later, in 1874, when the Department of Internal Affairs was formed and the Land Office placed therein, the documents in the custody of the secretary of the Commonwealth were returned. These latter records, among them commission books and letter of attorney volumes, are cited below.

RECORDS: BOUND VOLUMES

COMMISSION BOOK 1   [1777–1800]   LO micro.: 1.

Contains copies of commissions to office holders, charters, oaths of allegiance, a speech of George Washington to the Indians, and proclamations.

COMMISSION BOOK 2E2 [2   1800–1809]   LO micro.: 1.

Contains copies of agreements, corporations, and appointments to various offices including those in the counties of Bucks, Dauphin, Delaware, Fayette, Huntingdon, Lancaster, Mifflin, Montgomery, Northumberland, Northampton, Philadelphia, Washington, Westmoreland, and York.

LETTER OF ATTORNEY   D-2 VOL. 8   [1774–1777]   LO micro.: 25.125.

LETTERS OF ATTORNEY   NO. 1   [1777–1785]   LO micro.: 25.120.

LETTERS OF ATTORNEY   NO. 2   [1785–1789]   LO micro.: 25.120.

LETTERS OF ATTORNEY   NO. 3   [1789–1792]   LO micro.: 25.120.

LETTER OF ATTORNEY   [No.] 4   [1792–1795]   LO micro.: 25.120–21.

LETTER OF ATTORNEY   [No.] 5   [1795–1796]   LO micro.: 25.122.

POWER OF ATTORNEY   [No.] 5 [6]   1796–1798   LO micro.: 25.127.

LETTER OF ATTORNEY   [No.] 7   [1798–1807]   LO micro.: 25.125.

LETTER OF ATTORNEY   [No.] 8   [1807–1809]   LO micro.: 25.125.

---

[1]CR 14:378.

IV.G. Records

For the first 129 years of the Commonwealth, 1776–1905, no change occurred in the series of records used to transfer land to individual ownership. The five documents generated in the patenting process continued to be the application, warrant, survey, return of survey, and patent. Changes in the requirements for submitting applications and in the format of warrants occurred, however. The changes hinged upon whether the land was improved or unimproved at the time of application.

Between 1784 and 1794 the Land Office accepted applications for both improved and unimproved land. Requirements for a warrant and patent were the same as under the proprietary government. But between 1794 and 1817 the Commonwealth's new policy regarding settlement, improvement, and cultivation permitted the Land Office to accept applications only for improved land. Most of the remaining vacant land in the Commonwealth passed to private ownership under this regulation. After 1817 applications for both improved and unimproved land were accepted once again for all remaining vacant land in the Commonwealth.

Warrants likewise underwent changes. A variety of forms developed; each carried statements referring to the program or legislation under which the warrant was granted. A more subtle change occurred in the meaning of a warrant to survey versus a warrant to accept. Between 1794 and 1817, when applications could be accepted only for improved land, a warrant to survey came to mean a survey on a tract of improved land where no survey had been recorded. This differed from the earlier concept that a warrant to survey represented vacant unimproved land. Likewise, between 1794 and 1817 a warrant to accept meant that a survey had already been recorded, and the applicant for the patent was agreeing to abide by that survey. Often a warrant to accept was a second, or junior, warrant drawn on an abandoned warrant and survey.

Significant changes also occurred in the procedure for titling land. Because the Land Office lacked maps of warrantee tracts and had no idea whether land was vacant or not, the burden of proving the vacancy was placed upon the applicant. After 1807 the applicant was to trace his own chain of title to prove that no prior warrant had been granted. Carrying the burden of proof one step further, beginning in 1874 the applicant was required to publish his application in a local newspaper. This procedure gave a prior warrantee for the same tract of land an opportunity to file a caveat.

Other significant changes occurred with the records. Bowing to the needs of the public, the more important records were shared with the county offices. After 1792 deputy surveyors were required to keep available for local public use a book of completed surveys so that applicants could easily see what land was vacant. After 1816 a law required that patents be recorded in a special book in the county recorder of deeds office as well as in the state Land Office.

IV.G.1. Applications

By the era of the Commonwealth the application had become a formal document. The first in the series of records used to transfer land to private ownership, the application was submitted to request a warrant. Consequently an application should be on file for every warrant granted. The date of the application will be the same day as or earlier than the warrant.

During the early Commonwealth period, 1784–1794, applications were accepted for either improved or unimproved land. Each application was to specify whether the land was improved or not and to include a "particular description" of the desired tract. An application for improved land was usually called an entry. An entry was to state when the improvement had begun so that interest could be charged from that date. Certified by two justices of the peace of the proper county, the entry, or application, was then sent to the Land Office.[1]

Between 1794 and 1817 entries were the only type of application the Land Office could accept. The new policy requiring settlement, improvement, and cultivation, which was designed to stimulate ownership by such means, prohibited applications for unimproved land.[2]

After 1817, when most of the state's lands had been transferred to private ownership, the Land Office again accepted applications for unimproved land.

Another change in applications occurred in 1807 when the burden of proving the vacancy was placed squarely upon the applicant. Under this new arrangement the applicant was to conduct his own record search to prove that no prior warrant for the same land had been issued in his name or in the name or names of any person or persons under whom he claimed. The certified application presented the chain of title.[3]

Nearly seventy years later the applicant's responsibility was again extended. The new state land law of 1874 required the applicant to publish his application for three successive weeks in one or more local newspapers.[4] This procedure was designed to encourage caveats against applications. If the land applied for was held by another warrantee, a hearing on a caveat might avoid a court case. If the land was not vacant,

the applicant's money was refunded. A set of papers filed under the title "Escheats" within the Land Office collection and cited below contains records of applicants whose money was refunded.

Applications were accompanied by the purchase price of the land unless the requirement had been waived under a special program. Generally no warrant could be granted until the entire purchase price and fees had been paid. After the survey was conducted and back interest calculated, the Land Office adjusted the purchase price, and the applicant paid the outstanding balance. Until 1809 the purchase money was paid to the receiver general. After that position was abolished in 1809, the money was paid directly into the state treasury. In 1874, when the Land Office moved to the new Department of Internal Affairs, the purchase money was deposited with that department.

Applications were written in longhand until the early 1870s when printed forms were developed. Although the handwriting may be difficult to read, applications frequently contain more information than warrants. Especially if settlement dates are in doubt, applications should be consulted.

Although applications are not indexed in the warrant registers, they are filed chronologically. The date of the application was usually the date of the warrant, but occasionally the application was dated earlier. In some cases, when loose applications have not survived, a copy may be found in a bound application book.

RECORDS: LOOSE PAPERS

APPLICATIONS FOR WARRANT   1784 TO PRESENT   LO micro.: 7.28–101.

Filed chronologically. The date of the application usually corresponds to the date of the warrant. After the mid-1870s the application on file is accompanied by a proof of publication record. Microfilmed through 1957.

APPLICATIONS   LISTS   1785–1865   LO micro.: 16.1–2.

A collection of twenty-five folders of multiple applications on single sheets of paper, although a few single applications are interfiled.

APPLICATIONS FOR WARRANTS   5 MAY 1792–3 APRIL 1866.

A collection of several folders of applications for warrants that do not seem to have been issued.

APPLICATIONS FOR WARRANTS NOT ISSUED   26 AUGUST 1802–5 DECEMBER 1951   LO micro.: 16.11–13.

A collection of forty-one folders of applications for warrants that were not issued.

APPLICATIONS FOR WARRANTS CAVEATED AND NOT DISPOSED OF   1873–1882   LO micro.: 16.15.

A collection of seven folders of applications for warrants on which caveats were filed and action thereafter ceased.

APPLICATIONS FOR WARRANTS WITHDRAWN   1874–1912   LO micro.: 16.14–15.

A collection of forty-five folders containing applications that were withdrawn.

ESCHEATS   LO micro.: 20.1.

A collection of twenty-five folders containing records of applicants whose money was returned after their applications were invalidated.

RECORDS: BOUND VOLUMES

APPLICANTS   1784–1785   (Binding No. 99)   LO micro.: 25.116.

Arranged by county, this volume gives the following information: application date, applicant's name, number of applications, by whom they were given (or brought to the office), and situation.

RECORD OF LAND APPLICANTS   JULY 5, 1784–FEBRUARY 28, 1785   (Binding No. 100)   LO micro.: 25.116.
RECORD OF LAND APPLICANTS   MARCH 9, 1785–DECEMBER 31, 1785   (Binding No. 101)   LO micro.: 25.116
RECORD OF LAND APPLICANTS   FEBRUARY 1, 1786–DECEMBER 29, 1786   (Binding No. 102)   LO micro.: 25.116–17.

Arranged chronologically, these volumes give applicant's name, number of the application, location, and county.

LIST OF LAND APPLICANTS   MAR. 15, 1794   (Binding No. 103)   LO micro.: 25.117.

All applications in this volume are dated the same day and are for four hundred acres. They are for locations in Northumberland and Luzerne counties, and most applicants' tracts adjoin that of the previous applicant.

APPLICATIONS   1794   (Binding No. 104)   LO micro.: 25.117.

Gives the applicant's name, acres (four hundred in every case), and location.

[1]April 1, 1784, *SmL* 2:102.
[2]Ibid. 3:184, 5:22
[3]April 13, 1807, ibid. 4:472.
[4]April 14, 1874, *PaL*, 58–59.

IV.G.2. Warrants

The Commonwealth Land Office continued the practice of issuing warrants to order a survey. The warrant, the second in the series of documents used to transfer land to private ownership, authorized the deputy or county surveyor to survey vacant improved or unimproved land.

During the first century of the Commonwealth, while the Land Office was a separate government agency, the basic types of warrants were the warrant to authorize a survey and the warrant to accept a survey. For the first several years of the new government, these two types of warrants had the same definition as during the proprietary era. The warrant to survey was granted for unsettled unimproved land and the warrant to accept was granted for settled improved land.

After 1794, however, the definition of the warrants changed. Under the Commonwealth's policy of ownership by settlement and cultivation, in effect between 1794 and 1817, warrants for unimproved land could not be granted. Thus, during this twenty-three-year period the warrant to survey was granted for improved land that had not been surveyed. The warrant to accept was granted when the applicant for improved land could prove his chain of title from a survey that was already on file with the deputy surveyor or the Land Office.

Warrants to accept a previous survey were prepared at the time of patenting. Written by the secretary, the wording of the warrant was based on the original warrant and survey. More important, these warrants signified that the purchase price and all fees had been paid.

After 1817 the warrant to survey was again granted for either improved or unimproved land. Written by the secretary of the Land Office, the warrant was given to the warrantee unsigned and without the Land Office seal. The warrantee carried the warrant to the treasurer's office, where an account was opened and the purchase money collected. With warrant and receipt in hand the warrantee returned to the secretary's office, where the warrant was signed, a seal was affixed, and the warrant was recorded in a war-

rant book. The warrantee then carried the warrant to the surveyor general's office. There the warrant was filed until the survey was completed and the purchaser applied for a patent.

While land was still plentiful, the signing of warrants was considered to be a very important responsibility. Between 1781 and 1790 warrants were signed by the president of the Supreme Executive Council. Between 1790 and 1809 the governor signed all warrants. Transmittal forms prepared by the secretary of the Land Office to accompany the warrant as it was sent out for signature are part of the Land Office collection and cited below.

The forms of warrants granted during the Commonwealth era reflected the specific details of the special programs under which warrants were granted. For example, different forms of warrants were used for the Northumberland Lottery, Depreciation Lands, land east of the Allegheny River and Conewango Creek under the vacant land law of 1792, and land north and west of the Ohio and Allegheny rivers and Conewango Creek under the vacant land law of 1792. The differences in form were dictated by the applicable laws and terms of sale, but all warrants also included common features. They stated the purchase rate per one hundred acres, the time allotted for payment, and the laws affecting the land for which the warrant was granted.

All warrants that were granted are listed in the regular warrant registers or in registers specific to the program under which they were granted. Regular warrants can be accessed by name of warrantee and county of jurisdiction at the time the warrant was granted. An incomplete version of the regular warrant registers is published in *PA* (3) 24–26. Twenty-three counties are omitted, as well as all reference to survey and patent volumes.

Warrants for three special programs, the Northumberland Lottery, the Depreciation Lands, and the Last Purchase 1784, have been removed from the bulk of regular original warrants and filed by program. In this GUIDE the warrants for these programs are discussed and cited under

IV.E, Categories of Land. See the specific sub-section dealing with each program.

Original warrants have been laminated to assist in preservation and copied three times. One copy is an incomplete set of handwritten bound volumes authorized by the General Appropriation Act of 1911 and cited in the sources as Copied Warrants. A second copy is a set of microfilm prepared in the mid-1970s by the Church of Jesus Christ of Latter-day Saints. This microfilm is available through the Family History Library in Salt Lake City. A third copy is the set of Commonwealth-authorized microfilm prepared in the late 1950s and duplicated in 1988. The state microfilm is available for use in the State Archives Search Room and for purchase.

RECORDS: LOOSE PAPERS

ORIGINAL WARRANTS   LO micro.: 3.1–156.

Regular warrants for the period 1779–present are filed by county of jurisdiction at the time the warrant was granted. Within each county they are grouped alphabetically by the first letter of the last name and numbered chronologically. They are indexed in the warrant registers cited below. Microfilmed through 1957.

TRANSMITTAL OF WARRANTS   1781–1809.

A collection of transmittal forms signed by the secretary of the Land Office to accompany warrants sent to the president of the Supreme Executive Council (1781–1790) or the governor (1790–1809) for signing. The transmittal forms give the name of the payer, amount paid, amount of land, township and county, application number and date, and applicant's name.

WARRANTS WRITTEN BUT NOT ISSUED   (With index).

A collection of eight boxes of warrants that were never issued for one reason or another. A multivolumed index including search sheets gives the warrantee's name, county, and page number assigned to the warrant.

WARRANTS SIGNED AND SEALED, NOT PURSUED   (With index).

A collection of two boxes of warrants issued by the Land Office but never acted upon. A multivolumed index including search sheets gives the warrantee's name, county, and page number assigned to the warrant.

WARRANTS   DEPUTY COUNTERPARTS   (With index).

A collection of warrants that ordinarily would have been sent to deputy surveyors. A multivolumed index including search sheets gives the warrantee's name, county, and page number assigned to the warrant.

RECORDS: BOUND VOLUMES

WARRANT REGISTERS   [1733–present]   LO micro.: 1.1–5.

Arranged by county, these twenty-one volumes are the master indexes to the warrants and surveys. Entries are grouped alphabetically by the first letter of the last name of the warrantee and are then listed chronologically by warrant date. For each warrantee the following information is cited: warrant number; name; type; location; date; return date; acres returned; patentee's name; patent volume, number, and page; and survey series, book, and page. See Appendix C for a correlation of warrants by county to microfilm reels. Microfilmed through 1957.

WARRANT BOOK BEDFORD, GREENE, LUZERNE, TIOGA   (Binding Volume 146).
WARRANT BOOK LYCOMING, NORTHAMPTON, SOMERSET   (Binding Volume 147).

Contain listings by county of the warrants granted for the period 1792–1816. The following information is given: warrant number, warrantee's name, type of warrant, acres, and date.

COPIED WARRANTS   (RG-14).

Copies authorized under the General Appropriation Act of 1911. The project was not entirely completed for each county, but there are 175 bound volumes and 19 packages containing 313 booklets. They are organized in the same way as the original warrants, and the warrant registers serve as an index.

WARRANT BOOKS   (With partial index)   LO micro.: 25.108–16.

These sixteen volumes are chronological listings of warrants granted for the years 1775–76, 1781–1814, 1827–1848, and 1863–1888. A few of the volumes are indexed. Interim volumes are missing. The volumes give the date of warrant, to whom it was granted, and the acres, situation, county, and terms.

IV.G.3. Surveys

Surveys made during the Commonwealth era followed guidelines established in 1765 under the proprietors. The size of the tract in acres was authorized in the warrant, but a statement of the detailed measurements was not included. To determine the exact courses and distances, the tract had to be measured on the ground. The survey gave notice to everyone that the particular tract was claimed. The diagram of the survey indicating the courses and distances and adjoining owners was the third in the series of documents used to transfer land to private ownership.

The deputy or county surveyor conducted the survey by actually going upon the ground, measuring the land, and marking the corners. The marks on the ground were legal evidence of the actual survey and took precedence over the diagram. The deputy filed the official diagram of the survey in the surveyor general's office.

Submitted on paper at least 8 × 10 inches, the diagram was required to name the current adjoining owners and to indicate any change in adjoining owners between the warrant and the survey. The diagram was also to include all streams, roads, railroads, canals, and township and county lines, features that were not always drawn. Surveys conducted on warrants issued after June 1, 1814, and including an actual settlement carried a notation indicating when the settlement had commenced.[1]

After 1792 the deputy was required to keep a plat or unofficial diagram of the survey in a survey book in his local office. For a slight fee the book was to be available to the public. Passed from one deputy to the next, these books sometimes can be found in the county courthouse or in the county historical society.

Usually, surveyors ran all but the closing line and then calculated the acreage before running the final course and distance. In this way the surveyor could adjust the size of the tract by shortening or lengthening one or two of the lines.

Lines belonging to adjoining tracts that had already been surveyed were not rerun. Considered to be fixed, those lines could not be changed. Therefore, the latest survey in a given area was forced to conform to surveys already made. After 1792, if for some reason not enough vacant land existed for the survey to be made, the deputy surveyor completed a certificate stating the reason. These certificates were sent to the surveyor general and were used to authorize a refund of the purchase money. Cited below, these certificates are part of the Land Office collection.

Surveys were expected to contain the usual allowance of 6 percent for roads but often included more. The allowance was to be within the surveyed tract; thus, on a warrant of 400 acres, 424 acres would be surveyed. A leeway of 4 percent on top of the 6 percent, or a total of 10 percent in surplus, was permitted without extra purchase money, but land in excess of 10 percent had to be purchased. In 1817 a cap of 100 acres was placed on the surplus.[2]

Overlapping surveys were not uncommon, especially in mountainous or wooded areas. Frequently conducted years apart, overlapping surveys often occurred when the older tract represented unseated land. In other instances the surveyor may have plotted out a survey in his office from information furnished him by the purchaser. Although this was an illegal procedure, the Land Office accepted such surveys because no maps of warrant tracts existed.

The area of the tract surveyed was usually given in acres and perches. The distances were first measured in perches or rods. The acres were calculated by determining the number of square perches and dividing by 169.6, the Land Office acre. The whole number resulting was the number of acres. The remaining perches were figured by dividing the remainder by 106.3.[3] Refer to the chart below for area constants.

Often surveys were not made for many years after the warrant was granted. If a warrantee's tract was recognized as official by his neighbors, no survey was necessary until the owner decided to patent the land. Sometimes the tract was sold several times before the survey was made. If the warrant tract had been subdivided before the survey was made, more than one survey would result from the same warrant.

Chart 13. Surveyor's Measures

16.5 feet = 1 perch

1 perch = 1 rod

4 rods = 1 chain

1 chain = 66 feet

10 square chains = 1 acre

1 acre = 43,560 square feet

1 acre = 160 square perches

The Commonwealth made some effort to follow the federal public land guidelines of surveying in rectangular sections. Both Depreciation and Donation lands were surveyed in rectangular tracts before they were sold, and the remaining land within the Purchase of 1784 was surveyed as nearly as possible into tracts whose length was not greater than twice the width. Consequently the warrant tracts in northwestern Pennsylvania create a map of contiguous rectangular tracts.

Likewise, the amount of land on any navigable river or lake usually did not exceed more than one half the depth of the tract. The tract could extend to the low-water mark, but the public was permitted an easement between the high- and low-water marks.

When the survey was completed, the diagram was returned to the surveyor general. His office checked the calculations for accuracy before filing the survey with the warrant. Surveys with obvious errors, such as inaccurate acreage or insufficient information, were returned to the county surveyor for correction. A list of surveys returned to the county surveyors for checking was kept and is cited below.

The vast majority of original surveys from the Commonwealth period are on file in the Land Office. Copied surveys are also part of the Land Office collection. Beginning in 1856, under an 1833 legislative program to preserve old and defaced records, original surveys were hand copied onto large sheets of paper and bound into books.[4] Original surveys and copied surveys are filed under the same series, book, and page numbers. They are indexed in the warrant registers by the name of the warrantee.

RECORDS: LOOSE PAPERS

ORIGINAL SURVEYS   LO micro.: 6.1–190.

Original surveys numbered and filed at random in the same order as the copied survey volumes. The following series and book numbers are used: A to Z, A-1 to A-89, B-1 to B-23, BB-1 to BB-4, C-1 to C-234, and D-1 to D-114. Each survey is a drawing on a separate piece of paper accompanied by a verbal description. The drawing gives courses and distances and adjoining owners, and shows the name of the individual for whom it was surveyed, the acres, and, sometimes, significant geographic features. The endorsement "Retd" (Returned) and date on the reverse side refer to the date the surveyor general sent the return of survey to the secretary of the Land Office to prepare the patent.

DEPUTY SURVEYORS CERTIFICATES   LO micro.: 19.5.

A collection of thirty-four folders of certificates giving the reason the survey could not be made pursuant to the land law of 1792. The certificates are filed by the deputy surveyor's name.

RECORDS: BOUND VOLUMES

COPIED SURVEYS   LO micro.: 28.1– .

Copied surveys numbered and filed by series and book as follows: A to Z, A-1 to A-89, B-1 to B-23, BB-1 to BB-4, C-1 to C-234, and D-1 to D-90. Original surveys D-91 to D-114 have not been copied, but in-house search sheets and a partial index are available. Each copied survey faithfully reproduces the original survey including errors, but errors in the original are highlighted.

LIST OF SURVEYS RETURNED TO DEPUTY SURVEYORS FOR CORRECTION   LO micro.: 25.31.

Covering the years 1816–1822, this volume appears to consist of fragments of a more extensive volume. Information given includes the warrantee's name, warrant date, return date, and date when the corrected survey was received.

LIST OF SURVEYS RETURNED TO COUNTY SURVEYORS FOR CORRECTION   1860–1926   LO micro.: 25.31.

Lists all surveys not passing inspection in the Land Office and the reason for their return to the county surveyors for correction. Information given includes the surveyor's name, warrantee's name, warrant date, date returned, and date when the corrected survey was received, with remarks such as "Don't Table," "Excess Too Great," "Area Wrong," "Warrantee Not Named," and "Adjoiners Not Named."

LIST OF SURVEYS IN THE REJECTED FILE   (Binding No. 87).

Organized by county, this volume gives the warrantee, warrant date, and quantity, with remarks.

---

[1]Min. Bd. Prop., June 1814, Bk. 8; LO micro.: 25.23.

[2]*SmL* 6:427.

[3]Pennsylvania Department of Internal Affairs *Annual Report of the Secretary of Internal Affairs* (1909): 23.A. See also Knud Hermansen, "Pennsylvania Warrants, Original Surveys, and Patents" (Ph.D. diss., Pennsylvania State University, 1982).

[4]February 16, 1833, *PaL* 1832–33:46–47; Pennsylvania Department of Internal Affairs *Annual Report of the Secretary of Internal Affairs* (1885): 10.A.

IV.G.4. Returns of Survey

A return of survey was the fourth in the series of documents used to transfer land to private ownership. Always considered to be an internal document, the return of survey combined a restatement of the warrant and a written description of the survey. Prepared by the surveyor general at the request of the secretary of the Land Office, the return acknowledged that the balance on the purchase price, interest, and fees had been paid.

As an in-house document, the return of survey authorized the preparation of the patent and was tacit recognition that the land described in the return was privately owned. The phraseology from the return of survey was copied in the body of the patent.

Although the secretary used the return of survey to prepare the patent, the return was not eliminated in 1843 when the position of secretary was abolished. The surveyor general continued to use the return until 1868 as a check on the status of the patenting process.

In 1868, under the lien law, the return of survey took on a new format. Rather than a written description of the warrant and survey, the return contained a diagram of the resurvey and information to indicate whether the resurvey was of the whole tract or a portion of the tract and when the original survey had been completed.

Returns of survey for the Commonwealth period 1781–1870 are filed chronologically and indexed in the warrant register under the name of the warrantee. The endorsement giving a date and the abbreviation "Ret'd" or the word "Returned" on the reverse side refers to the date the surveyor general sent the return of survey to the secretary and is almost always an indication that a patent was prepared. It is important to remember that the return was prepared in the patentee's name.

Returns of survey for the period after 1870 were filed with the application packet.

Although book copies of the returns of survey for the Commonwealth period have never been made, the returns have been microfilmed. The microfilm user should be aware that many returns dated between January 1868 and August 1870 are not returns at all but rather applications for patents. The applications are part of a series of records for patenting unpatented land and are discussed in IV.E.4, Unpatented Land and Land Lien Dockets.

RECORDS: LOOSE PAPERS

RETURN OF SURVEY   OCT. 2, 1781–AUG. 1870   LO micro.: 5.13–117.

Handwritten records prepared in the surveyor general's office, giving a written description of the warrant and survey. The return of survey acknowledges the payment of the balance due on the purchase price and is dated the day it was sent to the secretary. The return authorizes the completion of the patent. Records dated between January 1868 and August 1870 were microfilmed with this collection but belong with the Applications for Patents (LO micro.: 4.1).

IV.G.5. Patents

The Commonwealth Land Office conveyed final land ownership to individuals through a patent. Retaining the proprietary term, the patent was simply an official document granting exclusive right to a particular tract of land. The fifth in the series of records necessary to convey state-owned land to private ownership, the patent was the final document.

In form the patent of the Commonwealth was the same as the patent of the proprietary era. Describing the tract in courses and distances, the patent summarized all the preceding records. The warrantee and warrant date, county, and township were all stated, as well as the purchase price. A tract name was also included until 1811–12. An added measure, the tract name was intended to make it easier to trace tracts when they changed ownership. For a citation of the tract name index, see the records below.

Following the proprietary example, the patent also stated the Commonwealth's reservation of "one fifth part of all gold and silver ore . . . , to be delivered at the pit's mouth clear of all charges." This reservation does not appear to have resulted in profits, but it was not rescinded until 1889.[1]

Before the patent was issued, the entire purchase price, interest, and fees had to be paid. Some exceptions to this rule occurred when mortgages were offered in special programs to encourage the patenting of land. After 1816 patents granted on mortgages were recorded at the county level.[2] The mortgage option is discussed in IV.E.1.a, Land Granted by the Proprietary Government.

Two copies of the patent were always prepared. The first copy, or original patent, belonged to the owner as with any other deed. The second copy belonged to the state. After 1816 each county was also required to keep a book in which patents to land granted by the Commonwealth were recorded.[3]

The responsibility for signing patents changed from official to official as follows: the president or vice president of the Supreme Executive Council, 1781–1790; the governor, 1790–1809; the secretary of the Commonwealth, 1809–1843; and, from 1843, the governor. The master of the rolls affixed the great seal of the Commonwealth on the original patent and bound the copy into a book.

After the position of master of the rolls was abolished in 1809, the patent books were sequentially in the charge of the secretary of the Land Office (1809–1843), the surveyor general (1843–1874), the Department of Internal Affairs (1874–1966), the Department of Community Affairs (1966–1981), and finally the state archives (1981–present). The book copies of the patents constitute the official legal record of the transfer of the tract from Commonwealth to individual ownership. The books have been indexed and microfilmed and are cited below.

In addition to the patents and the patent indexes, patent registers were kept by the secretary of the Land Office and his successors. The registers present a chronological listing of patents granted and other vital information and are cited below.

RECORDS: BOUND VOLUMES

PATENT BOOKS   SERIES P   [1781–1809]   (With indexes)   LO micro.: 15–39 (formerly 17–40).

Sixty-five books of official legal copies of the original patents, entered in chronological order. Many books have their own indexes. The patents are handwritten and contain the name of the patentee, a description of the tract in courses and distances, the tract name, and the warrant date and warrantee. This series was prepared by the master of the rolls.

PATENT INDEX   SERIES P   LO micro.: 1.16–18.

Four volumes of indexes to the P series of patents. Patentees' names are grouped in each index alphabetically by the last name and by the patent volume and book. For each patentee the index gives the patent date, patent book and page, acres patented, warrantee, warrant date, and county. The indexes are organized as follows:

Index vol. 1 = Patent books 1–19, 1781–1794.
Index vol. 2 = Patent books 20–35, 1792–1800.
Index vol. 3 = Patent books 35–43, 1799–1800.
Index vol. 4 = Patent books 44–65, 1800–1809.

PATENT BOOKS   SERIES H   [1809–Present]   LO micro.: 39–71 (formerly 41–79).

Eighty books containing official legal copies of original patents for the dates given. The patents are entered in chronological order, and several books have their indexes. The patents are handwritten until 1898, after which they are typewritten. The patents contain the name of the patentee, a description of the tract in courses and distances, the tract name until 1811–12, and the warrant date and warrantee. Microfilmed through 1957.

PATENT INDEX   SERIES H   LO micro.: 1.18–20.

Five volumes of indexes to the H series of patents. Patentees' names are grouped in each index alphabetically by the last name and by the patent book. For each patentee the index gives the patent date, patent book and page, acres patented, warrantee, warrant date, and county. The indexes have been microfilmed through 1957 and are organized as follows:

Index vol. 1 = Patent books 1–20, 1809–1823.
Index vol. 2 = Patent books 21–40, 1823–1839.
Index vol. 3 = Patent books 41–60, 1840–1865.
Index vol. 4 = Patent books 61–76, 1864–1903.
Index vol. 5 = Patent books 76–80, 1903–present.

TRACT PATENT NAME INDEX   LO micro.: 1.20–22.

Three volumes of indexes covering particular periods and arranged alphabetically by tract name. The following information is given: patent volume, book, and page; patent date; patentee; acres; warrantee; warrant date; and county. Each volume relates to a specific number of patent books as follows: 1781–1794, P1–P20; 1792–1800, P20–P36; and 1799–1809, P35–P65.

PATENT REGISTER   1781–1785   (Binding Volume 148; with index).
PATENT REGISTER   1786   (Binding Volume 129).
PATENT REGISTER   1873–1933.

Chronological listings of patents for the periods indicated. They give the following information: patent number, patentee, patent date, township, county, acres, and price.

---

[1]May 9, 1889, *PaL*, 175–76.
[2]*SmL* 6:309; January 25, 1816, *PaL*, 9.
[3]*SmL* 6:309.

Land Settlement, 1905–1990: Epilogue

The post-1905 period of land settlement in Pennsylvania focused on three primary concerns. Foremost in importance was completing title to unpatented land. Not far behind trailed the idea that the state was entitled to a fair market price for the land when it was patented. Directly intertwined with these concerns was the growing recognition of the necessity of building a forest reserve.

V.A. Twentieth-Century Policies

All unpatented land in Pennsylvania had evolved into three categories by 1905. Land was classed either as 1) unwarranted and unimproved, 2) unwarranted and improved, or 3) warranted and unpatented. The last two categories consisted of occupied land whose owners either had neglected to complete titles or were unaware that titles were incomplete. It was the first category, unwarranted and unoccupied land, that the state was anxious to identify and reclaim.

From the time of the first state land law in 1781 until 1905, the price of unwarranted land had been set by law. The price of $.2666 per acre had not changed since 1835. By 1900 the continually decreasing value of the dollar and the constantly increasing value of land made the price quite out of line with the true market value.

Concurrent with these developments was the creation of a state forestry commission. Having sold nearly all of its land, the state initiated a policy of reacquisition in 1887. By 1904 three

state forestry reservations had been created, but new legislation was needed to unify the state's land policy.

V.B. Public Land Law of 1905

The resulting land law of 1905, modified in 1909, revolutionized the method of considering and disposing of land. The century-old policy of requiring the applicant to prove the vacancy was eliminated. Reluctantly the Commonwealth accepted the responsibility of determining whether the land applied for was actually vacant. Basing its action upon the federal public land system of surveying prior to settlement, the Commonwealth introduced the practice of requiring that a preliminary survey be submitted along with the application. The survey was to show all adjoining tracts and give the names of current and warrant owners. From this information the Land Office searched its records and constructed a connected draft of warrant tracts based upon the original surveys on file.

If the Land Office investigation showed that the land was unwarranted and unimproved, officials referred the application to the Bureau of Forestry. Under the 1905 law the bureau had the right to preempt the tract for forest reservation or forest culture. One of the first states to engage actively in reforestation, Pennsylvania was at the forefront of the national conservation movement. Years of active land acquisition followed, and eventually the state became the owner of ever-enlarging state forests. Deeds to these forest tracts from grantors to the Commonwealth form part of the Commonwealth deed collection and are cited in the records under V.E, Commonwealth-Owned Land.

In another sense the law of 1905 was intended to be Pennsylvania's final effort to force the titling of land held by occupancy alone. With the purpose of the Commonwealth always being to encourage and protect preemption rights, the law gave squatters five years to apply for a warrant before preemption claims would no longer be considered. Squatters who applied are listed in a special volume cited in the records below under V.E, Commonwealth-Owned Land. Opposition to the abolition of preemption rights prevailed, however, and a new law on May 3, 1909, restored preemption rights to holders of unwarranted but improved land.

Obtaining a fair market price, one of the main thrusts of the 1905 legislation, was accomplished by eliminating the fixed price for land and substituting an appraisal system. A board of three impartial appraisers viewed the land applied for and submitted their notarized statement

---

Table 32. Research Aids: Twentieth-Century Legislation

Clepper, Henry. "Rise of the Forest Conservation Movement in Pennsylvania." *Pa. Hist.* 12 (1945): 200–216.

Pennsylvania Code. Harrisburg, 1970. See title 4, section 131 (Bureau of Land Records).

Pennsylvania Department of Internal Affairs *Annual Report of the Secretary of Internal Affairs* (1905, 1907): 18.A–28.A, 37.A–44.A.

Stephenson, John G. "Land Office Business in Pennsylvania." *Villanova Law Review* 4 (1959): 175–97.

Title 64, Public Lands. Vol. of *Purdon.* See pp. 1–115.

---

of value to the Land Office. An applicant was required to pay the price or abandon his claim.

Documents generated in the titling process under the 1905 and 1909 laws are cited under the appropriate headings in Section IV.

RECORDS: BOUND VOLUME

APPLICATIONS FOR VACANT LAND UNDER ACT OF ASSEMBLY APPROVED MARCH 28, 1905 [and May 3, 1909].

A chronological register by date of receipt giving the following information: applicant's name and address, quantity applied for, county, township, date when the report of investigation was filed, date when the report was referred to the State Forestry Reservation Commission, date when the report was received back from the forestry commission, date when a notice was forwarded to the applicant, appraisement per acre, amount of purchase money, date of receipt of purchase money, date of payment of purchase money, warrantee's name, and date of warrant.

V.C. Warrant Tract Maps

To facilitate the new procedures for warranting and patenting land and to locate untitled tracts, the Land Office initiated a warrant tract mapping program in 1907. Because land in Pennsylvania was not surveyed before it was settled, the Land Office had only single, unconnected survey drafts whose location relative to other tracts was known only by the name of the adjoining owners. The warrant maps were to provide for Pennsylvania what the range maps provide for the western federal land states—the location of each original survey.

Beginning with the western counties where tracts were surveyed in rectangular shapes before they were sold, Land Office draftsmen mapped one township at a time. As each county was

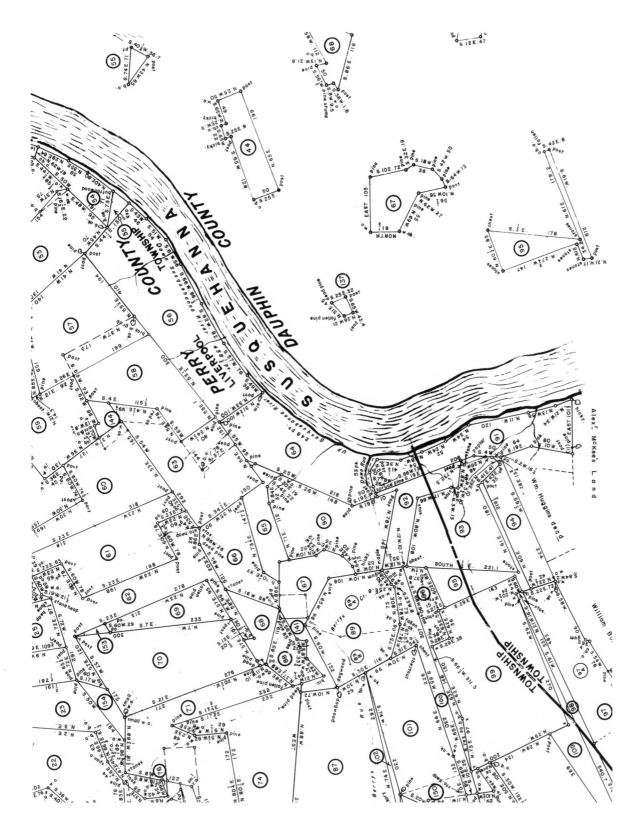

Segment of a warrant tract map for Perry County.

completed, the township maps for that county were bound together and published in a warrantee township atlas. Later, the atlas form was done away with, and each township map became available as an individual item as soon as it was completed.

The warrant map program is far from complete. Appropriations for the project were always minimal, and other projects often interfered. Ninety years after its inception, the construction of warrant tract maps remains an ongoing program. The major difference is the use of computer technology. Drawn on a scale of 1 to 100, the maps vary in size depending upon the number of tracts in the township. Some townships contain over 150 warrant tracts, others only 30 or 40. Information entered on the maps includes all information found on the original survey drafts, along with warrantees' names; warrant and survey dates; patentees' names; patent dates; township, city, and borough lines; and major geographical features. In effect these maps form a graphic warrantee register. If a township map has been completed for the geographic area being searched, a warrant tract map may be the place to begin an investigation. But researchers must realize that the information on the map covers a broad time span, and these maps represent warrant tracts over time.

As the warrant tract maps are completed, they are distributed by law to several repositories. The county commissioner and recorder of deeds offices receive a copy of the township maps of their county. The Pennsylvania State Library, Pattee Library of the Pennsylvania State University, and the Library of Congress receive copies of all township maps.

Maps are also available for sale from the Land Office. To determine the cost and availability of maps, write to the Pennsylvania State Archives.

V.D. Public Land Law of 1959

Although the Public Land Law of 1959 replaced the land laws of 1905 and 1909, no significant policy changes resulted. Procedures under that law currently in effect for warranting and patenting land are outlined in the following paragraphs.

Applications for unwarranted unimproved land are filed on forms provided by the Land Office and must contain a preliminary survey of the tract and adjoining tracts showing the warrantees and current owners. If the land is found to be vacant, the Department of Environmental Resources is notified and may take the tract for forest reserve by its preemptive right. In such cases the land is patented to the department without fee but following the same procedures as an individual applicant would follow. When the department waives its right, the applicant may proceed to advertise his intent and in so doing fulfills the additional purpose of proving the vacancy. An opposing claimant may file a caveat. If this happens, the application and the caveat go to the Board of Property for its decision based upon a hearing. After advertising has been completed, or when the proper applicant is determined, an impartial board of three appraisers places a valuation on the tract. As soon as the applicant pays the valuation price and other fees, a warrant to survey and a calculation form are issued to the applicant's surveyor. Upon return of the certified survey and calculations to the Land Office and their verification, a patent signed by the governor is issued in the name of the applicant.

Applications for unwarranted improved land follow the same general procedures but with some significant differences. Because this land is being claimed by settlement and improvement, the applicant must provide a chain of title dating from before March 28, 1905, the date after which preemption is not permitted by law. The applicant also swears to have met the legal definition of settlement and improvement by living on the tract and clearing and tilling the soil for gainful support. Obviously, unwarranted improved tracts are generally found in the more rural areas of the state. Since the Commonwealth has always supported preemption rights, referral of the application to the Department of Environmental Resources is not necessary in such cases.

Applications for tracts that were warranted and perhaps surveyed but not patented also follow the same basic procedures. An abstract of title, a preliminary survey, advertising, and a final survey must all be provided by the applicant. The tract, however, does not need to be appraised and purchased from the state since presumably the land was purchased at the time the warrant was granted. Instead, if the tract appears in the lien docket as warranted but unpatented prior to January 1, 1935, the applicant must pay a twenty-five-dollar fee to cancel the lien in addition to a flat fee for the patent.

Documents generated under the 1959 public land law are cited under the appropriate headings in Section IV. They have not been microfilmed.

V.E. Commonwealth-Owned Land

The Land Office is the custodian for all original deeds to land owned by the Commonwealth. These Commonwealth deeds form the reverse of all other Land Office records since they are records of the acquisition of land, not the sale of land.

Failing to set aside specific amounts of land for its own use, Pennsylvania needed to reacquire land for military and social purposes. This process began in the early nineteenth century. For example, as early as 1816, David Mead sold land to the state for the Meadville Arsenal, and in 1821 and 1822 the state bought land in Philadelphia for the Eastern State Penitentiary.

Land acquisition became more active in the twentieth century as state government grew in concept and size. Although the bulk of the property was controlled by the Department of General Services or its forerunners, the Forestry Commission and the Game Commission acquired so much land that their deeds are filed separately from those of other Commonwealth-owned land.

Deeds to Commonwealth-owned land are cited below by category and may be accessed by reference to the Master Register of Commonwealth Deeds also cited below.

RECORDS: LOOSE PAPERS

STATE FORESTRY RESERVE DEEDS   LO micro.: 2.1–63.

The original deeds to the Commonwealth for forestry land. Access is by file number, which can be found in the State Forestry Reserve deed register cited in the bound volumes below. Microfilmed through 1957.

GAME COMMISSION DEEDS   LO micro.: 2.64–70.

The original deeds to the Commonwealth for game land. Access is by file number, which can be found in Deed Register Game Preserve cited in the bound volumes below. Microfilmed through 1957.

COMMONWEALTH DEEDS   LO micro.: 2.71–142

The original deeds to land owned by the state other than forest and game land. Access is by file number, which can be found in the Master Register of Commonwealth Deeds cited in the bound volumes below. Microfilmed through 1957. These deeds fall under one of the following categories:

Armories	Military Camp Site (Mount Gretna)
Arsenals	Monuments
Aviation	Normal Schools
Bridges	Old Capitol Ground
Capitol Park	Parks
Executive Mansion	Penitentiaries
Fish Hatcheries	Pennsylvania Training Schools
Flood and Reclamation	Pymatuning Reservoir

Highways	Quarantine Station
Historical Parks	Reformatory
Home for Deaf Children	Soldiers and Sailors Home
Hospitals	Soldiers' Orphans' School
Independence Mall	State Police Barracks
Industrial Home Women	Tuberculosis Sanitoria
Insane Hospitals	Turnpikes

RECORDS: BOUND VOLUMES

STATE FORESTRY RESERVE   LO micro.: 1.11–14.

Four volumes arranged alphabetically by county, providing an index to deeds to land acquired by the Commonwealth for forestry reserves through 1957. They cite the Land Office file number, location of the tract, type of instrument, date, grantor, grantee, and county deed book.

DEED REGISTER   GAME PRESERVE   LO micro.: 1.11.

An index arranged alphabetically by county to deeds to land acquired by the Game Commission through 1957. It cites the land office file number, location of the tract, type of instrument, date, grantor, grantee, and county deed book.

MASTER REGISTER OF COMMONWEALTH DEEDS   LO micro.: 1.10–11.

Two volumes forming the index to the Commonwealth deeds through 1957. The following information is recorded: file number, location, type of instrument, area, date, grantor, grantee, and county deed book.

APPENDIX A

The 1759 Land Office Inventory and Transcripts

Key: Column headings should be read as follows:

Inv. # (Inventory number): the number of the original volume as it appears in Hughes' List (Binding No. 62) for titles under Secretary's Office and in Register of Old Rights (Binding No. 138) for titles under Surveyor General's Office; it is also the number of the transcript as entered in the copied volume.

Binding Title: the title embossed on the spine of the volume when it was bound in green in 1874. However, where two volumes of transcripts have been bound together, and both titles appear on the binding, only the applicable title is cited in this appendix.

Binding #: the number on the spine of the green bound volume.

Micro. #: the number of the Land Office microfilm reel.

Guide Subsection(s): The number(s) of the subsection(s) in which the volume is mentioned in this GUIDE.

Secretary's Office

A. *Bound volumes in the Secretary's Office in 1759 and the correlating transcripts (Green Books) made by John Hughes in 1759.*

Inv. #	Binding Title	Binding #	Micro. #	Guide Subsection(s)
1A	PATENTS BY ROYAL GOVENORS OF NEW YORK	none	25.32	I.C.
13	[Transcript:] Patents 1677–1682	26	25.5	I.C
2B	WARRANT BOOK NO. 3 1682–1684	15	25.3	II.D.1.a, II.G.3

215

Inv. #	Binding Title	Binding #	Micro. #	Guide Subsection(s)
13	[Transcript:] Proprietary Warrants	26	25.5	II.D.1.a, II.G.3
12	[Transcript:] Warrants Proprietaries 1–113 with Index	41	25.9	II.G.3
3C	WARRANT BOOK 1685–1691	14	25.2	II.G.3, II.G.6
17	[Transcript] Old Rights—Philadelphia, Chester, Bucks, New Castle, Kent and Sussex	23	25.5	II.F.1, II.G.3, II.G.6
4D	MINUTES OF PROPERTY [Book D]	(Proprietary Papers, folder 3)	23.1	II.F.1
10	[Transcript:] Minutes of Commissioners of Property 1689–1692	21	25.4	II.F.1
5E	MINUTES OF PROPERTY [Book E]	(Proprietary Papers, folders 3, 4)	23.1	II.F.1
10	[Transcript:] Minutes of Commissioners of Property 1689–1692	21	25.4	II.F.1
6F	MINUTE BOOK F NO. 6	none	none	II.F.1
10	[Transcript:] Minutes of Commissioners of Property 1689–1692	21	25.4	II.F.1
11	[Transcript:] Records Miscellaneous with Index	39	25.8	II.F.1
7G	COMMISSIONERS OF PROPERTY G-7 1701–1709	20	25.20	II.F.1
16	[Transcript:] Minutes of Commissioners of Property 1701–1709	20	25.4	II.F.1, III.G.5
8H	COMMISSIONERS OF PROPERTY H-8 1712–1720	21	25.20	II.F.1
	INDEX TO NEW MINUTES OF PROPERTY 1712–1720	6a	25.1	
17	[Transcript:] Old Rights—Philadelphia, Chester, Bucks, New Castle, Kent and Sussex	23	25.5	II.F.1, II.G.3, II.G.6
91	COMMISSIONERS OF PROPERTY I–9 1716–1732	22	25.20	II.F.1
6	[Transcript:] Warrant Register 1700–1705	22	25.4	II.F.1, III.F.1
10K	COMMISSIONERS OF PROPERTY 10-K 1732–1741	22	25.20–21	III.F.1

Inv. #	Binding Title	Binding #	Micro. #	Guide Subsection(s)
6	[Transcript:] Warrant Register 1700–1705	22	25.4–5	II.F.1, III.F.1
11L	WARRANT BOOK 1700–1715	117	25.108	II.G.3
8	[Transcript:] Warrants—Proprietaries and Commissioners 1700–1704	36	25.8	II.G.3
9	[Transcript:] Warrants 1704–1715 with Index	37	25.8	II.G.3
12M	WARRANT BOOK 1715–1741	118	25.108	II.G.3, III.G.2
	[Index separately bound as] WARRANT BOOK INDEX 1715–1741	none	none	II.G.3, III.G.2
2	[Transcript:] Warrants of Property 1715–1735	28	25.6	II.G.3, III.G.2
3	[Transcript]: Warrants 1735–1747	29	25.6	III.G.2
13N	PATENT REGISTER 1701–1728	5	25.1	II.G.6
6	[Transcript:] Patents 1701–1728	22	25.4	II.G.6
14O	PATENT BOOK 1732–1741	6	25.1	III.G.5
	[Transcript:] Warrants and Surveys 2[1]	none	25.128	II.E.1.b, II.G.5, III.G.4, III.G.5, III.G.6
15P	FRAGMENTS OF WARRANT BOOK 1a-1b	none	25.1	III.D.1, III.G.2
19	[Transcript: Warrants Copies 1729–1733,] Warrant Register 1733–1738	51	25.11	III.D.1, III.G.2
16Q	PATENT BOOK 1733–1744	2	25.1	III.G.5
11	[Transcript:] Returns of Surveys 1733–1744 with Index	39	25.9	III.G.5
17R	PATENT BOOK 1745–1753	3	25.1	III.G.5
16	[Transcript:] Minutes of Commissioners of Property 1701–1709	20	25.4	II.F.1, III.G.5
18S	[Missing: WARRANT BOOK S 1741–1752]			
	INDEX TO WARRANT BOOK S 1741–1752	4	25.1	III.G.2
24	[Transcript:] Warrant Register 1741 to 1752 Part 1 of 2 Pg. 1–300	57	25.12–13	III.D.1, III.G.2
	[Transcript:] Warrant Register 1741 to 1752 Part 2 of 2 Pg. 301–558 Index	57	25.13	III.D.1, III.G.2
19T	[Missing: WARRANT BOOK T 1752–1772]			

Inv. #	Binding Title	Binding #	Micro. #	Guide Subsection(s)
	INDEX TO BOOK T 1752–1772	153	none	III.G.2
23	[Transcript:] Warrant Register 1752–1759 with Index	54	25.12	III.D.1, III.G.2
20U	[Missing: PATENT BOOK 1753–1759]			
25	[Transcript:] Patents 1753–1759	60	25.14	III.G.5
21	LOTTS OF THE 4 STREETS &c. A CERTIFICATE OF THE DRAWING OF ORIGINAL PURCHASERS LOTS	(Philadelphia City Lots Folder)	21.1	II.E.1.b
	[Transcript:] Warrants and Survey 2[1]		25.128	II.E.1.b, II.G.5, III.G.4, III.G.5, III.G.6

B. Bound volumes (Green Books) John Hughes made in 1759 by copying loose original records in the Secretary's Office.

Inv. #	Binding Title	Binding #	Micro. #	Guide Subsection(s)
14	PHILADELPHIA CITY [Old Rights, Returns A–W], PHILADELPHIA CITY NEW RETURNS [A–W], LANCASTER COUNTY NEW RETURNS [A–B69]	Warrants and Surveys 2[1]	25.128	II.G.5, III.G.4, III.G.6
20	PHILADELPHIA COUNTY [Old Rights, Returns A–Y], BUCKS NEW RETURNS [A–L]	Warrants and Surveys 6[1]	25.129	II.G.5, III.G.4, III.G.6
4	RETURNS—CHESTER [Old Rights] A TO P-15 [Bucks Old Rights] A TO Z	32	25.6–7	II.G.3, II.G.5, III.G.6
22	RETURNS PHILADELPHIA A TO T CUMBERLAND A TO Z BERKS A TO Z CHESTER [Old Rights] P14 TO Z	53	25.11	III.G.4, III.G.6
21	RETURNS—BUCKS L-23 TO Z LANCASTER H-67 TO M-41	33	25.7	III.G.4, III.G.6
15	RETURNS—LANCASTER B-70 TO H-66	45	25.9–10	III.G.4, III.G.6
18	RETURNS LANCASTER M 42 TO S 207	48	25.10	III.G.4, III.G.6
3	RETURNS YORK A TO Z NORTHAMPTON A TO Z WARRANTS—1735–1747	29	25.6	III.G.4, III.G.6
1	RETURNS 1734–1760 BERKS, BUCKS, CUMBERLAND, CHESTER, LANCASTER, NORTHAMPTON, YORK	27	25.5	III.G.4, III.G.6
	PHILADELPHIA COUNTY NEW RETURNS [B–S]	Warrants and Surveys 9[1]	25.129	III.G.4, III.G.6

Surveyor General's Office

A. Bound volumes in the Surveyor General's Office in 1759 and the correlating transcripts (Green Books) made by John Hughes.

Inv. #	Binding Title	Binding #	Micro. #	Guide Subsection(s)
A1	RETURNS OF SURVEYS A-1 1684–1693	68	25.31	II.G.5
	[Transcript: not found]			
B2	REGISTER OF SURVEYS—1684	7	25.1–2	II.G.5
29	[Transcript:] Returns of Surveys	Warrants and Surveys 3[1]	25.128	II.G.5
C3	COPIES OF SURVEYOR GENERAL'S WARRANTS 1700	1	25.1	
	[Index bound in] PATENT REGISTER 1701–1728	5	25.1	II.G.6
	[Transcript: not found]			
D4	MARKHAM'S BOOK	17	25.3	II.F.2
	[Transcript: not found]			
E5	RETURNS [of Survey] PHILADELPHIA CITY LOTS NO. 2	93	25.36	
	[Transcript: not found]			
F6	DEPUTY SURVEYORS ORDER BOOK 1682–1693	none	25.36	II.G.4
19	[Transcript:] Old Rights 1682–1693 with Index	50	25.11	II.G.4
G7	WARRANTS 1682–1684	16	25.3	II.G.3
26	[Transcript:] Old Rights with Index 1682–1685	58	25.13	II.G.3
H8	RETURN OF SURVEYS 1701[–1720; 1733–1737]	18	25.3	II.G.5, III.G.4
	[Transcript:] The Copies of the Surveyor General's Returns 1700	Warrants and Surveys 4[1]	25.128	
	[Transcript:] Copies of the Surveyor General's Returns from October 29, 1733	Warrants and Surveys 5[1]	25.129	III.G.4
I9	WARRANT REGISTER 1743–1745	119	25.2	
	[Transcript: not found]			

Inv. #	Binding Title	Binding #	Micro. #	Guide Subsection(s)
K10	SURVEYOR GENERAL—RETURNS OF SURVEYS, NO. 5 1736–1740	75	25.32	III.G.4
15	[Transcript:] Returns of Surveys	Warrants and Surveys 7[1]	25.129	III.G.4
16	[Transcript:] Returns into Secretary's Office with Index	46	25.10	III.G.4
L11	RECORD OF RETURNS OF SURVEYS 1740–1747	76	25.32–33	III.G.4
27	[Transcript:] Returns 1740–1747	59	25.13–14	III.G.4
M12	RETURN OF SURVEYS 1748–1753	19	25.3–4	III.G.4
23	[Transcript:] Return Surveys June 1748 to June 1753 with Index	55	25.12	III.G.4
N13	[Missing]			
	[Transcript:] Returns Surveys 1753–1759	Warrants and Surveys 8[1]	25.129	III.G.4
14–17	[Missing]			
18	WARRANT BOOK NO. 18 1745–1746	12	25.2	III.G.2
19	[Missing]			
20	WARRANT BOOK 1752–1753 NO. 20	10	25.2	III.G.2
21	INDEX NO. 21 1751 LIST WARRANT BOOK	9	25.2	III.G.2
22	WARRANT BOOK NO. 22 1750–1751	8	25.2	III.G.2
23	[Missing]			
24	WARRANT BOOK 1747–1748	6c	none	III.G.2
25	[Missing]			
26	[Missing]			
27	WARRANT BOOK NO. 27 1733–1734	6f	25.1	III.G.2
28	WARRANT BOOK 1733–1737	6e	25.1	III.G.2

Inv. #	Binding Title	Binding #	Micro. #	Guide Subsection(s)
29	[Missing]			
30	[Missing]			
	[Transcript:] Directions of Reference in the City Draught of Philadelphia to the Lots of the Purchasers	Warrants and Surveys 2[1]	25.128	
31	PHILADELPHIA CITY LOTS NO. 31 HUGHES' LIST	165	none	III.E.4
32	RECORDED SURVEYS 1684 NO. 32	6d	25.1	II.G.5
33	NEW CASTLE COUNTY SURVEY NOTES, 1675–1679	none	471	I.C
	[Transcript: Albert Cook Myers, *Walter Wharton's Land Survey Register, 1675–1679* (see Table 2)]			
34	[Missing]			
	[Transcript:] Capt Wm Markham List of Papers Received pp. 1–70	61	25.14	II.G.5
35	[Missing]			
	[Transcript:] Account of Lots Returned 1698	61	25.14	II.E.1.b
36	STEEL'S RENT ROLL FOR PHILADELPHIA 1731	6b	25.1	II.E.1.b, II.F.4
37	[Transcript probably:] Caveat Books 1, 2, 3, and part of 4 1748–1769	2	25.14	III.F.1

B. Bound volumes (Green Books) John Hughes made in 1759 by copying loose original records in the Surveyor General's Office.

Inv. #	Binding Title	Binding #	Micro. #	Guide Subsection(s)
1	OLD RIGHTS—BUCKS NO. 1A TO 21A [21P]	24	25.5	II.G.3, III.G.6
2	OLD RIGHTS—BUCKS NO. 22 P TO Z WARRANTS—[Bucks] NO. 1A TO 39C	25	25.5	II.G.3, III.G.2, III.G.6
3	WARRANTS—BUCKS 1737–1749 C TO H	30	25.6	III.G.2, III.G.6
21	WARRANTS BUCKS H-141 TO M-241	52	25.11	III.G.2, III.G.6
4	OLD RIGHTS, CHESTER A-1 TO H-106	31	25.6–7	II.G.3, III.G.6

Inv. #	Binding Title	Binding #	Micro. #	Guide Subsection(s)
none	OLD RIGHTS, CHESTER H-107 TO T-55 [Manuscript no. 37180, Chester County Historical Society; LDS micro.: 0020886]	none	none	II.G.3, III.G.6
6	OLD RIGHTS, CHESTER T-56 TO Y-4 WARRANTS CHESTER A-1 TO F-38	34	25.7	II.G.3, III.G.6
7	WARRANTS CHESTER F-39 TO P-47	35	25.7–8	III.G.2, III.G.6
17	WARRANTS CHESTER P-48 TO S-111	47	25.10	III.G.2, III.G.6
	[Old Rights Philadelphia A-1 to F-768; missing]			
none	PHILADELPHIA COUNTY [Old Rights F-769 to H-1203, P-2421 to S-2441]	Warrants and Surveys 1[1]	25.128	II.G.3, III.G.6
10	OLD RIGHTS PHILADELPHIA I-1225–P2420	38	25.8	II.G.3, III.G.6
12	WARRANTS PHILADELPHIA A-1 TO H-38	42	25.9	III.G.2, III.G.6
13	WARRANTS PHILADELPHIA H-39 TO M96	43	25.9	III.G.2, III.G.6
18	WARRANTS PHILADELPHIA M-97 TO S-262	49	25.10–11	III.G.2, III.G.6
11	WARRANTS LANCASTER A-1 TO B386	40	25.9	III.G.2, III.G.6
24	WARRANTS LANCASTER B-387 TO C-444	56	25.12	III.G.2, III.G.6
14	WARRANTS—BERKS A-1 TO B-81	44	25.9	III.G.2, III.G.6

[1]The volumes titled Warrants and Surveys 1–9 in the Philadelphia City Archives are actually 1759 transcripts that have been rebound. LO micro.: 25.128–29.

APPENDIX B

Miscellaneous Papers

Boxes 22–41   LO micro.: 24.1–38.

A large collection of loose papers more historical than legal in value. A portion has been identified and indexed in a 3″ × 5″ card file retained in the Land Office. Topics vary widely, including applications for land, warrants to accept previous surveys, canceled patents, Asylum Company papers, town lot tickets, Board of Property decisions, proprietary manors, the Delaware and Schuylkill Canal, deputy surveyors' notes, Donation Lands, Land Office correspondence, Seventeen Certified Townships, and warrants and receipts. Many papers are marked "copy" or "duplicate"; others did not fit the established Land Office filing system or could not be identified. It is very doubtful that missing applications, warrants, surveys, or returns of survey will be found in these boxes, but historians of land-related topics may wish to examine this collection.

APPENDIX C

Numerical List of Land Office Microfilm

Note: Reel numbers in parentheses represent original 1957 microfilm series, now in restricted use.

Reel Numbers	Description
1–2	Commission Books
2–9 (3–10)	Patent Books A1-A20
9–15 (11–17)	Patent Books AA1-AA16
15–39 (17–40)	Patent Books P1-P65
39–71 (41–79)	Patent Books H1-H80
3428 (79)	Depreciation Lands Register
3428 (79)	Donation Lands Register
1–4 (formerly 1.1–5)	Warrant Registers

Warrant Register
- Adams
- York
- Allegheny
- Armstrong
- Cambria
- Fayette
- Greene
- Indiana
- Somerset
- Beaver
- Butler
- Crawford
- Erie
- Lawrence
- Mercer
- Venango
- Warren

Reel Numbers	Description

2   Warrant Register

—Bedford	—Cameron
—Berks	—Clearfield
—Schuylkill	—Elk
—Blair	—Forest
—Clarion	—Jefferson
—Bradford	—Lycoming
—Columbia	—McKean
—Montour	—Potter
—Sullivan	—Carbon
—Susquehanna	—Lackawanna
—Tioga	—Luzerne
—Wyoming	

3   Warrant Register

—Monroe	—Juniata
—Centre	—Mifflin
—Clinton	—Perry
—Cumberland	—Snyder
—Dauphin	—Union
—Lebanon	—Northumberland Lottery
—Franklin	—Baynton & Wharton
—Fulton	—Huntingdon

4   Warrant Register

—Lancaster	—Delaware
—Northampton	—Wayne
—Northumberland	—Pike
—Philadelphia	—Lehigh
—Chester	—Westmoreland
—Bucks	—Washington
—Montgomery	

Reel Numbers	Description
1.5–8	Lien Dockets
1.8	East Side Applications Register
1.8–9	West Side Applications Register
1.9	Last Purchase 1784 Register
	New Purchase 1768 Register
1.9–10	Old Rights (Bucks, Chester) Register
1.10	Old Rights (Philadelphia) Register
1.10–14	Master Register of Commonwealth Deeds
1.15	Erie, Franklin, Warren, Waterford, Sunbury, Beaver Town Lots, Reserve Tracts
1.16	Patent Index A-AA Series
1.16–17	Patent Index P Series

Reel Numbers	*Description*
1.18–20	Patent Index H Series
1.20	Tract Patent Name Indexes
1.21	Original Purchases Index
	Old Rights (Bucks, Chester, Philadelphia)
1.22	Seventeen Certified Townships Luzerne Index
2.1–142	Commonwealth Deeds
3.1–7	Original Warrants—Last Purchase (1784)
3.7	—Baynton-Wharton
3.7–8	—Northumberland Lottery
3.8–9	—Depreciation Lands
3.9–10	—Adams
3.10–15	—Allegheny
3.15–16	—Southeast Allegheny
3.16–17	—Armstrong
3.17–18	—Beaver
3.18–29	—Bedford
3.29–34	—Berks
3.34	—Blair
	—Bradford
3.34–38	—Bucks
3.38–39	—Butler
3.39–40	—Cambria
3.40	—Cameron
	—Carbon
3.40–41	—Centre
3.41–44	—Chester
3.44	—Clarion
	—Clearfield
3.44–45	—Clinton

Reel Numbers	Description
3.45	—Columbia
3.45–46	—Crawford
3.46–55	—Cumberland
3.55–57	—Dauphin
3.57	—Delaware
	—Elk
	—Erie
3.58–61	—Fayette
3.61–63	—Franklin
3.63–64	—Fulton
3.64–65	—Greene
3.65–70	—Huntingdon
3.70–71	—Indiana
3.71–72	—Juniata
3.72	—Lackawanna
3.72–84	—Lancaster
3.84	—Lawrence
	—Lebanon
3.84–85	—Lehigh
3.85–91	—Luzerne
3.91–93	—Lycoming
3.93	—McKean
	—Mercer
3.93–97	—Mifflin
3.98	—Monroe
	—Montgomery
	—Montour
3.98–108	—Northampton
3.108–24	—Northumberland

Reel Numbers	*Description*
3.124–25	—Perry
3.125–28	—Philadelphia
3.128	—Pike
	—Potter
3.129–31	—Schuylkill
3.131	—Snyder
3.131–32	—Somerset
3.132	—Sullivan
3.133	—Susquehanna
	—Tioga
3.133–34	—Union
3.134–35	—Venango
3.135–36	—Warren
3.136–41	—Washington
3.141–48	—Westmoreland
3.148–49	—Wyoming
3.149–56	—York
3.156	—Springettsbury Certificates
4.1–10	Applications for Patents, 1870–1957
4.10	Notice of Purchase of Lands by Dep't. Forests and Waters
4.10–11	Money and Fees to the Treasury, 1907–1917
4.11	Public Service Commission Agreements
5.1–114	Returns of Survey, 1733–1870
5.115–19	Returns of Survey, Miscellaneous and Town Lots, 1682–1759
5.119	Returns of Survey—Undated
	—Virginia Claims
	—Proprietary Manors
6.1–190	Original Surveys
7.1–4	Applications for Warrant—New Purchase

Reel Numbers	Description
7.5	—Preemption
7.5–101	—1734–1957
8.1–4	Donation Land Claimants, Lists, Miscellaneous, Patents
9.1–20	Seventeen Certified Townships
10.1–2	Holland Land Company
10.2–3	[Pennsylvania] Population Land Company
11.1–4	Commonwealth Town Lots
11.4	Proprietary Towns
11.4–5	Richard Peters's Tickets
11.6	Commonwealth Town Lots
12.1–8	Title Papers (Prepatent Deed Polls, 1811 Law)
13.1–11	Caveats
14.1–5	Proof of Settlement
15.1–4	Mortgages
16.1–2	Applications for Warrants
16.2–7	Applications—Islands
16.8–11	Islands, View and Appraisal
16.11	Applications—Riverbeds
16.11–13	Applications for Warrants Not Issued
16.14–15	Applications for Warrants Withdrawn, Caveated, Refused
16.15	Applications for Patents Refused
16.15–16	Applications for Release of Liens
17.1	Deeds (Burr, Foulke, Hoopes, Wilson, Parker, Wharton, Peters, Wilson)
18.1–7	Depositions
19.1–4	Deputy Surveyors Duplicate Commissions and Instructions
19.4–6	Deputy Surveyors Certificates
19.6–9	County Surveyors Election Returns and Oaths
20.1	Escheats
20.1–3	Certificates of Exoneration

Reel Numbers	Description
20.3	Appointments Unpaid Money (Unpatented Proprietary Grants, 1820)
	Certificates of Indebtedness, 1779–1781
20.3–4	Receiver General Certificates
20.4	Surveyor General Certificates
20.5	Surveyor General Correspondence
	Townships, Chester County and Miscellaneous
	Secretary of the Land Office Reports
	Land Office Procedure
	Field Notes
21.1	Proprietary Warrants and Philadelphia Lots
	William Allen's Papers
	James Logan's Correspondence
	London Land Company
	Baynton and Wharton
21.1–2	Melish Maps
21.2	Muster Rolls
	Roads and Rivers
21.3	Roads and Rivers
	Surveyors General Correspondence, 1682–1839
21.4	Philadelphia Lots
	Melish Maps
22.1–6	Board of Property, Petitions
22.6–34	Board of Property, Papers
23.1	Proprietary Papers
24.1–38	Miscellaneous Papers
25.1–14	Original Bound Volumes and 1759 Transcripts (Green Books)
25.14–20	Caveat Books
25.20–21	Original Bound Volumes and 1759 Transcripts
	Journal of the Commissioners, 1810

Reel Numbers	Description
25.20–21 (cont.)	Letters of Attorney
	Agricultural Land Minute Book
25.21–27	Board of Property Minute, Docket, and Fee Books
25.27–30	Index to State Lines and Roads
	County Surveyors, 1850–1871
	Deputy Surveyors' Lists of Returns
	Donation Lands
25.30–35	East Side Application Book
	Certified Townships Bound Volumes
	Surveyor General Letter Books
	Original Bound Volumes and 1759 Transcripts
	Lease and Release Books
	Surveys Returned for Correction
	Mortgage Books
	Donation Lands
25.35–37	Depreciation Lands
	Commonwealth Town Lots
	Island Books
25.37–107	Daybooks, Fee Books, Journals and Ledgers, Receiver General's Office
25.108–16	Original Bound Volumes and 1759 Transcripts
	Warrant Books
25.116–18	Application Books
25.118–19	Mortgage Book
	Nicholson's Court and Deed Books
25.120–27	Letters of Attorney Books
25.128–29	Warrants and Surveys 1–9 (1759 Transcripts in Philadelphia City Archives)
26.1	Maps, Roads, Rivers, Creeks
27.1–12	County Commissioners' Oath and Appraisals, 1835 Law
28.1–	Copied Surveys

Glossary

APPLICATION
A formal request for a warrant and the first in the series of documents used to transfer land to private ownership.

CAVEAT
A legal notice, or writ, that prevents an officer from acting until all litigants are heard.

DEED POLL
A deed made by one party only, usually to transfer the rights of the grantor to the grantee.

DIVESTITURE
In this GUIDE, the act of November 27, 1779, putting an end to all rights of the proprietaries in the public domain.

ENTRESOL
A low story between two larger ones, usually between the ground floor and the first story.

ENTRY
Early Land Office term for an application for improved land.

ESCHEATED LAND
Land returned to the proprietary or the Commonwealth government when the legal owner failed to hold the property, but not considered part of the public land and therefore not subject to public land law.

HEADRIGHTS
Per capita grants of land made either to Original Purchasers for each of their servants or to the servants themselves.

LEASE AND RELEASE
A pair of indentures acting as one and transferring land from the Crown to the proprietor and then to the purchaser.

LIEN
A right to hold property for payment of a claim.

LOCATION
Another word for an application formally entered in the books of the Land Office.

MANOR
A large tract of land usually subdivided and rented by the proprietor to tenants for a long term.

OVERPLUS LAND
The amount of land included in the survey beyond the amount authorized in the warrant.

PATENT
A final deed from the proprietary or the Commonwealth government conveying all rights to a particular tract of land.

PERCH
A linear or square unit of measure equaling one rod or one square rod, equivalent to 16.5 feet or 16.5 square feet.

PROPRIETARIES
Term used to refer to the multiple Penn heirs who had exclusive right to the colony of Pennsylvania.

PROPRIETOR
An individual who holds exclusive right to something; in Pennsylvania, William Penn, who held exclusive right to the colony.

QUITRENT
A ground rent originally intended to release the payer from feudal duties.

RETURN OF SURVEY
A restatement of the warrant and survey in words and the fourth in the series of documents used to transfer land to private ownership.

RIPARIAN
Pertaining to the bank of a river.

SEATED LAND
Land that is occupied, cultivated, or improved.

SQUATTER
A person who actually settled upon the land without the benefit of a warrant.

SURVEY
The measurement of the courses and distances of a tract of land and the third in the series of documents used to transfer land to private ownership.

UNSEATED LAND
Land that is privately owned but not cultivated, improved, or occupied.

WARRANT
An order to survey and the second in the series of documents used to transfer land to private ownership.

WARRANT TO ACCEPT A SURVEY
The type of warrant granted when the tract had been settled and improved before the survey.

WARRANT TO SURVEY
The type of warrant granted when the tract had not been settled and improved before the survey.

Index

Unless otherwise specified, counties, rivers, and towns are located in Pennsylvania.